BÉISBOL

Latin Americans and the
Grand Old Game

BÉISBOL

Latin Americans and the Grand Old Game

Michael M. Oleksak and
Mary Adams Oleksak

Masters Press

Published by Masters Press
5025 28th Street, S.E., Grand Rapids, Michigan 49512

© Copyright 1991 by Michael M. Oleksak and Mary Adams Oleksak

Library of Congress Cataloging-in-Publication Data
Oleksak, Michael M., 1957–
Béisbol : Latin Americans and the grand old game / Michael M.
Oleksak and Mary Adams Oleksak. — 1st ed.
    p.   cm.
Includes bibliographical references (p.) and index.
ISBN 0-940279-35-5 : $22.95
1. Baseball—Latin America—History.   2. Baseball—History.
3. Baseball players—Latin America—Biography.
I. Oleksak, Mary Adams, 1959– .   II. Title.
GV862.6.043   1991
796.357'098—dc20   91-10697
                        CIP

Distributed to the trade by
National Book Network
4720-A Boston Way
Lanham, MD 20706

Printed in the United States of America

For our parents

Eileen and Paul Oleksak
Ruth and Harroll Adams

CONTENTS

ACKNOWLEDGEMENTS

Many thanks to Tom Bast, publisher at Masters Press, for his confidence in this project; to Amy Wolterstorff, editor, and Anne Shuart, art director, for their thorough and enthusiastic work at Masters Press; to Tom Heitz, Librarian at the Baseball Hall of Fame in Cooperstown, New York, who emphasized to us the need for this work back in 1987; to Bill Deane and Pat Kelly for their help at the Hall of Fame Library; to David Rusk and Cappy Gagnon for their time and encouragement; and to Walter and Paul Blumberh, who many years ago pointed out that Roberto Clemente and Tony Oliva always got two or three hits a game.

FOREWORD

I've been lucky. During my 43 years of major league broadcasting, I've been able to watch many of the great stars from Latin America who have contributed so much to the game of baseball. I've admired these fine athletes, who had the courage to leave their own countries and cultures to come to a strange land. While I did not have the opportunity to follow all their careers closely, I did come to know many of these athletes personally.

Now, in *Béisbol*, Michael M. Oleksak and his wife Mary Adams Oleksak give readers insight into the lives and careers of these Latin American baseball players. This is the definitive text on the subject, and it is a book which has long been needed. The authors trace the development of the game in Cuba, the Dominican Republic, Mexico, Puerto Rico, Nicaragua, Panama, and Venezuela, countries which have contributed hundreds of talented players to the grand old game. *Béisbol* also reveals the difficulties the Latin American athletes faced as they battled to survive and succeed in Major League Baseball.

One of the deepest regrets I have about my own career is that I was unable to observe Roberto Clemente's tremendous athletic skills on a regular basis. Perhaps that is why I especially enjoyed the authors' treatment of this first Hall of Famer from Latin America. In addition to discussing Clemente's baseball career, the Oleksaks also highlight his humanitarianism.

Minnie Miñoso, Tony Pérez, Fernando Valenzuela, and many other baseball greats come to life in this book. The Oleksaks offer a fine segment on the careers of Luís Aparicio, another Hall of Famer, and Bert Campaneris, my candidate for one of the most underrated players. But, I think, my favorite personalities are two stars not well known in the United States: Martín Dihigo and Hector Espino.

Dihigo is the only Latin American from the Negro league era to be elected to the Baseball Hall of Fame in Cooperstown, New York. Also, he is the only player who is a Hall of Famer in four different countries—the United States, Cuba, Mexico, and Venezuela. Hector Espino, the great hero of Mexican baseball, holds the record for the most lifetime home runs in the minor leagues. Like many other Mexican stars, Espino—except for a brief excursion in the United States—stayed home to play the game and become a national celebrity.

Béisbol is an entertaining and authoritative book in part because Michael and Mary Oleksak have lived in Latin America; they have experienced Latin American culture and history firsthand. Certainly, their book has heightened my awareness of the Latin American contribution to baseball, and increased my respect for the many Latin American players who overcame often daunting odds to "play ball" in the United States.

Ernie Harwell

Lakeland, Florida
February 1991

PREFACE

Imagine being a fanatical baseball fan but living in a land where the only baseball news you could get was a few lines in the newspaper, a month-late copy of *The Sporting News,* and an occasional static-ridden play-by-play over Armed Forces Radio.

That's the situation I found myself in when the bank I work for transferred me to Buenos Aires. The song "Don't Cry For Me, Argentina" took on a new spin, since the whole country could not have cared less about my plight.

It wasn't long, however, until I was offered the chance to move from baseball purgatory to baseball heaven—the Dominican Republic. I jumped at that chance like Roberto Clemente going after a waist-high hanging curve ball.

My decision paid off immediately. Even as I rode in a taxi from the airport after landing in Santo Domingo, I talked baseball with the driver. It was 1983, and the World Series between the Orioles and the Phillies was in progress. All the cabbie wanted to talk about was Pedro Guerrero and Tony Peña. And when he wasn't bragging about them, he was telling me about Licey, his favorite winter league team.

The next day my morning newspaper confirmed that I was right. It was the *Listín Diario,* which dedicated over half its five-page sports section to U.S. and Dominican baseball.

When I got to the bank for my first day on the job, the managers and staff had some tough questions for their new arrival. They wanted to know if I thought Pete Rose or Tony Pérez should play first base for the Phils in the World Series. I knew right away that I was going to like the job!

One of the first rules of succeeding at a new job is to establish a good relationship with the boss. I found out immediately that this would be no problem. My supervisor, Freddy Jana, invited me to lunch with him and Jorge Bournigal, a local radio personality. Jorge knew more about baseball than anyone I had ever met. In fact, his friends call him the "Enciclopedia" because of his ability to recite baseball stats and stories. The Enciclopedia's face would light up as he told stories about his beloved Boston Red Sox and Ted Williams.

Soon the Enciclopedia and my copy of *The Baseball Encyclopedia* were going head-to-head at the Bournigal family finca, a modest ocean house where Jorge would go on weekends to escape his hectic schedule. He needed the change of pace after a week of doing his radio show, writing a daily sports column, editing the sports page of the *Ultima Hora* (a Santo Domingo daily), broadcasting the home games of the Estrellas Orientales, and translating major league games for local TV. Although Jorge needed a break from his schedule, he never seemed to want to get away from the game he loved. So I would grill the Enciclopedia on the players, events, and history of the game.

In Santiago, one of the game's biggest stars is Gold Glove catcher Tony Peña. One day when I was working with Freddy at the bank there, Peña and his wife dropped by. Suddenly the banking world went on a brief, unscheduled holiday. A visit by Tony Peña anywhere in the Dominican Republic is like having Tom Cruise walk into an American high school. The place was abuzz with excitement.

Peña was staying in shape by playing for his hometown Aguilas Cibaeñas in the Dominican winter league. Yet when we met, I could tell he was eager to give his language skills a workout too, because he immediately switched to English for our conversation. That eagerness to communicate paid off. When Peña signed with the Boston Red Sox in 1990, the Sox cited his good communication skills as a key factor in their acquisition of him.

All of these experiences in the Domincan Republic—meeting Jorge the Enciclopedia, seeing the Dominican love for baseball, getting to know people like Tony Peña—made my interest in Latin baseball soar. And that led me to begin looking for books on the subject. But I struck out in my search.

Then I toyed with the idea of writing a travel guide to help visitors who would come to attend the winter league games and to share with them my love for the game. I also planned to include information about the Dominican Republic's rich history, its fascinating museums, its delightful restaurants, and its sun-drenched beaches.

When I talked with Jorge about the idea, the dream grew. He had already done several articles on the top Latin players, so we decided that the book should also include profiles of the best Latin players.

However, that team effort never developed. Jorge's busy schedule and my unexpected transfer out of the Dominican Republic squashed all hope of collaboration. Another great idea went on the shelf.

I am not sure what the shelf life of an idea is, but this one definitely lived for two more years. It was reenergized shortly after Mary and I were married in 1986, when we received an impressive newspaper story from her family. The article recounted the story of a trip to San Pedro de Macorís by a writer from the Albuquerque *Journal.* Mary felt that if this woman from Albuquerque could make so much of one visit to the Dominican Republic, she could certainly contribute something valuable after spending four years there.

So, with new impetus and confidence, we got my old idea down, dusted it off, and set out to see if it was a project that needed to be done.

When we moved back to the States, we continued the search for writings which touched on the Latin baseball experience. We found pieces of the story in biographies of Latin stars, histories of Negro league players, and periodicals. The rest of the story, or rather, our interpretation of it, comes from our combined ten years of living experience in Latin America which taught us that Latin baseball, like Latin culture, moves to a different beat.

We hope that by sharing our insights on the century-long history of Latin baseball, we will increase the understanding between our two cultures and lead to further, badly needed, research on the subject. In this way we hope to repay at least in part the friendship and hospitality we received during our years in Latin America.

Michael M. Oleksak
Mary Adams Oleksak

Winchester, Massachusetts
February 1991

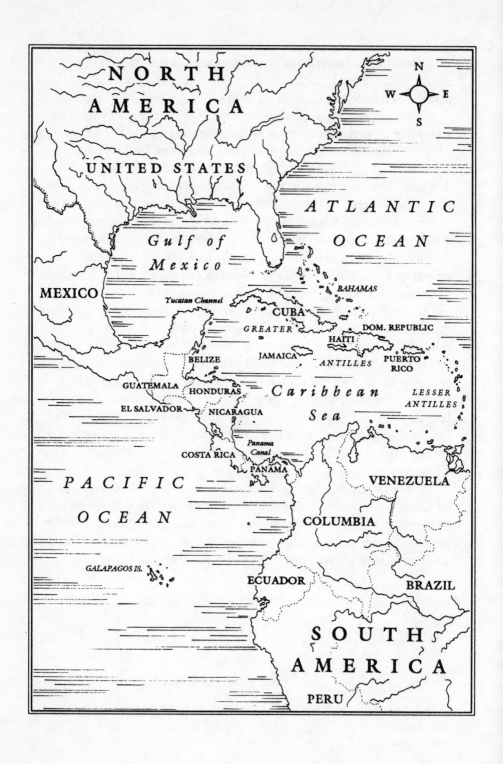

INTRODUCTION

Major league rosters of the 1990s will in-
clude the names Rijo, Canseco, Sierra, Guillén, Bell, Alomar,
Fernández, Franco, Galarraga, Guerrero, Higuera, Martínez, Palmeiro, Samuel, Santiago, and Tartabull.

Each of these Latin American players has, like his U.S. peers,
achieved the ranks of the majors by pushing the limits of his
individual talent. Yet these players crossed more than personal
borders to reach this height—they crossed the very boundaries that
define our "national pastime." In so doing, they built on the tradition
of Latin migration to U.S. fields that has become an indelible part
of the "grand old game."

Reminders of this tradition—and, indeed, of the importance of
Latin players in the major leagues—are never far from view. The
MVP in the 1990 All-Star Game was Dominican Julio Franco of the
Texas Rangers. At the end of the 1990 season, the World Series
MVP was another Dominican, José Rijo, in recognition of his
pitching, which helped Cincinnati sweep the powerful Oakland
Athletics.

Rubén Sierra of the Texas Rangers will throw out runners from
his right field position in the 1990s in a way that will remind fans
of another young Puerto Rican outfielder of the 1960s, Roberto
Clemente of the Pittsburgh Pirates.

White Sox shortstop Ozzie Guillén will pivot on a tough double
play at second base, and Chicago fans will remember the outstanding
performance of past Venezuelan shortstops Chico Carresquel and
Luís Aparicio in the 1950s and 1960s.

Chicago Cubs slugger George Bell will build on a record which
has already put him in the ranks of Dominican 200-plus home run
hitters along with Felipe Alou, Pedro Guerrero, and Rico Carty.

Puerto Rican catchers Benito Santiago with San Diego and Sandy Alomar with Cleveland will both probably continue as All-Star catchers until the year 2000.

In the 1990s, these young stars will add a 13th decade to the record of Latin Americans playing the grand old game. This record started with the very first professional baseball league formed in the United States, in 1871, which included a Latin player on its roster. This early trickle of talent swelled to a steady flow during the past 40 years. To date, over 500 of the 12,000 men to reach the major leagues have come from Latin America, from countries which have developed their own rich baseball traditions. Cuba, Puerto Rico, and the Dominican Republic have each contributed over 125 players to the majors. Venezuela, Mexico, Panama, and Nicaragua have combined for another 120. This blend of players has been enriched by a sprinkling of players from Colombia, Jamaica, the Virgin Islands, and the Netherlands Antilles.

The leagues in Latin America have done more than supply talent to the majors. At the beginning of the century, they provided the forum for black athletes to prove their worth against white major leaguers. In more recent times, the Caribbean has provided practice fields for managers, coaches, and even umpires seeking to prove that they have what it takes to reach the majors. Many a player has enjoyed the warm hospitality of the Caribbean and learned about the poorer nations beyond the U.S. borders.

The history of the interaction of the U.S. and Caribbean leagues has mirrored the political and economic history of the region. Wars, elections, dictators, and presidents have all played a role in the history of Latin baseball. But the one overriding theme throughout these many decades has been the poverty which afflicts our Caribbean neighbors and continues to make the attainment of a major league salary (even without bonuses) a near miraculous achievement of wealth.

Another strong theme throughout this story is the cultural differences which continue to separate the United States and Latin America. Latin players stand out not only because they speak a different language, but because of the way they view themselves and deal with their fellow players. This interaction is the subject of some amusing and some tragic tales.

The many stories about colorful Latin players enrich the history of U.S. baseball. This is important because baseball is an entertainment business. Latins are an untapped resource for the entertainment side of the business. To date, only a few major league clubs have developed their Latin talent beyond a "cheap reserve" status and recognized the potential of Latin baseball players as genuine personalities who increase the stadium draw and television receipts.

1

THE CUBAN
CONNECTION

Ask any kid to name the most important
Cuban-born baseball star of all time, and he might answer José
Canseco. Someone a little older might say Tony Pérez or Luís Tiant.
These men brought with them to the major leagues a style and a
personality that combined with their remarkable ability to make
them key figures in baseball history.

Yet there are other men from the time before television who are
as significant in baseball history.

Nemesio Guillot, for example.

In the late 19th century, Nemesio's parents sent him north from
Cuba to go to school in the United States. They realized that,
although their Cuban homeland was still a Spanish colony, the
young, expansive nation 90 miles to the north, just emerging from
its Civil War, would soon dominate the American hemisphere.
Experience in English would serve a young member of the upper
class well. Besides, the Catholic schools in North America were at
least as good as those in Mother Spain or the University of Havana,
founded in 1728.

When Guillot returned to Cuba in the summer of 1866, along with his new knowledge of the United States, he brought home some strange equipment, which he said was used to play a new game called béisbol. Soon he was teaching his friends this new game he had learned in the United States.[1]

Other U.S.-trained Cubans followed Guillot home with a similar passion for the game that had become the sport of choice among upper-class North Americans.

One of these initiates into this growing U.S. diversion was Esteban Bellán, who had learned the game at Fordham University in New York City. Bellán learned Nemesio's game so well that by 1869 he was playing for the Troy Haymakers. In fact, Bellán became a major leaguer in 1871 when he played third base, shortstop, and outfield for Troy, which at the time was a charter member of the National Association. He also played in the NA for the New York Mutuals. As "Steve" Bellán, the Cuban native hit .236 during this three-year stint in baseball's first pro league.

If Nemesio Guillot introduced baseball and Cuba to each other, Esteban Bellán performed the marriage. In 1874 he returned to his home country and helped organize the first recorded baseball game in Cuba. Bellán played third base for a team from Havana, which trounced Matanzas 51-9.[2]

Although the game did not provide much drama, the stage was set for baseball in Cuba, and the sport grew quickly. Only four years after the game's introduction, Havana, Matanzas, and a third team, Almendares, joined to form Cuba's first professional league, only two years after the formation of the National League in the United States. The Havana club dominated the new league, winning nine pennants between 1878 and 1892 under club founder Emilio Sabourín, considered by many to be a patriarch of Cuban baseball.

Besides becoming a professional sport, another change was taking place in Cuban baseball. Just as in New York, the game which began as a rich man's sport was rapidly gaining mass appeal. The equipment and the rules were so simple and accessible to the working classes that they soon formed their own teams.

This combination of professionalism and a growing interest from the lower classes led to an epidemic of baseball fever in Cuba. In the next few years, 75 new baseball clubs were founded. Wenceslao Gálvez y Delmonte, a ballplayer-turned-writer, predicted in 1889 that baseball would outlast bullfighting and cockfighting, centuries-old pastimes imported from Spain.[3]

But bullfighting and cockfighting were not the only aspects of Spanish colonialism threatened with extinction. In the late 1800s the Cuban people began to rail against the right of the Spanish to control their island. But Spain was not going to give in easily.

For three centuries Cuba had been a sleepy Spanish colonial outpost. When the world developed a taste for Cuban sugar and tobacco in the early 1800s, Spain shipped 200,000 Africans to the Caribbean island for the back-breaking chore of chopping the thick, splintery sugar cane with machetes. Soon sugar propelled Cuba's economy, supplemented by the cigar tobacco relished as the best in the world. The sugar and tobacco riches kept Spain's aging empire afloat, so while most Latin American countries won independence early in the 19th century, Spain clung to Cuba.

While baseball's popularity grew in Cuba during the last two decades of the 1800s, Spain's fell. The Cubans fought a series of wars for their independence starting in 1868. In 1895 Jose Martí, a poet and leader of the independence drive, founded the Cuban Revolutionary Party and sparked the last, bloodiest revolt. The United States sent the battleship USS *Maine* to protect U.S. property and citizens in the violent rioting against the Spanish. One night in February 1898, the *Maine* was destroyed with 260 crew members aboard. Soon the United States and Spain were at war not only for the "freedom" of Cuba, but also for the other remains of Spain's crumbling empire in Puerto Rico, the Philippines, and Guam. The fighting was over by August with the spoils going to the victorious United States.

Island Hopping

The decades of violence from the battle for independence drove many Cubans to seek refuge on Hispaniola, the quiet neighboring island to the west. Hispaniola was the site of Columbus's first settlement in the New World as well as the first hospital, monastery, and university. In 1697 the Spanish ceded the western end of the island to the French, which later became Haiti. The eastern two-thirds of the island remained the Spanish colony of the Dominican Republic.

It was to the Dominican side of the island that many Cubans fled during their protracted war of independence. The Cubans found Hispaniola quite similar to their homeland, and they bought up the low-priced sugar land in the southern part of the country to establish a modern sugar industry. Besides their expertise in growing cane, they also brought to the island the game that had won the hearts of Nemesio Guillot and Esteban Bellán: baseball.

Baseball and sugar production fit perfectly. During the six months it took for the cane to grow, baseball was a cheap and easy diversion for the laborers. The slow pace of the game suited the hot Caribbean days, allowing plenty of rest in the shade and only infrequent bursts of exertion. Bodies made strong by slashing the tough, wiry cane in the harvest were perfectly suited to action at home plate. In addition, the sugar mill owners wanted to field winning teams, so baseball skills brought a premium to workers who possessed them. The Cubans eventually sold out to U.S. investors, who continued their support of these "sugar leagues" for the next 20 years.

Go West, Young Men

Some of the Cubans who fled their nation during its violent drive for independence in the 1890s sailed west to Mexico's Yucatan Peninsula, which is closer to Havana than Santo Domingo is. There, just as in Hispaniola, the Cubans became baseball ambassadors. Boys introduced the game, with loose rules and playing styles, to the children in Mérida, and amateur teams were formed by upper-class children. However, the sport was quickly adopted by the working class, which still supports baseball today. Indeed, some of the local game's first stars were Mayan field workers toughened by their work among the gray sisal stalks grown for U.S. twine manufacturers.[4] Although the game also came into Mexico through other means, the Cubans' introduction of baseball represented one of the first inroads of the sport into the huge land to the south of the burgeoning United States.

To Another Spanish Isle

A third Latin American nation that got its first baseball lessons from Cuban expatriates was Puerto Rico. Both countries were still Spanish colonies in 1890 when Spain transferred one of its diplomats from Cuba to Puerto Rico. His son taught the game to Puerto Rico's children. As in Cuba, upper-class Puerto Rican students who studied in the United States also promoted baseball among their friends on the island.

Local newspapers first reported on Puerto Rican baseball in 1897, the same year Puerto Rico won its independence.[5] The people of the island had agitated for independence from Spain for more than 50 years. In 1897 they finally won a charter from the Spanish establishing rights of self-government. But before the charter was enacted, the United States declared war on Spain, and U.S. Marines landed in Puerto Rico in 1898. Although the war ended quickly, the U.S. soldiers stayed under the authority of the U.S. Congress, which hesitated to grant self-government to the island based on testimony that the Puerto Ricans were "poverty-stricken, illiterate, and wholly inexperienced in self-government."[6]

The first organized baseball game played in front of spectators in Puerto Rico was held on January 9, 1898, six months before the Marines arrived. Borinquen, a team that adopted the Indian name for Puerto Rico, played Almendares, named after the famous Cuban team. The game took place at a San Juan bicycle course, with a seat in the shade selling for 40 cents, a seat in the sun for 20 cents, and a bleacher seat selling for a dime. Actually, the game took three weeks to complete. On the first attempt, the game was called after three innings because of rain. The two teams tried again the next week, only to get washed out after four innings. Finally, on January 30, 1898, the game was completed as Borinquen defeated Almendares 9-3.

The two rain delays did not dampen the Puerto Ricans' interest in this newfangled game called baseball. By the turn of the century, teams all over the island organized to play the game. Baseball became a popular diversion for Sundays and holidays, and schoolboy teams played on Fridays as soon as classes were over.

Soon the advent of professional baseball began to put the game on an even higher level. Town teams began to play each other, with gate receipts covering expenses and the excess being divided among the players. The Almendares team reorganized and began playing for pay, and other teams such as Havana and San Cristóbal joined the pro ranks. Teams often played in El Morro, an old Spanish fort that stands on a finger of land in San Juan Harbor.

During these early days of Puerto Rican professional baseball, there were no organized leagues. Games were generally set up between any well-matched teams on the island. Despite the lack of a clear-cut league setup, newspapers reported three or four annual "Champions of Puerto Rico." And occasionally, promoters would set up what they called "National Championships."

South to Venezuela

A Cuban also brought baseball to a southern neighbor, Venezuela, so named because an early explorer thought the Indian huts built on piles over the shallow waters of Lake Maracaibo had the look of Venice. Colonial Venezuela was ruled from Santo Domingo and Bogota with benign neglect. Early on, the Spanish actually gave control of the area to a German banking house. After the Germans gave up their 50-year search for gold and silver, the small Spanish settlements enjoyed relative autonomy and developed an economy based on corn, beans, beef, tobacco, sugar, cacao, and hides. During the 17th century, Dutch pirates raided the Venezuelan coast, which came to be called the Spanish Main. For the first half of the 18th century, the Spaniards once again granted an economic monopoly in Venezuela, this time to a group of Spanish Basque merchants. The Spanish sent nobles to occupy the highest government posts, but locally born whites owned most of the land and dominated local politics. This local elite, called *criollos,* resented the Spanish nobles.

When Napoleon Bonaparte invaded Spain in 1808, the criollos saw their chance to break away from the weakened Spanish. In 1810 Venezuela and Argentina became the first Latin American countries to declare independence from Spain. Under leaders like Simón Bolívar, a man remembered for his dream of a united Latin America, the Venezuelans fought a long and destructive battle for freedom. Finally, in 1821, Venezuela won independence for itself, as did Colombia and Ecuador.

Venezuela had enjoyed six decades of freedom when Cuban ballplayer Emilio Cramer introduced baseball in 1895.[7] Cramer's

new sport gave Venezuelans a choice of Sunday-afternoon events—
bullfighting or baseball.

The game advanced slowly in Venezuela until 1922, when oil
was discovered under Lake Maracaibo. Royal Dutch Shell and
Standard Oil of New Jersey moved in to develop an oil industry,
producing great wealth and financing large public works projects.
Suddenly it was possible for Venezuela to afford something that
gave baseball a boost—it could now pay Americans imported from
the U.S. Negro leagues to play. Baseball began to take on an
international flair in the land of Simón Bolívar.

What began in eastern schools in the United States, spread
throughout Cuba and then to the Dominican Republic, Puerto Rico,
Mexico, and Venezuela, had come full circle. The U.S. game was
now being played by U.S. players on Latin soil.

2

INVESTING IN BASEBALL

The Cubans were not the only baseball missionaries who spread the game across Latin America. At the same time that Cuban emigrants carried the sport to the Dominican Republic, Puerto Rico, Venezuela, and Mexico's Yucatan, U.S. travelers won their own share of baseball converts in northwestern Mexico, Nicaragua, and Panama.

That some Latin countries learned baseball from the United States rather than from their Latin neighbors is not surprising. For 400 years, Spain prohibited trade among its American colonies. All trade had to be channeled through the mother country. Furthermore, Spain outlawed local industry in its Latin colonies to guarantee a market for Spanish goods, including wool, metal, glass, ceramics, and leather. So when these countries broke free from European domination in the 1800s, they needed to replace their only trading partner. To do that, they turned northward to the young but ever stronger neighbor, the United States.

At the same time, the United States was recovering from its Civil War, and it began to gain new confidence in its power and to develop its own identity in the world. Looking to the south, U.S. businessmen and politicians alike saw the possibilities of working with the emerging independent Latin American countries. When they traveled south to the "other" America for talks and trade, they took with them the sport that was rapidly becoming an institution in the Western Hemisphere.[1]

Mexico: Railway Spikes and Baseball Bats

Business and baseball penetrated Mexico, Nicaragua, and Panama for different reasons. In Mexico, it was trains. The Mexicans declared independence from Spain in 1821, but their territorial battles continued for years afterwards. Mexico lost land in several conflicts with the United States, and in the 1860s Mexico even had to fight off French conquerors. One victory in this struggle, on May 5, 1862, is celebrated annually by Mexicans as the "Cinco de Mayo."

After this period of unrest, Mexico was ripe for the strong hand of Porfirio Díaz, a dictator who took control of the country in 1876 and pushed it into the modern age. Under Díaz's iron rule, economic development came first.

To unify this huge nation, the government began stringing telegraph wires, cutting out roads, and laying railroad tracks. Within 30 years, more than 12,000 miles of railroad tracks crisscrossed Mexico.

When Díaz wanted railroads, he knew where to get the know-how—from the United States, which had finished its first coast-to-coast rail line in 1869. The northern railroaders brought more than sledgehammers, spikes, and railroad expertise with them. They also brought bats, balls, and baseball strategy. So it was that in the late 1870s in Nuevo Laredo, one of the first Mexican baseball games was played under the watchful eye of railroad construction supervisor Johnny Tayson.[2]

Sailors also helped turn Mexico into a baseball country. In the port city of Guaymas, which lies along the western coast, sailors from the U.S. ships *Montana* and *Newborne* taught local workers the game in 1877. Within just ten years, baseball had spread to the capital, where the Mexico Club was formed as weekend recreation. In a link harkening to baseball's introduction into the country, one of the Mexico Club's primary opponents was the Mexico National Railroad Club.

Nicaragua: Baseball Versus Cricket

Baseball was also transported to Nicaragua by the ships of commerce. Nicaragua became independent from Spain first as part of the Mexican empire, and then in the Federation of Central America. It broke off on its own in 1838 but did not develop a federal government strong enough to control the British and U.S. businessmen seeking to profit from the growing transport business between the Atlantic and Pacific oceans. When the Gold Rush started in 1848, thousands of prospectors made their way to California by steamship to Panama and Nicaragua and then across Central America before continuing north by steamship to San Francisco. British companies came into conflict with Commodore Vanderbilt's Accessory Transit Company, which provided boat service up the Rio San Juan and across Lake Nicaragua and then land transport for the last 14 miles to the Pacific. In 1850 the United States and Britain agreed in the Clayton-Bulwer Treaty that neither country would unilaterally exploit Nicaragua.

However, the treaty did not solve another burning controversy between the two countries—which sport would gain acceptance in Nicaragua, baseball or cricket. U.S. businessman Albert Adlesburg was disturbed to find that the British were teaching the Nicaraguans cricket. Adlesburg countered this British invasion with baseball as his weapon. In 1889 Adlesburg sponsored the first Nicaraguan baseball game, played in the city of Bluefields.[3]

Adlesburg's war was aided by young Nicaraguans who had gone to the United States to study and had learned about baseball in the process. David Arellano, for example, was a member of the first baseball team formed by the Managua Society of Recreation in 1890. Arellano, like Cuban-born baseball ambassador Esteban Bellán, had studied at Fordham University.

Two other U.S. students turned baseball missionaries were Marcial Erasmos Solis and Juan Deshón. Both were star pitchers for El Boer, a team that was founded in 1905 and is still competing today under the same name. Deshón is remembered in Nicaragua as the first pitcher for his homeland to throw curves, and he was the initial inductee into the Nicaraguan Baseball Hall of Fame.

Panama: Bully for Baseball

Just as the search for the shortest route between the two oceans led to Nicaragua's discovery of baseball, so it was with Panama.

Shortly after the dawn of the 20th century, U.S. president Theodore Roosevelt became convinced that the United States needed a more efficient means of transportation between the two oceans than the ground transport companies like that organized by Mr. Vanderbilt. The narrow 42-mile-wide strip of land that separated the east and west coasts of Panama seemed like the ideal place to build a canal. For centuries Panama had been the link between Spain and its colonies along the western coast of South America. Shipments from the merchants of Seville were exchanged in Panama for silver and gold to finance the Spanish crown. However, when Roosevelt tried to use this same route for his canal, Colombia, which had controlled Panama since the two countries broke away from Spain in 1821, refused to lease the land to Uncle Sam.

The Panamanians took matters into their own hands. On November 3, 1903, they declared their independence from Colombia. To punctuate the declaration, U.S. warships stood ready to prevent Colombian forces from landing. Within two weeks, the United States had been granted use and occupation of the Canal Zone.

Soon the North Americans were in the Canal Zone with picks, shovels, and baseballs. The game was a hit, and the Panamanians quickly formed local teams to take on the U.S. sailors and laborers. By 1912 Panama had its own league with teams sporting names as diverse as Mateo Iturralde, Tigrillo, Tosania, Walk Over, and El Palais Royal.

Between playing baseball and swatting mosquitoes, the laborers found time to dig the huge ditch, and in 1914 the first ship passed through the locks. Also that year, a second Canal Zone league was formed to play baseball from December through April, to coincide with the dry season. Canal Zone ballparks in Colón, Pedro Miguel, and Balboa were outfitted with grandstands for 2,500 to 3,000 spectators with the help of a $19,000 government appropriation.

The league got underway when President Porras threw out the first pitch.[4]

Ten years later, the visit by a team from the University of Havana (Equipo Caribe) generated even more enthusiasm for baseball. Although the Panamanian clubs lost the three-game series with Team Caribe, their presence inspired continued growth of league play.

By land, by water, by railroad, baseball spread throughout the Caribbean region by the beginning of the 20th century. Although the sport has been the strongest in Cuba, the Dominican Republic, Puerto Rico, Venezuela, Mexico, Nicaragua, and Panama, all former Spanish colonies, it is also played today in Colombia, the Virgin Islands, Central America, and the Netherlands Antilles.

3

VACATIONS IN THE SUN

Soon after baseball began to take hold in the countries south of the border, major leaguers discovered the value of a working winter vacation in the sunny Caribbean.

The New York Giants first sampled the tropical winter climate and enthusiastic fans of the Caribbean when they visited Cuba in 1890. Baseball excursions from U.S. teams to that island nation were short-lived, however. It was not the heat of the climate that put a stop to them, but rather the heat of political violence. During the Cuban struggle for independence from 1895 to 1898, major league teams were afraid to barnstorm there.

So, as did many Cubans during the revolution, the players who wanted to play winter baseball in the sun looked to Cuba's western neighbor, Mexico. During the early years of the new century, teams from Cuba and the United States frequently played each other along the U.S.-Mexican border. In the spring of 1907, the defending world champion Chicago White Sox—the Hitless Wonders—became the first major league team to train outside the United States when they made Mexico City their spring headquarters.

U.S. soldiers stayed in Cuba for three and a half years after the conclusion of the Spanish-American War. The soldiers withdrew under the terms of the Platt Amendment, which reserved for the United States the right to intervene at will to protect U.S. interests, a right the U.S. Congress exercised several times in the following decades. But baseball was already popular enough in Cuba to be unaffected by questions of Cuban independence and U.S. interference in internal affairs.

Cuba had settled down enough by 1908 for major leaguers to return. The first post-Spanish-American War barnstorming visit by a U.S. team was the brainstorm of José Massaguer of the Havana daily *El Mundo*. He arranged for the fifth-place Cincinnati Reds to travel to Cuba and take on Almendares and Havana. Whereas Almendares fielded an all-Cuban team, Havana boasted a few black players from the United States.

The Reds were unprepared for what happened. A 20-year-old Cuban fastballer, José "The Black Diamond" Méndez, shut out the Reds 1-0 and gave up only one ninth-inning infield single. Young Méndez threw a fastball and a sharp curve powered by the strong shoulders and forearms he developed chopping sugar cane. Méndez pitched twice more against the Reds and stopped them in seven innings of relief and then in a complete game shutout. Cincinnati won only four games and lost seven on its ill-fated trip.

The 1909 American League champion Detroit Tigers were the next northerners to be lured to Cuba by the prospects of balmy weather and extra income. Again the major leaguers found southern hospitality less to their liking than they had anticipated. Enhanced by players from the Negro leagues in the United States, the Cubans beat the Tigers in seven of the twelve games. Perhaps the losses resulted from the absence of Ty Cobb and fellow outfielder Sam Crawford, as well as the presence of a pitching staff that was not at full strength. For whatever reason, the Tigers were embarrassed when little-known Eustaquio Pedroza fired a ten-inning no-hitter at them.

These winter vacation losses by the Reds and Tigers to teams of dark-skinned Cuban and U.S. Negroes created an uncomfortable dilemma for many who had gone on record as opposing the integration of dark-skinned people into the major leagues. One of their arguments had always been that the game must be kept lily white to preserve the high quality of play. The Cuban teams' fine performances cast doubts on that already dubious theory.

Despite Detroit's poor showing in 1909, the team decided to go island-hopping again in 1910. This time the Detroiters brought along Sam Crawford for the 12-game schedule against Havana and Almendares. But Crawford was not enough, as old nemesis Eustaquio Pedroza leveled the Tigers again, this time no-hitting them for 11 innings.

The teams battled toe-to-toe through the first seven games. Detroit and the Cuban teams each won three times and one game ended in a tie. The series ended with a Ty too—Ty Cobb, that is. The Tigers' premier hitter journeyed to Cuba for the last five games.

In game eight of the series, the Cuban fans packed the Havana ballpark to watch Cobb hit two singles and a home run to lead Detroit to a 4-0 win. Cobb was hitless against Cuban pitching the next day, although he did reach first base once on a walk. Against José Méndez, Cobb struck out and singled. When the Cuban dust had settled, the Tigers had finally won a series—seven games to five.

But Ty Cobb did not leave Cuba as a happy winter vacationer. Although he performed well in front of the Cuban fans, he was outhit by three American Negroes playing for Havana. John Henry "Pop" Lloyd (inducted in Cooperstown Hall of Fame in 1977), Grant "Home Run" Johnson, and catcher Bruce Petway all exceeded Cobb's .370 batting average. After this series, Cobb vowed never to play against black men again, a promise he kept.[1]

Cobb's visit is remembered in Cuba not for his outstanding play, but for his wily twist of an umpire's arm. In one of the games, Bruce Petway threw Cobb out on a steal attempt. Cobb protested that second base was implanted farther than the standard 90 feet from first base. Cobb insisted that the umpire measure the base path. Cobb was proved correct when the tape measured 90 feet, 3 inches. The story lived on for years in Cuba, a famous footnote to the major league barnstorming tours.

Not long after the Tigers got back on the boat for their return voyage to the States, the world-champion Philadelphia A's sailed in. They met a familiar fate, losing three of the first four games to their Cuban hosts.

José Méndez was fast becoming a major nemesis for the major leaguers. Against Philadelphia, he twice defeated the A's great lefty, Eddie Plank. The A's recovered to take three of the final four games behind Jack Combs and Chief Bender to earn a split of the eight games in Cuba.

As this pattern continued, the major league teams began to scratch their heads about the success of the teams of Cubans and Negro league players. The A's, who had handily defeated the Cubs to take the World Series in five games, had to wonder what was happening if they could do no better than split the Cuban series.

Down but not out, the major leaguers kept coming. The other Philadelphia team, the Phillies, tried their hand at taking on the Cubans in 1911. Despite losing twice to (who else) José Méndez, the Philadelphia club took five of the eight games.

Next came the New York Giants under their intense manager John McGraw. It took only two games to get McGraw so steamed up that he threatened to send his players home. A 6-4 loss to Pedroso in the opener, coupled with a 3-2 loss to Adolfo Luque, set McGraw off. In a fiery speech to his charges, he berated them and warned, "I didn't come down here to let a lot of coffee-colored Cubans show me up. You've got to either play ball or go home."[2]

To help his cause, McGraw sent Christy Mathewson out to the mound to face Méndez in the next game. It was a classic pitchers' duel until the Giants got to Méndez late for four runs and five hits. Mathewson finished with a three-hit shutout and a 4-0 win.

The Giants were on a roll. They took eight of the last nine games and finished the series with an 8-3 record. The only other loss came when Mathewson again dueled Méndez and Pedroso and lost 7-4.

In a backhanded tribute that revealed the state of race relations in the early 1900s in America, McGraw remarked that he would have given $50,000 to get Méndez and "Strike" Gonzales, his catcher—if they had been white.[3]

The attitude was no different in the American League. The A's 50-50 showing against the Cubans in 1911 was more than American League President Ban Johnson could bear. He put a stop to the Caribbean barnstorming of his league's teams, remarking, "We want no makeshift club calling themselves the Athletics to go to Cuba to be beaten by colored teams."[4]

The final tally of the 65 games played in those years reveals the source of embarrassment for Major League Baseball. In four years of barnstorming against teams made up of Cubans and American Negroes, the all-white major leaguers could do no better than win

32 games, lose 32 games, and tie one. And José Méndez? He picked up eight of those victories for the Cubans.

Yet it was not too many years before the lure of the sunny island nations called the major leagues back for more.

This time, they took with them the greatest weapon of them all: Babe Ruth. At the prompting of Cuban promoter Abel Linares, who paid the Bambino $1,000 a game, Ruth accompanied John McGraw and the Giants for a renewal of the U.S.-Cuba series.

After playing two games against Havana, the Cubans unveiled their secret weapon. Almendares, a team the major leagues had faced before, had its own version of Babe Ruth. Cristóbal Torriente was an outfielder who was built like the Babe, with a powerful upper body and slender legs. In the first game, Torriente smashed three home runs. Then, late in the game, Ruth himself took the mound to face Torriente. The Cuban star stood in against his North American mirror image and belted a double.

When reporters dubbed Torriente "The Cuban Babe Ruth,"[5] the Bambino's response was that Torriente was "as black as a ton and a half of coal in a dark cellar."[6] Skin, not skill, was still the name of the game.

Another twist to the series came because of the location of many of the games, Oriental Park. This casino-racetrack, which stood on the outskirts of Havana, belonged to Giants owner Charles Stoneham and his manager, John McGraw. This connection with gambling, coming just a year after the Chicago "Black Sox" scandal, led Baseball Commissioner "Kenesaw Mountain" Landis to force Stoneham and McGraw to sell the complex in 1921.

Barnstorming was not the sole domain of the major leagues. The Cubans did it too. In 1916 José Méndez pitched in Puerto Rico and received a hero's welcome. And in the 1920s and 1930s, Puerto Rico hosted games between teams from the Negro leagues and the major leagues. Negro league stars such as Satchel Paige and Josh Gibson, along with Cuban greats like Adolfo Luque and Martín Dihigo, all spent some of their winter time in Puerto Rico. Later, Willard Brown and Roy Campanella also traveled to the island.

The irony of all this barnstorming activity is what it revealed to Negro league players who left the "land of the free" to play baseball where they were accepted. They were surprised to find that freedom existed just a few miles away to the south. In an emotional letter sent from Mexico, shortstop Willie Wells wrote, "I've found freedom and democracy here, something I never found in the United States. I was branded a Negro in the United States and had to act accordingly. Everything I did, including playing ball, was regulated by color. Well, here . . . I am a man."[7]

4

PUREST BARS OF CASTILLIAN SOAP

U.S. baseball in the early quarter of the 20th century had no rules barring Cubans from playing in the major leagues. The players simply had to meet two unwritten qualifications: They had to be white, and they had to be able to prove it.

The 20th century Cuban talent flow into Major League Baseball began in 1911, when Cincinnati Reds Manager Clark Griffith offered a tryout to Rafael Almeida, an outfielder playing for the New Britain franchise in the Class B Connecticut League.[1] Almeida arrived at the tryouts with an interpreter who also played some pretty good baseball. Griffith, after watching the two players in action, remarked, "I like his interpreter better." The Reds signed them both.[2]

Soon Almeida and his bilingual teammate, Armando Marsans, were standing on the field in the major leagues. Not since Vincente "Sandy" Nava (who was born of Cuban parents in San Francisco) played for Baltimore and Providence from 1882 to 1886, and Colombian Luís Castro played for the Philadelphia A's in 1901, had any Latin ballplayers set foot on a major league diamond.

But Almeida and Marsans did not arrive to the open arms of the baseball world. The majors had been segregated since the late 1800s when White Sox Manager "Cap" Anson had yelled, "Get that nigger off the field"[3] at Newark player George Stovey, a light-skinned black pitcher from Canada.

The people of Cincinnati were concerned that olive-skinned Almeida and Marsans were not truly white, and they were afraid the league would not accept them. So the Reds' management sent to Cuba for documents that would establish the players' pedigrees. With that documentation in hand, the Cincinnati newspapers certified the Cubans as "two of the purest bars of Castillian soap ever floated to these shores."[4]

Almeida lasted three seasons with the Reds and batted .270, but Marsans proved to be a speedy outfielder and lasted until 1918 in the major leagues, batting .269. He also starred for Almendares during the winters in Cuba. After Marsans batted .317 for Cincinnati in 1912, the Havana City Council awarded him a $200 gold medal as "Cuba's Greatest Player."[5]

Mike González, another white Cuban, followed Almeida and Marsans a year later. González debuted with the Boston Braves in 1912. He had good defensive skills, but he hit only 13 home runs and batted .253 in 17 seasons with Boston, the Reds, the Cardinals, the Giants, and the Cubs. After his playing days were over, González coached for the Cardinals for 14 years and even managed 23 games for them in 1938 and 1940. González was coaching third for the Cards in the 1946 World Series when Enos "Country" Slaughter raced home from first base with the winning run on Harry Walker's seventh-game hit.

González took his World Series ring, said goodbye to St. Louis, and returned to Cuba, where he bought out all his partners in the Havana Reds. González had owned part of the Havana team for many years, and he had managed the club each winter. He also became one of the first local bird dogs for the U.S. leagues. Indeed, it was González who first used the expression "Good field, no hit" when telegraphing his report on a prospect. Since that time, a "good field, no hit" label has been applied to many ballplayers, frequently Latin utility infielders.

Two other Cuban players to break the border barrier and land in the majors in the first quarter of the century were Jacinto "Jack"

Calvo and José Acosta. Calvo played outfield for the Washington
Senators in 1913 and 1920. Acosta pitched for the Senators from
1920 to 1922, compiling a 10-10 record. These two players stand
out as the only men to play in both the segregated majors and the
Negro leagues. In the Negro leagues, Calvo and Acosta played for
the Long Branch Cubans and the New Jersey Cubans. In a 1920
Cuban exhibition game, Acosta struck out Babe Ruth three times.
Black players in the Negro leagues hoped that the majors' acceptance
of Cuban players signaled a crack in the wall that kept them out of
the majors, but the white line remained in force.

Dolf Luque: The Best of the Bunch

The best of the Cubans to reach the major
leagues during this period was, undoubtedly, Adolfo "Dolf" Luque.
Born in colonial Cuba in 1890, Luque played third base as a boy on
school teams because of his good reflexes and strong hitting. He
watched with great interest when U.S. players visited Cuba. Luque
later attributed his success with his curve to watching Christy
Mathewson during a Giants' visit.

Luque was pitching and playing third for the Fe (Faith) Club in
Havana when Cuban promoter Abel Linares signed him in 1912.
Luque went north to play for Long Branch, a semipro team in the
New York-New Jersey League. The team members were all white
Cubans, although a few years later Long Branch converted into the
Negro league team that Calvo and Acosta played on. In his first
season, Luque played third base and outfield and pitched 27 games
for a 22-5 record. Long Branch won the league championship.

For the next five years, Luque bounced around the minor leagues
and had a quick cup of coffee with the Boston Braves in 1914 and
1915. Every winter he headed home to Cuba where he was a winter
league favorite. Luque reached the majors for good in 1918 with
Cincinnati, where he threw his first shutout, also the first by any
Latin major leaguer.

Luque's early years in the majors were not easy. On his first visit
to St. Louis, fans greeted him with chants of "Nigger!" Luque stood
five-feet-seven in a wiry 160-pound frame. He had blue eyes and a
long, thin face that looked suntanned, but certainly not black.
However, a "suntan" was different enough to arouse suspicion

among white fans still unaccustomed to foreigners playing their "national game."

If such hostility bothered Luque, his record did not indicate it. He went 6-3 in 1918 and 9-3 in 1919. He pitched twice in relief in the fixed 1919 World Series against the Chicago "Black Sox," allowing only one hit and no runs in five innings and earning another baseball first—the first Latin player in a World Series game.

After the 1919 season Luque managed and pitched for Almendares in the Cuban winter league. He had a 10-4 record, propelling Almendares to the Cuban championship.

Over the next few years, Luque produced both record highs and record lows. In 1922 he established the all-time record for futility by a Latin pitcher, losing 23 times against 13 wins. Yet the very next year he bounced back to establish the record for wins by a Latin hurler with 27 victories. Together, Reds teammates Eppa Rixey (21-5), Pete Donohue (20-15), and Luque (27-8) became the last trio of National League pitchers on one team to win 20 games in a season.

Luque's career, although brilliant with 193 wins and 1,130 strikeouts, was not without its controversial moments. And generally those incidents stemmed from his Latin temperament.

In August of his 27-victory season, Luque was on the mound at Redland Field, Cincinnati, against the defending champions, the New York Giants. The crowd filled every available seat, including those usually saved for the players, so benches were set up on the field. Bench jockeying was common in those days, but it was even more lively that day because the players sat so close to the batters. In the eighth inning, New York was leading 6-2 and Luque was pitching to Ross Youngs when the Giants' reserve outfielder Bill Cunningham rankled Luque with a particularly choice remark. Luque slowly removed his glove, placed the ball inside it, turned, and raced toward the Giants' bench. He swung and connected with the jaw of outfielder Casey Stengel, who was sitting next to Cunningham. A free-for-all broke out, and eventually both Luque and Stengel were led from the field. Moments later, Luque came running back onto the field, swinging a bat. Four policemen grabbed him and removed him from the park.[6]

From Luque's angle there was no choice but to fight. His Latin society had taught him to be "macho." In Latin culture, a man's dignity comes from his daring, his competitiveness, and his will to conquer. A man's swagger tells the world that he stands ready to take on all comers and even discourage a few bystanders. A man's pride leaves little room for conciliation. To Luque, the swagger and the daring that marked a macho man were part of the game.

In a more domestic dispute, Luque once challenged teammate Babe Pinelli to a duel. Pinelli, the Reds' third baseman (and later an umpire after his playing days were over), made the mistake of suggesting a different pitching strategy to Dolf. Luque grabbed a pair of scissors and stormed after Pinelli. Teammates blocked Luque, but he screamed, "You get taxicab. I get taxicab, then we get guns and have a duel." The laughter of his teammates reminded Luque that gun battles over pitching strategy were unheard of in Ohio, and he backed down. Luque and Pinelli later became friends.7

Another time Luque was fined $50 by the National League for chasing Brooklyn pitcher Tiny Osborne with a bat after Osborne tried to bean Luque. Against almost every batter he faced, Luque went for blood. Luque's 1957 obituary in the New York *Journal-American* recalled, "Few hitters ever liked to go to the plate against him. They knew that if they didn't crowd the plate, they didn't have a chance against him. And they knew that if they did, he might put knots on their heads or crack their ribs or their elbows or their knees."8

Perhaps it was his drive and courage that extended his career long past normal retirement age. In 1932 the New York Giants picked up the 42-year-old Luque for some relief help. With Luque in the bullpen, the Giants won the National League pennant and faced the Washington Senators in the 1933 World Series. In the fifth game, with New York leading three games to one, Giants Manager Bill Terry called on Luque in the sixth inning with the score tied 3-3. Luque pitched four scoreless innings, matched zero for zero by Senators ace reliever Jack Russell. In the top of the tenth, Mel Ott hit a solo home run for a 4-3 Giant lead. Luque retired the first two Senator hitters in order, but Senators player-manager Joe Cronin singled and outfielder Fred Schulte walked on four pitches. Terry visited the mound to see if Luque could finish off Joe Kuhel, a .322 hitter with 107 RBIs in the regular season. Luque told Terry, "Bill, you listen to Poppa. I see you in the clubhouse quick."

Luque struck out Kuhel on three pitches, the last a curve that broke down in the dirt. Kuhel missed it by a foot. "I fixed him! I fixed him! I gave him Number Two!" Luque yelled as he raced off the field. In the locker room, Luque paraded around with a bloody toe, split from his work on the mound. He called this moment his greatest thrill as a pitcher.[9] Luque finished his major league career in 1935 with a 193-179 record, 26 shutouts, and two world championships.

Luque kept pitching after he left the majors, and he made his last appearance on the mound in 1946 at age 56, when he relieved in the last game for Puebla in the Mexican summer league. After he threw a scoreless ninth inning to preserve a win over rival Veracruz, Luque strode off the field amid thunderous applause from the Puebla fans. The local press compared Luque to "the greatest of Mexican bullfighters," Rodolfo Ganoa.[10]

Luque's pitching knowledge assured him coaching and managing jobs long after his major league days ended. He could spot and correct a fault immediately. He developed Sal "The Barber" Maglie in Cuba in 1945-46 and in the Mexican league in 1946. Luque coached him to pitch close and hit the corners. He also taught Maglie the "fadeaway" screwball he had learned from watching Christy Mathewson 35 years earlier. Maglie "shaved" the hitters as Luque taught him when he later starred for the Giants, Indians, Dodgers, and Yankees.

It is difficult to get a good glimpse of the man under the hard, unyielding exterior known as Dolf Luque. One way to do that is through the story of Luque and fellow Cuban, Negro league pitcher José Méndez. After Luque's 27-9 season with Cincinnati in 1923, Cuban fans honored him with a parade and the gift of a car at home plate of Havana's Gran Stadium. Luque spotted Méndez sitting on a bench and said, "You should have gotten this car. You're a better pitcher than I am. This parade should have been for you."[11] Luque recognized that only a few shades of skin color enabled him, not Méndez, to travel first class and earn major league money. And he acknowledged the injustice of it all.

So it was that Dolf Luque was the only outstanding Latin in the majors during the first third of the 20th century. Not because he was the only Latin with enough talent. The Caribbean countries could have sent many of their young men to the "big time." No, it was something else. Dolf Luque was the only Latin with the right combination of great talent and skin light enough to blend into the snow-white rosters of the major leagues.

5

TOO DARK FOR
BASEBALL

Most people in the Caribbean islands and
Central America have some combination of African black, Spanish
white, and native Indian blood. The African slaves were freed in the
early 1800s, and in contrast to the United States, the descendants
of these slaves intermarried with the offspring of the Spanish
colonials as well as immigrants from the Mediterranean and the
Middle East, leaving at least three-quarters of the population of most
islands with mixed blood. Although the upper classes are still mostly
white, the rest of the population is comprised of people with varying
skin tones. Perhaps for this reason, Caribbean countries never
legislated discrimination as did the United States.

Nor was baseball ever segregated in Latin America. Thus, during
the decades of U.S. baseball segregation, the only place black and
white ballplayers could regularly compete was on Latin fields.
Problems arose when the top Latin players attempted to graduate
to the majors, where only the lightest skin was accepted. Of course,
it was harder to tell with the Latins. White Latins, with the olive
skin of the Spanish, were already darker than many North Americans

whose ancestors lived in northern Europe. The distinction between olive and light brown was a hazy one.

One of the first U.S. all-black professional teams, formed on Long Island in 1885, tried to capitalize on this. They adopted the name "Cuban Giants" and the players pretended to speak Spanish, hoping that somehow a foreigner would be less offensive to North American fans than a black man.

After the turn of the century, mixed teams of white and black Cubans barnstormed through the United States under names such as Cuban Stars, Stars of Cuba, and All Cubans (1905-1911). The Long Branch, New Jersey Cubans (1915), Cuban Stars of the National League (1923-1938), New York Cubans (1935-36, 1939-1950), and Havana Stars followed.

In 1920 black businessmen formed the first formal Negro league in the United States. The league consisted of nine teams, including a revised version of the Cuban Stars. The owners welcomed the Cuban club because it drew well, proving correct the Cuban Giants' assumption that fans were intrigued by the coffee-colored players from another land. Once the reputation of the Cubans took hold, the players sought better playing spots elsewhere in the league. Cubans who played in the Negro leagues also served as an information source for winter opportunities. Through them, word spread about the need for players on Cuban teams or lucrative openings elsewhere in Latin America.

The Cuban Stars were owned by Alex Pompez, the son of Cuban immigrants from Key West, Florida. Pompez began as a baseball manager and sports promoter in Key West, and eventually moved north. In Harlem, Pompez was a big operator in the numbers racket and acquired Dyckman's Oval, a Harlem baseball stadium and amusement park. Pompez later served on the Baseball Hall of Fame Committee that gave belated recognition to several Negro league stars.

Although the Cubans were attracted by the money of the U.S. leagues, they had to suffer the indignities of whites-only restaurants and water coolers, restricted hotels, hostile attitudes, and social rules unlike anything back home in Cuba.

José Méndez

Yet many Cubans endured U.S. segregation for a chance to show their talents before the U.S. fans. One such strong-willed star was

José Méndez, the old menace the U.S. barnstormers had so much trouble with. In 1909 he won 44 games and lost only two for the Cuban Stars.

After arm trouble forced him to switch to shortstop and the outfield, he played for the Chicago American Giants and the Detroit Stars. Between 1920 and 1926, he was player-manager for the Kansas City Monarchs. During the winter Méndez pitched in the Cuban league, winning 74 games and losing 25 (.747) in 13 seasons. His popularity in Cuba grew to a point where, if he entered a Havana restaurant after a big winter league win, all the patrons stood and applauded. After a brief illness, Méndez died in 1926. When Cuba established its Baseball Hall of Fame in 1939, José Méndez was a solid member of the first group of inductees.

Martín Dihigo: Hall of Famer

The Baseball Hall of Fame Committee inducted only one Latin ballplayer from the Negro league era: Martín Dihigo. He is also the only player to be afforded Hall of Fame status in four countries: the United States, Cuba, Mexico, and Venezuela. Although Dihigo was a big man at six-feet-three, 225 pounds, he was fast on the bases, he had a strong and accurate arm from the outfield, and he hit the long ball.

He also pitched very well. In fact, Dihigo played all nine positions. Negro league star and fellow Hall of Famer Buck Leonard said, "Dihigo was the best all-around player I have ever seen. He could run, hit, throw, think, pitch, and manage. He both knew the game and could play it. I was in the game 23 years, and I never saw anyone better than he was. And that includes not only the United States but also Puerto Rico, Venezuela, Colombia, Cuba, and Mexico."[1]

Dihigo first drew notice for his play against U.S. Negro league teams, which were in Cuba for winter ball. Oscar Charleston and John Henry Lloyd, two Negro league legends and future Hall of Fame inductees, recognized Dihigo's versatility and encouraged him to go north. Negro league fans first saw 18-year-old Dihigo on Alex Pompez's Cuban Stars in 1923.

Dihigo's accomplishments were chronicled in a book titled *Blackball Stars* by John Holway. By Holway's calculations, Dihigo won 256 games and lost 136, while batting .304. In 11 Negro league seasons, Dihigo played mostly for the Cuban Stars and the New York Cubans. From 1937 to 1947, he played each summer in Mexico, where his 119-57 record set a new mark for win-loss percentage. He threw a no-hitter for Veracruz in 1937, had a career ERA of 2.84, and batted .317. During the winters in Cuba, he starred for the Havana Reds and Santa Clara.[2]

Dihigo was frustrated by never having the chance to manage the Havana team, a job Miguel González kept for himself. Instead, Dihigo moved to Marianao, where he became a player-manager. While in this position, Dihigo persuaded Buck Leonard to play for him. Leonard later told of the hospitality extended to him and the other visiting players. At Dihigo's home in Matanzas, on an off day, Dihigo served a traditional celebration feast to his teammates. Leonard said, "They dug a hole in the ground and heated rocks on the bottom with a wood fire. They put a spit through the pig, put a cover over it, and then shoveled dirt over the whole thing. They left it in the ground a long while, until it was time to eat. Then they dug up the pig, and you never tasted anything so delicious. Martín was a superb host."[3]

Cuban President Fulgencio Batista heaped public praise on Dihigo in his prime for Dihigo's outstanding contribution to Cuban sports. In Dihigo's later years, after Fidel Castro took power, the former baseball great became Minister of Sports. From that post he encouraged Cuban youth to play baseball. When Dihigo died in 1971, he was regarded as a national hero, both for his baseball playing and for his work in Cuba on behalf of the sport.

Cristóbal Torriente

Another outstanding Cuban who played in the Negro leagues was outfielder Cristóbal Torriente, the player who had given Babe Ruth a run for his money during the barnstorming years. Torriente, a strong-armed lefty, had superb range and was a great bad-ball hitter. It was said that Torriente's skin might have been light enough for him to pass for white, if he had not had kinky hair. With the Havana Reds, the colorful Torriente often wore a red kerchief around his neck and bracelets around his powerful wrists.

After jumping to the U.S. Negro leagues, Torriente played for the Chicago American Giants, the Kansas City Monarchs, the

Detroit Stars, and the Cleveland Cubs (1919-1934). Along with Méndez, Torriente was elected to the Cuban Hall of Fame in 1939.

Luís Tiant, Sr.

Among the talented Cubans who graced the Negro leagues was a pitcher whose name is familiar to many baseball fans today. That name is Luís "Lefty" Tiant. From 1930 to 1947, Lefty hurled for the Cuban Stars and the New York Cubans. In one of Cuba's most memorable showdowns, Tiant defeated New York Giant ace Carl Hubbell in a winter exhibition.

Among Negro league fans, Tiant is remembered for one incident in particular. While pitching for the Cuban Stars against the Baltimore Elite Giants, Tiant kept a baserunner close to the bag at first with his deceptive pick-off move. After a series of particularly herky-jerky motions, Tiant threw to first. The batter, Goose Curry, fooled by Tiant's motion in the twilight, took a swing. The umpire paused, then yelled, "Strike!" When Curry spun around to protest the call, the umpire declared, "If you were stupid enough to swing, it's still a strike."[4]

The Tiant legacy of mound mastery later made the majors through the twisting and turning pitching style of Tiant's only son, Luís Tiant, Jr.

The segregation that kept Dihigo, Torriante, Tiant, and countless others out of the majors makes comparisons with the performances of other greats virtually impossible. New York fans in the 1950s, or even modern-day fans with long memories, can debate the comparative merits of center fielders Willie Mays, Mickey Mantle, and Duke Snider. But it takes an active imagination and a knowledge of obscure performance records to begin comparing José Méndez and, say, "Smokey Joe" Wood, or Lefty Tiant and Dizzy Dean, Cristóbal Torriente and Jimmie Foxx, or Martín Dihigo and any player with the versatility to match him. In a sport like baseball, where part of the joy of the game is in the "hot stove league" where fans argue and compare, that is a great loss indeed. And the loss was even greater to the talented players who couldn't play in the major leagues because their skin was too dark.

6

EL PRESIDENTE DOESN'T LOSE

Although many Americans long considered the talent of the Negro leagues to be insignificant, Negro players were honored in the Latin countries for their magnificent skills. In the Dominican Republic in the 1930s, the country's dictator even assembled the cream of this talent in the hope that he could shine in the reflection of their starlight.

This dictator rose out of a debt crisis not unlike the one later faced by many Latin countries in the 1980s. The borrowings by a previous corrupt dictator, Ulises Heaureaux, in the 1880s had been used for both national modernization and for the strong man's personal aggrandizement. When the debts soured in 1905, the U.S. military moved in and seized Dominican customs receipts to pay off the notes, keeping 55 cents of each dollar collected and returning 45 cents to the Dominicans. That economic disaster, combined with the assassination of respected President Ramón Cáceres in 1911, plunged the country deep into chaos.

After a long period of trouble, U.S. President Woodrow Wilson authorized the Marine Corps to take control of the Dominican

Republic in 1916. The Dominican leaders refused to bow to U.S. policies, so the country was ruled by martial law. The United States allowed free elections in 1924 and the Marines withdrew. When the Marines sailed away from the island, they left behind many successful public works projects, a constitutional government, and a strong National Guard.

Unfortunately for the Dominicans, that National Guard was used by one man as a vehicle for consolidating power and gaining election as president in 1930. That man was Rafael Leonidas Trujillo Molina.

Trujillo, "The Boss"

One of the most violent dictators ever seen in Latin America, Trujillo dominated every aspect of Dominican life. His police force spied on the citizenry and controlled all travel within the country. Little or no emigration was allowed. With his strong-arm tactics, he wrested from investors most of the businesses, factories, and plantations in the country. Trujillo's family became the largest owner of sugar land and of rum manufacturing facilities, which made liquor from the sugar water and molasses produced from the cane. He ensured that every child learned about "the benefactor, Papa Trujillo." To guarantee that no one would forget his power, he ordered every Dominican home to display a portrait of himself, graced by the caption, "In This House, Trujillo is the Boss." No one was safe from Trujillo's clutches. It was so bad that Dominican men sought every excuse to keep their wives and daughters from Trujillo's sight, lest they catch his eye.

Although there were many issues for which Trujillo marshalled support from the Dominican people at the point of gun, he encountered little resistance when it came to baseball. Trujillo was, like most Dominicans, an ardent baseball fan. During the 1930s he encouraged visits by major league teams such as the Cincinnati Reds. After he changed the name of Santo Domingo to Ciudad Trujillo in 1936, any team from that city had to do justice to the dictator's name. He stacked the teams in the capital with the best players, including Dominicans, imported Cubans, and Negro league players.

In the summer of 1937 Trujillo staged the grandest tournament ever seen in the country. He combined Licey and Escogido (two teams that had enjoyed a reputation for baseball excellence since the early part of the century) into a team called Los Dragones. The Aguilas Cibaeñas from Santiago and the Estrellas Orientales, representing San Pedro de Macorís, provided competition for Los Dragones. Trujillo paid big salaries to top Negro league and Cuban stars who were distributed among the three teams. His representative, Dr. José Enrique Aybar, offered Satchel Paige $30,000 to bring a group of eight players to Ciudad Trujillo. Aybar told him, "You may take what you feel is your share and divide the rest."[1]

The Negro leaguers who joined Paige included Josh Gibson, Martín Dihigo, Cool Papa Bell, Chet Brewer, and Dan Bankhead. Trujillo's offer of hard cash advances, good salaries, and transportation for spouses lured the best players from the Pittsburgh Crawfords and other Negro league teams. The Crawfords, the Negro league's strongest team in 1936, were decimated by Trujillo's actions.

Trujillo used force and fear to keep his expensive imports in line and to ensure a championship for his team. One evening at the end of the 1937 season, pitcher Chet Brewer attempted to call on his friend Paige, a rival in the upcoming 1937 championship series. Brewer could not find Paige anywhere. When he inquired, he was told that Trujillo had locked up his players in jail to keep them out of trouble the night before the big series.

In *Invisible Men: Life in Baseball's Negro Leagues,* Donn Rogosin tells another story about Trujillo's dominating ways. "When Trujillo's team lost a series to Santiago, his players returned to their hotel to discover a squad of angry militia men. 'El Presidente doesn't lose' shouted the militia men, firing their rifles in the air. 'You know you are playing for El Presidente,' they shouted, and more shots rang out. Cool Papa Bell and other Ciudad Trujillo Negro leaguers were terrified, and they swept the next series against Santiago."[2] In the 1937 finals, Trujillo's team won the championship. The very next day, the players boarded a Pan Am Clipper (telling people as they went that they were eager to get away from the guns) and returned to the United States, where they barnstormed for a short time as the Trujillo All-Stars.

A few months later, basking in his victory and ever-growing control over the Dominican people, Trujillo ordered a systematic and premeditated extermination of 18,000 Haitians living in the Dominican Republic. The Haitians had long been used as migrant workers to supplement Dominican labor in the grueling sugar cane harvest. Many Haitians then stayed on in the country, living on the fringes of Dominican society. Their patois language, derived from French, made them stand out, as did their dark black skin, for there was much less intermarriage in Haiti than in the Dominican Republic.

Dominicans held a century of resentment for the Haitians, a result of the frequent wars between the two countries. But this shocking massacre was too much for almost everyone. In the aftermath of the carnage, Trujillo's power was questioned, and he was forced to pull back, hide behind a puppet president, and profess no interest in international relations. Full-scale war with outraged Haiti was avoided only when surrounding American republics intervened and forced Trujillo to pay a large indemnity to Haiti. As a result, for the next decade, Dominican baseball, like all phases of Dominican life, withdrew into a cocoon of fear and repression.

7

HOW TO RECRUIT A SENATOR

While the Dominican Republic languished behind a wall of political oppression, Cuba thrived. Cuba, a U.S. protectorate and virtually a colony under the Platt Amendment, received from the United States preferential treatment in purchasing its products as well as large investments in its economy. During Prohibition, improved airplane service from Miami made it easier for rich Americans to gamble in Havana casinos and play on Cuban beaches. By 1928 American businesses owned 75 percent of Cuba's sugar interests and controlled its utilities and tourism.

When sugar prices tumbled during the Great Depression, Cuban workers saw their wages fall. They joined with local intellectuals and professionals in protest against the governing "Platistas," whom they resented for allowing the United States to gain control of Cuba. Eventually, conservative military officer Fulgencio Batista wrested control of the Cuban political machine. Batista took power in January of 1934 and dominated Cuban politics for the next 25 years.

Unlike his neighbor Trujillo, Batista did not try to halt the flow of Cuban talent to the U.S. leagues. He was the perfect ally for Clark

Griffith, who recognized that Cuban baseball fields were as fertile and promising as the fields of sugar cane that made American businesses rich.

Griffith, who was the owner and patriarch of the Washington Senators, first observed Latin talent as the young manager of the Cincinnati Reds. He had broken significant ground when he signed Marsans and Almeida for the Reds in 1911, just before moving on to manage the Senators. In 1921 Griffith purchased part of the Senators and was named president. His son Calvin was a catcher for Bugle Laundry, a weekend semipro team in Baltimore. Through that association, Clark Griffith became friends with Joe Cambria, the man who owned the laundry and managed Griffith's son's team, and who later played a significant role in enabling Cuban baseball players to break into the major leagues.

Joe Cambria, Scout Extraordinaire

Cambria was something of a controversial figure. Born in Massachusetts, he played semipro baseball before moving to Baltimore. In the early 1930s Cambria bought the Albany franchise in the International League for $5,000. Soon after, Baseball Commissioner Kenesaw Landis cited Cambria's Albany operations for irregularities when it was discovered that he had held back some contracts from the league office until he was sure the players would make the club. Griffith intervened and defended Cambria.[1]

When the Depression set in, wherever possible Griffith cut expenses on the Senators, especially bonuses and salaries, which made up most of the ball club's costs. In an effort to secure inexpensive ballplayers, Griffith sent Cambria to Cuba in 1934. Cambria's first prospect was Roberto "Bobby" Estalella. In Cuba Estalella was called "Tarzan" because of his gigantic home runs. Within a year of his signing, Estalella was playing for the Senators. The Cuban slugger played an aggressive but awkward third base for Washington, and he became a fan favorite. Often fans would call the Washington offices before deciding whether to come out to the park—they wanted to know if manager Bucky Harris was going to start Estalella at third base.

If Estalella did play, it was an adventure. For example, he would sometimes stop ground balls with his chest or his chin. But his limited English cost the Senators on occasion, like the time he was told to let a bunt roll foul, and the language barrier frustrated Harris's instructions from the dugout.[2]

Between 1936 and 1939 Estalella bounced around in the minor leagues. In 1941 he moved to the St. Louis Browns, was traded back to the Senators, and then was sold to Philadelphia in 1943. During the war, he played for the A's. He finished his career with 44 home runs and a .282 average over parts of nine major league seasons.

Pedro "Preston" Gómez, who played in eight games for the wartime Washington Senators and later became a major league manager, was one of the 400 Cubans signed over the years by Joe Cambria. Gómez recounted to Richard Goldstein, author of *Spartan Seasons*, "Joe normally scouted the teams that were playing in Havana. But his secret was that he had former players he knew in every town, what you'd call bird dogs. They'd contact him when they saw a boy that looked pretty good, and Joe used to go to that town. The majority of American scouts, they'd only stay in Havana, but Joe traveled all over the island. He always had one fellow with him, he was the guy who would kind of translate. I do feel Joe understood the Spanish language, but I don't think he spoke Spanish. He used to sign 10, 15, sometimes 20 a year. The ones he thought had a chance to play in higher baseball, even to play on the major league level, he'd send to the Washington club. The other ones he'd send to various minor league clubs; his friends were always looking for ballplayers."[3]

In 1937 Cambria sold his Albany franchise for $65,000 to the Giants for transfer to Jersey City. Then he purchased the Trenton team of the New York-Penn League and signed Senator outfielder and five-time stolen base leader George Case. Cambria also invested in shares of the Salisbury, Maryland, and Springfield, Massachusetts, franchises. While scouting in the United States, Cambria also discovered Senator standout Mickey Vernon.

During his 25 years of scouting in Cuba, Cambria's efforts may never have led to a Senator pennant, but he did save money for the Griffiths. Rubén Amaro, former Philadelphia Phils scouting director, explained how Cambria arrived at tryout camps in a limousine, dressed in a white linen suit, and smoking a cigar. Amaro said, "Cambria had Cuba all to himself, so the Washington Senators

monopolized the talent. All these kids were desperate to sign."[4]
Indeed, Cambria became such a famous figure that a local cigar
company named one of its products "Papa Joe" after him.[5]

As Preston Gómez observed, Joe Cambria achieved this
dominance without ever learning Spanish. This deficiency led to many
amusing exchanges over the years. One spring Cambria showed up at
the Senators' training camp in Orlando with a big, powerful pitcher
he had tracked into Cuba's interior to sign. Cambria introduced the
player, Roberto Ortiz, as "faster than Walter Johnson and a longer
hitter than Jimmie Foxx." Manager Bucky Harris asked Ortiz where
he wanted to play. Ortiz, who did not understand English, gave him
a blank look. Harris, none too patient after his experiences with
Roberto Estalella, turned to Cambria and said, "You ask this guy
whether he's a pitcher or an outfielder. Let's see what he wants to
do."[6] But Cambria was no help at all. The best he could do was to
shout the question in English, to which Ortiz could only respond with
a bigger shrug and a blanker look. How this exchange ended is not
known, but someone finally decided on the outfield for Ortiz. It may
have been the wrong decision, for he hit only .255 with six home runs
in six years for Washington.

One of Cambria's most successful finds in Cuba's winter league
was Venezuelan pitcher Alejandro "Patón" Carrasquel. Carrasquel
passed for a white player in the majors in 1939, although fans and
opponents heckled him for his slightly dark skin. Early in his career,
he tried to anglicize his name to Alex Alexandra, but the press called
him "Carrasquel, the Venezuelan." He won 50 games and lost 39
from 1939 to 1945 for the mediocre Senators.

Despite the large number of Latins on the Senators, life was not
easy for Carrasquel and his fellow migrant baseball players. The
Latin players lived apart from the white players, spoke Spanish, and
were shunned by their teammates. And no wonder, given the
attitude of their manager. In 1940 Harris said, "They're trash.
They're doing no good and they aren't in place here. They don't fit.
They've all got to show me something and show me quick or I'm
cleaning out the joint. If I have to put up with incompetents, they
better at least speak English."[7]

Ossie Bluege took over the Senators in 1943, and in 1944 he
designated the mature Carrasquel to interpret and smooth relations
between the Senators' many Latin players and the outside world.

Joe Cambria had such a lock on the Cuban market that he was even credited with scouting Fidel Castro. According to Clark Griffith, "Uncle Joe scouted Castro and told him he didn't have a major league arm."[8] Rubén Amaro made this observation, "Cambria even turned Fidel Castro down twice. He could have changed history if he remembered that some pitchers just mature late."[9]

Rafael Avila, scouting supervisor in Latin America for the Dodgers, said, "A lot of people resented Cambria because he signed so many players for the Griffiths and so many got released. But I don't. He gave the opportunity to a lot of my people that no one else was willing to give."[10]

Cambria proved with Carrasquel and Estalella that Latin America was a cheap and plentiful source of talent. His Latin connections became more attractive than ever when the United States joined World War II and the military called up players into its service. Almost 50 Cubans got their chance at the big time during the war years, signed by the Senators and a few other teams.

The wartime search for talent also extended to other countries. Jesse Flores followed Mel Almada and José Luís "Chile" Gómez as the third Mexican-born major leaguer when he was called up by the Cubs in April 1943. Puerto Rico provided its first two players to the majors in 1943 when pitcher Hiram "Hi" Bithorn made the Cubs' roster, and two months later, Luís Olmo joined the Brooklyn Dodgers in the outfield. Venezuela's second major leaguer, "Chucho" Ramos, made a brief appearance at first base for Cincinnati in 1944. Most of these Latins were considered only temporary replacements during the war and were to be demoted when the soldiers returned home for the 1946 season.

8

PANCHO VILLA AND THE MEXICAN INVASION

When returning U.S. servicemen pushed aside their Latin replacements after World War II, Mexico provided the displaced players with a lucrative summertime alternative in its strong leagues supported by enthusiastic fans.

It had been 70 years since Porfirio Díaz's railroad construction and economic programs had first brought the sport to Mexico, and in that time baseball had grabbed a premier position on the Mexican sporting scene.

As a former soldier, Díaz enjoyed military support and significant investment by U.S. businessmen. The wealthy upper class gained the most during the Porfiriato. The Díaz government arranged by law for the largest landholders to continue to acquire more property, and land held by Indian villagers for centuries was handed over to large plantation owners. Soon, a handful of Mexicans owned most of the country's land.

In 1908 Díaz made statements to the foreign press intimating that Mexico was ready for democracy. The Mexican people took him at his word and demanded elections. Díaz reneged on his promise, however, and popular sentiment forced him to flee to Paris. After Díaz left, rival groups fought for 13 years for control of the country. More than 250,000 people died in battles for cities, factories, and farms across Mexico.

Pancho Villa's Invasion

During this period of turmoil, one revolutionary rose to prominence. His name was Pancho Villa. Fearing U.S. involvement, Villa defiantly led an incursion across the border and into New Mexico in 1916 and killed 17 American soldiers. U.S. Army General George Pershing led an unsuccessful search for Villa in the hills of Mexico. To this day, Mexicans proudly assert that theirs is the only country other than England to invade the territory of the continental United States.

In 1924 the bloodshed finally ended, and modern Mexico was born. The political group in control adopted the name of the Institutionalized Revolutionary Party (PRI). The government wrote a constitution which set Mexico apart by establishing agrarian reform, affirming extensive labor rights, nationalizing many industries, and mandating universal education. The PRI has held power in Mexico since that time by borrowing the symbols of the Indians and peasants, while involving labor, business, and the armed forces. In this way, the PRI candidate has won the presidency every six years. During the relative stability of the years since 1924, Mexicans have developed a strong sense of nationalism and independence, despite their constant awareness of their larger neighbor to the north.

One of the first presidential candidates put forth by the PRI was Abelardo Rodríguez. Rodríguez grew up playing baseball. Later, while studying at the University of Arizona, he started at second base for the Wildcats and in fact showed such promise that the Los Angeles Angels of the Pacific Coast League offered him a contract in 1920. His family, however, decided that his future lay in Mexico, which was probably a wise decision, since Rodríguez rose to be president of Mexico in 1932, thanks to the support of popular Mexican politician Lázaro Cárdenas.

Thus, Rodríguez left the distinction of being the first Mexican to reach the major leagues to fall on another youngster, Baldomero

Melo "Mel" Almada. Almada played baseball while growing up in Sonora, Mexico, and he made his start in U.S. ball in the Pacific Coast League. He was brought up by the Boston Red Sox in 1933, for whom he hit .341 in 14 games. In a career that stretched across nine years, Almada batted .284 for the Red Sox, the Senators, the Browns, and the Dodgers. Another Mexican, infielder "Chile" Gómez, played briefly for the Phillies in 1935 and 1936, and for the Senators in 1942.

After the revolution ended in the early twenties, the Mexican Baseball League was organized for summer play. In the early years, teams played mostly on Sundays, and eventually the league evolved to include minor league systems across the country. During the 1930s Mexican teams, occasionally supported with Cuban players, assembled for exhibitions against Negro league squads and other U.S. teams. Cubans Martín Dihigo, Lázaro Sálazar, and Agustín Bejerano excelled in these games and against some U.S. major league barnstorming teams, one including Jimmie Foxx. These games provided Mexican fans with top quality baseball and offered ballplayers the chance to earn some extra money during the Depression. In 1937 Connie Mack and the Philadelphia A's trained in Mexico City and Veracruz. The Mexicans defeated the A's twice during their stay.

Mexican baseball reached a turning point in 1940 when millionaire Jorge Pasquel and his four brothers took over the Veracruz Blues (Club Azules de Veracruz) of the Mexican Baseball League. The Pasquel brothers and their three sisters were Veracruz natives. Their father, Francisco Pasquel, owned a customs brokerage and part of the most profitable cigar company in Mexico. After successfully running the Veracruz lottery, the Pasquels turned to baseball, their passion.

In the early 1940s the Pasquels recruited Josh Gibson, Willie Wells, Buck Leonard, Ray Dandridge, and Booker McDaniels to play in the Mexican league. They paid the players well and encouraged them to bring along their families. Then, during World War II, the Pasquels lost Quincy Trouppe and Theolic Smith to the U.S. military draft. So Jorge Pasquel, with his numerous contacts in government, arranged a loan of 80,000 Mexican workers to the United States in exchange for these important players.[1] He also lured such great black stars as Roy Campanella, Satchel Paige, Monte

Irvin, Chet Brewer, and Johnny Taylor. Jorge Pasquel had seen the
enthusiam of Mexican fans in 1944 when 48-year-old Rogers
Hornsby played a few games there, especially when Hornsby broke
up his final game with a grand slam homer. Following the war, as
the U.S. servicemen returned to their prewar teams in the United
States, Pasquel recognized that Latin ballplayers would be relegated
to the minors or put back on the bench. He saw this as a recruiting
opportunity.

Jorge Pasquel's Invasion

Pasquel grabbed the position of league presi-
dent and urged the addition of new teams in San Luís Potosí and
Torréon to the existing six franchises (Mexico City, Veracruz,
Monterrey, Nuevo Laredo, Tampico, and Puebla). To fill the expanded rosters for the 98-game summer schedule, Pasquel made his
move. In the tradition of Pancho Villa, he invaded the United States.
Pasquel's invasion was not a quest for political advantage, however;
it was a quest for players to be distributed throughout the Mexican
league.

Pasquel's first targets were the Latins who enjoyed a brief touch
of major league glory during World War II. He snapped up Roberto
Ortiz, who left the Senators; Rene Monteagudo, who left the
Phillies; Luís Olmo, from the Dodgers; and Nap Reyes from the
Giants. Cuban pitcher Tommy de la Cruz left the Reds, and Cubs
pitcher Adrián Zabala abandoned the Cubs. Even Patón Carrasquel,
who had earned his major league slot long before the war, broke his
newly signed contract with the White Sox to go to Mexico. Dolf
Luque came from Cuba to manage the Puebla team. Pasquel gave
the Latins a chance to say no to the U.S. minor leagues, walk away
with their heads held high, and still play summer baseball for big
salaries. It was also refreshing for them to be able to play in Latin
America and to speak Spanish.

If Pasquel had stopped there, his raid would not have attracted
much attention. But he did not stop—he made ready for his next
incursion into baseball territory. He wanted to sign white major
leaguers to play in Mexico, a move which got the attention of the
major league executives. Pasquel and his smooth-talking brother,
Bernardo, attracted pitchers Max Lanier and Fred Martin as well as
infielder Lou Klein from the St. Louis Cardinals. Catchers Mickey

Owen and Ray Hayworth came from the Brooklyn Dodgers. Shortstop Vern Stephens left the St. Louis Browns, and pitchers Sal Maglie and Harry Feldman, outfielder Danny Gardella, and second baseman George Hausmann all left the New York Giants. Max Lanier told reporters, "Gentlemen, Mr. Pasquel offered me so much money I couldn't afford to turn him down."[2]

At the peak of his successful raiding, Pasquel declared, "We get about 15 telegrams a day from United States players asking for a chance to play in Mexico. We'll contract about a dozen more foreign players during the next four weeks. Maybe I'll ask [Baseball Commissioner] Happy Chandler if he wants a job down here."[3]

Tom Gorman, Giants pitcher and later a major league umpire, described what it was like to be wooed by Pasquel. "When I arrived in Laredo, Bernardo Pasquel met me at the Palace, the only hotel on the American side of town. He told me his brother Jorge wanted to see me in Mexico City. They had a plane waiting. When we got there, the Pasquels made me feel like Babe Ruth. A Cadillac met us at the airport." Gorman took a bow between innings at a baseball game and then moved on to Jorge Pasquel's office where, as Gorman recalled, "he opened a drawer of his desk and took out a wad of bills, most of them thousands. He counted out $20,000 and laid it out on the desk as he had promised."[4] Gorman pitched all of 1946, despite an early-season arm injury, with the help of Novocain injections.

Pasquel enjoyed tweaking the nose of U.S. baseball so much that he announced he was going to invite Joe DiMaggio, Ted Williams, Bob Feller, Stan Musial, and Hank Greenberg to join his league. Pasquel's gloating and posturing offended the major league executives as well as Commissioner Chandler. Finally, Chandler put his foot down and announced that players in Pasquel's "outlaw" league would be banned from organized baseball in the United States for five years if they did not return by Opening Day 1946.

The commissioner's threat, coupled with local conditions that left something to be desired, soon diminished the lure of big money for a few players. Vern Stephens returned after delivering the game-winning hit in his only game. Stephens complained, "It was like a concentration camp in Mexico. Everyone with six-shooters on the hip. The low caliber play and the high altitudes got me down. So did the 'No spikka da English.'"[5] Stephens signed a new contract with the Browns and was not suspended. Mickey Owen also left before completion of his Mexican contract.

Despite Pasquel's vision and drive, the Mexican league could not compete on the major league level. Limited seating capacities in the stadiums (Mexico City held 22,000; the rest averaged 8,000) made it impossible for Pasquel to recoup his expenses, and he lost huge amounts of money in 1946. When he started cutting back salaries in 1947, few of the U.S. players returned. Although the players who jumped to Mexico were to be barred from U.S. Organized Baseball for five years, a lawsuit by Danny Gardella permitted players to return in 1949. Among the players who were banned, Sal Maglie had the biggest impact upon his return. Between 1950 and 1953, The Barber won 59 games for the Giants.

But as Maglie and the others regrouped and moved ahead, Pasquel's fortunes plummeted. At a 1951 playoff game between Veracruz and San Luís Potosí, Pasquel was hit by a rock thrown by a fan. Veracruz won the championship that year, only its third since 1940, but Pasquel gave up control of the team and stepped down as Mexican league president. Jorge Pasquel was a disillusioned man when he died in 1955 in the crash of a plane he was piloting.

Jorge Pasquel's legacy to Mexicans and Mexican baseball is that he headed the only foreign league to successfully raid the U.S. major leagues. Like Pancho Villa, he was not afraid to stand up to the giant nation to the north. These victories may be symbolic at best, but they remain important victories to the Mexican people.

✠✠✠✠✠✠✠✠✠✠✠✠✠✠✠✠

9

JACKIE ROBINSON OPENS THE DOOR

World War II was over, and it was time for a fresh start in Major League Baseball. Much of the wartime replacement talent was pushed to Mexico, the minor leagues, or out of baseball. The major league rosters needed to be revitalized. As the flood of victorious soldiers returned home to take up their places in the elite ranks of politics, business, and sport, they were bolstered by an absolute confidence in the supremacy of the United States. This combination of national euphoria and a clear slate in baseball gave Brooklyn Dodgers General Manager Branch Rickey the courage to put into action a plan he had been developing for several years. He was determined to break the major league color barrier.

One idea he considered was to bring up a dark-skinned Latin. Since major leaguers had played alongside Latins for many years, Rickey wondered whether the tan-like skin color of a Latin might be less shocking to white baseball executives, fans, and players as the darker skin of a U.S. black.

One of Rickey's candidates was Cuban shortstop Silvio García. In preparation, Rickey interviewed García to see how he might hold up under pressure in the spotlight. When Rickey asked García how he would react if a white man slapped him, García responded, "I kill him."[1] End of interview. And end of Silvio García's chance to play for Branch Rickey. Instead, the Dodger boss chose Jackie Robinson, a young black U.S. Army veteran.

As the nation celebrated V-J Day, Rickey launched his plan. He announced that Jackie Robinson would play in the 1946 season on the Dodger farm team in Montreal. In 1947 Rickey added Don Newcombe, Roy Campanella, and Roy Partlow. To avoid any outcry against the black players, the Dodgers held their spring training in Cuba that year. Even in racially integrated Cuba, the Dodgers hedged their bet, separating the four black Montreal players by housing them in a second-rate Havana hotel. The Brooklyn players and the white Montreal players stayed at the Havana Military Academy, an upscale private school. Food for the white players was flown in from the United States, while Robinson got sick from local restaurant food.[2]

The Dodgers' venture into integration did not make much of a splash in Cuba that spring. The Cubans were more excited about Almendares, managed by Dolf Luque, because it had just won the hotly contested Cuban championship. Besides, light-skinned Latin major leaguers, established Negro league stars, and local Cuban favorites had all played in Cuba that winter. Therefore, seeing the major league's first black rookie prospect was not much of an attraction. Weakened by his stomach problems, Jackie Robinson did not play very well anyway. The Cubans had seen many black players who were far better.

Robinson was in better form when the Dodgers moved on to Panama for more exhibition games. Panamanian promoters had guaranteed $35,000 in receipts if Robinson accompanied the team. The response of the Panamanians was as enthusiastic as the Cuban response had been apathetic. The thought of a black man with the chance to move up to the majors captured the imagination of the people of Panama. For instance, when the Jackie Robinson-less Dodgers played the winter league champion, General Electric, only 2,000 fans attended. But when Montreal and Robinson showed up for their crack at GE, 6,000 fans packed the ballpark. During the Panamanian series, Robinson rose to the occasion, hitting .519 in the 12 games played. From then on, the people of Panama followed Robinson's successes throughout his career.[3]

Not long after the 1947 season began, Robinson was called up to Brooklyn. Throughout the year he faced racial tension and abuse, yet he persevered to win the National League Rookie of the Year Award. The following spring he returned with the Dodgers to Latin America. This time, Brooklyn held spring training in Ciudad Trujillo, Dominican Republic. As in Panama, Robinson was a flesh-and-blood underdog whom the fans cheered. They knew that Robinson had opened a door upon which many Dominicans could never even have knocked.

Felipe Alou, a Dominican who starred in the major leagues in the 1960s, recalled Robinson's visit. "I remember when Jackie Robinson came to our country in 1948. It was the first year after he played with the Dodgers. I was 13 then, and it was a proud moment. To see Robinson in the Brooklyn lineup gave us hope. We didn't have much besides baseball. No college scouts came looking there for football or basketball players. But there was a black man out there with a major league uniform on. He beat us, too. Our Dominican All-Stars had the Dodgers beat 2-1 into the ninth when Robinson hit a liner over second with a man on and raced around the bases. How he could fly!"[4]

Minnie Miñoso

The man who could fly had flung open a door that allowed any player, with any skin color, to rise to the top of the sport. The first dark-skinned Latin to pass through the door opened by Robinson was a Cuban, a man named Saturnino Orestes Arrieta Armas.

Armas's family, poor and illiterate, worked the sugar cane fields in Cuba. When sugar prices collapsed during the Great Depression, his family was forced from its comfortable home into a dirt-floored shack that stood by the fields at La Lonja, near Matanzas. Saturnino, who took up baseball at age nine, recalls, "I see Dihigo play one day and I say to myself, 'I want to be as great as he is.' Dihigo great man. Everyone in Cuba worshipped him. That's how I come to play baseball."[5]

Armas wore uniforms made from cotton flour sacks, used shabby gloves, and hit with splintered bats handed down from his stepbrothers. Because he always played ball with his stepbrothers, people called him by their name, "Miñoso." Later, when Armas reached the United States, the name "Miñoso" gave rise to the nickname "Minnie." Thus Saturnino Orestes Arrieta Armas became known as Minnie Miñoso.

From age 10 to age 14, Armas received his only schooling. He then took a job cutting cane with a machete at La Lonja plantation. On the plantation, Armas organized and managed his own baseball team, aggressively fining teammates 50 cents for each missed sign. He fielded every position when needed and even suited up as the catcher when no one else volunteered. One day, however, he was hit in the elbow by a bat. Mamá Armas laid down the law: either give up catching or give up baseball. He gave up catching.[6]

Within a few years Armas's mother died, and Armas moved to Havana to live with his sister. There he worked in the Ambrosia candy factory and played on the company team. At the tryouts, the manager asked him what position he played. Armas chose third base because, "I see three good outfielders, then I see old man playing third. I hit good, so I stay on third. I hit .367."[7] His scrambling speed allowed him to turn routine ground balls into hits and doubles into triples. He could steal bases almost at will. From Ambrosia, he moved on to Partagas, the semipro team of a cigar company, and he worked part time making cigars. Then he played for two years for a mining team in Santiago, Cuba.

A scout with Club Marianao of the Cuban winter league spotted and signed Miñoso in November 1944. In his first game with Marianao, Miñoso replaced the injured third baseman in the seventh inning and promptly dove into the stands to chase a foul pop. In the top of the ninth, Miñoso singled off Cuban ace Ramón Bragaña to drive in the winning run. In the bottom of the ninth, Miñoso made two stops at third to preserve the win. Miñoso quickly became a favorite of the Marianao fans. For the season he hit .301 and was named Rookie of the Year.

Next it was off to the United States for Miñoso. Alex Pompez, owner of the New York Cubans in the Negro league, signed up the professed 23-year-old for the 1945 season. But Miñoso was not prepared for the big-city bustle he found in New York. Pompez wisely assigned Silvio García as Miñoso's roommate. Silvio, the Cuban who had been a little too fiery for Rickey's integration plans, was a perfect guide for Miñoso. "García," Miñoso said later, "showed me how to live, how to eat, how to play in New York."[8]

Miñoso hit .294 for the champion New York team and was invited to play in front of 48,112 fans at the Negro league All-Star Game. Miñoso, himself very dark skinned but more accustomed to the varying skin colors of the Caribbean, was surprised by the make-up of the crowd, saying, "I never saw so many Negroes in all my life."[9]

On the basis of his Negro league success, Miñoso was given a tryout with the St. Louis Cardinals, but was not signed. However, when a Cleveland scout saw Miñoso play, he paid Pompez $25,000 for the contracts of Miñoso and Puerto Rican-born José "Pantalones" (Pants) Santiago. Miñoso went to 1949 spring training with the Indians.

Sportswriters noticed that Miñoso did not speak English, and they wrote humorously about his performance during team calisthenics. Miñoso tried to anticipate manager Lou Boudreau's orders, but he was totally out of sync with the other players, jumping instead of squatting, stretching instead of touching his toes.[10]

Although sportswriters loved Miñoso, they were free with the kind of condescending writing that many Latins later found insulting. The writers found Miñoso enthusiastic, accessible, and colorful in his comments and stories. And he was not ashamed of his Spanish accent. But the press was always merciless in phonetically transcribing his quotes, "Me play" and "You boys be my friends."[11]

Even when Miñoso's English improved, the treatment was the same. As with Luque before him, the writers portrayed Miñoso as a cross between Tonto and Amos & Andy. One writer called him the "Katzenjammer Kid." These quotes made good copy and probably made Miñoso less threatening in the newly integrated world of baseball. Unlike Luque, however, Miñoso had a tolerant manner and enough experience in big cities with his buddy García that he let these insults roll off. Minnie Miñoso proved himself not only to be a fine baseball player but also a strong man—strong enough to take the insults that came his way.

It seems that Miñoso purposely used his wide-eyed innocence to deal with the foreign and hostile world of Major League Baseball. When Cleveland demoted him to San Diego after 16 at-bats in 1949, Padres President Bill Starr recounted, "I had heard that Miñoso had a lot of trouble with the English language. People said he couldn't speak a word of it. I went over to him, shook hands, and told him that we were happy to have him with our team. I told him about our team, baseball in the Pacific Coast League, and so on. Miñoso didn't say a word. Then I asked him, 'Do we owe you anything for expenses?' 'Expenses?' he asked. 'Yes.' Then he rattled off a list: hotel expenses, transportation, meals, tips. I was surprised. He really understood what I was talking about when I mentioned money!"[12] This former sugar cane field worker may not have had perfect grammar, but he knew how to take care of himself.

After spending the 1949 and 1950 seasons with San Diego, Miñoso was traded to the Chicago White Sox, where he was the Sox's first black player. Within 24 hours of his arrival, Miñoso hit a two-run home run in his first at-bat to spark a 4-2 win against Vic Raschi and the hated Yankees. Miñoso played third base in that 1951 season, batted .326, scored 112 runs, and led the American League in triples with 14 and stolen bases with 31. Attendance jumped by 500,000 that year, and the White Sox improved by 21 games. White Sox Manager Paul Richards said, "He hit a home run the first time at bat for the White Sox, and he hit one the last time up as the season ended. In between, he was better."[13] Miñoso's enthusiasm inspired White Sox fans to chant, "Go, Go," anticipating a steal. The "Go-Go Sox" tag stuck through the 1950s.

Miñoso's black South Side Chicago fans honored him at the end of his rookie season on September 23, 1951, with Minnie Miñoso Day at the park, and they showered him with gifts of a television set, a radio, a camera, and a new Packard. Despite this fabulous season, the Baseball Writers Association of America voted its Rookie of the Year Award to the Yankees' white third baseman, Gil Mc-Dougald. McDougald outhit Miñoso in only one category, with 14 home runs to Miñoso's 10. White Sox General Manager Frank Lane said, "If ever there was a Rookie of the Year, it was Minnie in 1951. The fact that McDougald was picked over him was, in my mind, a grave miscarriage of justice. And I'm not just saying that because he's on my ball club. You figure this out. When it came to picking the Most Valuable Player that year, the same men who tabbed McDougald Rookie of the Year ranked Miñoso fourth behind Yogi Berra, Ned Garver, and Allie Reynolds. McDougald finished ninth in their poll."[14]

There was no question about where Miñoso stood with the baseball fans back home in Cuba. Upon his return, he received a hero's welcome at José Martí Airport. Cuba's President, the Army Chief of Staff, and the Mayor of Havana presented Miñoso with a key to the city, a symbol of admiration for the Cuban who electrified Major League Baseball. At a ceremony in Marianao, Miñoso was given more gifts, including a trophy, another television, another radio, another car, as well as a $10,000 house. Minnie Miñoso was not just a rookie of the year in his homeland—he was man of the year.

Miñoso played three months with Marianao in the Cuban winter league, and then went home to his old neighborhood. There he gave his stepfather a week off from the cane fields by working in his place. Each day, he loaded cane onto the oxcarts as he had done years before. Only this time, his shiny new Packard was parked at the cane field's edge.

Miñoso starred for the White Sox in the 1950s, twice more leading the American League in triples and stolen bases, and regularly batting .300. His fans formed the Minnie Miñoso Cuban Comet Club. One of the thrills the Cuban Comet gave his fan club was his hitting stance. He would hang over the plate, almost daring the pitcher to plunk him. His stance caused him to be hit by more pitches than anybody ever had, and it earned him a hairline skull fracture from Yankees pitcher Bob Grim. Miñoso joked with the White Sox trainer that a coat of white paint on his face and arms would make him a little harder to hit, but White Sox Manager Paul Richards explained, "He crouches and crowds the plate. He's completely fearless up there. He doesn't give a darn whether they hit him or not."[15] But he must have cared a little, for when the pitching got too tight the Katzenjammer Kid occasionally released the bat about halfway through his swing.

Back in Cuba Miñoso led Marianao to league championships in 1956-1957 and 1957-1958. But he missed earning a pennant in the United States when he was traded to Cleveland for the 1958 and 1959 seasons. During his exile, the White Sox won their first pennant in 40 years in 1959. Miñoso returned to Chicago in 1960, then finished with the St. Louis Cards, the Senators, and then back to the White Sox in 1964. Miñoso became a player-manager in Mexico, but after Fidel Castro assumed power, Miñoso never returned to Cuba. He played with his son, Orestes, Jr., with Puerto Vallarta in the Mexican league, and the father-son duo hit back-to-back homers to win a game in 1975.

The White Sox invited Miñoso back in 1976 to join the coaching staff. He also played in a few games that year and delivered a base hit to become the oldest player to hit safely in a game. In 1980 Miñoso became baseball's only five-decade player when he fouled out and grounded out in two appearances. Miñoso was invited back for 1990 by Chicago, but Commissioner Fay Vincent felt that, at age 67, Miñoso's appearance was only for publicity's sake, and he vetoed the idea.

Miñoso finished with a .298 average, 186 homers, 1,136 runs scored, 1,023 runs batted in, and 1,963 hits. Because he did not become a regular until age 28, he did not post Hall of Fame numbers. Rollie Hemond, one-time White Sox general manager, said, "If Miñoso had begun his major league career at age 21 or 22, he would have, I'm quite sure, accumulated an impressive array of statistics for consideration for enshrinement in the Hall."[16]

Miñoso got a late start because he had to wait until Jackie Robinson could courageously swing open the door for men of color to play Major League Baseball. Although his age cost him a spot in the Hall of Fame, it probably helped him deal with the challenges of the major leagues once he finally arrived. His maturity and easygoing personality inspired a warm and enthusiastic following. Minnie Miñoso, like Jackie Robinson before him, helped smooth the way for acceptance of the many black and Latin players who would soon follow.

10

A NEW WORLD SERIES

While Major League Baseball was embarking on the grand enterprise of racial integration, the Caribbean Latin leagues were conducting their own experiment in political integration. The Caribbean goal was not to mix blacks and whites, but Latins and Latins. For while the Latin American countries held a common Spanish heritage and shared a passion for baseball, they had rarely mixed it up on the ball field as professionals.

The stage had been set by the close of World War II, however. By then, professional winter leagues had been formed in four Caribbean countries. However, the competition in these leagues was limited by the small size of the countries. Cuba and Puerto Rico, for example, had populations smaller than some U.S. cities. The local population could provide just so much talent and could support only a handful of teams. The Venezuelan patriot Simón Bolívar had pointed out 140 years previously that there was much to be gained if Latins could organize themselves. In a way, Jorge Pasquel also gave Latins a brief taste of an independent identity for Latin baseball. Thus, following the lead of history, the first Latin championship competition was formed in 1948 among the teams representing Cuba, Puerto Rico, Panama, and Venezuela.

The idea of a national league was not a new one. Cubans had established a professional winter league in the previous century. But no other country followed Cuba's example until the 1930s, when Puerto Rico organized its first league.

Puerto Rico

Life in Puerto Rico between the Spanish-American War and the late 1930s was an economic roller coaster. As a commonwealth of the United States, the island nation had at first benefited from U.S.-led development of the sugar and tobacco industries, but that stream of economic aid was reduced to a trickle during the Depression, plunging two-thirds of the Puerto Ricans into unemployment.

In these difficult times, baseball provided a diversion for the people. In 1930, to encourage this interest, the strapped local government nevertheless voted to build a new stadium, later named Sixto Escobar Stadium after a Puerto Rican boxer who held the bantamweight championship of the world.

The Sixto Escobar Stadium became the base for many of the games of the Puerto Rican league, founded in 1938. The league consisted of six teams: the San Juan Senators, the Mayaguez Indians, the Ponce Lions, the Guayama Warlocks (Brujos), the Humacao Greys, and the Caguas Natives (Criollos). Each team was allowed three non-Puerto Rican players, or "imports." All imports were from the United States except for Ponce's three Dominican players. Perucho Cepeda (father of future major leaguer Orlando) won the first batting title with a .365 average and led the Guayama Brujos to the first Puerto Rican championship. Cepeda won the batting title again the next year, while leading Guayama to another championship. During World War II, the U.S. military drafted many Puerto Rican players, forcing teams to merge and schedules to be shortened.

The end of the war may have brought boom times to the United States, but Puerto Rico's postwar economy was more of a bust. Agricultural production never really picked up, and many people lost their jobs. The jobless began to exercise their rights as U.S. citizens and move to more economically secure parts of the United States. To counteract this flow, the government established Operation Bootstrap, which provided U.S. tax incentives to build manufacturing facilities in Puerto Rico. These incentives, combined with low labor costs, slowly built up an industrial base. Just as in the 1930s, however, the economic troubles did not hurt baseball. Rather, baseball provided cherished relief from troubles. During the 1950s, Puerto Ricans saw some great baseball, fueled by competition with their Caribbean neighbors.

Adding to the excitement was Buck Canel, a popular broadcaster. Canel was born and raised in Staten Island, New York, and learned Spanish from his father. When the 43-year-old Canel first arrived in Puerto Rico in 1946, he discovered that he was already famous on the island for his radio translations of United Nations proceedings and speeches by Franklin D. Roosevelt and Winston Churchill from New York for NBC. But even more important, Canel was known for his broadcast of major league games to Puerto Rico. Fans loved his precise call of local games, but they were surprised by his neutrality. They could not understand how he could call the games without being passionately partial to any one team. After a few years, a Cuban radio network offered Canel a lucrative contract to broadcast the winter league in Havana. He turned it down to stay in Puerto Rico.

Some of Canel's fame stemmed from a verbal twist he put on a popular commercial product. Whenever the bases were loaded, Canel called it a "Situacíon Don Q" on behalf of that Puerto Rican rum company. Don Q paid Canel $100 each time a grand slam was hit following Canel's declaration. Soon "Situacíon Don Q" was being used to describe any tense, precarious, or potentially rewarding situation in everyday Puerto Rican life.[1]

Baseball fanaticism reached fever pitch in Puerto Rico in 1954 when Willie Mays flew in for the winter season. Mays had won the batting title with the New York Giants by batting .345 the summer before, and had capped the season with a remarkable catch on the dead run with his back to home plate. "The Catch," as it has since become known in baseball folklore, was made on a long fly ball hit by Vic Wertz, and sparked the Giants' four-game sweep of the Cleveland Indians in the World Series. Mays was offered $1,000 a month plus expenses to play for Santurce, which was the limit a major league player could receive. But Puerto Rican fans bet that Mays would not show up after his fine season to play winter baseball in their country. After all, no star of his caliber had ever played in the Puerto Rican winter league.

But Mays did arrive, and when he landed at the crowded San Juan airport, still-skeptical Puerto Ricans changed their wagers. Now they bet on how soon he would leave the island. Mays found a familiar face on the Santurce team. Giants coach Herman Franks was the team manager, and he made Mays feel welcome. Franks took Mays aside and said to him, "I told Roberto Clemente in left and Bob Thurman [Cincinnati outfielder] in right to give you plenty of room on any ball you call for."[2]

In addition to Clemente, Mays, and Thurman, Santurce rounded out its talented team with Rubén Gómez, winner of a 1954 World Series game for the Giants, slugging first baseman George Crowe, and St. Louis Browns pitcher Bill Greason. Mays started quickly, hitting safely in his first five games. Then, in Game Six, he was held hitless by a rather obscure pitcher for the team from Mayaguez—a man by the name of Tommy Lasorda. Commenting on his success with Mays, Lasorda said, "I teased him with the first pitch, making it good enough to hit at but not good enough to overpower. Maybe I've discovered his weakness."[3] Two weeks later, Mays hit his first home run of the season off the same Mayaguez teaser, Tommy Lasorda. Willie Mays, the man they said would not stay, won the Puerto Rican batting championship with a .395 average.

Venezuela

As in Puerto Rico, Venezuelan baseball remained an amateur adventure for the first half of the century. In 1940 the Venezuelans sent their first team to the World Amateur Championship, which was played in Hawaii. The Venezuelans finished fifth, but the very next year the Venezuelan team surprised everyone by upsetting heavily favored Cuba to take the tournament. This victory made national heroes out of the players. Venezuela continued to do well in the amateur competition, winning it in 1944 and 1945.

These victories laid the foundation for the formation in 1946 of the Venezuelan winter league, which included four teams: Cervecería Caracas (representing a local brewery), Vargas, Magallanes, and Venezuela. The leadoff hitter in the inaugural game was

Magallanes's star shortstop, Luís Aparicio, Sr., father of future Hall of Famer Luís Jr. The Magallanes pitcher, major leaguer Alejandro "Patón" Carrasquel, pitched a complete game for a 5-2 victory over the team named Venezuela.

Five days later Carrasquel's nephew, Alfonso "Chico" Carrasquel, debuted at shortstop for Cervecería Caracas. In the seventh inning of a scoreless game, Carrasquel hit a solo home run to lead Caracas to a 2-0 win, and fans all over Venezuela began a love affair with Carrasquel. Their hero soon moved to the majors, where he enjoyed a ten-year career until 1959. His biography, published in 1986, was titled *Idol for all Time (Idolo de Siempre)*.

In March 1947 the New York Yankees visited Venezuela for a four-game exhibition series. Touring with the Yankee club were legends Yogi Berra, Phil Rizzuto, Tommy Henrich, and Allie Reynolds. In the first game of the series, the Yankees led 2-1 in the ninth inning when Vargas's import Lloyd Davenport hit a two-run, game-winning double to win the game for the home team. Although the Yankees swept the next three games, Venezuelan fans were proud of their country's showing against a team that had won 87 games in the American League the previous summer.

As Venezuelan professional baseball developed, the political situation changed. The country's flirtations with democracy were interrupted in 1948 when the military stepped in and took over. The army promoted one of its own, Marcos Pérez Jiménez, to lead the country. He built a strong secret police system while enjoying the support of the U.S. government. Jiménez used oil revenues to build superhighways and other parts of the country's infrastructure. The works included a new multipurpose stadium, built in 1951 for the Bolívar Games. The Estadio Universitario, as it was named, is still the principal stadium in Caracas.

The Caracas team in the Venezuelan winter league changed hands in 1952 when Cervecería Caracas confirmed through a market survey that the fans of the team's biggest rival, Magallanes, refused to drink Cervecería's beer. The team was promptly renamed the Caracas Lions, and Hall of Famer Martín Dihigo managed them to the league championship.

In the mid-1950s the league added six new teams and split into two divisions: the Oriental and the Occidental leagues. As the 1950s drew to a close, the political life of Pérez Jiménez ended too. He was forced out of office, setting the stage for the 30-plus years of democratic succession Venezuela has enjoyed since.

Panama

Following the Venezuelan pattern, Panama also built its first national leagues in the amateur arena. The Panamanians sent their first national team to the Central American and Caribbean Games in El Salvador in 1935. The team finished the regulation round tied for first place with Cuba and Nicaragua, but finished second to Cuba in the playoff.

In 1936 the Panamanians took another step toward improving baseball in their country. They hired Negro league shortstop Bill Yancey to form a team for the Berlin Olympics, which was including baseball as an exhibition sport. Yancey set up two national teams called the Atlantic Side and the Pacific Side. The teams enjoyed such success that more than a dozen Panamanians from these teams ultimately became Negro league players. In fact, 20 years later, Panamanian pitcher Pat Scantlebury joined the Cincinnati Reds and became the last black player to go from the Negro leagues directly to the major leagues.

Panamanian baseball turned pro in 1946. The teams in this new winter league for pay took their names from commercial sponsors: General Electric, Spur Cola, Chesterfield, Carta Vieja, and Cervecería Balboa. General Electric, whose team consisted of both locals and imports, was the strongest team until 1948 when it broke up and its players were distributed to the other four teams.

A New Alliance

As these winter leagues began springing up around the Caribbean, the competition for players grew. The leagues realized that they needed to establish rules governing recruiting. In August 1948 representatives from Cuba, Puerto Rico, Panama, and Venezuela met in Havana and agreed to stop pirating players from each other.

The group also decided to cap off their own seasons with a tournament among the champions of each country's winter league. To make the competition even stiffer, the countries agreed that each team could bring along five reinforcements from the rosters of the defeated teams in their league. They then developed a round-robin, 12-game format, which ensured that each team would face all others twice. These tournaments were scheduled for the end of the winter league seasons, but well before major league training camps got underway.

Since the North American major leagues considered their own championship to be the World Series, the founders of this new tourney had to qualify it by calling it the *Caribbean* World Series. The first Caribbean World Series was held in 1949 at the Estadio del Cerro in Havana. As 25,000 Latin American baseball fans watched in anticipation, the president of the U.S. minor leagues, George Trautman, threw out the first pitch.

Caribbean World Series Summary, 1949–1960

1949 Site: Havana

Champion: Cuba—Almendares

Highlights: Almendares swept all six games. Managed by Philadelphia A's catcher Fermín "Mike" Guerra, the team was led by Al Gionfriddo, Monte Irvin, and Sam Jethroe in the outfield. At first base for the champs was Chuck Conners, who would later go on to TV stardom in his title role in *The Rifleman*.

1950 Site: Puerto Rico

Champion: Panama—Spur Cola

Highlights: Spur Cola did not fare well in 1949, but bounced back in 1950. After six games, Panama and Puerto Rico were tied with 4-2 records. Spur Cola Manager Wayne Blackburn called on Negro leaguer Chet Brewer to pitch the playoff, while Puerto Rico's manager and Dodger outfielder Luís Olmo sent fellow Dodger Dan Bankhead out to the mound. A six-run third inning spelled the difference for Panama in its 9-3 victory. Brewer recalled, "We were the poorest country of all of them. The other players laughed at us when they had the pregame ceremony. We looked like boys in our knickers. But we had some real ballplayers."[4] Back in Panama, the players were heroes. The dramatic win was Panama's first and last in the Caribbean World Series.

1951 Site: Venezuela

Champion: Puerto Rico—Santurce

Highlights: Rubén Gómez and José "Pantalones" Santiago each won two games on the mound.

1952 Site: Panama

Champion: Cuba—Havana Reds

Highlights: Manager Mike Gonzáles led the Reds to a six-game sweep. Tom Fine no-hit Cervecería Caracas for the only Caribbean World Series no-hitter. Fine also pitched a series-clinching 11-3 win over Panama.

1953 Site: Cuba

Champion: Puerto Rico—Santurce

Highlights: Santurce swept the series in six games. Leading pitchers were Alva "Bobo" Holloman and Ellis "Cot" Deal (two wins) and Rubén Gómez (one win). Second baseman Junior Gilliam batted .545, and Willard Brown slammed four home runs and batted in 13 runs.

1954 Site: Puerto Rico

Champion: Puerto Rico—Caguas

Highlights: Manager Mickey Owen used players such as smooth-fielding first sacker Vic Pellot Power along with Félix Mantilla, Carlos Bernier, Jim Rivera, and Luís Márquez.

1955 Site: Venezuela

Champion: Puerto Rico—Santurce

Highlights: Willie Mays. In the third game, Mays broke out of a 0-12 slump to win the game with a home run. In his final 19 at-bats, Mays had 14 hits to bat .469.

1956 Site: Panama

Champion: Cuba—Cienfuegos

Highlights: Caribbean World Series sluggers pounded out 29 home runs in 12 games. Camilo Pascual and Pedro Ramos won two games each for Cuba.

1957 Site: Cuba

Champion: Cuba—Marianao

Highlights: Minnie Miñoso and Solly Drake led Marianao to the title. Jim Bunning pitched two of Marianao's five victories.

1958 Site: Puerto Rico

Champion: Cuba—Marianao

Highlights: Manager Nap Reyes and his crew defended their title as Minnie Miñoso and José Valdivielso took hitting honors. Pedro Ramos won two games on the mound for Marianao. Other outstanding performances were seen when:

- Juan Pizarro (Puerto Rico Caguas) struck out 17 in one game.
- Humberto Robinson (Panama's first major leaguer) won two games, including a 5-0 shutout of Cuba.
- Victor Pellot Power hit .458.

1959 Site: Venezuela

Champion: Cuba—Almendares

Highlights: The host country's Oriente team was led by Norm Cash, who had two home runs and eight RBIs. Almendares was led by Tony Taylor, Carlos Paula, Rocky Nelson, Willie Miranda, Orlando Peña, Mike Cuellar, Camilo Pascual, Tommy Lasorda, and Art Fowler. Pascual won the series-clinching game over Venezuela 8-2.

1960 Site: Panama

Champion: Cuba—Cienfuegos

Highlights: Camilo Pascual won two games, ending his Caribbean World Series career with six wins, no losses, and two shutouts. Tommy Davis of Puerto Rico hit .409 and his brother Willie hit .333 for the Venezuelan Rapiños.

11

ROARING FIFTIES IN CUBA

The strong Cuban teams that dominated the Caribbean World Series came out of a golden decade in Cuban baseball and society. In the 1950s U.S. tourists rediscovered Cuba. Movie stars made feature films there, and Ernest Hemingway's writing, fishing, and drinking exploits on the island became legendary. Cruise ships from Miami brought adults to a playland of beaches where white-coated waiters served rum drinks. After dinner, guests wandered into casinos for roulette and blackjack. And nearby was the dance floor where the visitors could join the conga line or dance the limbo, the rumba, and the cha-cha.

This glamorous night life was not enough to draw Cuban fans away from Havana's Gran Stadium or away from their radios as they followed the winter league action. In the early 1950s theater, restaurant, and nightclub owners petitioned Cuban President Prío to reduce the number of winter league night games from six to three each week, in an attempt to increase local trade, but their pleas fell on deaf ears. Cuban fans filled the local stadiums wearing the blue of Almendares, Havana's red, Cienfuegos's green, and Marianao's brown. Team songs filled the air as fans whistled, clapped, shouted, and sometimes even charged the field to inspire their favorites. Skyrockets were launched from the stands. Men bet on everything from individual pitches to the final score. Women learned to love the game from radio. At one Ladies' Night game between bitter rivals Havana and Almendares, fights between female fans of the two clubs caused police so much trouble that no future night-time promotions were scheduled for the Cubanas.

The energy and emotion of Cuban ball astonished visiting U.S. players. No one was more surprised than Tommy Lasorda, who pitched in Cuba in the early fifties. One night he approached the plate to question a couple of ball/strike calls by Cuban home plate umpire Orlando Maestri. As Lasorda approached, Maestri opened his jacket enough for the pitcher to see a large handgun stuck in his pants. "Maestri," Lasorda yelled as he turned and hurried back to the mound, "you're the best damn umpire I've ever seen."[1]

The success of the winter league was only part of the story of Cuban baseball in the decade. The summer addition of Minor League Baseball to the Cuban experience was a vital new development. Some minor leagues, including the Florida State League, had suspended play during World War II because of a talent shortage. When the leagues started up again, Clark Griffith and his family saw their chance. They teamed up with Havana baseball promoter Roberto Maduro and formed a team called the Havana Cubans. The Cubans became part of the Class B Florida International League, which consisted of five other teams, all in Florida. The Griffiths had taken talent out of the country for their Washington Senators team, but now they were beginning to develop it for U.S. competition right in Cuba.

The Havana Cubans played in Gran Stadium, which was built in 1946. This modern stadium presented an impressive setting for the momentous merger of Latin baseball into U.S. organized ball. The stadium seated 35,000, had an impeccable surface, and boasted a lighting system of major league caliber. The large field with prevailing wind from straightaway center was a pitcher's paradise. Fans and writers rode elevators to upper-level, glassed-in boxes. From the very start, Havana led the league in attendance.

The Havana Cubans spent eight years in the Florida International League. From 1946 to 1953, Havana won four regular-season titles and two playoff championships. Future Washington Senators from the first Havana Cuban teams included Julio Moreno, Connie Marrero, and Frank Campos. Future White Sox reliever Luís Aloma also played for the Cubans. Fans rooted for the Cubans against the Florida clubs with fury. Play was competitive and fiery—so much so, in fact, that in one 1949 game in Havana, Miami Manager "Pepper" Martin, former St. Louis Cardinals "Gas House Gang" member, was fined and suspended for choking an umpire.

The Washington Senators often drew from the Cuban talent pool. Youngsters on the Havana farm club in the early 1950s who were called up by Washington included brother pitchers Carlos and Camilo Pascual. At age 16, Camilo was the youngest prospect ever signed by Joe Cambria. He went on to gain 174 victories in an 18-year major league career. Sandy Consuegra, a 16-game winner with the White Sox in 1954, Julio Becquer, and Juan Delis also climbed to the Senators from Havana. Native Cubans and former major leaguers Bobby Estalella, Sandy Ullrich, and Gil Torres extended their careers by playing with the Cubans. Torres's father, Ricardo, had been a utility player for Washington from 1920 to 1922 and one of the majors' first Cubans. With the Cubans' success in the Class B League, and the fan enthusiasm at league-leading levels, Bobby Maduro knew Havana was ready for a step up in U.S. baseball.

Maduro outlined his case to the International League in 1954, asking for approval to create the Havana Sugar Kings to replace the Havana Cubans. Maduro cited the one million paid admissions during the previous Cuban winter and promised to pay an extra $60,000 to each of the other league teams to cover travel costs to Cuba. Finally, he agreed to clean up the gambling, which was as common in Latin ballparks as rum and Cokes. The league agreed, and the 1954 schedule was arranged so Canadian teams Montreal, Toronto, and Ottawa, and U.S. teams Rochester, Buffalo, and Syracuse, would visit the Havana Sugar Kings during the season for two five-game series.

Unfortunately, political trouble lay ahead for Cuba—trouble that would not bode well for baseball. Behind the music and magic of the 1950s, the dictatorship of Fulgencio Batista had gone sour. Batista had returned to power in 1952. Although he had taken a leading role in social reforms in the 1930s, Batista was cruel and corrupt in the 1950s. The poor who worked the sugar fields suffered, and the middle class became disillusioned by his abuses. Some Cubans resented the U.S. presence in business, government, and tourism, for they saw it as an extension of the Batista regime.

Fidel Castro emerged to offer an alternative to Batista's abuses. Castro was born to a family of some means, attended private school, and studied law at the University of Havana, where he pitched on the school team. While in law school, he became involved in national politics. After he set up his law practice, Castro tried to run for political office. The elections were canceled, though, by the pro-Batista military coup. Castro petitioned Cuban courts for Batista to be imprisoned for 100 years for treason and, failing in that, planned his first attack against the government in 1953. As the revolution marched west toward Havana from Santiago in 1958, Castro's supporters called the movement the fulfillment of José Martí's 1890s dream of Cuban independence. The 33-year-old revolutionary became the leader of Cuba in early 1959.

After the revolution, attendance at the 1959 home games of the Havana Sugar Kings was well below what it had been in previous years. Rumors circulated that the team would be transferred to Jersey City for financial reasons. Castro encouraged fans to attend games, and some new promotions were attempted to boost attendance. In the July 29, 1959, issue of *The Sporting News*, Castro was quoted as saying, "The Sugar Kings are a part of the Cuban people. It is important for us to have a connection with Triple A ball."[2]

To kick off a celebration of the one-year anniversary of the birth of Castro's drive on Havana, Castro pitched both innings for the "Barbudos" ("Bearded Rebels") in a special preliminary exhibition before a Rochester-Havana game. Two days later, on July 26, 1959, the Rochester-Havana game was shortened after rifle bullets fired into the air in celebration reportedly grazed third base coach Frank Verdi and shortstop Léo Cárdenas. The game was called in the 11th inning, tied 4-4, and, although neither Verdi nor Cárdenas was hurt and Cuban fans had not intended to cause harm, the Rochester team left the island.

Cool heads in the International League front office decided to complete the schedule despite protests over the safety of playing in Castro's Cuba. This allowed the Havana Sugar Kings to win the Junior World Series with Castro in the stands, cheering Havana on to victory over Minneapolis.

After five years of middle-of-the-pack performance for the Cubans, winning the International League championship over Minneapolis was a triumphant climax to the development of Cuban baseball. The team's stars included pitcher Mike Cuellar, infielders Léo "Chico" Cárdenas and Octavio "Cookie" Rojas, Puerto Rican reliever Luís Arroyo, Venezuelan outfielder Pompeyo Davalillo (brother of major leaguer Vic Davalillo), and Carlos Paula.

The triumph was accomplished in the eye of a storm. Although Castro had initially changed little in the country, going about business as usual, he soon declared himself a communist. He expropriated all U.S.-owned property, including sugar mills, oil refineries, utilities, banks, and ranches. Private land and the businesses of many Cubans were seized as well.

Many Cuban professionals and their families felt they had little choice but to leave their beloved homeland, and many fled to the shores of Florida, 90 miles to the north. Throughout the 1960s, families continued to flee to the United States, including the families of a couple of youngsters named José Canseco and Rafael Palmeiro. Not until the late 1980s did those two players become famous as two of the last of the Cuban-born major leaguers.

Castro initially assured the Maduro family that their extensive holdings in Cuba, including Gran Stadium, were safe. Nevertheless, in 1960, the International League hierarchy, in response to the nationalization of U.S. businesses, transferred the Havana franchise from Cuba to Jersey City, New Jersey. Castro denounced the move as another aggressive action by the United States government. Baseball, loved in Cuba as in the United States, became another political tool in the ongoing diplomatic battle between the United States and its island neighbor.

The move represented Cuba's last great movement of baseball talent to the United States. Many of the players on that 1959 International League championship team went on to the major leagues and did not see their families or friends for more than a decade. One of them, Cookie Rojas, became the second full-time Latin manager when he took over the helm in California. With this honor, he followed in the footsteps of Preston Gómez in Houston and San Diego.

Castro's decisions ended the glorious period of professional baseball in Cuba. U.S. teams no longer traveled to Cuba to play against local teams in front of the savvy Cuban fans. The Caribbean World Series, with Cuba as the powerhouse, halted after the February 1960 contests. In the 12 years of the Caribbean World Series, Cuba won 51 of 71 games for a .718 average, took 7 of the 12 titles, and was undefeated in 3 of the 12 tournaments. Only Puerto Rico, in 1953, also swept a series. Cuban pitchers threw 10 of the 20 shutouts thrown in the 142 games played.

When Castro choked off the Cuban talent pipeline, he created a vacuum in the Latin baseball world and put an end to the golden age of baseball in Cuba.

12

THE DOMINICAN DIMENSION

A few miles east of Cuba, across the waters of the Caribbean, the Dominican people still suffered under the absolute control of the ever-imposing Trujillo. Trujillo's reign was not without successes, however, as the dictator's family built roads, buildings, and factories throughout the country. The government focused on improved agricultural production and education, and emphasized personal hygiene. And even though Trujillo controlled most key businesses, the country prospered and paid off all its foreign debt. Yet all was not well. Despite the economic gains, the people railed at Trujillo's oppression, but Domincan opinion was silenced by Trujillo's censors.

Dominican organized baseball lay dormant in the years following the grand tournament in 1937. The spark that began to revive it was the Brooklyn Dodgers' decision to hold training in Ciudad Trujillo in 1948.

In 1951 Trujillo advanced Dominican baseball further by allowing a summer league with the four long-standing Dominican teams: Licey, Escogido, Estrellas Orientales, and Aguilas Cibaeñas. The league competed from 1951 to 1954, with Licey winning two titles and Estrellas and Aguilas one each. The summer schedule for the league meant that if Dominicans were allowed to join U.S. baseball, then the quality of local play would be sacrificed. But Trujillo was the boss, and he kept the Dominican players at home. The summer schedule also meant that Dominicans did not participate in the wintertime Caribbean World Series.

The Dominican league changed course when it switched to a winter schedule in 1955 and invited major leaguers to participate. Escogido, owned by Trujillo's brother-in-law, stocked the outstanding local and imported talent: the brothers Felipe, Matty, and Jesús Alou; Juan Marichal; Ossie Virgil; plus imports Frank Howard, Stan Williams, Bill White, Willie Kirkland, Willie McCovey, and Andre Rodgers. Escogido won the league title each year from 1955-56 through 1960-61, with only one Licey title in 1958-1959 to break the streak.

As always, the Trujillos took winning seriously. At one Escogido game, Trujillo's brother, an army general, exploded when Escogido shortstop Andre Rodgers botched an infield throw. General Trujillo stopped play and ran out of the stands to reprimand Rodgers. However, Rodgers was not a Dominican, as Trujillo assumed, but a Bahamian who took great offense at the arrogance of the gesture.

Once the Dominican league switched to the winter season, it was no longer necessary to keep local talent at home. Trujillo realized that the best Dominicans could play in the United States in the summer, bring great prestige to their country, and return to play for local fans during the winter.

Trujillo just barely missed attaining the distinction of sending the first Dominican to the majors. Ossie Virgil, a Dominican refugee who left for New York at an early age, had become a U.S. citizen by the time he reached the majors. Virgil grew up playing baseball in the Bronx, spent two years in the Marines after high school, and then made his way up to the New York Giants in September 1956. In 1958 he became the first nonwhite to join the Detroit Tigers.

In the late 1950s, Trujillo approved construction of ballparks in Santo Domingo, Santiago, and San Pedro de Macorís, all modeled after Miami Stadium (now Bobby Maduro Stadium) in Miami. He also put his son Ramfis in charge of the negotiations for Dominican players. Ramfis gave audiences to a number of clubs, but the initial victories were scored by Giants scout Alex Pompez, whose links with Latin ball stretched back 40 years to the first Negro leagues. Pompez teamed up with Horacio Martínez, a baseball coach at the University of Santo Domingo, to sign the first two Dominican exports: Felipe Alou and Juan Marichal.

The Road Begins for Alou

Felipe Rojas Alou grew up in Haina, a rough-and-tumble port near the nation's capital. He and his two younger brothers, Mateo and Jesús, made their bats on a lathe set up in the family barn. Jesús Alou explained, "I don't know how poor the DiMaggios were, but we were poor Dominicans, and that's poor. My father was a carpenter and blacksmith. He used to make horseshoes and fix the plows for other people. We all helped him in the shop, and he was very busy all the time, but no money was coming in because everybody was poor around there."[1]

Alou was fortunate enough to have an uncle in Trujillo's army who lived comfortably in the capital. His uncle brought Felipe to Ciudad Trujillo so he could go to high school. From there, his athletic ability gained him admission to the University of Santo Domingo. In college Alou participated in track and field as well as baseball. In 1955 he accompanied a Dominican team to the Pan American Games, where his long home runs caught the eyes of a number of major league scouts. But Felipe's coach, Horacio Martínez, called the shots and steered him to sign with the Giants.

When Alou traveled to Lake Charles, Louisiana, in 1956 to play in the Evangeline League, he was one of five dark-skinned players sent by the Giants to integrate the team. Those dark-skinned players were driven out after five games. Alou did not understand the controversy. Describing his feelings toward this treatment, Alou wrote, "Back in the Dominican Republic there was never any talk concerning a race problem or racial inequality. Furthermore, my mother is a Caucasian, the daughter of a Spaniard who had migrated to the Dominican Republic. My father is a Negro, the grandson of a slave who had most likely been imported from Africa to work on the farms. There had never been anything wrong with a man merely because of the color of his skin."[2]

Alou moved to the Florida State League, but he could not move away from racial problems. He did get some assistance, however. Puerto Rican pitcher Julio Navarro took him under his wing and provided support. Alou recalled, "Navarro, had he wanted to, could have passed as a white man. He counseled me daily, telling me about things I could and could not do, places I could and could not go because my skin was tan, something that supposedly made me inferior to people whose skin was white. Patiently, Navarro kept brainwashing me, telling me about how Jackie Robinson and others had survived and succeeded, telling me that there wasn't anything I could do about the race situation and that I should learn to live with it. He said, 'Patience, Felipe. You must have patience.'"[3]

Thus counseled, Felipe moved on in 1957, first to Minneapolis and later to Springfield, Massachusetts. Of those days he wrote, "I was now playing in the northern part of the country, and there were no more signs bearing the vicious word *Colored*. I could eat in any restaurant I wanted, could sit in any seat on any bus and not have to worry about a thing. Cold as it was, I soon took a liking to Springfield and still regard it as one of the finest cities I have ever known."[4]

Marichal Moves Up

The route to stardom also soon took fellow Dominican Juan Marichal through Springfield. Marichal grew up on the north coast of the Dominican Republic and, like the Alous, came from a humble background. Marichal's father died in 1941, when Juan was three, so his mother raised Juan, his three older brothers, and his older sister on the family farm, which provided a diet of rice and beans, sweet potatoes, eggplant, onions, peppers, corn, tomatoes, lettuce, and milk from four cows.

Juan's brothers made him a shortstop as a youngster, but as Juan moved from sandlots to the Montecristi team, he began pitching. A rival team in Manzanillo, sponsored by the United Fruit Company, hired Marichal away for $18 a week. Marichal pitched the winning game for Manzanillo in the finals against the Dominican Air Force team. Right after the season, the Air Force drafted Marichal to ensure that he did not hand them another defeat. He starred for the Air Force team in 1957, then was released to Escogido, Trujillo's winter league team. That is where he was when the big league scouts spotted him. Once again, Pompez and Martínez ruled the day and sent Marichal to the United States under a Giants' contract.

Marichal first played in Michigan City, Indiana, where he won 21 games. Then, in 1959, it was on to Springfield, Massachusetts, Felipe Alou's favorite town. In Springfield, manager Andy Gilbert suggested a change in Marichal's delivery that eventually enabled him to become the best Latin pitcher in major league history. Gilbert realized that Marichal's delivery needed adjustment and advised him to stop throwing sidearm. "You'll ruin your arm," he told him. "Start coming overhand. Kick higher with your left foot as you rear back to throw. That will bring the ball down because the body force will be coming down as you release the ball."[5] Gilbert also helped Marichal develop a screwball to complement his fastball, sinker, slider, curve, and change-up. Finally, Gilbert made Marichal run countless numbers of laps in the outfield to strengthen his legs.

The Big Time for Felipe

Alou, still one step ahead of Marichal, left Springfield for Phoenix for the 1958 season. In June the Giants, who had moved from New York to San Francisco, called him up, and Alou arrived in San Francisco the night before his first major league game. For three years he had traveled all over the United States, far from home and everything familiar. The night before his major league debut was no different from any other night except for the telegram he received from his boyhood friend Roque Martínez, who worked in a cement factory back home in the Dominican Republic.

Felipe was touched that such a poor man would spend so much money to wish him luck. The telegram told Felipe that Martínez had been praying for him to become a major leaguer and a Christian. Martínez recommended passages from the Bible, which Alou carried with him. The next day, with the guidance and encouragement of Giants reliever and Christian minister Al Worthington, Felipe knelt down in the middle of the Giants' clubhouse and became a Christian. Like almost all Latin Americans, Felipe was already a nominal Christian. To this day, most Latins are baptized, married, and buried by the Roman Catholic Church. However, being raised in the church does not always produce a spiritual enlightenment of the kind experienced by Felipe that day.

When he stepped to the plate, Alou hit the first big league pitch he saw, a fastball from Cincinnati's Brooks Lawrence, for a sharp single to left field. The next time up, he hit the first pitch for a double. The Giants put Alou in left field because a man named Willie Mays occupied Alou's usual center-field spot. Puerto Rican rookie Orlando Cepeda became Felipe's roommate.

Marichal Marches to the Majors

Meanwhile, Juan Marichal moved on from AA Springfield in 1960 to AAA Tacoma, Washington, where local reporters called him "Laughing Boy" for his "ever-present grin and sunny disposition."[6] In July the press reported, "The big Giants called up Juan Marichal, . . . one of the most personable and likeable of the Tacoma players." When San Francisco Manager Bill Rigney gave Marichal his first start, he retired the first 19 Phillies hitters and had a perfect game for 7⅔ innings. Only a Clay Dalyrymple double spoiled Marichal's 2-0, 12-strikeout debut.

Marichal moved into a house near Candlestick Park owned by Blanche Laverne "Mama" Johnson. He was joined in September by Felipe Alou's younger brother Matty (Felipe lived with his new wife in a house nearby). Mama Johnson lectured Marichal and Alou on how to get along in the United States. Matty Alou recalled, "If we didn't pay attention to what she said, she'd grab her dish mop and give us a swat. She'd tell us, 'You want to make good in this country, you learn to speak English. Nobody makes shaving commercials in Spanish.'"[7]

While Alou and Marichal were making their mark in the National League, trouble was brewing back home. On May 30, 1961, assassins successfully completed their plot to kill General Trujillo. The Trujillo era, increasingly corrupt and violent, ended with his death, leaving a leadership vacuum that led to battles among competing political factions. Fighting and strikes raged into the fall and caused cancellation of winter baseball one month into the season.

The following spring Marichal reported to the Giants' training camp but asked permission to return to the Dominican Republic and marry his fiancée, Alma Rosa. He was worried about her safety because her father had been an acquaintance of Trujillo. The Giants granted Marichal his wish, and he was off to get married. The couple enjoyed a two-day honeymoon in the Hotel El Embajador, a showpiece during the Trujillo years. Then the newlywed Marichal returned to shut out Warren Spahn and the Milwaukee Braves 6-0 on Opening Day.

During the 1962 season Felipe Alou led the Giants with a .316 average, and Marichal finished 18-11 as San Francisco pulled into a first-place tie with the Dodgers on the season's last day. Marichal started the third and decisive game against Los Angeles for the National League pennant. Still suffering from a late-season ankle injury, Marichal pitched seven innings and left trailing 3-2. In the ninth inning, Matty Alou, Harvey Kuenn, Willie McCovey, Felipe Alou, Willie Mays, Orlando Cepeda, Jim Davenport, and José Pagán combined three walks, two singles, a forceout, a sacrifice fly, a wild pitch, and an error to score four runs for a 6-4 pennant-clinching playoff win.

Marichal started Game Four of the World Series against Whitey Ford and allowed two hits and no runs through four innings. While bunting with two strikes, he fouled a fastball off his index finger, smashing his finger so badly that he was unable to play for the rest of the series. Felipe Alou batted .269 in the seven-game series.

Although San Francisco lost the final game 1-0, and the series went to the Yankees, Felipe and Matty Alou and Juan Marichal returned to the Dominican Republic as national heroes, the first Dominicans ever to play in a World Series. Thousands of people walked, rode donkeys, and took buses 20 miles out to the Santo Domingo airport to greet the stars upon their arrival.

After an abbreviated, two-week effort at a winter season, the Domincan league was called off because of fighting among rival political groups. A series of unauthorized exhibitions was later scheduled, with Felipe, Matty, and Juan participating. For their appearance in the series, the trio was fined $250 each by Baseball Commissioner Ford Frick. Felipe Alou was outraged. "They do not understand that these are our people and we owe it to them to play for them," he complained. "Juan and I were big names. We had just played in the World Series. How could we say no to people who came out as many as 17,000 and 19,000 to see us? Besides, it was the only way lesser-known players in the Dominican Republic could make any money."[8]

Technically, Frick was right. The three Giants had clearly defied the rules by playing a professional exhibition while under a major league contract. Yet Frick was also shortsighted. He ignored the fact that the Dominican baseball fans, who were as ardent as their North American neighbors, would naturally be thrilled to see the first Dominicans who had played in a World Series. It was all the more exciting for the Dominican fans because their three countrymen had played together, on one team. The players' appearance could have been a wonderful opportunity for the Giants and for the major leagues to show how their representatives, these players, went home to comfort their countrymen, who were struggling to form a democratic government amid the political chaos that followed Trujillo's assassination. The appearance by the players had the makings of a public relations dream but instead was made a nightmare by Major League Baseball on a technicality.

The Giants were also shortsighted in their postseason negotiations with Felipe Alou. He asserted, "You don't offer a guy who hit .316 a $2,000 raise. That was what they offered me for being their best hitter on a team that won the pennant. Finally, I made them give me close to what I wanted, but I had to go through a lot of bad letters. They wrote things like, 'Do you think you'll make that kind of money in the Dominican Republic?'"[9] Because Alou went home to his own country each winter, it was somehow easier to think of him as a migrant worker of professional sport, a cheaper source of labor who should be glad to have the major league job.

The three Domincan stars grew close. Matty, who had been a caddy at the Santo Domingo Country Club, taught Felipe and Marichal how to play golf. In 1963 Felipe and Matty were joined by their younger brother Jesús, and all three played in the outfield together for three games during the season, the first time in major league history that three brothers played in the same game. The close-knit group was soon broken up, however. Following the 1963 season, Felipe was traded to the Milwaukee Braves in a seven-player deal. Felipe questioned the trade publicly: "Had the Giants resented my leadership of the Latin faction of the club? I was not a leader in any formal sense, but probably did serve as spokesman for the Latins on our team, a role I did not particularly enjoy. Had the Giants resented my speaking out concerning their treatment of, or, as I felt, mistreatment of Matty after he had been hurt? Matty had been injured during spring training in 1963, and I felt the condition of his left knee warranted more medical care than he received."[10]

Back in the Dominican Republic, calm was restored and winter baseball resumed in 1963-1964 and 1964-1965, with the championships going to Licey and the Aguilas del Cibao, two rivals who had been dominated in the previous decade by Trujillo's Escogido team. But in 1965, the country was disrupted again by political violence. In late April the events were brought home to the Giants in San Francisco. During a home game, the Western Union employee who transmitted Giants' games back to two Dominican radio stations announced over the Candlestick Park public address system that first one, then the other, Dominican radio station had been taken by rebels. The country was cut off from the outside world. Several days later U.S. Marines landed in Santo Domingo, close to the Hotel Embajador. It was a difficult time for Dominicans in the United States, so far away from family and home.

The Giants and the Dodgers were locked in a tight pennant race when they met for a four-game series in Candlestick Park in August 1965. The Giants lost two of the first three games in extra innings. In the fourth game, Sandy Koufax faced Juan Marichal in a duel of baseball's best pitchers. Maury Wills of the Dodgers led off with a bunt single, then scored the first run of the game. When Wills came to bat in the second inning, Marichal knocked him down with a pitch. Next it was Willie Mays's turn. When he batted in the second inning, Koufax threw a pitch well over his head, all the way to the screen.

Tension was building as the Dodgers led 2-1 in the third inning. Marichal was the lead-off hitter that inning. When catcher Johnny Roseboro fired the ball back to Koufax close to Marichal's head after the first two pitches (Juan later said it nicked his ear), the Laughing Boy grew angry. He turned to Roseboro and asked, "Why did you do that?" According to Marichal, Roseboro answered, "You." Marichal took a swing with his bat at Roseboro and hit him in the head, opening a two-inch gash and setting off a wild melee.

Home plate umpire Shag Crawford reported, "Naturally both dugouts emptied. We finally got Roseboro away, but then Marichal went crazy. He went down the first base line, swinging the bat like a wild man. The Giants were in front of him and the Dodgers were behind him, but nobody would make a move on him because of the bat. I came up on the home plate side, trying to get a shot at him. I waited until he raised the bat to swing again, then I dove at him. I hit him around the neck, grabbed the bat, and we both went down. That's when both teams jumped on him."[11] Roseboro tried to get back into the rumble but was grabbed by Willie Mays. When the inning continued, Mays hit a three-run home run off the shaken Koufax for a 4-3 Giants' win.

In his autobiography, Roseboro explained that the tension had built up with Marichal during the first innings of the game. Roseboro wanted to put some pressure on Marichal, but "Koufax was constitutionally incapable of throwing at anyone's head." So, after the second pitch, "I dropped it, picked it up and in pegging it back to Sandy, I threw it about two inches past Juan's nose. . . . It was intentional all right. I meant for him to feel it. I was so mad I'd made up my mind that if he protested, I was going after him. He protested, so I started out of my crouch. . . . I went to hit him with a punch and he hit me with his bat."[12] Dodger Manager Walt Alston said, "I thought it had knocked Roseboro's eye out. There was nothing but blood where his left eye should have been. Dodger pitcher Howie Reed said, "If he doesn't get suspended indefinitely, there's no justice."[13] In the end, National League President Warren Giles suspended Marichal for eight games and fined him $1,750. Marichal had always been a tough player, but there was no precedent for this outburst. He later apologized, saying that feeling the ball brush his head pushed him over the edge.

So affected was the Giants' pitching by Marichal's absence that Matty Alou had to be called on in one game to pitch two innings against Pittsburgh. Marichal finished the season with a 22-13 record, ten shutouts, and a 2.14 ERA, but the Dodgers won the pennant by two games.

In 1966 Felipe, Matty, and Marichal enjoyed career-best years. Felipe starred for the new Atlanta Braves as he led the National League in hits (218), runs scored (122), and at-bats (666); he batted .327 and hit 31 home runs. Younger brother Matty, traded in the off season to the Pirates, won the National League batting crown with a .342 average under Pittsburgh's expert tutor, manager Harry Walker. Felipe's teammate and fellow Dominican Rico Carty finished third in the batting race with a .326 average. It was the first time two brothers ever finished 1-2 in a batting race, and it marked the first time that three non-U.S. citizens led a league in hitting.

Marichal started 1966 with a 9-0 record in ten starts with nine complete games and a 0.59 ERA. He kept his concentration despite booing and hate mail over the Roseboro incident. Marichal finished the season 25-6 with a 2.23 ERA, and *Time* featured him on its cover with the heading, "Baseball's Best Righthander." The Dodgers won the pennant again by two games, and Sandy Koufax (27-9, 1.73, 317 strikeouts) won all 20 votes for the Cy Young Award, given to baseball's best pitcher each year.

Still, Marichal earned respect with his mound work. Hank Aaron described what it was like to hit against him: "The foot's up in your face, and that's bad. Then he comes through like a fullback charging. He lunges right off the hill. Sometimes he even stumbles from the force of his delivery. With all that confusion of motion, it's a problem seeing the ball, but his control is a bigger thing. He can throw all day within a two-inch space, in, out, up, or down. I've never seen anyone as good as that."[14]

Marichal's autobiography, *A Pitcher's Story,* was published in 1967, and he was comforted by the strong response. Mama Johnson's advice seemed to pay off when Marichal earned a contract to promote apple juice in San Francisco. The only problem was that Marichal's accent made "Saxon Apple Juice Will Make You Strong" sound more like an endorsement for sex and apple juice.[15]

In 1968 Marichal joined Lefty Grove, Bob Feller, Hal Newhouser, and Sandy Koufax as the only pitchers since the advent of the lively ball to win 25 or more games in three seasons (25-8 in 1963, 25-6 in 1966, 26-9 in 1968). Marichal won more games than any other pitcher in the decade (191). In 1971 Marichal pitched for the National League in an All-Star Game for the eighth and final time. In 18 All-Star Game innings pitched, Marichal won two games, lost none, allowed only one earned run, and had an ERA of 0.50.

Felipe Alou was traded to Oakland in 1970, where he enjoyed a productive season before being sent to the New York Yankees. His Yankee manager, Ralph Houk, said about Alou, "He's a great influence to have around the ball club. He helps the club just by his presence, his class, and his ability to do everything as a professional.

Felipe plays every day like a pro. He does the little things that win games, but only a manager and some other players notice."[16]

Felipe was released in 1974 after three pinch hitting opportunities with the Milwaukee Brewers. He said he expected his release, "because no Latin player who bats under .240 in the big leagues is forgiven."[17] Alou finished off his career with a .286 average, 2,101 hits, and 206 home runs, tied for the most among Dominicans through 1990. He has since managed extensively throughout the Montreal Expos minor league system, coached for the Expos at first base, served as a hitting instructor, and is a future major league managerial candidate. He managed winter teams in Venezuela and the Dominican Republic and guided Escogido to the 1990 Caribbean World Series championship in Miami.

Felipe's brother Matty also finished his career in 1974, with a .307 average, 31 home runs, and 1,777 hits. Youngest brother Jesús retired in 1979 with a .280 average, 32 home runs, and 1,216 hits. No other brother combination in baseball history has eclipsed 5,000 hits. Felipe Alou is still a pillar of the Christian community, and he commands respect in both the U.S. and Dominican baseball communities.

In 1983 *The Sporting News* selected Marichal as the best pitcher on its All-Time Team for the 50 years of All-Star Games. Marichal retired in 1975 with a 243-142 record, six 20-win seasons, and 52 shutouts. Marichal was elected to Baseball's Hall of Fame in 1983, the only Dominican so honored and the first Latin elected by the normal voting process of the baseball writers. On July 10, 1983, the San Francisco Giants retired Marichal's number, 27. Marichal gave his acceptance speech at the Hall of Fame in English, and then in Spanish for the broadcast of the event back to the Caribbean. Marichal, now a director of Latin American recruiting for the Oakland A's, is looked upon as a senior statesman in Dominican sports and society.

13

HOWIE HAAK AND HIS PROUD PIRATES

When the major leagues opened their rosters to dark-skinned players, the stage was set for the truly modern baseball era. This was not the modern era as measured by superficial elements like the lively ball or outlawed spitballs or big gloves, but a modern era in which no skin-color barriers could block players from the sport's highest plateau. When black U.S. players were finally accepted, it might have seemed logical that this would give fewer opportunities to talented Latins. But it did not.

At the same time that black players were allowed to play in the major leagues, the U.S. economy was moving into a boom period. As young men enjoyed more opportunities than ever to go to college and get good jobs, fewer and fewer were willing to gamble on the long odds of the baseball lottery—the slim chance that they would actually reach the big time. The competition for talent also increased with the growth of professional football and basketball leagues. In the United States, boys play baseball in the off seasons of football and basketball. In the Caribbean, boys play baseball year-round.

The postwar league expansions also greatly increased the need for talent, not only in the major leagues, but also in the extensive yet lower-paying farm systems. The poorer countries to the south were ideal sources for filling minor league rosters with rookies willing to play the lottery for low bonuses or even none at all. The cost of this Latin talent also decreased with modern jet travel. A flight from New York to Los Angeles can be longer and more expensive than a flight to San Juan, Santo Domingo, or even Caracas.

Roberto Clemente

The major league scouts headed south in record numbers after 1950. One trip by Brooklyn Dodgers scout Al Campanis turned up the best Latin and certainly one of the best players ever to play Major League Baseball, Roberto Clemente. Campanis and Santurce Cangrejeros owner Pedrín Zorilla found Clemente in an open tryout at Sixto Escobar Stadium. It was immediately obvious to them that the young high school student was a natural. Campanis returned after Clemente's graduation in 1954 and signed him for $10,000. Clemente's father, a foreman on a sugar plantation in Carolina, Puerto Rico, sent his son off to the United States with these words of caution: "Buy yourself a good car and don't depend on anyone."[1]

Dodger Minor League Manager Max Macon was instructed to hide Clemente for a year on the Montreal roster. Under baseball rules at the time, any player signed for over $4,000 had to remain all year on the parent club roster or be subject to an irrevocable draft after the season, so the Dodgers, in order to give Clemente a year of seasoning at Montreal while attracting as little attention to him as possible, decided to bench Clemente during hitting streaks and play him during slumps. Macon dutifully followed orders, which made Clemente depressed and disillusioned. As it turned out, the Pittsburgh Pirates learned about Clemente anyway. Pirates President and General Manager Branch Rickey sent scout Howie Haak up to check him out. On Haak's recommendation, the last-place Pirates selected Clemente as the first choice of the special draft the next spring. Clemente later admitted, "I didn't even know where Pittsburgh was."[2]

The following winter Clemente returned to Puerto Rico and Santurce, forming a dynamic pair with Willie Mays in his stint on the team. Clemente said, "Mays also helped me. He told me not to allow the pitchers to show me up. He suggested I get mean and if the pitchers knocked me down, get up and hit the ball. Show them."[3] Mays helped Clemente with the basket catch and shoestring catch, which Clemente later perfected to complement his powerful throwing arm. Clemente's winter in Puerto Rico left him with an unfortunate legacy, however, because while there he was in a car accident which left him with back pains that were to plague him throughout his career.

In 1955 Clemente broke into the major leagues with the Pittsburgh Pirates. From the very start, he displayed the fiery, unforgiving pride that is developed in Latin men by their culture. One day in his rookie year, a New York City sportswriter approached Clemente and said, "Roberto, you had a fine day and a fine series here. As a young fellow starting out, you remind me of another rookie outfielder who could run, throw, and get those clutch hits. Young fellow of ours, name of Willie Mays." Clemente paused for a long moment and responded, "Nonetheless, I play like Roberto Clemente."[4]

In the early years, Clemente's only close friend on the Pirates was Cuban outfielder Román Mejías. Then teammate Bob Friend introduced Clemente to a Pittsburgh postman, Phil Dorsey. Since Clemente stayed with the Pirates for his whole career, the two became very close and Clemente became a frequent visitor to the Dorsey family home. Clemente, in turn, entertained the Dorseys at his own house. Phil Dorsey recalled, "When I went to Puerto Rico, he'd take the money from my wallet, so I couldn't spend a cent of my own, and tell people, 'This is Phil, my brother from Pittsburgh.'"[5]

This is a side of Roberto Clemente rarely reported in the United States. In fact, the U.S. press rarely uncovers the depth of Latin players' personalities because of the players' constant migration back and forth to their off-season homes and their continuous travel during the baseball season. It is a side that goes a long way toward explaining the Latin character. Latin society defines the individual in terms of dignity, in contrast to the North American definition, which focuses more on freedom and independence. Each Latin jealously guards his inner dignity. He will not be rushed. He will not be insulted, nor will he do anything he feels is beneath him. Traditionally, Latin societies have worked on the basis of power rather than law. In such a society, it is not what you know but who you know. Thus, Latins define themselves in terms of family and friends—and they show them a greater degree of loyalty than is commonly seen in North America. Clemente felt indebted to Phil Dorsey for taking him into his home and, in turn, wanted to treat Dorsey as well as he could when he visited Puerto Rico.

In 1960 Pittsburgh won the National League pennant and the World Series. Clemente led National League outfielders with 19 assists and batted .314 with 16 home runs. In the series, he hit safely in all seven games. When U.S. sportswriters voted for the National League MVP after the regular season ended, Clemente finished eighth. Series hero Bill Mazeroski later said, "Roberto worked as hard as anybody on the team in 1960, and he was broken-hearted at finishing no better than eighth in the balloting for Most Valuable Player in the National League. Our shortstop, Dick Groat, was the winner. Our third baseman, Don Hoak, finished second. Roberto was as valuable as either of them. It affected him as a person and made him bitter."[6]

But Clemente was not afraid to speak out against the media's treatment of Latins, just as he was not afraid to protest the segregated hotels of the South. In a 1961 interview, Clemente shared some of his feelings. "Latin American Negro ballplayers are treated today much like all Negroes were treated in baseball in the early days of the broken color barrier. They are subjected to prejudices and stamped with generalizations. Because they speak Spanish among themselves, they are set off as a minority within a minority. And they bear the brunt of the sport's remaining racial prejudices."[7]

Yet as disappointed as Clemente was with the balloting for MVP, he didn't let it slow him down once he stepped onto the field. In 1961 he banged out 210 hits, scored 100 runs, smashed 23 home runs, and knocked in 89 runs. About that season he said, "After I failed to win the MVP in 1960, I made up my mind I'd win the batting title in 1961 for the first time. I did, with a .351 average."[8] His 210 hits made him the first Pirate with 200 or more hits since Paul Waner did it in 1937, yet he only moved up to fourth in the MVP balloting.

Buck Canel, the well-known Spanish broadcaster in Puerto Rico, recalled, "You know Clemente felt strongly about the fact that he was a Puerto Rican and that he was a black man. In each of these things he had pride. But it was a beautiful, uncompromising kind of pride, because I never heard him—and you must remember that I am fluent in Spanish—I never heard him make a slurring remark about anyone's color or religion. In this he was remarkable. On the other hand, because of the early language barriers, I am sure that there were times when he thought people were laughing at him when they were not. It is difficult for a Latin-American ballplayer to understand everything said around him when it is said at high speed, if he doesn't speak English that well. But, in any event, he wanted very much to prove to the world that he was a superstar and that he could do things that in his heart he felt he had already proven."[9]

A clinical psychologist working with the Pirates said, "No one drives himself like Clemente. I've never seen a more intense person. If Clemente were a football player, he'd make Ray Nitschke look like a pussycat."[10] Clemente won batting titles in 1964 (.339) and 1965 (.329). In 1966 Clemente batted .317 and did not win a batting title, but he was finally voted the National League's Most Valuable Player. He reached career highs in home runs with 29 and runs batted in with 119. Pittsburgh stayed close in the pennant race but finished third. When Clemente won the 1967 batting title (.357), it was the highest National League average since Stan Musial's .376 in 1948. His fourth title put him in an elite group with Ty Cobb, Honus Wagner, Stan Musial, Ted Williams, Rogers Hornsby, and Harry Heilmann, who each won at least four batting titles.

Clemente's problems with the press were compounded because he discussed his physical maladies with the reporters. Over the years, he detailed to them his troubles with tension headaches, tendon problems in his heel, a bout with malaria, a strained instep, bone chips in his elbow, a curved spine, a chiropractor's opinion that one of his legs was heavier than the other, hematoma of the thigh from a lawn mowing accident, pains in the back and neck from the car accident, a paratyphoid infection from hogs on a farm he owned, severe food poisoning, and insomnia. Pittsburgh General Manager Joe Brown said, "The local press felt he was a malingerer. It wasn't true, but even some of the players, the manager, and the coaches didn't want to recognize that the injuries were real."[11]

Clemente finished the 1960s with the decade's highest batting average at .328. In July 1970 Pittsburgh held Roberto Clemente Night at the new Three Rivers Stadium. That night, Clemente said, "I began life in 1934 when I was born in Puerto Rico and I began another life in 1955 when I started playing baseball in Pittsburgh. I have two loves. My family—my father and mother, my wife and children [three boys]—and my fans in Pittsburgh and Puerto Rico."[12] In 1970-1971, Clemente played his final of 15 Puerto Rican winter league seasons for Santurce, Caguas, and San Juan, and finished with a .323 average.

The Pirates won the National League East division title in 1971. Clemente batted .341 in 132 games during the season, then went 6 for 18 in helping Pittsburgh defeat San Francisco in the National League playoffs. In the World Series against Baltimore, Clemente picked up for a slumping Willie Stargell. After the two teams split the first six games, Clemente homered off Mike Cuellar in the fourth inning of Game Seven. Pittsburgh added an insurance run in the eighth inning and held on for a 2-1 win to take the series.

For the series, Clemente hit .414 with two home runs, a triple, two doubles, and seven singles in 29 at-bats. When the World Series was over, Clemente was voted Most Valuable Player, and he finally heard the praise he had earned over his long Pirate career. He said, "There was never any problem about the people misunderstanding the Latin players. But the writers, at first, they thought Latins were inferior to the American people. Now they know they can't be sarcastic about Latins, which is something I have fought for all my life."[13]

Clemente reached 3,000 hits in September 1972 and led the Pirates to their third consecutive divisional title. After Pittsburgh was swept by Cincinnati in the playoffs, Clemente went to Nicaragua in November with the Puerto Rican team for the World Series of Amateur Baseball. When a devastating earthquake hit Nicaragua a month later, Clemente heard reports that dictator Somoza's soldiers and black-marketeers were looting Red Cross packages. Clemente organized his own relief effort, hired a pilot, and chartered a plane to deliver food and clothes to Managua from San Juan on New Year's Eve. But tragically, the plane crashed soon after takeoff, killing

Clemente and the crew. Puerto Rico went into a state of shock and mourning.

Tearful tributes to the fallen Clemente, with his young sons dressed in his Pittsburgh "21" uniform, recalled the scenes ten years earlier of John Kennedy, Jr., saluting the passing casket of his father, the slain president. A special election was called among the Baseball Writers Association of America to vote Clemente into the Hall of Fame by waiving the five-year waiting period. Of the 424 votes cast, 393 approved Clemente's induction. Those opposed only requested that the voting take place after the normal five-year wait. With this overwhelming vote, Clemente became the first Latin ballplayer elected to Baseball's Hall of Fame.

At the induction ceremonies in August 1973, Commissioner Bowie Kuhn said, "He was so very great a man, as a leader and humanitarian, so very great an inspiration to the young and to all in baseball, and to the people of his proud homeland, Puerto Rico."[14] The Commissioner's Award, given to the player who best exemplifies the game of baseball on and off the field, was renamed the Roberto Clemente Award in recognition of the work he did with many charities. Roberto's wife, Vera, accepted the plaque on her husband's behalf and called the election "Roberto's last triumph, dedicated to the people of Puerto Rico and Pittsburgh and to baseball fans all over the United States."[15]

Manny Sanguillen

One of Clemente's closest friends on the Pirates—and a devoted protégé—was fellow Latin Manny Sanguillen. Sanguillen had a solid 13-year career, but was often overlooked because he played in the shadow of Johnny Bench and even Clemente himself. Howie Haak scouted and signed young Sanguillen for the Pirates, as he had Clemente years before. "He was a boxer when I first heard about him from his high school coach in Colón, Panama, [Sanguillen's goal was] to coach young athletes and go into religious work," remembered Haak. "It took a little coaxing and a modest bonus to get him to sign."[16] Sanguillen had grown up in a poor family with an alcoholic father. He had become inspired by a Bible school run by a Canadian preacher, Elmer Fehr. Sanguillen was a great athlete in school, but he did not learn to play baseball until he joined a team at Fehr's school.

Sanguillen started his professional career in Batavia in the New York-Penn League, where he hit .235 in 99 games. He recalled, "When I first broke in at Batavia, I used to take a lot of pitches. Howie Haak told me that I better learn to swing at the first pitch. I think I got a lot of hits on bad pitches."[17] During his major league career, Sanguillen was called the best bad-ball hitter since Yogi Berra. Sanguillen's manager, Tom Saffell, drilled him on defensive skills and counseled him on his baseball future. Sanguillen said, "I thank Tom Saffell and Howie Haak for talking me out of going home. I knew nobody. I had no friends. After the season, I had only $500 to take home. I made $350 a month, but I had only $500 to take home, so I think again, I better quit baseball. But Haak talked me into staying."[18]

By 1967 Sanguillen was in Pittsburgh, but after 30 games he broke a finger and spent the next season at Columbus. He won the first-string catcher's job with Pittsburgh in 1969 and batted .303 in 129 games. The next year, Sanguillen caught every game in September's pennant race and batted .325 for the year, third best in the National League. Sanguillen credited the Pittsburgh organization for his success, saying, "Danny Murtaugh, Don Leppert, and Bill Virdon helped. Virdon taught me to hit well. Clemente, [Matty] Alou, and [José] Pagán always talk to me and show me what to do. I have many friends. I am happy now."[19]

Despite Sanguillen's strong performance, the media focused on power-hitting Johnny Bench, who hit .293 with 45 home runs and 148 RBIs. Sanguillen hit only seven home runs with 61 RBIs to go with his .325 average. Roberto Clemente boosted Sanguillen publicly while taking a swipe at the press, saying, "Sure, I think Manny is super, better than any catcher around, but they always write about Bench. When the sportswriters write about a black or a Spanish player it's always something controversial. When they write about white players, it is usually nice, the human interest stuff."[20]

Pittsburgh won the National League East in 1970 by five games, but Cincinnati swept Pittsburgh in three games in the playoffs. Sanguillen enjoyed a strong year in 1971. He knocked in 81 runs and hit .319, his third straight season over .300.

Sanguillen also made the most of his seven home runs. Because of his bright personality and take-charge position on the field, teammates enjoyed ribbing Sanguillen. They especially liked to kid him for his home run trot. Teammate Richie Hebner said, "Sometimes it takes Manny five minutes to circle the bases after a home run. It is good for TV commercials. They get in four or five commercials after every one of Manny's homers." Sanguillen responded, "I like to take my time after a home run. I can never tell when the next one will come."[21]

Sanguillen's wide smile was captured in pictures often as Pittsburgh drove to the division title in 1971. Manager Danny Murtaugh praised him, saying, "Bench is the number one catcher in baseball and Sanguillen is right behind him. Bench has that explosive bat, the home run bat. Sanguillen is a better line drive hitter. There is no way to pitch him [Sanguillen] either. He will hit a double to left on a pitch that seems headed for his head. He will hit a line drive off an ankle-high pitch. Defensively, Manny can do it all. He has learned the hitters. He calls a good game."[22]

In the 1971 postseason, Sanguillen was errorless against San Francisco and Baltimore. His hitting (4 for 15 in the playoffs; 11 for 29, .379 in the World Series) was overshadowed by Roberto Clemente's terrific series, but his catching was valued by the pitching staff. Steve Blass, who threw the complete-game 2-1 win in Game Seven against Baltimore, said, "Sanguillen's deceptive in that he puts more into catching than people realize. You think of him as a hitter who can throw well, but he can spot my own weaknesses before I can. I pitch from a three-quarter delivery. If I drop below that, I'm in trouble. Manny notices any little change. In the seventh game of the World Series, my slider wasn't working at first, but Manny didn't give up on it. It started coming around in the fourth inning and he called for it 80 percent of the time the rest of the way. The Orioles had seen how bad it was earlier and were surprised."[23]

Pittsburgh won its division for the third straight season in 1972, but after it lost in five games to Cincinnati in the league playoffs, Sanguillen left for Puerto Rico to play winter ball with Clemente. When Clemente's plane crashed into the sea after takeoff on New Year's Eve, Sanguillen dove numerous times in scuba gear to look for the body. Sanguillen said, "When he died, it was so big in Puerto Rico people stopped everything. Nobody had any more parties for

New Year's. Everybody went to the beach to try to find him. Try to find the body or at least something."[24]

The next spring, Pirates management assigned Sanguillen to take Clemente's job in right field. Sanguillen said, "The Bible says respect the law and to do it, you have to listen to the boss. The boss wants me to play right field, I play."[25] Sanguillen lasted in right field until an injury to Milt May moved him behind the plate. Manny recalls, "I was not in shape to catch every day. My legs were often soft because you use different muscles when you play outfield. So when I went behind the plate, I forgot all about hitting. I was worried too much about catching the ball. It was embarrassing. I was not catching well because I was out of shape and I was terrible at the plate. It was not a good season."[26] Pittsburgh finished under .500 and in third place.

In 1974 Sanguillen caught 151 games and Pittsburgh again won its division. In 1975 Sanguillen batted .328 in 133 games. He was named to the All-Star team for the third time, and Pittsburgh won its fourth division title in five years. After Pittsburgh missed the 1976 division title, Sanguillen was traded to Oakland for manager Chuck Tanner in an unprecedented baseball transaction. Sanguillen was a jack-of-all-trades for Oakland, playing catcher, first baseman, outfielder, and designated hitter. Pittsburgh reacquired him after the season for three players.

Sanguillen returned as a reserve, pinch hitting and occasionally catching. When Pittsburgh won the 1979 National League pennant, Sanguillen spoke reflectively, "In a way, the Latin player is always in the shadow. They say Clemente proved himself in the 1971 World Series. He was 37 years old then. He had been great for a long time. He had been great for 17 years. Here he was, 37 years old, and they said he had to have a great World Series or else people would not know how great he was. He was so ashamed. He'd tell me, 'Oh, when I was younger, I was so much better.' But I'm glad I'm here, I thank God I'm one of the Pittsburgh Pirates."[27]

Sanguillen's opportunity to help the Pirates in the clutch came in Game Two of the World Series. Down 1-0 in the series, manager Tanner called for Sanguillen to pinch hit with runners on first and second, two out, in the top of the ninth of a 2-2 tie. Tanner said, "I felt he could handle Stanhouse. I know Manny likes pitches that are off the plate. I know Stanhouse likes to throw that pitch. I told him if he got an inside pitch to jerk it out. I wanted somebody who could put the bat on the ball, and I knew Manny could make contact. He helped us win four or five games this year with hits. He was involved in every game. He was always on the bench encouraging the younger players. Like tonight. He gave them a big lift. He did not want to go back to Pittsburgh down two games."[28] Sanguillen slashed a 1-2 pitch to right field to knock in the winning run. Pittsburgh held Baltimore in the bottom of the ninth to even the series.

Sanguillen gave this testimony to the 1979 World Series: "Anything we do in this series, we are doing for Roberto Clemente. Roberto was with me in spirit. My hit, all I do to help the club is for him. I wasn't thinking about Roberto when I was at the plate, but after the game, after we won, it came to mind. If Roberto was alive, he might be a coach or manager, but he is still with us. God took him away from us, but I still have Roberto in my heart."[29]

Pittsburgh won the 1979 World Series in seven games. Sanguillen did not play after the 1980 season and finished his career with a .296 average. Research by Bill Deane at the Baseball Hall of Fame reveals that only four catchers had higher batting averages while playing in more games than Sanguillen: Mickey Cochrane (.320), Bill Dickey (.313), Ernie Lombardi (.306), and Gabby Hartnett (.297), good company for a kid from Colón, Panama, who wanted to be a coach.

Sanguillen and Clemente were the products of analysis by Pittsburgh scout Howie Haak. After Clemente's success in the 1950s, Branch Rickey sent Haak off to Latin America to find other players like them. Haak, a catcher in the St. Louis Cardinal organization in the 1930s, explained to Kevin Kerrane, author of *Dollar Sign on the Muscle*, "The Senators had been signing Cuban ballplayers for years, and they got into Latin talent for the same reason we did—to save money. The first year I got [Ed] Bauta and [Román] Mejías from Cuba and [Manny] Jiménez and [Julián] Javier from the Dominican, for about a thousand dollars of bonus money, total. This was when bonuses for American players had gone through the roof. The next year I went to Venezuela and Panama, and then I started to spend three or four months a year in Latin America. I was the first scout who went to all the countries."[30]

Over the next three decades, he also signed Diómedes Olivo, Carlos Bernier, Felipe Montemayor, and Rennie Stennett. In the 1970s he signed Omar Moreno, Tony Armas, Tony Peña, Luís

Sálazar, Luís de León, and Cecilio Guante. Even though these players blossomed into major leaguers, Haak's first contact with them was in less-than-perfect Spanish. Haak explained, "I know enough Spanish to run tryout camps down there, because most of the league games are on Sundays and you could go to 50 games and not see any prospects, unless someone has tipped you off. So I conduct these camps, like the camps the Cardinals had in the States back in the 1930s with maybe 400 kids. First, I make the kids run, and anyone who can run the 60-yard dash in seven seconds or less gets to throw. The ones who can throw get to hit. And then the ones who can hit, or at least have bat speed, get signed."[31]

Haak also points out the challenge of geography. "Venezuela's the toughest country to get around in because it's so big and its terrain is so rough. It took me three planes and a 200-mile drive to get to Tony Armas's house. His father was well-to-do. I think he worked for the government and was very intelligent, but he had more chicken and cattle than I've ever seen. Tony slept in a hammock in the living room. He was special. He had great ability, he was intelligent, and he was a fine, fine person. One of the best."[32]

Experience with Latin scouting taught Haak many lessons about the special problems of Latin players. For example, Haak said the best talent he ever signed was "probably a kid named Manny Girón, out of Panama. He may have had the best arm I ever signed, but he was also the poorest kid I ever signed. His father was a fisherman. They lived in a hut on the ocean. When I came for the father's signature, he was actually up in a coconut tree. The hut had a dirt floor, the kitchen was the living room, and there was one bedroom for eight children. Now, you think he would have been happy to come to the States, but after he got there he would finish throwing and sit there on the grass and cry like a baby. He just wanted to go home. He went and came back, but the last time he left, I never heard from him again."[33]

Unlike North America, where people tend to move around a lot, most Latin Americans live close to their families all their lives. By extension, the friendships they form last a lifetime. This close circle of family and friends gives the Latin a sense of security and confidence that is not easy to leave behind. Thus, while their visas require them to leave the United States at the end of the season, most would go home anyway.

This migrant status makes it difficult for Latin players to learn English. The process can be complicated, because most of these men did not learn their own language through formal education. Thus, they have no basis for undertaking the study of a foreign system of conjugation and sentence structure.

Of course, Haak asserts, "Homesickness is more than just language. You'd be surprised. Many of these boys don't like our food. They don't eat their meat the way we do. They chop it up. They're crazy for rice. All these things."[34] The poorer countries ringing the Caribbean customarily eat a tiny fraction of the meat served at the average North American table. The more common source of protein is beans, eaten in combination with a starch. In the Caribbean, the starch is rice, grown in the warm tropical fields. In Venezuela and Mexico, corn and wheat are more common. Central American customs vary from the hot lowlands to the cooler mountain regions. A human body raised on beans and vegetables revolts when fed a diet of heavy pork or beef.

Ultimately, however, it is not by language or cultural adaptation that Latins will be judged in Major League Baseball. It is by their performance, a product of talent and work ethic. Baseball's unarguable statistics make performance measurement easier. It is by these statistics that Roberto Clemente is judged to be among the best players ever to play the sport, and it is by these statistics that many other Latins have proved their ability and the legitimacy of their own nations' baseball legacies.

14

THREE
WORLD-CHAMPION
LATINS

More than 500 Latin-born players have reached the major leagues. Some of these Latins have been good enough to stand out in the universe of all players, while others had mediocre careers. Whereas any player's performance speaks for itself, the day-to-day performances do not make headlines, at least outside the team's area. With 162 regular-season games, fans cannot see, personally or even on television, the performance of all players. National prominence comes only through playing in a handful of big media cities like New York, Los Angeles, or Chicago, or through outstanding efforts in the playoffs or World Series.

Since Latin players first broke into the big time, World Series play has provided a stage for them to perform in the national spotlight. But even when a Latin does make his way into the spotlight, stardom does not come easily. A strong performance may put a Latin in front of microphones, where poor English and heavy accents cut short interviews. With different backgrounds and values, the enthusiasm of a country kid from Venezuela may seem peculiar compared to an Iowa farm boy's glee. And after the season is over, these migrant workers of baseball return home, far from the microphones and cameras of America's nightly news crews.

The only pre-television Latin to play on a World Series championship team was Dolf Luque, who pitched in two games for the Cincinnati Reds in their tainted 1919 victory over the Chicago White Sox. Luque played on another championship team in 1933, when he closed out the Washington Senators for the New York Giants. Although the color barrier fell in 1947, it took 21 years after Luque for the next Latin to play on a world-champion team, when Puerto Rican pitcher Rubén Gómez won his start in the New York Giants' four-game sweep of the Cleveland Indians in 1954. Gómez was followed in quick succession by a line of Latins contributing to World Series victories:

- Cuban Sandy Amoros batted .333 for Brooklyn in 1955 when it defeated the Yankees.
- Puerto Ricans Félix Mantilla and Juan Pizarro played for the 1957 champion Milwaukee Braves.
- In 1960 Hall of Fame outfielder Roberto Clemente hit safely in all seven games to help the Pirates defeat the Yankees.
- Puerto Rican reliever Luís Arroyo and Panamanian outfielder Hector López were standouts for the 1961 champion New York Yankees. López returned with the Yankees as they repeated in 1962.
- In 1964 Dominican Julián Javier played second base as St. Louis took the title.
- Hall of Fame shortstop Luís Aparicio, Jr. anchored the Baltimore infield in its four-game 1966 sweep of Los Angeles.

Luís Aparicio

Luís Aparicio, a diminutive shortstop who had a huge major league career, was a quiet, serious Venezuelan who brought the excitement of the stolen base back to baseball in the 1950s and excelled during a long career in the infield.

Aparicio was born while his father was away playing baseball. His father was considered one of the finest shortstops in Venezuela and turned down a contract with the Washington Senators in 1939. Aparicio explained, "My father didn't like to fly." Luís Jr. had to overcome his own obstacles. "My mother hated baseball. She used to tell me, 'No baseball,' and I remember what happened the first day I got a uniform. I folded it up nicely and I put it away while I went to school, maybe in the sixth grade. When I came home, I couldn't find it, and she said to me, 'I burned the uniform, Luís, and I don't want you to play that game,' and that was the start of it."[1]

Aparicio played on an amateur level while he diligently studied typing, English, accounting, and business administration. After he completed his studies, he joined the Venezuelan winter league on the Maracaibo Gavilanes, a team owned by his father and his uncle Ernesto. On the side, he worked as an accountant for the local pharmacy. In November 1953 the elder Aparicio gave way to Luís at shortstop, handing his glove over in a special presentation before the game. Aparicio Sr. gave his son a warm hug, sent him out to short, and moved over to first base for a few games before retiring. In February 1954 young Aparicio was chosen for Venezuela's Caribbean World Series team.

One of the teams in the Venezuelan league, Magallanes, had a manager, Red Kress, who also coached for the Cleveland Indians. Kress asked Cleveland General Manager Hank Greenberg to send a scout to look at Aparicio. Frank Lane, the White Sox general manager, was also impressed by Aparicio. Cleveland made the first offer, contingent upon Aparicio's 1954 spring training performance. But Lane called his Venezuelan contact, Pedro Morales, owner of the Caracas team. Lane said, "If the White Sox don't get Aparicio, you don't get [Chicago and Venezuelan shortstop Chico] Carrasquel next season. We'll buy Aparicio's contract for $6,000 and pay him $4,000 to play for one of our farm clubs this season."[2] Aparicio later said, "White Sox—Indians—what do I know? I was only a kid. All I want is the big leagues."[3]

Aparicio did not suffer from the racial slights darker-skinned Latins endured. With his English-speaking skills and business background, Aparicio was better prepared for the big leagues when Chicago opened a roster spot for him after only two years in the minors. Venezuela's star shortstop, Chico Carrasquel, stood in his way, though. Carrasquel said, "In 1955 he [Aparicio] was playing really well in spring training. Then they sent him to Memphis. At the train station, I saw he didn't feel too good, he felt bad. 'Don't worry,' I told him. 'You're young. Maybe in two more years, you'll be on the train going to Chicago.'"[4]

But Aparicio waited only one more year, because Chicago traded Carrasquel to Cleveland. Aparicio said, "Chico was my hero. It's a strange thing. He's a real good friend of mine. He's a real good friend of my father."[5] Friendship aside, Aparicio, 21 years old on Opening Day 1956, said he was ready. "It is the same bat, the same ball, the same game as it is in Venezuela. These are the same plays my father has taught me. I do not feel so strange, even in this new country. I trust my manager to know if I am ready, but I think I am ready for the American League, for any league. Anyway, I was not afraid. It is baseball, the game I love and get to know a little better all the time."[6]

In Aparicio's rookie season, teammate Jim Rivera introduced him to Sonia Llorante, Rivera's cousin. She said, "He's very gentlemanly. That's what I first liked about him. He's very gentle. In a way, he's almost shy. The first time he met me he brought me an orchid. He wrote every day. He called me quite often, too. He wrote to my father in Puerto Rico. My mother liked him right away. In four months we were married."[7]

Aparicio's rookie year was also a success on the field. His enthusiasm led him to the front of the league in stolen bases, putouts, assists, and errors, and landed him the Rookie of the Year Award. Aparicio's double play partner, Nellie Fox, seven years older than Aparicio, became his teacher and role model. Aparicio started chewing tobacco like Nellie, and even named his son Nelson after Fox.

White Sox Manager Al Lopez paid tribute to Aparicio's fielding skills: "At shortstop, you must pick up the ball clean or you don't throw the man out. It is the most important position. First, second, third, you can knock the ball down. At third you don't need good hands. At second you don't need good hands or a good arm. At first, all you need is to be able to catch the ball. Shortstop requires the most ability: catching, arm, hands, experience. Luís has great hands, great arm, great speed. He covers ground from all the angles, positions. I've seen some great shortstops, but he does everything well."[8]

In June 1959, as the "Go-Go" White Sox ran away with the American League pennant, Lopez said, "I go back a ways and I've seen Glenn Wright (Brooklyn), Leo Durocher (Cardinals), Lou Boudreau (Cleveland), and Phil Rizzuto (Yankees). Luís is as good as any of them and he could get better."[9] Aparicio stole 56 bases, the most by any American League player since 1943 and 35 more than runner-up Mickey Mantle. Aparicio was the top speedster on the Go-Go Sox. The Dodgers defeated Chicago in the World Series in six games, but Aparicio recognized the importance of the exposure he got. He said, "I was lucky to be in the World Series after only four years. Some guys don't get there after ten years. You see your club in the World Series, everyone cheers for you in your home town."[10] Aparicio returned to Venezuela a hero and played for his country in the Caribbean World Series, where he hit a grand slam. The Gillette razor company hired him to do a shaving commercial in English, evidence of Aparicio's increased visibility.

Chicago traded Aparicio to Baltimore after the 1962 season. The 1964 Orioles challenged the Yankees, but its young team fell two games short. A couple of years later, though, before the 1966 season, the Orioles traded pitcher Milt Pappas and two other players for Cincinnati outfielder Frank Robinson. On his first day in the batting cage in spring training, Robinson started hitting pop-ups. Aparicio, an infield chatterbox and cheerleader from shortstop, yelled, "Ah, I thought we got a home run hitter and instead we got a guy that pops up. Bring back Pappas."[11] Robinson shrugged off this barb from the diminutive Aparicio to hit 49 home runs, with 122 RBIs and a .316 average. Robinson won the Triple Crown and led Baltimore to the American League pennant. In the World Series, the Orioles combined superb pitching with solid fielding to sweep the Dodgers in four games. Many Venezuelan fans made the trip to Baltimore to see their darling Aparicio.

After the 1967 season, Chicago management gave in to the White Sox fans who had criticized the earlier Aparicio trade to Baltimore by getting him back. Luís spent three seasons with a weak Chicago team and then was traded to Boston. Aparicio hit safely in his first seven games with Boston, and batted in 12 runs in his first 12 games. Then everything fell apart. He did not hit safely in his next 44 at-bats, the longest streak of outs for a non-pitcher in Red Sox history. The streak attracted national attention. When Sherm Feller, the Red Sox public address announcer, offered Aparicio a mezuzah—a scroll symbolic of the Jewish faith in the Almighty—Aparicio deadpanned, "Can I hit with it?" When Aparicio finally singled to break the streak, President Nixon sent him a letter of congratulations, which read in part, "In my own career I have experienced long periods when I couldn't seem to get a hit regardless of how hard I tried. But in the end I was able to hit a home run."[12]

Aparicio recovered from the slump to raise his average from .150 to .232 by the time the season ended. During the season, he broke the all-time record for games played by a shortstop. Ted Williams said, "You might have wanted a shortstop with more power—say Joe Cronin or Ernie Banks—on some particular team. But for doing the job with brilliance over a long period of time, I would have to take Aparicio."[13]

Aparicio's Boston club threatened Detroit late in the 1972 season. In a crucial three-game series, Luís fell rounding third base and cost the Red Sox a big inning. Detroit pitcher Mickey Lolich recovered to stop Boston and lock up the Tigers' divisional title. It was a rare baserunning gaffe for the dependable Aparicio. Even so, Aparicio was still named for the fifth time to *The Sporting News* American League All-Star Team.

During spring training in 1974, Aparicio was released by Boston. After 19 years in the majors, he accepted the release graciously: "The game's been good to me. Anyway, I have a wife and five kids who are happy about it. I'd have to give a lot of thought to playing somewhere else. I can look at it this way: I went out with a pretty good year (.271 in 1973) and everyone says a man should quit while he's ahead."[14]

For his career, Aparicio played 2,581 games, stole 506 bases, participated in a major league record 1,553 double plays, and had 2,667 hits in 10,230 at-bats (.262). In Venezuela Aparicio played eight seasons in the Venezuelan Occidental League and 13 seasons in the Venezuelan winter league. Brooks Robinson described Aparicio as follows: "Here is a guy who had a real impact on the game for the years he played. He was the greatest base stealer of his time. He was certainly the greatest shortstop I saw in my 30-odd years of playing baseball. Take a look at what he did. He led the league something like eight times in fielding and assists."[15]

Baseball writers elected Aparicio to the Hall of Fame in 1984, and the White Sox retired his uniform number, 11, before his Hall induction. In his acceptance speech, Aparicio said, "I thank my father, to whom I owe the first secrets I learned from the profession. I worked hard to do my best for my team, for the fans, for all those who also love this game, and for baseball itself. That is why for me to be among the greatest players in baseball history will always mean much more than I can say."[16]

Orlando Cepeda

When the St. Louis Cardinals played in the 1967 World Series, they, as had Aparicio's Orioles the year before, boasted a son of the early Latin leagues. Like Luís Aparicio, Sr., Perucho Cepeda avoided the United States, but for different reasons. His son, Orlando, explained, "Father never came to the States because of the race problem. Negroes were having a tough time then. Father had a bad temper. He would get mad. He would fight. He would have been thrown in jail if he came here to play. He used to say that."[17]

Perucho played so well he was called "the Puerto Rican Babe Ruth," but his style was more like Ty Cobb's, with slashing hits and the use of his spikes as weapons on the bases. Perucho was a baseball idol in Puerto Rico during the 1920s and 1930s. He played in Puerto Rico with Negro league stars Satchel Paige and Josh Gibson, who were also occasional houseguests of the Cepedas.

In his autobiography, *High and Inside,* Orlando explained that his father played ball for pay only three months a year. "The rest of the year," Orlando wrote, "he was a municipal water tester, earning $140 a month. On that, he had to feed and clothe two families. In 'ours,' there was my mother and me and my brother Pedro. Then there was his 'other family.' My father had a woman on the side, and six children with her. Everyone knew it, and no one made much fuss over it. Those were different times, and it was not an unusual situation."[18] In those older times, it was common for any man who could afford it to have two families in this manner. Today this practice is much diminished, although Latin men, like European men, have a looser view of marital fidelity than North American society purports to have.

Pedro Zorilla, Santurce owner and Giants scout, signed Orlando Cepeda in 1955 for $500. Cepeda was assigned to the Class D Salem, Virginia, Giants, and said, "I was three nights on the bus, getting

there. Sometimes, when the bus stopped and I was hungry, somebody white would get off and go get some food and bring it to me.
What my father had said about the United States seemed only too
true. Of course, I was traveling through the worst part—the Deep
South—but that didn't make much of an impression on a 17-year-
old."19

By 1958 Cepeda had reached the Giants in their new home in
San Francisco. Cepeda got his first major league hit in the April 15
opener when the Giants hosted the Dodgers in Seals Stadium.
Cepeda hit a solo, third-inning home run off Don Bessent to support
a six-hit 8-0 shutout by Cepeda's countryman, Rubén Gómez. Bill
White's departure for the army opened up first base for Cepeda all
season. Cepeda batted after Willie Mays in the Giants' lineup and
hit 25 home runs, batted .312, had 96 RBIs, and led the league with
38 doubles. He was unanimously voted National League Rookie of
the Year and finished ninth in National League Most Valuable Player
voting.

The San Francisco fans and Cepeda, both new to Major League
Baseball, hit it off just right. Mays was perceived as a New York star,
while fans adopted Cepeda as their own. Although Mays hit .347,
San Francisco fans voted Cepeda the team MVP over the "Say Hey"
kid.

Like his father, Orlando's temper flared occasionally. In a 1958
game, Cepeda's roommate, Rubén Gómez, hit Pirate batter Bill
Mazeroski, then was hit in the back by Pirate pitcher Vern Law.
Walking to first base, Gómez engaged in verbal combat with
Pittsburgh Manager Danny Murtaugh. Cepeda, loyal to his friend
and countryman Gómez, exploded out of the San Francisco dugout.
Only a tackle from behind by Willie Mays prevented a bat-swinging
battle. The next winter, Gómez and Cepeda were teammates on
Santurce when another brawl erupted. Gómez hit Mayaguez batter
Joe Christopher with a pitch early in the game. Mayaguez fans hurled
bottles, fruit, and insults, and Cepeda charged into the stands.
Santurce owner Pedro Zorilla put up $500 bail money to keep
Cepeda out of jail. San Francisco management decided to trade away
Gómez to keep Cepeda out of trouble.

In 1959 Willie McCovey entered the San Francisco scene. Both
McCovey and Cepeda were power hitters and first basemen, so Giant
management shuffled Cepeda between first base and left field, with

four games at third base in a failed experiment. Even so, Cepeda was named to the National League All-Star Team and finished at .317, with 25 home runs and 105 RBIs.

After a year of managerial turmoil in 1960, San Francisco hired former Giant World Series star Alvin Dark to manage in 1961. Dark, an intense leader, demanded San Francisco's players push themselves to achieve their goals. Cepeda and his teammates responded with some incredible power hitting. In an April 30, 1961, game against Milwaukee, Willie Mays hit four home runs, José Pagán hit two, while Felipe Alou and Cepeda hit one each. Mays's four home runs and the Giants' eight tied major league records. On July 4 Cepeda had eight RBIs in a Wrigley Field game against the Cubs, and on August 23, five Giants, including Cepeda, homered in the ninth inning of a 14-0 win over Cincinnati. Despite all the heavy San Francisco artillery, Cincinnati won the pennant by eight games. Cepeda led the National League with 46 home runs and 142 runs batted in, both new marks for Latin players. Cepeda also batted .314, but the MVP Award went to Cincinnati's Frank Robinson.

As the 1961 season unfolded, some baseball people compared Cepeda to great right-handed hitters Harry Heilmann and Rogers Hornsby, as well as Negro league slugger and former Cepeda houseguest Josh Gibson. When speculation focused on Cepeda's chance to break home-run records, Dark said, "I don't think about Cepeda's hitting 60 or more home runs—and he doesn't either. He just hits the ball and it goes. He's a born hitter. He has everything to become one of the greatest right-handed hitters."[20]

In 1962 Cepeda played 162 games and hit .306 with 35 home runs. His fast start contributed to San Francisco's first National League pennant, won after a playoff with Los Angeles. In the decisive third game of the playoff, Cepeda hit a ninth-inning sacrifice fly to tie the game, and San Francisco scored twice more to win the pennant. Cepeda was hitless in the first three games of the World Series against the Yankees, was benched for the next two, then had three hits and two RBIs in the sixth game to tie the series 3-3. Cepeda was on deck when McCovey lined out to end the series.

Manager Dark set up a plus-and-minus system to rate the Giants' performances. Dark explained, "Our players get a plus anytime they do a little extra to help win a game. Anytime a player misses a sign or fails to drive in a runner from third with less than two out in a key spot, he's charged with a minus."[21] Single pluses were earned for early-game successes, with biggest points earned for clutch plays late in the game. When asked about Cepeda after the 1962 season, Dark answered, "Cepeda had 40 more minuses than pluses. A terrible record, especially for the last half of the season."[22]

San Francisco management blamed fatigue for Cepeda's last-half slump in 1962, and restricted his winter league play. Cepeda blamed his problems on a knee he injured playing basketball as a youngster. He said, "The knee hurt me all the time and I always aggravate it when I slide or stretch or even hit. Some people think that because we are Latins—because we did not have everything growing up—we are not supposed to get hurt, but my knee was hurt. Dark thought I was trying not to play. He treated me like a child. I am a human being, whether I am blue or black or white or green. We Latins are different, but we are still human beings. Dark did not respect our differences."[23]

This feeling that Major League Baseball had still not relegated racial considerations into the past was not Cepeda's alone. During the 1964 season, Dark was quoted in *Newsday* by Stan Isaacs as saying, "We have troubles because we have so many Spanish-speaking and Negro players on the team. They are just not able to perform up to the white ballplayer when it comes to mental alertness. . . . You can't make most Negro and Spanish players have the pride in their team that you get from white players. And they just aren't as sharp mentally. They aren't able to adjust to situations because they don't have that mental alertness. One of the biggest things is that you can't make them subordinate themselves to the best interests of the team. You don't find pride in them that you get in a white player."[24] Dark later retracted those inflammatory statements, but he was fired after the season. Giants Coach Herman Franks replaced Dark, but Cepeda was not appeased. He viewed Franks as nothing more than an extension of Dark.

In 1965 Cepeda finally had knee surgery, which kept him out almost the whole year. The next year, San Francisco traded Cepeda to St. Louis for left-handed pitcher Ray Sadecki, and the trade was traumatic. Cepeda said, "I knew it was going to happen, and I even had been hoping that it would. But it still hurt. I remembered those first days in San Francisco when the fans cheered me even on my bad days. I loved the city then, as I do today. I sat at my locker and cried."[25]

Cepeda's reputation preceded him to St. Louis. He remembered, "The other players were not too sure about me. From everything they had heard, I was temperamental, bad for a team, a troublemaker, a clubhouse lawyer. I had to prove myself, to myself and to the other players. I had to prove that everything they wrote and said about me in San Francisco was wrong."[26]

Cepeda's effort transformed him into a key force in the clubhouse. He played cha-cha records to dispel the gloom after losses, and he created a new cheer for "El Birdos," his St. Louis Cardinals teammates. Cepeda shouted "El Birdos!" and his teammates yelled "Yeah!" After repeating the cheer three times, Cepeda usually said something nasty about Giants Manager Franks, to the delight of El Birdos. His performance was also helped by the St. Louis trainer, who made a special effort in caring for Cepeda's knee. Cepeda batted .325 with 25 home runs and 111 RBIs, and was the first unanimous MVP in league history. The Cardinals finished in first place, 10½ games ahead of Franks's Giants for the National League pennant.

St. Louis took the World Series in seven games over Boston. However, a late-season slump by Cepeda carried into the series, and he went 3 for 29. Dominican Julián Javier enjoyed an outstanding series (9 for 25, .360), breaking up Jim Lonborg's no-hitter in Game Two with one of his three doubles in the series. Lou Brock and Bob Gibson also starred for the Cardinals. The Cardinals would not have reached the World Series without Cepeda, so he proudly joined the growing list of Latin World Series champions.

The Cardinals repeated as National League champions in 1968, but lost to Detroit in seven games in the series. Cepeda moved to Atlanta for the 1969 season and, after another knee operation, resurfaced with the Boston Red Sox as a designated hitter for the 1973 season. Cepeda reluctantly retired after the 1974 season with 379 home runs and a .297 average. Only one other Latin ballplayer has hit as many major league home runs.

Cepeda's successful career did not lead to a successful retirement. Once out of the game, he became depressed. As he wrote in *High and Inside*, his ex-wife was hassling him for alimony money, and he was drinking heavily and smoking marijuana every day. One of Cepeda's friends, the best man at his wedding, asked him to smuggle

60 pounds of marijuana from Colombia, convincing Cepeda that "Everybody knows Orlando Cepeda in Puerto Rico. You know yourself they never look in your bags when you come home."[27] However, when Cepeda did try to smuggle the marijuana, customs officials stopped him and arrested him. A year later, Cepeda was convicted and sentenced to five years in jail. He was released after ten months, spent time on parole, and worked to rehabilitate himself and restore his name in the baseball world. He has worked clinics and served as White Sox batting instructor for a year. In 1989 the San Francisco Giants hired him to work in player development.

At one time, Cepeda generated numbers worthy of a Hall of Famer. The knee injuries cut down his playing time and ultimately cut short his career. The drug smuggling arrest will probably keep him out of the Hall of Fame.

Mike Cuellar

The next Latin to bask in the World Series limelight was Miguel "Mike" Cuellar, a Cuban southpaw who opened the 1969 World Series for the Baltimore Orioles. Cuellar's long journey to the World Series began in sandlot ball in Santa Clara, Las Villas, Cuba. As a young man, he hurled a no-hitter in a sugar mill amateur baseball league and continued playing while in the Cuban Army. Bobby Maduro spotted Cuellar on the Army team and signed him up for the Havana Sugar Kings. Maduro was confident that Cuellar would be attractive to the Sugar Kings' parent team, the Cincinnati Reds. However, Joe Cambria of the Washington Senators said at the time that Cuellar would not make the majors because of his limited pitching repertoire.

Cuellar led the International League with a 2.44 ERA in 1957, and the next year he pitched five shutouts. In the winter, he pitched for Almendares and won a game against Panama in the Caribbean World Series. In 1959 the Reds called up Cuellar to pitch a couple of games, then returned him to Cuba and the Sugar Kings. Cuellar followed the Sugar Kings when they moved to Jersey City in 1961. After that, he slumped and became a baseball nomad, moving to Syracuse, Indianapolis, and down to Monterrey, Mexico. Maduro's confidence was unbroken: "Cuellar's going to be just like [Orlando] Peña and like a lot of other Cuban players. They all do well at the start of their careers, then slump for three or four years, then come back stronger than ever."[28]

Cuellar kept moving. He went to Knoxville, to Jacksonville, to winter ball in Nicaragua, and, eventually, to the St. Louis Cardinals in 1964. Rubén Gómez taught Cuellar the screwball at Jacksonville, a pitch with a history dating back to the days of Dolf Luque. But the Cardinals returned Cuellar to the minors after a brief look in 1965, before trading him to Houston, where he finished second in ERA to Sandy Koufax in 1966. In 1967 he went 16-11 and was named to the All-Star team. However, the Astros' management prohibited Cuellar from his accustomed off-season training, pitching in the winter leagues. Cuellar said, "When I go to spring training, I can't throw the baseball five feet. It was the first time in ten years that I missed winter ball. I tell them that's why I got a sore arm and won only eight games the next year and they didn't like it."[29]

This argument surfaces whenever a Latin ballplayer enjoys a big season or a poor season—the front office becomes concerned that the player will get tired. Often, the solution is to prohibit winter ball. What the front office men never recognize is that most Latin ballplayers would prefer to play winter ball, and their countrymen who read about them all year put great pressure on them to play. Furthermore, there are no construction, insurance, or sales jobs like those available to U.S. ballplayers that would pay them better than winter baseball. Finally, most players see it as a great way to stay in shape in the off season. Nevertheless, today fewer established Latin major league stars play extensively in the winter to avoid injury and to protect their rich contracts.

After the 1968 season, Houston traded Cuellar to Baltimore for outfielder Curt Blefary. Oriole superscout Jim Russo said, "Sore arm, my eyeball. He pretended to have a sore arm because they wouldn't let him pitch winter ball in Puerto Rico after he won those 16 games. You can't do that, take winter ball away from the Latins. They've been playing it since they were 15 and 16 years old. Their arm muscles actually stiffen up if they lay off in the winter season. That's what happened to Marcelino López when he was with the Angels."[30] Whether Cuellar had a sore arm or pretended to have a sore arm, he enjoyed winter ball and resumed play after joining the Orioles.

Cuellar proved himself worthy of the Orioles' confidence. His teammates found him cheerful and playful while in uniform. His catcher, Elrod Hendricks from the Virgin Islands, said, "Man, he's always fooling around. I remember the time Reggie Jackson hit one of his pitches over the center-field fence. It was like it was shot out of a cannon. For the next few pitches, Mike kept making these strange faces and talking to himself. Finally, I walked to the mound and asked him what was the matter. 'Nothing,' he said. Then he looked over his shoulder at the spot in center field and asked with a big, wide grin, 'That thing come down yet?'"[31]

With the media, though, Cuellar was reserved. He answered questions with a "yes" or "no." In his early years in the pros, the press quoted Cuellar phonetically, and he disliked the impression it left with readers. The ability to learn a foreign language seems to come easier to some people than to others. Most people in Cuellar's position react the same way: If they are embarrassed by their accent, they try not to speak. It takes a special personality to throw caution to the wind and just try to communicate, like Minnie Miñoso did. The only other option for Latin ballplayers is to perfect their English, a task made more difficult by their nomadic lifestyle and their lengthy visits home in the off season.

Ultimately, Cuellar's pitching spoke for itself. In 1969 Cuellar went 23-11 and won the Cy Young Award. The Orioles dominated their American League competition in the regular season, winning 109 games, taking their division by 19 games, and sweeping the Minnesota Twins in three games in the league championship. Cuellar was chosen to open the World Series against the New York Mets and responded with a complete game six-hitter to stop the Mets 4-1. He returned in Game Four and gave up one run in seven innings, but had no decision as the Mets won 2-1. Cuellar was the Orioles' most effective pitcher of the series, with 13 strikeouts and a 1.13 ERA. Even so, the Mets stunned the heavily favored Orioles in five games.

In 1970 Cuellar led the American League in wins with 24 (24-8), starts (40), complete games (21), and winning percentage (.750). Nonetheless, Jim Perry of the Twins won the Cy Young Award. Baltimore entered the playoffs determined to make up for its loss to the Mets the previous year. Cuellar was ineffective in the playoff opener against Minnesota and left before Baltimore took the lead for good. In the World Series against Cincinnati, Cuellar started Game Two after an opening Oriole win, but did not get past the third inning. The Orioles rallied to win for a 2-0 series lead, then split the next two games. When Cuellar was slated to start again, the Orioles held a 3-1 series lead.

The Reds scored three runs in the first inning off Cuellar in Game Five, but Orioles Manager Earl Weaver and pitching coach George Bamberger decided not to pull him, as they had in Game Two. Weaver knew that Cuellar pitched better in warm weather. "In the first and second innings, he's given up more runs than in any other innings all season. We have tried everything to bring him out of it. He's warmed up longer and thrown harder. Next season, we might run him up and down the track a few times to work up a sweat. When he came up to the dugout at the end of the first inning and wiped off his face with a towel, I knew he'd be all right. By that time he was warmed up." His catcher for Game Five, Andy Etchebarren, mentioned another reason: "Between innings we (Bamberger, Cuellar, and Etchebarren) huddled in the runway behind the dugout and decided to forget the screwball and rely more on the curve and slider."[32]

Whatever the reason, Cuellar held Cincinnati scoreless for the last eight innings while Baltimore piled up nine runs for a deciding 9-3 series clincher. As Cuban Dolf Luque had done 37 years before for the New York Giants, Cuellar was on the mound for the final out to gain the world championship for his team.

In 1971 Cuellar was one of four Oriole pitchers to win 20 games, the first time since the 1920 White Sox that this happened. But Cuellar (20-9), Jim Palmer (20-9), Dave McNally (21-5), and Pat Dobson (20-8) fell to the Pittsburgh Pirates in seven games in the 1971 World Series. Cuellar lost the seventh game after giving up a home run to Roberto Clemente and an eighth-inning RBI double by José Pagán.

Cuellar won 143 games between 1969 and 1976 for Baltimore. Opposing managers were frustrated that their players could not hit him. After a 1971 game against Cleveland, Indians Manager Alvin Dark complained, "Cuellar's fastball could have been caught barehanded. He couldn't have blackened your eyes from three feet away the way he was throwing. There's no way we shouldn't have hit him." Bamberger defended Cuellar's style, saying, "Hitting is all timing, so Mike uses a lot of different speeds. He really fouls up the good, strong hitters because, let's face it, most hitters are good fastball hitters."[33]

Cuellar was the major leagues' best Latin left-handed pitcher. He had a career .587 winning percentage, with 185 wins and 130 losses, a 3.14 ERA, and 36 shutouts. For six years he teamed with Dave McNally and Jim Palmer to make up the best pitching staff in baseball.

Luís Aparicio, Orlando Cepeda, and Mike Cuellar filled important roles on world championship teams. Aparicio played terrific defense and reintroduced the stolen base as an effective offensive weapon. Cepeda provided an explosive bat to the middle of some devastating lineups. Cuellar was a masterful pitcher who frustrated hitters with his style and repertoire of pitches. The careers of these men stand out among the Latins who have reached the majors for their individual performance, but also something extra. Their contributions to World Series championship teams brought Latin talent into the spotlight, the mainstream of baseball.

15

THE MOUSTACHE GANG AND THE BIG RED MACHINE

In the mid-1970s, two well-assembled, colorful teams dominated baseball. The hard-driving, fighting, non-conformist, moustachioed Oakland Athletics took three consecutive World Series from 1972 to 1974 with power hitting, strong pitching, and an ability to overcome their stingy owner and poor fan support. In the second half of the decade, Oakland skidded and its best players defected, and the Cincinnati Reds stepped forward as baseball's best team. The Big Red Machine, precise and professional under manager Sparky Anderson, swept aside all opposition in 1975 and 1976 on the way to World Series titles. Both teams featured strong Latins who influenced their successes.

Indeed, during the 1970s, Latin-born players starred on every World Series winner. Mike Cuellar clinched Baltimore's 1970 World Series title. Roberto Clemente and Manny Sanguillen sparked the 1971 Pirates. Later in the decade, Puerto Rican pitcher and 20-game winner Eduardo Figueroa anchored the New York Yankees' rotation on the 1977 and 1978 World Series winners. When Pittsburgh won the decade's last World Series title in 1979, four Latin players contributed to the title: Panamanians Manny Sanguillen, Rennie Stennett, and Omar Moreno joined Mexican pitcher Enrique Romo to form the Latin contingent of the Pirate "family."

Oakland and Bert Campaneris

In Oakland, the Latin player in the bright lights for the world-champion A's was Cuban Dagberto Blanco Campaneris. Campy was on board for the entire wild ride that took the green and gold from last place as the Kansas City A's to three championships as the Oakland A's and on into the unknown as free agents.

Campy was born in Pueblo Nuevo, Matanzas, Cuba, into a family with seven other children. His father, a former catcher, worked in a rope factory. Like his father, Campaneris started behind the plate, but he was too small for the position. As a boy, Campaneris played in the Cuban equivalent of Little League, then graduated to a local semipro team, where he played the outfield.

By chance, Campaneris was out of the country playing in an amateur tournament in Costa Rica when U.S.-trained forces invaded Cuba in 1961. While at the tournament, Campaneris and his teammate Tito Fuentes were signed by an A's scout, Félix Delgado. After the tournament, the young players returned home but were able to slip out of the country early in 1962, just before Castro sealed off Cuba from the outside world.

Campaneris's deal carried with it a conditional signing bonus—he had to survive 60 days in the organization—but he almost did not last through the first day. When the team equipment manager, Al Zych, saw the skinny young prospect, he almost sent him away. Said Zych, "I thought maybe it was a gag or something."[1]

Soon the 60-day limit faded into memory. In an August 1962 game for Daytona Beach, the ambidextrous Campaneris pitched two innings, left-handed to the lefty batters and right-handed to the right-handed hitters. He struck out four and gave up only one run. Campaneris also played the outfield, all infield positions, and catcher in 1962. After minor league stops in Binghamton and Birmingham, Kansas City A's management decided he was ready for the big time.

With only two summers of living experience in the United States under his belt, Campaneris's English was still weak. His baseball performance offered an escape from the embarrassment over language and the loneliness of being so far from home with no chance to return. When called up to Kansas City, Campaneris relieved his frustration in his major league debut against Minnesota pitcher Jim Kaat. On July 23, 1964, Campaneris hit Kaat's first pitch of the game for a home run, only the second player in major league history to homer in his first at-bat. Later, in his fourth at-bat in the seventh inning, Campaneris homered again, making him the second player in history to debut with two homers. His quick start immediately endeared him to A's owner Charlie O. Finley.

Finley, anxious to boost attendance for the lowly Athletics, promoted a unique demonstration of Campaneris's versatility in September 1965. With the California Angels visiting Kansas City, Bert Campaneris became the first major leaguer to play all nine positions in the same game. He pitched the first inning and gave up a hit, two walks, and a run. His cousin, José Cardenal, popped up against him. After the game Cardenal said, "What could I do? I promised his mother I'd never hit a homer off him."[2] In the ninth inning, Campaneris strapped on the catching gear and squatted behind the plate. In a close play at the plate, burly Ed Kirkpatrick steamrolled Campaneris and dislocated the catcher's shoulder. In between, in innings two through eight, Campaneris had played each of the other seven positions.

Three years later, Venezuelan César Tóvar duplicated the nine-positions-in-the-same-game feat for the Twins. In a way, both Campaneris and Tóvar paid tribute to the versatility of Hall of Fame utilityman Martín Dihigo.

Campaneris's first full major league season had ended with his team in last place, but he led the league in triples and stolen bases, putting an end to Luís Aparicio's nine-year reign as American League stolen base king. An exile from his own country, Campaneris headed off after the season to join the Leones de Caracas in Venezuela. He said, "It was better, living with Spanish people, speaking Spanish, where I'm at home."[3]

After a last-place finish and dismal attendance figures in 1967, Finley moved the Athletics to Oakland. Leaving a town after a last-place finish may have seemed desperate, but Finley knew his minor league system held some choice prospects. Oakland meant a fresh start for the A's, and Campanaris was up to the challenge.

In his early days with the Athletics, Campaneris had shown good range at shortstop, but he bobbled many grounders and often threw the ball too hard to his double-play partner. But as time went on, he improved. In Oakland, new manager Bob Kennedy moved Campaneris to left field after Campaneris made two errors in one game. He stayed there until he misplayed a ball. With that, Finley intervened and ordered Kennedy to return Campaneris to short, saying later, "I didn't need any manager who was wet behind the ears telling me about Campaneris. I'd seen Campy play shortstop for years before I hired Kennedy."[4] As it turned out, Campaneris was not to play long for Kennedy, because even though Kennedy managed Oakland to an 82-80 record and sixth place in 1968—the first time in 13 years the A's finished over .500—Finley fired him.

Campaneris enjoyed playing baseball, but he missed his family. In August 1968 he married a 24-year-old typist from Kansas City. With a home life and more exposure to the English language, Campaneris began to give interviews in English.

In 1969 a broken finger kept Campaneris out for four weeks and he missed the stolen base title for the first time in five years. Seattle's Tommy Harper took it with 73 bases stolen to Campaneris's 62. With Reggie Jackson's 47 home runs and stronger pitching, the A's rose to second place in the American League West. Then, in 1970, Campaneris hit 22 home runs, a career high, and teammates Sal Bando, Rollie Fingers, Dick Green, and Catfish Hunter helped the A's develop into a deeper team. These players had been together in the A's minor league system and rose to the major leagues as a unit. Oakland finished second again to Minnesota in 1970.

In 1971 Finley hired Dick Williams, his 11th manager in 11 years. Williams asked the players to forget the reputation as a disciplinarian he had earned when he managed Boston to the "Impossible Dream" pennant in 1967. Somehow, Williams found the right combination of control and freedom in leading the young and wild Athletics to the top. Vida Blue won 24 games as a rookie, while Joe Rudi, Gene Tenace, and Darold Knowles developed into top contributors. Bert Campaneris set the table with bunt singles and chop hits, then upset pitchers with his base-running threat. He slid aggressively, using his spikes to upset fielders and to kick balls from gloves. The A's played hard on the field and in the clubhouse, where youth and familiarity led to locker room wrestling matches that made the papers. Williams allowed blacks to have Afros and Latins to speak Spanish. When Finley offered players $300 each to grow moustaches for Moustache Day at Oakland Coliseum, Williams joined in and let his whiskers grow, too.

Oakland won 101 games and the American League West title in 1971, but Baltimore swept Oakland in three games in the playoffs. The fighting spirit that always seemed to be present on the team reared its head in the off season as Jackson and Blue spoke out against Finley's meager salaries.

In 1972 Campaneris stole 52 bases for his sixth stolen base title and led all shortstops in assists. After winning the division by 5½ games, Oakland faced Detroit in the American League playoffs.

Oakland won the first game; in the second, Campaneris singled twice, stole second both times, and scored twice. In the seventh inning, Detroit pitcher Lerrin LaGrow hit Campaneris in the ankle with a pitch. Campaneris responded by sailing his bat over LaGrow's head. Tiger Manager Billy Martin led the Detroit charge out of the dugout, but was headed off by the third base umpire as the rest of the Tigers battled the A's. The home plate umpire restrained the five-feet-ten, 160-pound Campaneris from attacking six-feet-five, 220-pound LaGrow.

After the game Baseball Commissioner Bowie Kuhn suspended Campaneris for the rest of the playoffs but not for the World Series, saying that it would unfairly penalize his teammates and Oakland. Campaneris said, "I don't understand. He tried to hit me, so I tried to hit him. That's not fair? I was wrong, maybe, but suspended?"[5] When Oakland met the Reds in the World Series after clinching the pennant against Detroit, Pete Rose told Campaneris, "Campy, I just want you to know that bats don't carry too well in this park."[6]

In the World Series Campaneris had only five singles in 28 at-bats and no stolen bases against Johnny Bench. But Oakland survived Campy's bad series as catcher Gene Tenace took over as Oakland's batting hero. The A's defeated Cincinnati in seven games to win the World Series.

Oakland repeated in 1973, winning its division by six games over the Kansas City Royals. Reggie Jackson led the league in home runs and RBIs, and Oakland pitchers Blue, Hunter, and Ken Holtzman each won 20 games. Before the playoffs Baltimore pitcher Jim Palmer said, "I think the key to beating Oakland is keeping Campaneris off base. He can manufacture some cheap runs—get on, steal a base, steal another, and score on an infield out, or something like that."[7] Palmer was right. Campaneris hit .333, stole three bases, scored three runs, and hit a home run in the bottom of the 11th inning to win the third game. Oakland won the American League pennant in five games.

Campaneris's hot streak continued into the World Series against the Mets. He batted .290 with a triple, a home run, three stolen bases, three RBIs, and six runs scored. He had a game-winning single in the 11th inning of Game Three. His home run came off Jon Matlack in Game Seven, with a man on base and no score in the third inning. It was Oakland's first home run of the series, and it put the Athletics ahead to stay. Reggie Jackson also enjoyed a good series, batting .310, with a triple, three doubles, six RBIs, and three runs. He followed Campaneris's homer in the third inning of Game Seven with a two-run shot of his own.

Jackson won the traditional prize of a car as the World Series MVP. He said, "Hell, I've got six cars now. I'd have voted for Campaneris." Campaneris said, "I expected to win. My teammates told me I'd win. I've never been so disappointed in my life."[8] The sportswriters, drawn to Reggie Jackson's marquee name, persisted in transcribing Campaneris's speech phonetically and denied him his best shot at individual postseason glory.

After the win over the Mets, manager Dick Williams had a surprise for his team: He announced his retirement. Williams was replaced by Alvin Dark, the old nemesis of Orlando Cepeda and the Latin contingent of the San Francisco Giants. Dark had managed for Finley in 1966-1967 in Kansas City, but Finley fired him when Dark withheld public support for the fining and suspension of a player. In 1974 Finley and Dark buried the hatchet and Oakland won the division by five games, captured the playoffs in four games over Baltimore, and took the World Series in five games from the Los Angeles Dodgers. No team had won three straight World Series since the 1956-1958 New York Yankees.

In 1975 Catfish Hunter left the A's for a long-term, multi-million-dollar agreement when Finley's failure to pay a $50,000 bonus was ruled a breach of contract. Dark managed Oakland to another division title, but lost the playoffs in three straight to Boston. After the 1975 season Reggie Jackson and Ken Holtzman were traded, while the rest of the team waited for their contracts to run out so they could declare free agency and move away from the tight-fisted Finley.

Alvin Dark retired in 1976 and new manager Chuck Tanner decided the Athletics would run after the division title. Campaneris stole 54 bases, including a club record five in one game at Boston. Charlie O. Finley later paid high tribute to Campaneris: "You can talk about Reggie Jackson, Catfish Hunter, and Sal Bando, all those great players . . . but it was Campy who made everything go."[9]

After 1976, and 13 years with the A's, even Campaneris gave up on Finley, declared free agency, and moved to Texas. During his long career with the A's, Campaneris was named to the All-Star team five times, led the league in stolen bases six times, and sparked the Oakland offense to three consecutive World Series titles. Because he kept himself in extraordinarily good health, Campaneris lasted until 1983, when he batted .322 in 59 games for the New York Yankees, ending his 19-year career on a high note. Campaneris was a six-time All-Star, finished with a .259 average, and made the Athletics feared as a running team. He ranks 11th on the all-time stolen base list, with 649. Campaneris joined Lou Brock, Ty Cobb, Honus Wagner, and Willie Wilson as the only players with 30 or more stolen bases in ten consecutive seasons.

Although the A's were colorful and successful, the strongest team of the 1970s was the Cincinnati Reds. The Reds' front office felt discipline and Midwestern values were best reflected by short hair, no moustaches or beards, and an emphasis on the team rather than the individual player.

Just as Bert Campaneris served a vital role with the rough-and-tumble A's, so too did two more Latin stars assist the Reds' drive for supremacy: Tony Pérez and David Concepción.

Tony Pérez

Like Campaneris, Atanasio Rigal Pérez signed a professional contract just before Fidel Castro slammed the door on Cubans leaving for the United States. As a youngster in Camaguey, Cuba, Pérez was a shortstop on a sugar factory team.

The Reds signed him in 1960 at age 17 and assigned him to Geneva in the New York-Penn League. A few weeks later, the Reds signed 19-year-old Cincinnati native Pete Rose, whom they also sent to Geneva. Rose said about Pérez, "We started the same year, 1960, in Geneva, New York. Reno DeBenedetti was our manager. I came to play second and Doggie [Pérez] had to move to third. He was built just like Davey Concepción is now, really skinny. He was just out of Cuba, didn't speak much English, but he was a good guy in the clubhouse, even then. Then he filled out. It's funny, because he never had the big forearms power hitters have, he was just strong in the bottom." [10]

After four seasons in the minors, Pérez got a late-season shot with the Reds in 1964. Despite only batting .080 in 12 games, a strong spring in 1965 convinced manager Dave Bristol to platoon Pérez at first with Gordy Coleman. Pérez's chance to shine came in 1967. After a strong winter season with Santurce in the Puerto Rican winter league, an injury to Reds third baseman Deron Johnson opened that spot to Pérez. He immediately hit safely in 17 straight games, and was named by Walter Alston to back up Richie Allen at third base on the National League All-Star Team. In the 15th inning of a game that set strikeout records in Anaheim's late afternoon sun, Pérez homered off Catfish Hunter to give the National League a 2-1 win. His wife, Pituka, and 14-month-old son, Víctor, cheered from the stands as Pérez received his first national attention. Pérez finished the season with a .290 average, 26 home runs, and 102 RBIs. He was voted Reds team MVP. Johnson was traded after the season.

When Pérez's performance slipped in 1968, Reds management fell into the old front office habit of barring Latin players from winter ball. They feared it would wear him down. Pérez proved to be the exception to the rule on Latins and winter baseball, for he seemed to benefit from the rest. Pérez returned for a big 1969, Cincinnati's last season in Crosley Field, with 37 home runs and 122 RBIs. First baseman Lee May hit 38 home runs and Johnny Bench joined the team as its catcher. This strong force inspired the Cincinnati nickname "The Big Red Machine." The Machine's time, however, had not yet come, and the Reds lost the division on the last weekend to Atlanta.

In the off season Reds' management hired 36-year-old, white-haired George "Sparky" Anderson to replace manager Dave Bristol.

One of Anderson's first big decisions was to keep a skinny, 20-year-old Venezuelan shortstop.

David Concepción

David Ismael Concepción grew up in the state of Aragua, just west of the capital of Caracas in Venezuela. His father drove a truck and dreamed of his son becoming a doctor. Concepción, who was tall and thin, was much more interested in basketball, which he played all through school. After he graduated from high school, Concepción worked in the loan department of a Venezuelan bank and played baseball during his free time for his home-town Aragua team. The team's manager, Wilfredo Calviño, scouted for Cincinnati and signed him in September 1967. Concepción received no bonus and, in fact, had to spend $44 to buy a glove and shoes before he headed north.

When Concepción arrived in the United States, he faced the dilemma every Latin faces when he comes to the United States for baseball. He said, "The United States was so big it scared me. They have people going to the moon. In my town people don't even go to Caracas. I was lost, afraid. When I left for the ballpark, I was shaking. I ask myself 100 times what I came here for. I have no friends. I speak no English. I was more lonely than ever before. But I play good baseball. And what do I do if I go home—drive a truck?"[11] Concepción was better educated than most Venezuelan truck drivers, but he took the chance to pursue his dream in the United States.

During two years in the minors, Concepción added 15 pounds to his 140-pound frame. Still, when he arrived at Cincinnati's 1970 spring training camp, Tony Pérez nicknamed him "Flaco" ("Skinny"). Nonetheless, Concepción's fielding drew rave reviews from Sparky Anderson, who said, "Dave Concepción can field a ground ball with a pair of pliers,"[12] and predicted, "Within a couple of years, the kid will be the best shortstop in the league."[13]

The Big Red Machine Takes Off

The Reds exploded in 1970, winning 70 of their first 100 games. Johnny Bench hit 45 home runs and batted in 148 runs to be named league MVP. First baseman Lee May hit 34 home runs. Right fielder

Pete Rose and center fielder Bobby Tolan each batted .316. Pérez hit 40 home runs, batted .317, and knocked in 129 runs. His batting coach, Ted Kluszewski, said, "Pérez has the most uncomplicated, level swing in baseball."[14] Bench had his own explanation: "See that rear end on him? That's what generates his power." His only blemish was a league-leading 35 errors at third base.[15]

Concepción shared time at short with Woody Woodward in 1970, and batted .260. When Cincinnati swept Pittsburgh in the playoffs, Pérez and Concepción reached their first World Series. Unfortunately, Pérez had hurt his hand and was held to one hit in 18 at-bats. Concepción played Games Three, Four, and Five against the Orioles, hitting a triple and two singles in nine at-bats with three RBIs. The combination of Brooks Robinson's phenomenal fielding and strong Baltimore pitching stopped Cincinnati in five games.

After the season fans in Pérez's adopted home, Puerto Rico, held "Tany (short for Atanasio) Pérez Night" in January 1971. Over 15,000 fans honored Pérez with praise and gifts, which included a car. Pérez responded with home runs in both games of a double-header sweep by his Santurce team. Santurce later reached the Caribbean World Series.

After a disappointing fourth-place finish in 1971, the Reds considered trading Pérez. Instead, they sent first baseman Lee May, along with Jimmy Stewart and Tommy Helms, to Houston for second baseman Joe Morgan, Dominican center fielder César Gerónimo, pitcher Jack Billingham, and two other players. This trade added some important parts to the Big Red Machine.

Pérez moved to first base and hit 21 home runs with 90 RBIs. Concepción still struggled at the plate, though, following a .205 season in 1971 with a .209 average in 1972. However, Johnny Bench, Pete Rose, and reliever Clay Carroll led the Reds back to the World Series in 1972. After winning the division by 10½ games and edging Pittsburgh in five games in the playoffs, the Reds faced off against Oakland. Pérez batted .435 (10 for 23) to lead Cincinnati, and Concepción hit three singles and a triple in 14 at-bats. Nevertheless, Oakland defeated Cincinnati in seven games, winning Game Seven 3-2.

After the 1972 season, Concepción returned to Aragua in the Venezuelan winter league to work on his hitting and hit .306 with Aragua. When Concepción returned to the Reds in the 1973 season,

Sparky Anderson convinced him to build on this new hitting success at the plate. Anderson said, "Dave, in the past, always used a 38- or 40-ounce bat. He thought he could handle them, but he couldn't. Well, we finally convinced him this spring. We talked him into swinging a lighter bat. He's more comfortable at the plate."[16] Concepción's roommate, Tony Pérez, also influenced Concepción. He said, "Tony, he's like my brother. He tells me when I do good and when I do bad. He shows me what to eat, how to live here. He helps me grow up."[17]

By now Pérez had become a U.S. citizen, which enabled him to visit his family for the first time in ten years without fear of being detained in Cuba. Pérez said, "I took clothes, shoes, food, medicine . . . everything I think my family might need."[18] His father was 76 years old and ill, and feared he might never see Tany again. Pérez's two brothers, both of whom worked in a sugar factory, helped him with his 17 bags on the train trip from Havana to Camaguey.

Pérez returned to strong form in 1973, hitting .314 with 27 home runs and 101 RBIs. Sparky Anderson paid tribute to Pérez, saying, "If there's a runner on second base, there isn't anybody I'd rather see walk to the plate than Tony Pérez. He turns mean with men on base."[19] Concepción also opened the season well, batting .500 for the first two weeks of the season. Pérez said, "For three years I keep telling Concepción not to get down on himself, but he didn't listen. What I tell Dave went in one ear and out the other. Now, though, he's hearing me."[20] Concepción was fortunate to have a mature friend like Pérez to help him through his first years in the United States. This was unlike many of the first Latins who came to the majors who played on teams with no other Spanish-speakers. A youngster like Concepción could have been buried without a guardian.

Concepción improved, .287 in 1973, and was named to the All-Star team. This success was cut short on July 20, however, when Concepción broke his ankle sliding into third.

The Reds finished the season by reaching the playoffs once again, this time against the New York Mets. Their hopes for another World Series appearance were dashed, however, when Pérez was held to two hits in 22 at-bats, and the Reds fell in five games.

In 1974 Reds management worried that, despite Pérez's 28 homers and 101 RBIs, his .265 average indicated that his time had passed, and they considered trading him. There was no doubt, however, about Concepción—it was clear his time had come. He won his first of five Gold Gloves and batted .281 with 14 home runs, 82 RBIs, and 41 stolen bases. Teammates Joe Morgan, Johnny Bench, and César Gerónimo also each won Gold Gloves. It was a disappointing year for the Reds, who lost the division by four games to the Dodgers, but the table was set for successful seasons in 1975 and 1976.

In April 1975 *The Sporting News* featured Concepción on its cover, which led Sparky Anderson to remark, "David Concepción's picture is going to be on the cover of *The Sporting News,* and he's going to be tough to live with. You know what, though? [Coaches] Ted Kluszewski, Alex Grammas, and [Concepción's wife] Delia should be in the picture with him. They're all a big part of the success Concepción is experiencing today."21

Pérez, meanwhile, answered the trade rumors by working out intensely over the winter in Puerto Rico. He ran on the beach, pumped iron in the gym, and took two inches off his waistline. He arrived for spring training in super condition.

Cincinnati roared to 41 wins in 50 games early in 1975. Bench, Morgan, Gerónimo, and Concepción all won Gold Gloves again. Morgan also won the first of two consecutive National League MVP awards. Concepción batted .274 and stole 33 bases. In August Pérez batted in the 1,000th run of his career, and he finished with 109 RBIs for the season. The Reds won the division by 20 games with a 108-54 record.

In a three-game sweep of Pittsburgh in the playoffs, Concepción went 5 for 11 with a home run in the clinching third game. Pérez was 5 for 12 (.417) with a home run and four RBIs. The Reds had their third shot in six years at winning a World Series.

In a series that absorbed the country, Cincinnati defeated Boston in seven games. The series began with the teams splitting the first four games. Pérez was 0-14 in the series, so Sparky Anderson moved Bench to cleanup and dropped Pérez to fifth for Game Five. Pérez responded with two homers and four RBIs to push the Reds to a 6-2 win and a 3-2 lead. Then, in Game Six, Carlton Fisk hit a 12th-inning home run for a 7-6 Red Sox win. In Game Seven at Fenway Park, with the Red Sox ahead 3-0 in the sixth inning, Pérez started the Reds' comeback with a home run off a Bill Lee "Eephus" pitch with Bench on base to cut the Boston lead to 3-2. Rose singled to tie the score in the seventh. Joe Morgan followed with a single off Jim Burton in the ninth to drive home Ken Griffey to win the game 4-3 and give Cincinnati its first World Series championship since 1940.

It had been a series marked by good pitching, clutch hitting, and outstanding fielding. Concepción hit only .179, but he had a home run, four RBIs, and three stolen bases. Pérez also batted a low .179, but he provided support through three homers and seven RBIs. After Pérez hit two home runs in Game Five of the series, Los Angeles *Times* columnist Jim Murray wrote, "He finally joined the people he belongs with: the Ruths, Gehrigs, Mantles, Berras. . . ."[22]

Concepción's long reach cut off many erstwhile singles over the years, but his powerful arm led to many throwing errors. In 1974 Concepción had 30 errors at short. He reduced the total to 16 in 1975, but the total was rising again in 1976, even though he led the National League in putouts and assists.

Concepción's main fielding rival, Philadelphia's Larry Bowa, needled him before a June 1976 series by asking him, "Is your first name Elmer?" Concepción answered, "Why do you say that?" Bowa responded, "I thought it had to be Elmer. Every time I look at the box it says 'E-Concepción.'" After Concepción robbed Bowa of a hit and turned in a great defensive game, he yelled to Bowa, "Elmer's Glue. That's me."[23]

In 1976 Concepción batted .281 and won the Gold Glove, as did Morgan, Bench, and Gerónimo, making the middle of the defense solid gold. Dan Driessen, at 23, frequently replaced the 34-year-old Pérez at first base, rekindling trade speculation. Pérez finished the season with 19 home runs, 91 RBIs, and a .260 average. This was the tenth consecutive season Pérez had more than 90 RBIs.

The Reds defended their divisional title, winning 102 games, and followed that by sweeping Philadelphia in three games in the playoffs. In the 1976 World Series sweep against the New York Yankees, Concepción batted .357 (5 for 14) with a double, triple, and three RBIs, batting safely in all four games. Pérez batted .313 (5 for 16) in the series. The Reds' win was an historic one, because since divisional play began, no other team has swept all postseason games. The press flattered the Reds with comparisons to the 1927 Yankees, a team considered by many to be baseball's all-time best.

Before the 1977 season, the Reds traded Tony Pérez and reliever Will McEnaney to Montreal for 36-year-old pitcher Woody Fryman and reliever Dale Murray. McEnaney had saved the last games of both the 1975 and 1976 World Series. The Associated Press quoted an omniscient Reds fan, who said of Pérez's departure, "It was a mistake. It's going to be hard for the body to function without the heart."[24]

Sure enough, Cincinnati finished ten games behind Los Angeles in 1977. Joe Morgan later said, "He could do it in the clutch. Johnny Bench, Pete, me, we got the MVPs, but Tony was just as valuable as we were. He was important in the clubhouse and on the airplanes, too. When they traded him before the 1977 season, I got upset. The first month and a half of that season, we kept getting into situations that he had always come through in. We kept waiting for him, and waiting, but there was no Tony. Tony was in Montreal. There's no doubt in my mind that if he'd played for us in '77, we would have won our third straight World Series."[25]

After three years in Montreal, Pérez declared free agency and moved to Boston in 1980. There he contributed 25 home runs, 105 RBIs, and much more. His years in the sport had built his confidence and insight, and had prepared him for the leadership role he assumed in Boston. The Red Sox had waited until 1959 to integrate, a full 12 years after Jackie Robinson's debut, and had not done much in the ensuing 20 years. In 1980 Pérez observed, "On the entire 25-man roster, the Red Sox have one black and one Latin, and I'm the one." Jim Rice was on the disabled list and as Tony said, "Mike Torrez? A Mexican from Topeka, Kansas, is not a Latin."[26]

Pérez also spoke up in August when Boston trailed by 12½ games. "It doesn't look like anyone cares. Win or lose, they all feel the same way. They come to the park every day, and winning and losing makes no difference. I have seen more things with this team than I have ever seen happen on other teams. On other teams, someone puts a stop to them. Here, nobody cares."[27]

In 1982 Pérez was awarded the prestigious Roberto Clemente Award by the Baseball Commissioner's office for his contributions to baseball. The following year, Pete Rose helped lure Pérez to the Philadelphia Phillies. There, the two teamed up with another ex-teammate, Joe Morgan, for a season that culminated in a National League pennant and World Series appearance for the Phillies. It was the fifth World Series for Pérez. Rose said, "The Reds misjudged what Tony did off the field. He was great communicating with players. He could talk to the blacks and the whites and the Latins. They all respected him. To me, the downfall of the Big Red Machine came when Tony was traded to Montreal after the 1976 season."[28]

Without Perez, the Reds' Concepción toughed it out. In 1978 he hit .301, the first Reds shortstop since 1913 to bat .300. Concepción and his teammates won the National League West with a late-season rush in 1979, making the sixth division title for Cincinnati in the decade. In the playoffs, however, they were swept by Pittsburgh.

Concepción won five Gold Gloves in the decade and patented his unique one-bounce throw from the hole off AstroTurf. He explained, "I first saw that when Brooks Robinson did it at Riverfront in the World Series of 1970. He got a ball hit down the line way behind third base and got rid of it, bang! Like only he could do. It bounced, but Boog Powell dug it out, and they got the runner. I could hardly believe it. I don't think Brooksie meant it—he had no chance, you know—but I thought about it that winter. I could still see the play. Then I had elbow trouble the next spring, so I began trying it—but on purpose, you know, to protect my arm. Our first baseman—it was Lee May; Pérez was later—didn't complain, and I kept on with it. On turf, it's a good play. Brooks Robinson started it, but I registered the patent."[29]

Concepción was proud of his role on the highly publicized Reds. He said, "Everyone knows that Bench, Morgan, Rose, and Seaver all got the publicity here. But in Venezuela, I am Número Uno. I make the people proud. When I play in the World Series it goes all over the world, and the people, they know that it is Davey Concepción from Venezuela. It is good for my country."[30]

During the 1980s Concepción signed a five-year contract, the biggest in club history up to that time. His former teammate, Pete Rose, returned to manage the Reds in 1984, bringing Tony Pérez back with him. Both Pérez and Concepción enjoyed strong production under Rose. Pérez started 1985 with 13 RBIs in his first 23 at-bats. In May 1985 he became the oldest player in history to hit a grand slam and finished the year with a .328 average. He was signed for 1986 and enjoyed himself at Tony Pérez Day, a ceremony at Riverfront Stadium celebrating the 16 of Pérez's 23 seasons in the majors spent with the Reds. Friend and roommate Dave Concepción led the tributes. At the next Reds game, Pérez hit the 379th home run of his career, tying Orlando Cepeda for the most by a Latin.

In the 1980s Concepción began serving as a utility player. He completed his 19th season with Cincinnati in 1988. Hoping to play 20 big league seasons, Concepción rejected the Reds' offer of retirement and was released. Oakland's Dave Parker, a former teammate of Concepción with Cincinnati, said, "They knew Concepción wanted to play 20 years. They could have carried him one more year. If the Reds had turned their backs on Rose, he never would have reached 4,000 hits. . . . If Pete Rose carries the clout people think he does in Cincinnati, how can they treat Dave Concepción, his friend, like that?"[31]

Concepción tried to catch on with the California Angels in 1989 but was cut at the end of spring training. He returned to Venezuela, where he managed the Tigres de Aragua, the Venezuelan winter league team he played on for 23 years. In the late 1970s Venezuelan sportswriter Rubén Mijares said, "In Venezuela, we like to say we have had the best shortstop in the major leagues for the past 25 years. First there was Carrasquel, then there was Aparicio, and now there's Concepción."[32]

Pérez and Concepción were key members of the Big Red Machine while Campaneris anchored the infield of one of baseball's most colorful teams. Their performance brought credibility and attention to all Latin American players. All three players will be remembered as stars of the 1970s, and Pérez certainly deserves election to the Hall of Fame.

16

CLOSE, BUT NO CIGAR (EXCEPT FOR LUÍS)

Some Latin players miss out on the postseason accolades heaped on men like Pérez, Cuellar, Concepción, and Campaneris. Through trades or contract obligations and financial decisions, these players never win a championship. They may spend entire careers with mediocre teams. Fortunately, baseball's painstaking records of individual performance ensure that superior players will eventually be noticed, even when ballplayers toil in less-media-saturated cities like Seattle or Houston or Cleveland. Such was the case with Rod Carew, Tony Oliva, Luís Tiant, and José Cruz. Although these Latin stars never played for a World Series winner, they came painfully close. Their career performances deserve a look back and a round of applause, especially for first-ballot Hall of Famer Rod Carew.

Rod Carew

Rod Carew was one of the most unforgettable hitters of all time. He grew up in Gamboa, Panama, in the black section of town. As he described it in his autobiography, *Carew*, "The Canal

135

Zone was segregated. When the Canal was built, starting in the late 1800s, a lot of whites from the southern states in America came down as organizers and laborers. They brought some of their racial attitudes with them. Workers were also recruited from the black populations of the West Indies—my grandparents included. Living quarters, schools, and even toilet facilities were separate. . . . To this day, white people live in one section, blacks in another. The commissary was where most of the people in Gamboa did their shopping. A partition divided it in half, and the whites shopped on one side, the blacks on the other. . . . I can't remember ever being called a racial name in Panama. But we knew enough to stay out of the white area."[1]

Carew remembered, "Jackie Robinson was a hero down there. Even neighbors who knew nothing about baseball idolized him. This was the early 1950s. Only a few years before, Jackie had become the first black in Major League Baseball; there still weren't very many others. My neighborhood was all black, so it was natural for black players to be favorites."[2]

When Rod was 14, his mother moved the family to New York City in search of better job opportunities. Carew's first experiences as a teen in New York were much the same as those experienced by ballplayers from the Caribbean or Latin America. He recalled, "I didn't speak a whole lot of English then, and my classes were in English. I had a terrible year. I'd walk around the streets and wish I were back home in Panama. In Panama there was room to play and room to run and room to breathe. But this was a crowded new world, and it was tough to understand."[3]

Life improved when Carew found an activity he remembered from home, baseball. One of Carew's teammates on a sandlot team told his father, a Minnesota Twins bird dog, about the young Panamanian, which resulted in a secret tryout during batting practice before a Twins-Yankees game at Yankee Stadium. After Carew hit a number of balls into the seats, Minnesota Manager Sam Mele exclaimed, "Get him out of here before somebody sees the kid!"[4] The Twins signed him after graduation from high school for a $5,000 bonus. After three years in the minors, Carew sufficiently impressed Twins owner Calvin Griffith in spring training and made the club.

Carew's teammate in his rookie year, veteran pitcher "Mudcat" Grant, advised him, "For a black guy to survive in the major leagues,

he has to go out there and play if his leg is broken, if he's dying.
Look around: You don't see many black guys sitting on the bench
up here. You go out there and play until they drag you from the
field."[5]

Carew missed his first chance to reach the World Series his rookie
year when Minnesota dropped the last two games of the 1967 season
to Boston, to finish one game behind the Red Sox. Carew batted
.292 and was voted American League Rookie of the Year.

When the 1969 season started, Billy Martin was the new Minnesota manager. Martin, a former second baseman, took an interest
in Carew, who at the time was having some personal difficulties
because his parents had just separated. In one game Carew walked
off the field and into the clubhouse. Martin said, "I followed him
into the clubhouse and found him there crying. He told me about
his mom and dad. I'd had some experiences with that, coming from
a broken home myself, so we talked." Carew returned Martin's
affection. "He was my teacher," said Carew. "He was like a second
father to me. I was young back then. I was quiet. People thought I
was moody. Billy tried to get me to joke more with the guys, to take
things less seriously. He'll always have a special place in my heart."[6]

Billy Martin also spent time helping Carew on the field. One
unusual thing he taught his young hitter was how to steal home.
Carew said, "Although I stole a lot of bases in the minors, I had
stolen only 5 and 12 in my first two seasons with the Twins. All I
knew about stealing home was that Jackie Robinson had done it so
spectacularly. I remember seeing newspaper photos of him, with a
big hook slide and a lot of dust around home plate and the catcher
lunging at him. That spring, Billy worked with me for hours on
stealing home. We had it timed to the split second."[7] As a result,
Carew stole home seven times in 1969 to tie Pete Reiser's major
league record.

Also in 1969 Carew switched his approach to hitting, going to
a 36-ounce bat from a 34-ounce model. He said, "I opened my stance
and forgot about hitting homers. All I do now is think 'base hit,'
and I don't care how I do it, even if I bunt it, drag it, chop it, or
slash it."[8] Carew batted .392 in early June and finished at .332 to
win his first batting title. He beat his roommate and teammate, Tony
Oliva, who tied for second at .309. Carew said, "It was like beating
my teacher. You can learn so much about hitting by watching Tony.

During my first season, I hit to left field a lot, but I did it by slapping the outside pitches to left. I watched Tony inside-out balls to left, especially inside pitches, and I tried it the next season."9

The Twins won the American League West title by nine games in the 1969 season, and Carew had his second chance to reach the World Series. But Carew was only 1 for 14 in the playoffs, and Baltimore swept Minnesota in three games.

In early 1970 Carew and his girlfriend, Marilynn Levy, announced their engagement. Levy, from a Jewish family in Minneapolis, had dated Carew for a couple of years. Carew's first visit to the Levy home took place during the Passover holiday. Marilynn explained about that visit, "My little nieces put up a sign on the wall at the seder, 'Guess Who's Coming to Dinner?' It was a popular Sidney Poitier movie of the time about mixed marriages. I took my mother to see it to prepare her."10 Carew and Levy married later that year.

Early in the season Carew's leg was broken when Mike Hegan made a dive at him to break up a double play. He pinch hit a few times late in the season and Minnesota won the division again. But Carew's third chance to reach the World Series slipped past when Baltimore again swept the Twins in the playoffs. Carew struck out in his only pinch hitting appearance in the championship series.

After a slow start in 1971, Carew rallied to finish at .307, but even so the Twins finished in fifth place. After the season Carew returned to Venezuela, where his previous year's winter league play had been cut short by knee pain. This time Carew led the league at .355, managed the team when Aragua Manager Vern Rapp left in November, and guided the team to second place in the Caribbean World Series.

Through the 1974 season Carew won four American League batting crowns, yet the Twins took him to salary arbitration and won the right to pay him only $120,000 instead of his requested $140,000. Carew was disillusioned and felt unappreciated. Nonetheless, he was named team captain in 1975 and moved to first base, replacing Harmon Killebrew in both cases. He also won his fifth batting title with a .359 average, 14 home runs, and 80 RBIs.

Carew began to make some noises about leaving Minnesota. "I've got nothing against the Twins," he said. "In fact, I've enjoyed playing in Minneapolis because it doesn't have the rush and bustle of other towns. But sometimes I get tired of playing on a third- or fourth-place team. I'd like to get into the World Series before I retire. And playing in those big towns helps with off-season employment. In New York and L.A. and Chicago, ballplayers get to do different things during the off season. But I haven't gotten any requests for endorsements in Minneapolis."[11]

Despite the isolation, Carew began receiving the attention one would expect for future Hall of Famers. In March 1977 he received the Roberto Clemente Award for his work with the Mental Health Association, the March of Dimes, and the Leukemia Foundation. Carew started the year hot and improved, batting .388 in mid-June. Chicago White Sox shortstop Alan Bannister quipped, "Carew is the only guy I know who can go 4 for 3."[12] Texas Ranger pitcher Gaylord Perry kidded, "Greaseball, greaseball, greaseball. That's all I throw him, and he still hits them. He's the only player in baseball who consistently hits my grease. He sees the ball so well. I guess he can pick out the dry side."[13]

Sports Illustrated and *Time* featured Carew on their covers in his pursuit of .400. Ted Williams, baseball's last .400 hitter, was quoted in the *Sports Illustrated* article: "When I first saw Carew in the late sixties, I didn't think he had the talent. He was a little too lackadaisical to suit me. He swung at bad balls, and he didn't make contact that much. He still looks lackadaisical. It's his style. He's so smooth he seems to be doing it without trying. I think the only reason Carew hasn't received the credit he deserves—I suppose I doubted his ability myself for this reason—is that he's a singles hitter."

Williams continued, "He's a classic straightaway hitter, and historically, the highest-average hitters were straightaway hitters. Good form, good plate coverage, good style, a quick bat. Doesn't give the appearance of being aggressive at the plate, but I think he is. He doesn't pull, but he hits anything. Now, accepting his speed and unique abilities, knowing he's a singles hitter, it figures Carew is going to get more pitches to hit. As a manager, I preferred not to see him on first base, knowing the commotion he could cause. You pitch to him and you've got a chance. Even if he connects, he doesn't figure to beat you with one swing. But the advantage in his getting better pitches means getting a better shot at fattening his average."[14]

The excitement over Carew's pursuit of .400 carried to the White House, where Carew presented one of his bats to Minnesota native

Vice President Walter Mondale. A Minnesota congressman entered two newspaper columns praising Carew's bat skills into the *Congressional Record* in Washington. When the season ended, Carew slipped to .3880, the highest average since Williams's .3881 in 1957. He also batted in 100 runs, scored a league-leading 128 runs, and had 239 hits, the highest total since Bill Terry's 254 in 1930. Carew was honored as the American League MVP in 1977.

After the 1977 season, Minnesota lost two of its best players, Larry Hisle and Lyman Bostock, to free agency and higher pay. When Carew asked for his contract to be renegotiated, Griffith refused. Even worse, he offended Carew in the process by calling ballplayers greedy and blaming Carew for his stupid bargaining in 1976. Carew requested a trade. Despite the turmoil, Carew won his seventh batting title, hitting .333 in 1978.[15]

In February 1979 Carew finally got the contract he deserved, but it took a trade (in which he was sent to California for four players) to accomplish it. As a condition of the trade Carew got a five-year, $4 million contract. California won the Western Division and Carew batted .412 in the playoffs (7 for 17), with three doubles and four runs scored. But California was defeated in four games by Baltimore. Baseball's top hitter for the 1970s (.343) was stopped short of the World Series for a fourth time.

In 1982 the Angels won the American League West again, this time with a 93-69 mark. Carew helped the cause by batting .319, the 14th consecutive time he cleared the .300 mark in his career. In the American League playoffs, Carew came as close as he would to the World Series. California won the first two games in Anaheim, 8-3 and 4-2, but Milwaukee won the next three games at home 5-3, 9-5, and 4-3 in the decisive game. Carew was 3 for 17 in the five games. With two out and a runner on second in the top of the ninth, Carew grounded to shortstop Robin Yount to end the game. Carew's fifth and best chance to reach the World Series disappeared.

Carew played three more seasons with California and played in his 15th and final All-Star Game in 1984. In 1985 Carew reached 3,000 hits on the same day Tom Seaver won his 300th game. Carew and Seaver had each been Rookie of the Year in their respective leagues in 1967. After the season the Angels did not re-sign Carew and, curiously, no other team expressed interest. An arbitrator found this lack of interest to be more than coincidence and fined the owners for collusion. Sadly, Carew's career was aborted by an unfair act by baseball's owners, and not by his own decision.

Among Latin ballplayers only Carew and Clemente have reached 3,000 hits. Carew explained, "Another honor related to that 3,000th hit came in November 1985 when I was asked by the government in Panama to return for a celebration. As part of the event I was given that nation's Medal of Honor by the Panamanian president, and my number, 29, was permanently retired. That means no player, at any level and in any sport, can wear that number in Panama. It was a heartwarming experience for someone who has purposely kept his Panamanian citizenship in hopes of giving the youth of that country a role model. The sights and sounds of that trip will never be forgotten."[16]

Rod Carew barely missed the World Series, but his career has earned him a spot among baseball's great players. Only Ty Cobb with 12 and Honus Wagner with eight won more batting titles than Carew's seven. He finished his career with 3,053 hits (12th all-time) and a .328 average. In January 1991 the BBWAA announced Rod Carew's election to the U.S. Baseball Hall of Fame on the first ballot, an honor accorded only 22 players in the Hall.

In tribute to the hard work that elevated Carew to the Hall of Fame, his former manager Gene Mauch said, "Rodney was an awful lot like two players I know—Ralph Kiner and Ted Williams. They practiced probably more than any player I saw before I met Rodney, and Rodney practiced just like they did. It wasn't something that just happened. For all the hits he got, he got 25,000 more in batting practice."[17]

Tony Oliva

One of Carew's teammates and an important influence in his early years in Minnesota was Tony Oliva, a Cuban who overcame injuries and isolation to put in record performances in the 1960s. One of ten children, Pedro Oliva began playing baseball in a local league in Pinar del Río, Cuba. Famous Washington Senators and Minnesota Twins scout Joe Cambria heard about Oliva on one of his many trips to Cuba and gave him airfare for a tryout in the United States, but Oliva could not find his birth certificate and authorities told him it would take a week to get a replacement. Instead of waiting, Pedro borrowed his brother Antonio's certificate, and Pedro Oliva, Jr., became Antonio "Tony" Oliva.

Oliva told his parents he would return in six months. Six days later Cuban rebels started the Bay of Pigs invasion, and shortly thereafter Castro prohibited travel by Cubans to and from the United States. Only Oliva's anxiousness to make the tryout got him out of Cuba before politics took over. Tony Oliva was the last Cuban prospect signed by Cambria in his 25-year Cuban scouting career.

Oliva had never been away from his family. He had never visited a big city like Havana, let alone a huge U.S. municipality like New York City. He spoke no English, and he was a baseball innocent who had never seen a professional game. His throws from the outfield were sidearm, and they often bounced to one side.

Three days after his arrival in the United States, the Twins gave Oliva his first tryout. Unimpressed, they turned him away and offered him to the Houston Colt 45s, who also turned him down. Oliva called the Charlotte Hornets, another Twins farm club, but they weren't interested, either. Finally, the Wyethville, Virginia, Twins in the Class D Appalachian Rookie League signed him after the Charlotte general manager placed a call. In Wyethville, Tony Oliva began to hit.

In 1961 Oliva hit .410, and when he was moved up to Charlotte in 1962, he batted .350. At the tail end of the season, Minnesota called him up and he had four hits in nine at-bats. Once Oliva arrived in the majors, the story of his brother's birth certificate came out. The Twins informed the Commissioner's office and immigration authorities in St. Paul, who assured them that Oliva would not be deported, nor would they lose their rights to him.

After he batted .304 with Dallas/Fort Worth in 1963, Minnesota called him up for good. Oliva's first roommate with the Twins, Puerto Rican first baseman Vic Power, said this about the young Oliva when he first came up: "He knew nothing about [major league] baseball. He never heard of Mantle or Ford. I said Whitey Ford is pitching tomorrow and he asked what color he was. He just knows to swing the bat and catch the ball. He's never satisfied. He gets one hit, he wants two. He gets two hits, he wants three."[18]

Oliva lived out of four suitcases and was in and out of hotels. Because he could not return to Cuba, Oliva traveled to Puerto Rico each winter to play winter league ball. Oliva described his solitude in the United States. "Sometimes I get lonely between seasons, being away from home. Other players are always glad to see the season end so they can go home. When the season is over, I can't go back to Cuba, and I have no wife or family here. Sometimes between seasons I call my parents by telephone. I have told them that if they want me to come home, I'll come home. But my mother tells me to stay in America because I have a big opportunity."[19]

Those close to Oliva admired his attitude, even though loneliness played a large part in his early years in the United States. Twins owner Calvin Griffith said, "He has a cheerful disposition and a positive approach toward life as well as baseball. You never see Tony brooding. In fact, I can't recall that I have ever seen him without a smile on his face."[20]

Few rookies in baseball history have had Oliva's impact. In 1964 he established a rookie hit record with 217 and is the only American League rookie to win a batting title (.323). He also led in doubles and runs scored, and he hit 32 home runs. Calvin Griffith said, "Oliva could become another Mickey Mantle or Al Kaline. I'm trying to go way back, but I can't remember anyone I've seen who hit just like him. He's bent over, standing deep in the box. And he has a golf swing—he swings from the inside out, driving the fastball to the left and pulling the curve."[21]

In May Oliva hurt his middle finger while sliding in a game in Boston. He wrapped the finger and switched to a knobless bat. Sometimes he released the bat on his follow-through, which gave him a reputation as a bat thrower. Minnesota management prohibited Oliva from playing winter ball so the finger could heal. Oliva was disappointed and said, "I tell them I play baseball all year 'round ever since I was a little boy. I tell them the finger doesn't bother me that much. I ask them how you get tired doing something you love to do? I say let me play. I ask what will I do with myself if all winter I don't have baseball? I get fat. I think about 70 games I could be playing with a Puerto Rican team and I get unhappy. Next time I play winter baseball. I'm not tired."[22]

Oliva led Minnesota to the American League pennant in 1965. Despite the finger injury, he won his second batting title, becoming the only player in baseball history to win titles his first two years. In fact, Nap Lajoie, Ty Cobb, and Ferris Fain were the only players ever to have repeated as batting champions. By the World Series Oliva had an injured knee to add to his finger woes. Still, the Twins pushed Los Angeles to seven games before falling to Sandy Koufax. Oliva batted only .182 and did not play on another World Series team. After the season he finally had an operation on the troublesome finger.

In 1967 Oliva took on new roommate Rod Carew and helped him get over disappointments, like losing the American League pennant to Boston on the last day of the 1967 season. In 1968 Oliva's season ended early when he separated his shoulder diving in the outfield. But in 1969 and 1970, Oliva, Carew, and Harmon Killebrew led the Twins to the American League West titles. Oliva was close to batting titles through the rest of the decade and carried a career batting mark of .308 into 1970. He led the American League in hits five times through 1970.

In June 1971 Oliva suffered a serious knee injury and doctors cut into his knee for the third time. His roommate, Rod Carew, said, "From then on, every time he swung he was in pain. He took as many as ten shots before a game during the season to relieve the pain so he could play. Before each game he took two or three painkilling pills. Yet he led the league in hitting that year (.337). And all this time people were saying, 'Tony is not really hurt that much; after all, look how he's hitting.' It was the old story that a black guy can't really get hurt."[23] In July 1972 Oliva underwent his fourth knee operation. By that time, Oliva admitted, "There was nothing left of the knee, just bone on bone."[24] Oliva did not play outfield again.

Even to bat as a designated hitter, Oliva suffered. Carew said, "On the road he'd carry a big, brown suitcase filled with electric massagers for his knees. They were awful. I'd hear him crying in the middle of the night from the pain. Yet people didn't believe he was suffering. A typical Latin, they'd complain, dogging it. Well, Oliva played until he couldn't walk. He'd ruined his health and lost his livelihood trying to live down the lies and rumors."[25]

Oliva returned for a final try as designated hitter in 1976. He said, "I hurt my knee in the prime of my career. I don't know if I could have beaten out Rod Carew for any batting titles in the last four years, but I do know I'd have had about 50 more home runs and 150 more RBIs. With better statistics, I'd have a better chance to get into the Hall of Fame. If I'd played in New York, Chicago,

José Méndez, ace Cuban pitcher, defeated many barnstorming major league teams in Cuba from 1908 to 1912. He pitched for several U.S. Negro league teams from 1908 to 1926, including the Kansas City Monarchs.

(Collection of Charles Monfort)

After the 1937 tournament in the Dominican Republic, Trujillo sent an All-Star team to tour the United States in a series of exhibition games on the Negro league circuit.

(National Baseball Library, Cooperstown, NY)

The 1942 Washington Senators included (left to right) Cuban outfielders Roberto Ortiz and Roberto Estalella, Venezuelan pitcher Alejandro Carrasquel, and manager Bucky Harris. Only Latin players with light skin played in the majors before the color line was broken in 1947. *(Collection of Charles Monfort)*

The 1948 Almendares Cuban winter league team featured (left to right) pitcher Aristónico Correoso, outfielder Santos Amaro (father of major leaguer Rubén Amaro), pitcher Ramon Bragaña, and catcher Gilberto "El Chino" Valdivia.

(Collection of Charles Monfort)

All-around Cuban standout Martín Dihigo, inducted in the U.S., Mexican, Venezuelan, and Cuban Halls of Fame, pictured in the 1940s while managing the Chileros de Xalapa of the Mexican summer league.

(Collection of Charles Monfort)

Mexican third baseman Felipe Montemayor batted for Cienfuegos in Havana's Stadium del Cerro in an October 12, 1952 Cuban winter league game against Cuban pitcher Mike Forieles. Almendares catcher was Fermín "Mike" Guerra and the umpire was Orlando Maestri. Montemayor homered.

(Collection of Charles Monfort)

Roberto Clemente was originally signed by Al Campanis of the Brooklyn Dodgers after his performance at this tryout in Puerto Rico in 1953. A big turnout at tryouts is common throughout Latin America.

(National Baseball Library, Cooperstown, NY)

Many U.S. ballplayers have enjoyed warm hospitality during their winter baseball seasons. Tommy Lasorda pitched in Cuba and in Puerto Rico, and managed the Dominican Republic's Licey team to a Caribbean World Series title. He's shown here after landing a prime catch in Puerto Rico in 1956.

(Puerto Rican News Service)

Almendares players, management, and followers celebrated the 1958–1959 Cuban winter league title. Cuban players who posed for the camera include pitcher Orlando Peña (holding camera), pitcher Carlos Pasqual (top right), and infielder Tony Taylor (seated behind Peña). U.S. pitcher Tommy Lasorda (standing behind Peña) also raised a glass. *(Collection of Charles Monfort)*

After Fidel Castro (above, left) overthrew the Cuban government, he assured 60 Cuban ballplayers, including Minnie Miñoso, that they could return to their U.S. major league teams despite the break in diplomatic relations between the United States and Cuba. Many Cuban players never returned to their homeland again. *(UPI Photo)*

Dominican brothers (left to right) Jesús, Matty, and Felipe Alou combined for 5,094 hits and a .291 average in the major leagues from 1958 to 1979.

(UPI Photo)

Roberto Clemente's son (left), family, teammates, and fans paid tribute to him after he died in a plane crash in December 1972, en route to assist Nicaraguan earthquake victims.

(National Baseball Library, Cooperstown, NY)

Panama-born Rod Carew (above, left) won his third of seven batting titles in 1973. Joe Cronin presented the "Silver Bat" on behalf of the American League. In 1991 Carew was elected on the first ballot to the Baseball Hall of Fame in Cooperstown, New York. *(UPI Photo)*

Luís "Lefty" Tiant, Sr., ace Cuban pitcher in the 1930s and 1940s, threw out the first pitch before an August 1975 Boston Red Sox game in Fenway Park. Tiant and his wife were allowed out of Cuba during a diplomatic thaw in 1975, and watched son Luís (right) lead Boston into the World Series.

(UPI Photo)

José Cruz batted .292 for 13 seasons in Houston, but was appreciated more by Puerto Rican winter league fans than by baseball followers in the United States.
(National Baseball Library, Cooperstown, NY)

Mexican sensation Fernando Valenzuela has won the National League Rookie of the Year Award, the Cy Young Award, a Gold Glove, a World Series ring, and has thrown a no-hitter.
(© 1991 Los Angeles Dodgers, Inc.)

or Los Angeles I'd have a better chance, too, because of more publicity. I want to get in. I didn't used to think about the Hall of Fame. Now I think about it a lot because it means so much to me. Especially when I think I could be kept out because of this."[26] Oliva finished with a .304 career batting average and 220 home runs.

Oliva has managed in the winter leagues in Mexico and Colombia. He has coached in the Minnesota system at the minor and major league levels, and he has been credited with the development of Kirby Puckett, turning the chunky outfielder into a home run hitter. Puckett paid tribute to Oliva after Minnesota won the World Series in 1987, saying, "It would take me ten years to tell you everything Tony has taught me."[27] So, although Oliva may be kept out of the Hall of Fame for his bad knee, he has given something back to baseball, the reason he left home and family so many years ago.

Luís Tiant

Another Cuban player who became a man without a country because of Castro's politics was Luís Tiant. Tiant came from a baseball family. His father, Luís Sr., known as "Lefty," was a premier pitcher in the 1930s. Lefty played in Cuba, in the Dominican Republic, and in the U.S. Negro leagues for the New York Cubans. He was one of the finest spitball pitchers in the Negro leagues. At age 42, after his arm gave out, Luís Sr. became a furniture mover to support his wife and child, Luís Jr.

Luís Jr. played ball in Havana neighborhoods with his friends, graduating from old corks and cigarette packs stuffed with newspapers to a youth league and a Juvenile All-Star team. Tiant said, "When I was 17, in 1957, I told my parents I wanted to quit school and play baseball. My mother said O.K. My father said no, because he was a pitcher, too, and he said there was no place in the major leagues for a black man. I said I'd find my place."[28]

Tiant Jr. caught the eye of Mexican scout Bobby Avila, the 1954 American League batting champ who scouted for the Cleveland Indians. Avila knew the Tiants and was confident that Luís Jr. could make it, even though both the Havana Reds and the Havana Sugar Kings had turned him down. Avila recommended Tiant to the Mexico City Tigers' general manager in 1959. Cleveland scouts also monitored Tiant's progress.

In 1960, during Tiant's second season in Mexico, he met María del Refugio Navarro, the left fielder on a women's softball team. They dated until he returned to pitch for the Havana Reds in the Cuban winter league. Tiant received permission from María's family to marry her, and they were wed in August 1961. They hoped to honeymoon in Cuba, but Tiant's parents advised the newlyweds to stay away because of Castro's politics and the restrictions placed on travel.

On the mound Tiant adopted some of his father's delivery quirks. When he made his major league debut in 1964 against New York, the Yankees sat up and took notice. Tiant allowed only three hits and struck out 11 Yankees. Afterward, New York shortstop Tony Kubek said, "We were amazed by him. He had so many trick deliveries and motions that we never really found out where the ball was. Maybe that's one of his big secrets. He gets the batter watching his body motions and you lose the ball. Then, when you see it, it's too late. And he could throw so hard, too."[29] Tiant shut out the Yankees 3-0.

After that first year Tiant returned to Mexico, his new off-season home, to his wife's family. Letters and an occasional holiday phone call were exchanged by Tiant and his parents. In one of his letters, Luís Sr. told his son to "get skinny," so Tiant went on a strict diet and started exercising. In 1966 Tiant responded with five shutouts but finished the season in the bullpen. So much for fatherly advice.

Tiant's wife chose to stay in Mexico with their children, so Tiant was separated from both his parents and his own family during the season. He compensated for his loneliness with a wild sense of humor. One of the favorite pranks he pulled on his Indian team-mates was to sneak up on a teammate reading a newspaper and set it on fire. Once, when Max Alvis dropped his burning paper and started stamping it out, "Fireman Tiant" ran in with his hat on backwards, screaming in his high voice like a siren and spraying a fire extinguisher madly around the room.[30]

In 1968 Tiant achieved stardom. During one stretch he threw four consecutive shutouts, and in another three-game stint he struck out 41 batters, tying a record. In two of those games he fanned 32 batters, also for a new record. Arm stiffness curbed his late-season production, but Tiant still finished at 21-9 with a 1.60 ERA, the lowest American League ERA since Walter Johnson's 1.49 in 1919.

Tiant's 1.60 also broke Stan Coveleski's Cleveland record of 1.82 from 1917. Tiant finished with 264 strikeouts and started in the All-Star Game for the American League.

If the off season is approaching, the controversy over the winter league is not far behind for Latin players. Cleveland General Manager Gabe Paul tried a novel approach to the problem. Paul and Manager Alvin Dark paid Tiant not to pitch winter ball in 1968. That didn't work, however, for Tiant lost eight of his first nine starts in 1969. He said his arm wasn't hurting, just weak. Teammate Juan Pizarro said, "It's no mystery. It is only that Looie did not pitch winter ball last year. I know. When your arm gets used to pitching all the time, something happens to it when you lay off like Tiant did." Tiant finished with a 9-20 record and was traded by new General Manager Alvin Dark to Minnesota after the season.

Tiant fit in well with his new teammates. He said, "I am quiet until I know what is going on. Before I just say 'hello' to Mr. Killebrew. Now I joke with him." In fact, he teased the Twins' slugger, calling him "Baby Killy." Tiant would stand in front of the clubhouse mirror and sing in his high-pitched voice, "Six-foot-two, eyes of blue, you good looking son of a gun." Tiant was, of course, only five-feet-eleven and did not have blue eyes. He also called everybody "Buddy Boy," although his English was sometimes difficult for his new teammates to understand, especially with his ever-present cigar jammed in his mouth.[31]

In 1970 Tiant started at 6-0 for Minnesota and was hitting .435 when X-rays showed a hairline fracture in the back part of his shoulder, an unusual position for a pitcher's injury. Minnesota released Tiant after the season, and after a short trip to the minors, he resurfaced with Boston where he captured the hearts of the Red Sox fans. In 1972 Tiant fashioned a 15-6 record and a commanding 1.91 ERA to again lead the American League. No Boston pitcher had put together an ERA under 2.00 since Carl Mays had done it in 1917.

Tiant made 1972 fun in more ways than one for his Sox teammates. The target of most of his gags and jokes was Tommy Harper, his former Indian teammate. Harper, a shy person, remembered his thoughts on learning that he had been traded to Boston. "There was no doubt in my mind he was going to get there early, just to put something in my locker or to set up some kind of joke on me. Just thinking about him doing something like that made me laugh. And sure enough, the moment I walked through the door I could hear that high, squeaky voice, yelling and screaming, telling everyone in the room that 'the ugliest man in the world just joined our team.' I looked at him, and he looked at me, and we laughed so hard we cried."[32]

After a particularly painful loss during the season in which Harper committed a crucial error, Tiant disappeared into a bathroom stall. A few minutes later Tiant flushed, then screeched in his highest voice, "Bye, Tommeee!" causing the locker room to explode in laughter.[33]

As the Red Sox developed in the 1970s, Tiant became a good role model for the younger Latins on the team. Tiant said, "It is difficult for the Latin ballplayer. But I don't think of myself as a leader. What I can do is pass on some of my experiences, on and off the field. I have come here the hard way. I've been at the bottom and learned to know who your friends are. I know what it's like to think about being released out of the game and, like Latin players who don't have the college background of the American player, worry about having to go back to Mexico or Cuba and work in a factory."[34]

In a surprise move, Fidel Castro allowed Tiant's parents to leave Cuba in August 1975, during a diplomatic thaw with the United States. The media and fans mobbed the Boston airport as the time approached for the emotional reunion. During the hot pennant race, television carried it as the lead story all over baseball-crazy New England. The Red Sox management invited "Lefty" Tiant to throw out the first ball from the mound in a late-August game, and the fans roared their approval for "Lefty" and his son, Luís.

After a key 2-0 shutout of Baltimore late in the season, Tiant said, "I'll be 35 in November and who knows how long I'll last? An injury and maybe I'm done tomorrow. So I want to pitch in the playoffs and World Series. It means a great deal. I've had a lot of things come to me, but to pitch in the series is something you get close to maybe once in a lifetime." The Red Sox won their division and headed for the playoffs against Oakland.[35]

Tiant opened the playoffs with a 7-1 three-hitter over the A's, allowing only a late unearned run. When Boston clinched the pennant after the next two games, Tiant was named to open the World Series against Cincinnati. For his "once in a lifetime series,"

Tiant was masterful, shutting out Cincinnati 6-0 on five hits. Tiant started the six-run seventh inning with a single, then scored the game's first run. He missed the plate on the first pass, was prodded by on-deck hitter Carlton Fisk to return, and tiptoed back past Reds catcher Johnny Bench to score. Fisk reminded the press of the American League's designated hitter rule and said, "You gotta understand, Luís hasn't been on the basepaths in three years."[36]

After rain caused some postponements, Tiant started Game Three. He threw 160 pitches and struggled, but won Boston's second game 5-4. The Red Sox had lost the other three games when Tiant took the mound for Game Six. Although Tiant was removed in the eighth inning trailing 6-3, the Fenway Park fans stood in applause as he left the mound. Boston rallied to win Game Six in one of the most dramatic contests in World Series history. Bernie Carbo's pinch-hit three-run home run and Fisk's 12th-inning home run brought the Red Sox into a 3-3 tie with the Reds. But Cincinnati won the series in the ninth inning of Game Seven 4-3.

After the 1976 season Tiant's parents died within a few days of one another and were buried near Boston. Tiant moved to the Yankees as a free agent for two years, then pitched briefly with the Pirates and the Angels. He finished his career in 1982 with a 229-172 record, 49 shutouts, 2,416 strikeouts, and four 20-win seasons. Tiant deserves consideration in Hall of Fame voting, but whether or not he makes it, he will be remembered as one of the most popular Latin players of all time.

Even though Tiant never won a World Series, his smiling face, with Fu Manchu moustache and cigar, made for popular photographs from the team whirlpool. Tony Oliva also enjoyed a corner of the spotlight, with batting titles in his first two years and a World Series appearance in 1965. Carew drew attention with his seven batting titles and four playoff appearances, even though he never reached the World Series. Although none of the three played for a world-champion team, all three benefited from the exposure of postseason play.

José Cruz

Rod Carew, Tony Oliva, and Luís Tiant were far better known than José Cruz. Cruz's style, his team, his stadium, his city, and even his name worked against him. In a strange way, even his talent had a reverse effect. Cruz's consistent play never grabbed headlines. His team, the Houston Astros, never played in a World Series. His stadium, the Astrodome, discourages power hitting. Most of his career was spent in Houston, not a media center. Each winter, he disappeared from the U.S. press and went home to Puerto Rico. And the name Cruz itself became a liability when, for a while during his career, it became almost as common as the name Smith. To top it off, Cruz's best years started in his late twenties, when most players begin to decline, a phenomenon confusing to the media. A look back at his career confirms that Cruz ranks among the best Latin players to play in the majors.

José Cruz played baseball, softball, basketball, and ran track in high school in Arroyo, Puerto Rico, a small fishing village on the southeastern coast of the island. José and his two brothers, Hector and Tommy, played in the Puerto Rican winter league. At age 19, José was signed by the St. Louis Cardinal organization, and he rose through the Cardinals' system in four years. When he reached St. Louis in 1970, he was the first major league player with the name Cruz. Soon his brothers Tommy and Hector, as well as unrelated Julio (United States), Victor (Dominican Republic), Todd (United States), and Henry (Virgin Islands) all came up to the majors. By the end of José's career, he was again the only Cruz in the majors, but by then fans were hopelessly confused.

José Cruz played as a part-timer with St. Louis through 1974, when the Cards sold him to Houston for $20,000 to complete a late-season trade for Claude Osteen. Tim McCarver, Cruz's teammate, said, "The Cardinals sure made some great decisions back then, didn't they? They got rid of Steve Carlton because they wouldn't pay him $10,000 [more] and they sold José Cruz for $20,000."[37]

After he was traded, Cruz said, "Of course, I was happy to go where I could show what I could do. I didn't think St. Louis had the patience with Latin players. The Latins seem to take more time to develop than the Americans. Here so many go to college and play. Over there, all they have is the ability."[38]

Cruz's point about late development of Latin ballplayers has been espoused before. The change of language, food, and culture, and the distance from family and friends could have an impact on the maturity and progress of a Latin ballplayer. Also, the competition level for U.S. youths who enjoy high school ball, American Legion play, and other summer leagues may be higher. As overwhelming percentages of Latin, white, and black aspirants alike fail to reach the majors, a more detailed study would be needed to determine whether Latin ballplayers actually do mature later than other players in the talent pool.

In spring training 1976, Astros hitting coach Deacon Jones explained, "I told José, 'If you hit ten home runs and bat .260, you haven't lived up to your potential, but if you hit four or five homers and bat .300, you help the team tremendously.'"[39] Cruz answered perfectly to his teacher's request, responding with a .303 average, 28 stolen bases, and four home runs.

That winter Cruz was named Puerto Rican league MVP and led Caguas to the Caribbean World Series. In 1977 Cruz stole 44 bases and had 17 home runs with a .299 average for the Astros. After the season he returned to Caguas and was named league MVP again. Cruz played almost every game in the winter league for 21 years, saying he owed it to his fans. Even in Puerto Rico, Cruz performed consistently.

The 1979 Astros made a serious run at the National League West title. Cruz led the team in hitting with a .315 average and in RBIs with 83, yet he received no MVP votes. The new label attached to Cruz was "the most underrated player in baseball." Cruz recognized the problem and said, "I've had some good seasons, but sometimes I think the press underrates me. I want to lead the league in hitting. I did it in the Puerto Rican league after being second or third many times. Now I want to do it here."[40]

When the Astros won the National League West in 1980, Cruz's shot at glory and national exposure in the World Series was blocked by the Philadelphia Phillies. In a tense five-game playoff series, four games were won after the losing team came from behind. Four games also went into extra innings. In the final game, Cruz rallied his team from a 7-5 deficit in the eighth inning with a two-run single. He remembered, "So we went into extra innings for the fourth straight game, tied 7-7. But that's all we could do. The Phils scored an extra run in the tenth inning and won it 8-7. I can't think of a game I've been in that hurt more to lose than that one."[41] For the series, Cruz batted 6-15 (.400) and took a record eight walks.

In Cruz's other postseason play with the Astros, Houston lost a divisional playoff in 1981 and lost the 1986 National League playoffs to the Mets, so Cruz was never able to play in the World Series. In 1983 Cruz finished with a .318 average, but was hitless in his last two games and missed the batting title by five points. To this day, the Houston Astros have neither played in the World Series nor had a batting champion.

Cruz performed well through the 1980s. In 1984, at age 37, he batted .312 with a career-high 95 RBIs. All of his 12 home runs were hit on the road, away from the cavernous Astrodome. Cruz explained, "I change my hitting style every time we go on the road. At home, I go for singles and doubles. On the road, I swing harder. I sometimes go for home runs."[42]

In 1985 the 38-year-old Cruz batted .300 for the sixth time in his career. Only Pete Rose had more hits at age 38 than José Cruz. Perhaps the feat went unnoticed because Cruz did not look his age. His dark, wavy hair kept its natural color through his late thirties. He did not smoke and rarely drank, and he kept his six-feet, 185-pound body in great shape. Ironically, 1985 was Cruz's first and only All-Star Game at-bat. Because of the dearth of publicity, fans and managers ignored him year after year.

Nevertheless, Puerto Rican fans embraced Cruz. His Houston teammate and winter league manager Art Howe said, "The people love him there. He always goes home to play after the major league season ends. And, unlike some others, he plays every day and gives his best." Cruz explained, "I feel I have an obligation to the people who see me play here. Those people cheer for me all summer. I don't need it. I play because they love me and I care about them. I want to do something to thank them."[43]

When Houston did not offer Cruz a contract after the 1987 season, he signed with the New York Yankees. He held the all-time Astros record for most total bases, RBIs, hits, games, at-bats, singles, and triples. After 13 years of consistent and outstanding performance for Houston, the Astros sent him away without ceremony. When Cruz left the majors in 1988, he had a lifetime .284 average, 165 home runs, 317 stolen bases, 1,036 runs scored, and 1,077 RBIs. His strong hitting lacks the accompanying fielding or home run production that might carry him into the Hall of Fame, but

Cruz remains a strong role model for young Latins with his steady, disciplined approach to life and baseball.

17

MEXICAN INDEPENDENCE, HECTOR ESPINO, AND FERNANDOMANIA

While players from the more easterly Latin countries were making their mark across the sports pages of the United States, the Mexican spirit of independence kept Mexico's baseball stars at home. Even when the Mexican summer league became a part of the U.S. minor league system in 1955, the accord was reached in order to prevent a repeat of Pasquel's player raids, and not necessarily to increase the chances of Mexicans playing in the United States. This agreement is still in effect today—Mexican summer league teams carry no more than two U.S. players per roster.

This U.S.-Mexican agreement recognized the high level of play by the Mexicans, and it also acknowledged Mexico's financial ability to lure players out of the U.S. system. With 82 million people, Mexico is the largest of the Latin baseball countries, large enough to do things its own way.

Unlike all the other teams in the U.S. minor leagues, the Mexican league teams own their players and have no binding affiliation with a major league organization. Under this setup, major league teams must purchase the contract of each Mexican player. Prices asked are often high enough to make up for lost future revenues from the player's box office appeal. Furthermore, the price is usually high enough to remind the U.S. teams that they cannot take advantage of the Mexican league.

These high prices discourage major league teams from buying too many top Mexican stars. Although the majors have willingly paid the price for about 40 eventual major leaguers over the years, U.S. fans have missed some of Mexico's top stars, like pitcher Ramón Araño, first baseman Angel Castro, outfielder Epitacio Torres, and pitcher Jesús Valenzuela. While American League fans enjoyed the glovework of third baseman Aurelio Rodríguez for 17 years, Mexican league fans watched his brother, Francisco Rodríguez, for 20 years. Both also played Mexican winter ball in the Pacific Coast League.

Hector Espino: One Who Stayed Home

Appropriately, the most enduring Mexican slugging star of all time was kept hidden from U.S. fans not by the system, but rather by his own strong will.

In 1964 Bobby Maduro, former owner of the Havana Sugar Kings, scouted Hector Espino for the Los Angeles Dodgers and signed him for a late-season stay with the Jacksonville Suns. Espino hit three home runs and batted .300 in 100 at-bats, but was reportedly miserable in the United States. Maduro said, "He couldn't adjust to things here, the food, the manner of living, anything."[1]

The St. Louis Cardinals bought his contract from Monterrey in early 1965. As is the practice in Mexico, this "signing bonus" went to his team, while Espino would receive a normal starting salary in the United States. The way Espino saw it, Monterrey owner Anuar Canavati was requiring him to go back to the lonely, uncomfortable existence of bus rides in the minor leagues while Canavati lined his own pockets. Espino demanded a ten percent cut of the contract price. Canavati refused, then suspended Espino for not reporting. Eventually, Espino gave in and boarded a plane to go to the Cards' spring training camp in Tampa, Florida. He flew as far as Dallas, thought better of it, and returned to Mexico for good. He later said, "I don't regret it. If he [Canavati] had gratified me with some type of bonus from the sale of my contract, I would have gone. But under the circumstances, I couldn't. If I had to do it over again, I would do the same thing."[2]

The Mexican press called Espino the "Rebel of Chihuahua." In response to this treatment by the press, Espino countered, "They have not treated me as well as they should have. They called me names and criticized me for who I am, for fighting my contracts. They always sided with Canavati and wrote what he said, instead of what was really happening. I fought for my contracts because I knew what I was worth."[3]

Espino's exchange has a familiar ring to anyone who reads sports pages during baseball's summer domination of U.S. newspapers. It sounds like George Bell when Toronto Manager Jimy Williams removed him from the outfield to become a full-time designated hitter, or Orlando Cepeda's verbal battles with Alvin Dark and Herman Franks. Because public confrontations are reserved in North American culture for what are defined as substantive issues, U.S. sportswriters try to read some deeper significance into these arguments, couching them in terms of black versus white, Spanish versus English. What they miss is what the Mexican sportswriters saw in the clash between Espino and Canavati: a contest between two men that is to be observed and enjoyed by outsiders.

Mexicans would explain such a contest in terms of a bullfight, a very Spanish custom that has survived to this day in their country. The Latins see the bullfight as a morality play evoking the daily struggles of the universe between the strong and the weak, the powerful and the powerless. They jeer and whistle the matador if he flinches at the bull's passing horns, and they cheer the bull's blind bravery in pursuing his tormentors even as blood streams from his neck. A brave bull is respected for his dignity and fighting spirit. Such respect is not diminished by his loss of the contest through death, for the spectators know that the odds were against him all along. What U.S. sportswriters miss is this Latin view of the drama in everyday life. Twenty years later, Espino was still proud of his refusal to give in on that ten percent to Canavati. Like Bell and

Cepeda, he made the stand he felt he had to make to preserve his pride and dignity.

Espino played baseball every summer from 1961 to 1985 with the Monterrey Sultans. He played each winter in the Mexican Pacific Coast League with the Naranjeros (Orangemen) of Hermosillo. His combined record in the summer and winter leagues was more than 760 home runs, a career batting average over .330, 18 batting titles, and 11 home run titles. Twice he batted over .400.

Mexico joined the winter Caribbean World Series for the first time in 1971. After five tournaments without winning the title, Espino's Hermosillo team won five of its six games to win in 1976. Espino batted .321 with seven RBIs in six games and grew in stature in the eyes of his countrymen. Winning this winter championship over Venezuela, the Dominican Republic, and Puerto Rico solidified Mexico's reputation in Latin baseball.

Monterrey General Manager César Faz said, "Espino turned Mexico into a playground where he could play baseball, where he could hit home runs. Everywhere he went he turned the country upside down. It was like a fairy tale."[4] Espino had a good chance of living such a fairy-tale life in the United States as well, to earn a big salary after a few big home-run seasons, but the dollars he gave up could not have bought what he received in return. In his 25-year career, he was never far from his friends and family. His salary put him at the level of the upper middle class, enabling him to have a comfortable lifestyle including good food, stylish clothes, and a well-furnished home with servants. Best of all, he was the master of his own destiny. His stardom in Mexico meant that his fate was never in question; he would never be a victim of a migrant worker status in a foreign land.

Ironically, many Latin players endure the hardships of their years in the United States in the hope of returning to a year-round life such as that achieved by Espino. Such a life is only possible in Mexico, where the baseball leagues stand in an armed truce with the majors to the north. The Mexicans had agreed that they would not repeat the Pasquel invasions. In turn, the U.S. owners are limited in their cherry picking by being required to pay market prices for Mexican talent.

When asked in 1985 to reflect upon his great career, Espino said, "Hitting a home run is great satisfaction, but it is momentary. You have to live in reality. My records will not last forever. Even my home run records will be broken by someone, sometime. The satisfying thing, the thing I'm most proud of, is that I've played 24 years. Not too many people go that long in these leagues."[5]

Espino's humility is overshadowed by his record in the eyes of Mexican fans. Today Espino's nickname is no longer "Rebel of Chihuahua." Now he is "Superman of Chihuahua."

Children all over Mexico imitated Espino and followed his exploits. One child, a little boy in a tiny farming village on the west coast of Sonora, sometimes skipped school to play baseball and listen to his hero Espino on the radio. Some of his friends played soccer. His 11 brothers and sisters worked in the fields to earn extra money. But all Fernando Valenzuela wanted to do was play baseball.

Fernando Valenzuela: The One Who Left

By age 15 Fernando Valenzuela had quit school and signed a $250 contract to play professional baseball for three months with a Sonora team. By age 17 he had been spotted by Mike Brito, a Los Angeles Dodgers scout who sported a wide-brimmed Panama hat and smoked an ever-present cigar. The next July, in 1979, Dodger General Manager Al Campanis saw Valenzuela, then playing for the Puebla team, and offered $60,000 for his contract. The Yankees bid $100,000 and Campanis almost dropped out of the bidding, but returned with $120,000 and won the rights to Valenzuela.

Because of the large Mexican-American community in southern California, Dodger owner Walter O'Malley had always dreamed of bringing a Mexican star to Los Angeles. But even O'Malley could not have imagined the impact that Fernando Valenzuela and "Fernandomania" would have on Hispanics, Major League Baseball, and almost all of North America.

Valenzuela started the climb to Chavez Ravine by pitching in Lodi, California. He was lonely and unable to speak English. To make matters worse, he missed his girlfriend, Linda Margarita Burgos. He pitched only 24 innings, but impressed Dodger management enough to enlist Dodger farmhand Bobby Castillo, an Hispanic from the East Los Angeles barrios, to teach Valenzuela the screwball. After a good summer in 1980 with San Antonio, Los Angeles called on Valenzuela to shore up a depleted pitching staff. In ten relief appearances for the Dodgers, he permitted no runs. Fernandomania was just a winter away.

On Opening Day 1981, with all the other Dodger starters ill, injured, or unavailable, manager Tommy Lasorda selected his rookie pitcher Fernando Valenzuela to pitch against Houston. The crowd did not even cheer for this unknown hurler when he walked to the mound. But by the end of his five-hit, 2-0 shutout, the fans were on their feet chanting, "Fernando, Fernando!"

When Los Angeles hit the road, Valenzuela pitched two more shutouts and gave up only one run in another win. He pitched five shutouts in his first seven starts and soon reporters from all over the United States and Latin America were following the Fernando story. Each time he pitched, he drew 9,000 more fans than normal for stadiums across the National League. His parents were flown up from Mexico as guests of the Dodgers to see him pitch in sold-out Dodger Stadium. By May 8 unheralded rookie Fernando Valenzuela was a remarkable 7-0 and had allowed only two runs. His career ERA stood at 0.22.

Fernandomania struck the nation. Special press conferences were called after each of his starts. One reporter asked Valenzuela what his chances were to win the Cy Young Award. Valenzuela shrugged his shoulders and asked, "What's that?"[6] *Playgirl* Magazine named him among the ten sexiest men in the world.

Yet a player strike was looming on the baseball horizon, and soon the players voted to walk out. Just before they did, though, Valenzuela was offered $50,000 for a poster contract, a sum $8,000 higher than his 1981 salary. When the baseball players' strike started in June, Valenzuela returned to Mexico and gave a clinic for 25,000 children. Mexican President López Portillo received him. A couple of weeks later he joined presidents Reagan and López Portillo in Washington for lunch. Tommy Lasorda, Dodgers manager and former winter league pitcher, said, "It is good for the Dodgers. It is good for baseball. It is good for Mexico. It is good for our relations with Mexico. And it is very good for Tommy Lasorda."[7]

One reason Valenzuela intrigued fans was that he did not look like a top athlete. Explaining his ample waistline, he said, "Sure, I drink a few beers, but not that much. What I do is eat a lot—steaks, salads, avocados, Mexican food, carne asada, beans, rice. I do like to eat."8 Another marvel was that Fernando could only communicate with the media through a translator. In the onslaught of publicity, Valenzuela remained cool. He said, "It's nice, but I didn't think I would be a star. I don't know how long it can last. All I want to do is maintain what I have. I'll take whatever comes."9 After a while Valenzuela moved out of his hotel room and into the home of Mike Brito's family.

After the strike was settled in August, Valenzuela was named to start the 1981 All-Star Game in Cleveland. He permitted a couple of hits but no runs in his only inning of work. Valenzuela finished the season with a 13-7 record and 2.48 ERA. He also led the National League with 11 complete games and 192 strikeouts, and he set a National League record for rookie pitchers with eight shutouts, all in an abbreviated season. He was voted a Silver Slugger Award for his batting prowess and was seriously considered for a Gold Glove. A lack of baserunning speed was the only apparent flaw of this gifted player.

By virtue of the best first-half National League West record, the Dodgers were awarded a spot in the Divisional Series. They traveled to Houston for the first two games of the best-of-five divisional series. Nolan Ryan defeated Los Angeles 3-1 in the opener, which Valenzuela had left in the ninth tied 1-1. The teams split the next two games, and Valenzuela started the fourth game on three days' rest. Pedro Guerrero homered in the fifth and Valenzuela pitched a four-hitter to win 2-1. Jerry Reuss won the fifth and deciding game 4-0 to win the division for L.A. No team had ever rallied in the postseason from a 2-0 deficit to win a five-game series.

The Dodgers won the first game of the best-of-five playoffs against Montreal 5-1. Valenzuela started the second game on three days' rest and lost 3-0 to Ray Burris. The teams split the next two games, and in the fifth and deciding game for the National League pennant, Tommy Lasorda started Valenzuela. A first-inning Montreal run stood up to a fifth-inning Valenzuela RBI until the ninth, when Rick Monday hit a dramatic Dodger home run. Valenzuela gave up three hits in 8⅔ innings until Bob Welch relieved for the last out of the 2-1 win for the National League pennant.

The New York Yankees won the first two games of the 1981 World Series in New York. When the teams returned to Dodger

Stadium, Lasorda called on Valenzuela to stop the Yankees. Los Angeles knocked out Yankee starter Dave Righetti by the third inning, but Valenzuela struggled as well, giving up four runs through three innings. Lasorda decided to stick with Valenzuela, even though he had thrown 100 pitches through the first four innings. Instead, Lasorda changed catchers, pulling Steve Yeager in favor of Mike Scioscia. Scioscia caught Valenzuela in the regular season and playoffs and even learned a few Spanish phrases to communicate with the young Mexican. Sure enough, Valenzuela settled down and held the Yankees scoreless the rest of the way for a 5-4 win. Lasorda said, "Fernando was like a sharp poker player who had to bluff his way through."[10] In this game Valenzuela pitched to Yankee third baseman Aurelio Rodríguez, marking the first time two Mexicans faced each other in a World Series game.

The Dodgers won two more one-run games in Los Angeles, then blew out the Yankees 9-2 in New York for the 1981 World Series championship. Valenzuela was 3-1 in the postseason, winning games against Houston, Montreal, and the Yankees. He pitched three complete games in his five starts with a postseason ERA of 2.21. It was a storybook end to a Cinderella season.

After the season ended, Valenzuela, the young boy who had never even heard of Cy Young, became the first rookie to win the award named for that great pitcher. Valenzuela was elected Rookie of the Year and finished fifth in MVP voting. *The Sporting News* named him the Major League Pitcher of the Year. Valenzuela became a hero over all of Mexico. His endorsement of the candidacy of Miguel de la Madrid for the presidency of Mexico made front-page headlines. When he married his girlfriend Linda Burgos in Mérida, a Caribbean port city on the Yucatan Peninsula, on December 29, the wedding was broadcast over Mexican radio. Mike Brito served as his best man and later revealed that the couple had been engaged for some time, "But now that Fernando has a better position, they got more serious."[11]

That winter Valenzuela pitched a couple of games with Navajoa, the Mexican Pacific League club near his home in Sonora. Hermosillo won the championship of the Mexican Pacific League and invited Valenzuela to start Mexico's opening game against Ponce of Puerto Rico. Through seven innings, Valenzuela had a no-hitter. His Dodger teammate, Candy Maldonado, opened the eighth with a double to right, and a few batters later Valenzuela was lifted for reliever Marty Decker. Decker induced a double-play grounder and preserved the shutout 14-0. Valenzuela also pitched the tournament's last game against the Dominican Republic. He allowed only a home run by Escogido's Tony Peña and left in the eighth with a 1-1 tie. Escogido jumped on Valenzuela's successors to eventually win 7-2. Valenzuela closed his only Caribbean World Series appearance with a record of 1-0, one earned run in 14⅓ innings, two walks, and 11 strikeouts.

In Valenzuela's spectacular rookie season, he was paid only $29,000 by the Dodgers because his minimum major league salary was reduced by the strike. He earned another $300,000 through endorsements, however. For his sophomore year, the Dodgers could pay Valenzuela what they wanted. Valenzuela and his agent asked for $1 million a year and threatened to hold out. When asked about Valenzuela's contract demands, Tommy Lasorda explained, "He wants Texas back."[12]

Valenzuela began 1982 as a holdout, but then signed for $300,000. He was 21 years old entering the season. Pete Rose said, "Hell, Fernando is still learning the league. He's not afraid of anybody or anything. I've never seen anything like him. When you're ahead of him, he throws screwballs and breaking balls, but when he's ahead of you, he'll try to throw the fastball to you. He'll throw 3-1 screwballs, 2-0 screwballs, and 3-2 and 2-0 curveballs."[13] At midseason, Mets Manager George Bamberger said, "Fernando may be the best pitcher in baseball right now. And I'm talking about right now, not last year."[14] He went 19-13 with a 2.87 ERA, four shutouts, 285 innings, struck out 199, and finished third in the Cy Young voting. Best of all, his wife Linda gave birth to Fernando Jr. on September 30.

During the winter Valenzuela won a $1 million contract in arbitration. Just as he had been the highest-paid sophomore in the history of the game, Valenzuela was now the winner of the highest arbitration award to date. The Dodgers had offered $750,000, but Valenzuela made a strong case. In the arbitration hearing, Tommy Lasorda called Valenzuela a "manager's dream" on videotape. In another clip, general manager Al Campanis recalled how Walter O'Malley, the late Dodger owner, always hoped the Dodgers could find a player of Mexican descent to involve the large Mexican-

American community in Los Angeles. Campanis said, "We found Fernando and we're so lucky. Mr. O'Malley must be looking down and smiling."[15]

The Dodgers won the National League West in 1983 and faced Philadelphia in the playoffs. During the regular season, the Dodgers beat the Phils 11 times in 12 games, but they lost the opening game of the series 1-0 at home. Valenzuela pitched the second game and won 4-1, striking out five in eight innings. The Dodgers lost the next two games and the pennant in Philadelphia.

In 1984 Fernando was again named to the All-Star team. During his tour on the mound, he struck out Dave Winfield, Reggie Jackson, and George Brett in one inning. Only six pitchers in All-Star Game history ever struck out the side. In the regular season, he struck out 240 hitters, the most by a Dodger since 1969. But Valenzuela suffered from a lack of support in a 12-17 season; the Dodgers scored one run or less in 13 of his last 27 starts.

Fernando returned to form in 1985, but Dodger batters again gave him little support. He set a major league record with 41⅓ scoreless innings at the start of a season. The Dodgers scored only eight runs in those five starts, five in one game, so his record was only 2-3. Still, Valenzuela was named Pitcher of the Month in April, the only time the award has been given to a pitcher with a losing record. In May Valenzuela prepared to face Dwight Gooden and the Mets in a nationally televised game in Shea Stadium. Before the game, Lasorda remembered, "I told Fernando there would be 89 million people in the United States and 140 million Mexicans watching him." Valenzuela answered, "I better get a new hat, a new haircut, and a new pair of pants."[16] Valenzuela defeated Gooden 6-2, one of Gooden's few losses in his 24-4 season.

Valenzuela finished 1985 with five shutouts, 14 complete games, and a 17-10 record. The Dodgers won the National League West and Lasorda named Valenzuela to start the League Championship Series at home against John Tudor and the St. Louis Cardinals. Valenzuela pitched 6⅓ innings and gave up one run in the 4-1 victory. The Dodgers won the second game, but St. Louis won the next two at home to tie the best-of-seven series. In the fifth game, Valenzuela gave up two first-inning runs, then allowed no runs over the next seven innings. He left after eight innings with the game tied 2-2. In the ninth, Ozzie Smith homered off Tom Niedenfuer to give

St. Louis the fifth game. The Cardinals won the series and the pennant with Jack Clark's ninth-inning, three-run home run in Game Six.

Valenzuela's image remained strong after five years in the public spotlight. He served as spokesman for a program aimed at Hispanics in Los Angeles-area schools. He took one day each homestand during the season to visit local schools, where dropout rates are as high as 50 percent. He always finished his speech by asking the kids, "What's my best pitch?" to which they would answer, "Be smart! Stay in school!"[17] Even though Valenzuela dropped out of school at age 15, his presentation was convincing enough to influence Los Angeles children to pursue their education.

The Dodgers and Valenzuela avoided arbitration in March of 1986 by settling on a three-year, $5.5 million contract. Manager Al Campanis said, "This is truly an international event. We signed an outstanding Mexican pitcher at an Italian restaurant in the middle of Chinatown."[18] The contract made Valenzuela the highest-paid Latin ballplayer to date.

The deal demonstrated Fernando's value as a player, but also his value as a marketer for the Dodgers. The O'Malleys and Dodger management are among the few who have recognized and profited from their local Latin audiences. Fernando's community work draws praise from all groups in the city, but it has also established a link with the nearly five million Latins in California, most of whom share Fernando's Mexican roots. This link is strengthened by Tommy Lasorda's interviews in Spanish and by a strong Latin contingent in the dugout.

The 1986 season opened well for Valenzuela as he threw back-to-back two-hitters against Montreal and Philadelphia. During the All-Star Game, Valenzuela equaled a record set by screwballer Carl Hubbell 52 years earlier. Valenzuela struck out five consecutive batters: Don Mattingly, Cal Ripken, Jesse Barfield, Lou Whitaker, and Ted Higuera. When Valenzuela faced Higuera, it marked the first time two Mexicans faced each other in an All-Star Game. Valenzuela pitched for the National League All-Stars in a total of five games from 1981 to 1986. He did not pitch in the 1983 game, although he was chosen to participate. In his 7⅔ innings, he did not allow a run.

When Valenzuela defeated Houston 9-2 with a two-hitter on September 22, 1986, he became the first Mexican pitcher in major league history to win 20 games. After the contest Astro Phil Garner said, "Fernando never beats himself. He pitches well, he hits well (.220 on the year), and he helps himself with his glove. He's one tough pitcher."[19] A couple of days later Milwaukee's Ted Higuera became the second Mexican 20-game winner.

Valenzuela completed 20 games in the 1986 season, eight more than any other National League pitcher. He also led the league in wins with 21, was second in innings with 269, and second in strikeouts with 242. Baseball writers voted him second in the Cy Young voting as well, behind division-winning Houston's Mike Scott. He was voted a Gold Glove for his excellence in fielding. However, the Dodgers scored three runs or less in 15 of his 1986 starts, dropping Valenzuela to 7-8 in those games. The Dodgers dropped to fifth place in the National League West.

Valenzuela did not miss a turn in the rotation for over six years, racking up 99 wins, 68 losses, a 2.94 ERA, and 26 shutouts through 1986. His career was a model of strength and consistency, and he did not give up easily. Valenzuela said, "I don't like being pulled from a game. As a pitcher, you like to think you can do the job on the mound, especially in the close games. There's always a tendency to think you can stay within reach of the other team and eventually win. After a few minutes on the bench, you realize that the manager is looking after the benefit of the team, and you settle down."[20]

Valenzuela gained his 100th win in April 1987. He posted a record of 14-14 for a second consecutive fifth-place Dodger team. Speculation arose that Valenzuela was overworked. He admitted that his shoulder was bothering him, that it was tight for much of the year, but he did not miss a start. His screwball, once called Fernando's Fadeaway, was flat, and batters were laying off it outside. The fastball had slowed up. He set a single-season Dodger record by walking 124 batters. He again led National League pitchers in complete games, with 12, and was third in innings pitched, with 251. He still struck out 190 batters, fourth in the National League, but his ERA rose to a career-high 3.98.

The Dodgers opened the 1988 season with new acquisitions Kirk Gibson, Jesse Orosco, Jay Howell, and Alfredo Griffin. Coming off his so-so 1987 season, the media no longer besieged him for interviews, but Valenzuela kept his sense of humor. He asked one reporter, "You want to talk to me? No? O.K., no interviews today."[21] Lasorda tabbed Valenzuela to pitch the 1988 opener at home against San Francisco, and the Giants beat him 5-1. As the season continued, the Dodgers scrapped to a lead in the National League West and Valenzuela labored. He did not miss a turn through the spring and early summer, but a number of theories were tossed about to explain his ineffectiveness: He used glasses to drive, but not to pitch; could it be his eyes? His father was dying of cancer; could the problem be concentration? He had pitched so many innings; could his arm be tired at age 28? The screwball worked in part by surprise; were hitters no longer fooled? [22]

Valenzuela was 5-8 with a 4.39 ERA when he started against Houston in Dodger Stadium on July 31. He had difficulty warming up before games, and compensated in his motion for the initial shoulder pain. In the fourth inning something gave in his shoulder. He gave up a fifth-inning home run to light-hitting catcher and countryman Alex Treviño, and Lasorda took him out. Specialist Dr. Frank Jobe called the injury "a stretched anterior capsule of the right shoulder" that did not require surgery. The Dodgers placed him on the 21-day disabled list, which broke his string of 255 straight starts without a missed turn.

In late September Valenzuela started a game in San Diego before the Dodgers clinched the National League West title. He pitched three passable innings, but the layoff was noticeable. On the last day of the season he relieved for four innings, his first save since 1980. He finished the season at 5-8 with a 4.24 ERA. The Dodgers debated activating him for the National League playoffs against the New York Mets, but chose Ricky Horton, another left-hander obtained in a late-season trade. Valenzuela was in uniform throughout the playoffs, and threw out the ceremonial first pitch before the first game, but after that he sat in the dugout and watched as his teammates knocked off first the Mets, then Oakland, for the world championship.

After struggling early in 1989, Valenzuela registered a 10-13 record and still suffered from a lack of Dodger run production. He signed a one-year, $2 million contract for 1990. Dodger management cited Valenzuela's leadership on the team and community involvement as reasons to sign him. In many opinion polls Valenzuela was named baseball's best left-hander of the 1980s.

In July 1990, against St. Louis, Valenzuela joined Juan Marichal (June 15, 1963) and Juan Nieves of Puerto Rico (April 15, 1987) as the third Latin hurler to pitch a no-hitter. Valenzuela finished the year with a 13-13 record. Through 1990, Fernando had a 141-116 record and a 3.31 ERA.

No matter what happens to Fernando Valenzuela's career, he has a record, on and off the field, that qualifies him for stardom. His achievements off the field serve as an example for Latin players and major league leaders of the economic potential of the previously ignored Hispanic audience for U.S. baseball.

Nearly three-fourths of the 18 million Latins living in the United States have roots in the baseball countries around the Caribbean. Most of these are concentrated in southern California, Texas, New York City, and Chicago, each of which has two or three major league teams. However, except for the Dodgers, no organization has capitalized on the market opportunity sitting in its clubhouse. When properly nurtured and developed, these teams' Latin stars are a strong draw for local Hispanic populations, the fastest-growing segment of the U.S. population.

In New York City this audience is dominated by Dominicans, Cubans, and Puerto Ricans. In much of the rest of the country the Mexican population is the predominant Latin group. Access to these local populations is simplified by the strong Spanish language television stations that have prospered across the country, each with myriad talk shows and news programs that mirror the English language stations. Given this type of commercial potential, it is understandable that the Mexicans remain so protective of their native talent.

The next step beyond the cultivation of the Latin players as stars of the Spanish media is, of course, the conquest of the English language media in the United States. The commercial potential for such success was first forseen by the owners of Negro league teams, whose "exotic" imports from the Caribbean intrigued the local fans. Wisps of this possibility have been seen in the media success of Minnie Miñoso, Luís Tiant, Roberto Clemente, and Fernando Valenzuela. Will baseball continue to strengthen this vital thread in the Latin American connection?

18

THREE DOMINATING DOMINICANS

In the face of Mexico's protection of its talent and Castro's embargo, the major leagues have turned to the Dominican Republic for Latin American talent. In an accident of history, the Dominican Republic was opened to the outside world at the same time Cuba was pulling back into the shell of communism.

After Trujillo's assassination in 1961 in the Dominican Republic, an interim government was named and organized elections were scheduled for 1962. The first election's winner was Social Democrat Juan Bosch. However, the military, filled with Trujillo loyalists, overthrew Bosch and his reformist government within a year. When Bosch's forces launched a counteroffensive in April 1965, the U.S. ambassador sent back reports that sentiment could swing to communism in the Dominican Republic, as it had in Cuba. On the ambassador's advice, President Lyndon Johnson sent in the U.S. Marines. The violence continued, and the 1965-66 Dominican winter baseball league was canceled.

When new elections were held, the winning presidential candidate, Joaquín Balaguer, a former member of Trujillo's government, told the nation he aspired to be "the Marichal of the Presidential Palace." Balaguer encouraged a period of great public works. Higher sugar prices and loans from international banks and organizations paid for schools, dams, and roads, elevating the country out of the primitive state it had suffered in under Trujillo. The Dominican Republic has since diversified its crop base, but it still depends heavily on sugar. A large portion of the sugar crop each year is purchased by the U.S. government at subsidized prices.

One of the great sugar regions of the country lies to the east of Santo Domingo, where emigrating Cubans introduced baseball at the end of the 19th century. Although it does not by any means have a monopoly on baseball ability, it has become known for its concentration of talent. Especially well-known for its baseball players is the sugar town of San Pedro de Macorís.

Rico Carty

One of the first stars to come out of this now-famous town was Rico Carty. Carty's father was a foreman of the Consuelo sugar mill outside of San Pedro, and his mother was a midwife. Carty recalled his modest start in baseball, saying, "In those days we made our own gloves out of old cement bags, our bats from branches of the guasma tree, and for balls we just picked up a stone."[1]

Carty gave up baseball for a couple of years for boxing, another popular sport in the Dominican Republic. Four of his uncles were boxers and Carty's father was a trainer. By age 15 Rico had won his first 17 fights, 12 by knockout. Before his 18th fight Carty ate a big meal. In the third round he caught a couple of good body shots, then took a clean punch to the nose and threw up rice and beans all over the ring. That was Rico Carty's last fight. He returned to baseball, a somewhat less upsetting sport.

Once he chose baseball, Carty stuck with it. Although he faced serious injury and illness many times in his career, he overcame the obstacles each time. His strong personality and fighting instincts got him into occasional trouble, but he frequently escaped because of his sense of humor and enthusiasm.

Carty was playing in the Consuelo sugar mill leagues when he was chosen for the 1959 Dominican team, which was to travel to the Pan American Games in Chicago. Before the team departed, Rafael Antún, owner of the San Pedro winter league team, the Estrellas Orientales, cut a deal to sign Carty for the Milwaukee Braves and the Estrellas. Antún and the Braves did not want to lose him after the U.S. scouts spotted him.

Sure enough, as Antún and the Braves had feared, the scouts flocked to Carty at the games. Carty could not speak English, but he understood they were all talking about money and baseball. He said, "I was just a dumb kid and didn't know anything. I signed with the Cardinals, Giants, Yankees, Braves, Cubs, and Dodgers and with all four teams in my country. I just wanted to play ball." Minor League President George Trautman resolved the situation. Carty explained that Trautman "said it was O.K. because I had not taken any money from any of the teams. So when I got my choice of who I wanted to play for, I chose the Braves because they were my favorite team. They gave me $2,000."[2]

After three years in the Braves' farm system, Carty made a big impression with Milwaukee in 1964, batting .330 in 130 games with 22 home runs and 88 RBIs. He also made his mark by leading the charge in an on-the-field brawl against the Mets and catcher Chris Cannizzaro. Carty said, "I saw him charging [Braves teammate Lee] Maye, so I went out there. When a thing like that comes up, you have got to defend your friend. But that's all—no more fighting. I was a little too hasty and it won't happen again—unless somebody picks on me."[3] Carty displayed the same loyalty to a friend as did Orlando Cepeda when he defended his friend and teammate Rubén Gómez. Carty put the baseball world on notice that Rico Carty would not be picked on.

Carty had back problems in 1965 and his lack of speed limited his outfield range. He rebounded in 1966 to finish at .326, behind fellow Dominicans Matty and Felipe Alou in the batting race. Carty was sometimes called a hot dog, to which he responded, "A lot of ballplayers will try to ignore the fans while a game is on, but I cannot be that way. I have always gotten along well with the fans. When they wave, I wave too. I like the little ones best, the kids. When I see that tiny little hand go up waving to me, I just have to wave back. I cannot help myself."[4]

While playing for Atlanta, Carty caused a stir one day because of his relaxed manner and inquisitive nature. A relief pitcher was warming up to replace an injured hurler, so Carty went behind the left center-field fence to the Indian tepee where the Braves' mascot sits. When the new Atlanta reliever was ready to pitch, there was no left fielder. Carty said, "I went into the tent to see what makes all that smoke. I decided that was a good time."[5]

Carty's personality continued to have its hot side. One night, while the team was traveling by air, Carty was joking in Spanish with some Latin teammates. Henry Aaron asked if they were talking about him, and he told Carty to speak in English. Carty took offense and called Hammerin' Hank a "black bleep." Aaron failed to see any humor in the remark, so he threw a punch at Carty. He missed him, but hit the the inside of the plane, denting it. Onlookers separated the two until Carty got free and threw a right at the still-restrained Aaron, hitting him right between the eyes.[6]

Besides his trouble with his temper, Carty also suffered one physical setback after another. In 1968 he contracted tuberculosis and missed the entire season. Fans, including Dominican President Balaguer, sent flowers and get-well wishes. In 1969 Carty dislocated his shoulder for the second time. After he healed, his hitting caught fire, and he batted .381 with 22 RBIs, many in clutch situations.

Carty's hot bat sparked Atlanta to a ten-game winning streak and 17 wins in 20 games to win the National League West title. In the wild clubhouse celebration that followed, so much champagne flowed that Carty hid under a table, beaming, "Everything is lovely, just lovely."[7] The Braves later lost to the Mets in three games in the National League playoffs, and the postseason champagne never flowed again for Carty.

Carty's strong performance continued on into 1970. In April he started a 31-game hitting streak, which was the longest ever for a Latin, and the third longest in National League history up to that time. Although he was left off the All-Star ballots for the 1970 All-Star Game, the fans voted Carty to a starting outfield position, the first ever write-in winner. He won the National League batting title with a .366 average, the highest since Stan Musial's .376 in 1948. Carty joined Bobby Avila, Roberto Clemente, Tony Oliva, Matty Alou, and Rod Carew as Latin batting title winners.

Still, he was plagued by physical problems. In December 1970 he crushed his kneecap in a winter league outfield collision. In February, during his recovery, Carty contracted pleurisy, an inflammation of the tissues surrounding the lungs, and in April he suffered from phlebitis, which caused a blood clot in his leg and set back his recovery.

To complete his disastrous 1971 season, he and his brother-in-law ran into trouble one night while returning from Carty's barbecue restaurant in Atlanta. The Dominicans stopped their car when two white men started shouting at them. Two policemen who happened by reported the two whites as saying, "These niggers were harassing us." Carty threw a punch and a brawl broke out. Carty was beaten by the two men, and suffered two black eyes and bruises all over his body. After an internal investigation, the Atlanta police chief announced, "This case involved the worst case of misconduct by a police officer I have ever seen." He announced that the white men were off-duty policemen who had been drinking, and that one of the uniformed policemen had been charged with brutality against blacks earlier that year. Charges against Carty were dropped and all three policemen were fired on September 2, 1971. On September 6 Carty's barbecue restaurant was burned by a fire of suspicious origin. The restaurant was not fully covered by insurance.[8] Rico Carty was undoubtedly thrilled to see 1971 come to a close.

Carty's foot speed, limited already by injury, was reduced in 1972 by his knee injuries and a hamstring problem. After the season, despite a career batting average of .315, Atlanta traded Carty to Texas for pitcher Jim Panther. Yet the more things changed, the more they stayed the same. Carty's jaw was broken by a pitch in winter ball, then he broke his left instep while breaking up a double play in June. In August he was sold to the Cubs, then to Oakland, which cut Carty from the roster while he was playing winter ball in the Dominican Republic.

But Carty still wanted to play Major League Baseball. The road back first took him to Mexico, where he batted .354 for Cordoba in the Mexican league. In late 1974 the Cleveland Indians noticed that he was healthy again and offered him the contract he wanted, which covered 1975. He said, "I had a couple of offers to go back to the major leagues, including one from the Phillies because Greg Luzinski got hurt, but I told them no because I didn't think they'd give me a fair shake. What I wanted was a contract for the following season [1975], too, because if I didn't get one, where would I be? But no one would give me one except [Cleveland General Manager Phil]

Seghi. I never met him before, but he seemed like an honest man, so I went to Cleveland and signed with the Indians."[9] Carty batted .363 in 33 games for the rest of 1974, but had $600 stolen during a game against Milwaukee. From then on, he played with his wallet in the back pocket of his uniform.

Carty's perseverance paid off, and he went on to play for five more years. He finished his career with Toronto in 1979 with a .299 career average, 204 home runs, and a slugging average of .464. In the Dominican winter league, Carty finished as the all-time home-run leader with 59 and a .301 average. He has coached during his retirement and maintains his contacts in the United States. "I have my green card so I have to be in the States every year," he explained. "Most ballplayers in the big leagues have the green card. If they don't, they're fools."[10] A green card allows players to stay beyond the season in the United States and presents employment opportunities that are not available at home.

César Cedeño

One of the next big stars to come from the Dominican Republic was César Cedeño, who rocketed to success at a very young age. Cedeño was born in Santo Domingo in 1951 and enjoyed a more comfortable upbringing than many Latins who have reached the majors. His father owned a small grocery store, which enabled the family to buy a car and a television set. Cedeño said, "I guess we were considered rich in Santo Domingo. Here, in America, we would be somewhere in the middle."[11] Cedeño's father expected him to become an engineer.

By age 15 Cedeño attracted attention for his play in Dominican amateur leagues. Bird dog Epy Guerrero tipped off Pat Gillick, the Houston Astros' scouting supervisor for Latin America, about Cedeño. Gillick and Guerrero saw Cedeño play, invited him for a tryout in San Pedro de Macorís, and decided to sign him. Cedeño's father's signature was needed because his son was still a minor. Gillick knew that the St. Louis Cardinal scout had offered $1,000 as a signing bonus, so Gillick went for broke and offered $3,000. The senior Cedeño signed the Astro contract just as the Cardinal scout pulled up to the curb with permission to offer more money. Gillick told him, "You're a few minutes too late."[12]

Cedeño started in Covington, Virginia, in 1968 at age 17. He said, "There are not many Spanish speakers in Virginia, but when you're young, everything is interesting. I worked hard to learn English. I watched TV-cowboy movies and cartoons. I learned English from "The Flintstones."[13]

Although Cedeño burned up the minor leagues the next two years, Houston General Manager Spec Richardson said, "We were determined to bring César along slowly. We didn't dare risk hurting the talent he had, and we wanted to make sure he was ready, both physically and mentally, before we exposed him to the majors. But the team wasn't going well and our outfield couldn't seem to put it together. . . . Finally we just couldn't wait any longer. We had to call him up."[14] The 19-year-old Cedeño became a major leaguer on June 18, 1970, less than three years after he was signed for only $3,000. In 90 games for Houston his first season, Cedeño batted .310 and stole 17 bases.

In the off season César married his longtime sweetheart. "At first I thought I'd wait until I made a reputation and more money, but I could see myself enjoying this life too much if I didn't marry. I did not want to be tempted to enjoy too many of the off-field activities. It could affect my play."[15]

In 1971, his first full season, Cedeño hit 40 doubles, 10 home runs, and batted in 81 runs. Over the winter he worked to improve his .264 average and 102 strikeouts. In 1972 he was hitting .360 at the All-Star break and pulled more All-Star votes than Roberto Clemente, Hank Aaron, and Willie Stargell. Houston fans dubbed the Astrodome "César's Palace." Although leg injuries slowed him in late season, Cedeño finished 1972 with a .320 average, third in the National League. He led the league in doubles with 39, and finished second in total bases and third with 55 stolen bases. He also won his first Gold Glove for his spectacular center-field play.

Manager Leo Durocher said, "César's our superstar. No doubt about that. Right now he's as good as Willie Mays when I first saw Willie. He can hit, and he has the same tremendous arm and the ability to make great catches. I don't know if he can keep this up for 20 years and I'm not saying he'll be better than Mays. No way anyone can be better than Mays. But I'll say Cedeño has a chance to be as good, and that's saying a lot."[16]

The next year Cedeño again batted .320 to finish behind Pete
Rose in the National League batting race. His new manager, Cuban
Preston Gómez, said, "This young man can be as good as he wants
to be. He can do everything in the field."[17] Cedeño won another
Gold Glove, but he also started drawing criticism for hot dogging.
After a diving, game-ending catch to seal a win over the Dodgers,
Cedeño lay on the field until his teammates came over. When they
reached him, he was giggling on the ground, "I just thought I'd lie
here for a while, so I'll get a big hand when I go in."[18] Whatever
his flaws, the Astros felt so certain of Cedeño's future they traded
away former star center fielder Jimmy Wynn.

Off the field Cedeño's life was nothing to laugh about. His
marriage broke up, and then he married a woman from Houston.
When he returned to the Dominican Republic for winter ball with
the Estrellas Orientales, more trouble came.

On December 11, 1973, five days after the Wynn trade, Cedeño
checked into a motel with a 19-year-old Dominican woman. He had
been drinking, and he ordered a couple more beers from room
service. About ten minutes later there was a shot and the woman
was dead. Powder burns were discovered on the woman but not on
Cedeño, confirming his testimony that she was looking at the gun
and it went off accidentally when he struggled to take it from her.

Cedeño called the motel manager to tell him of the shooting,
then left in his sports car. A few hours later, he turned himself in to
the police. He told them that he purchased the gun after he had been
robbed of several thousand dollars worth of jewelry one week earlier.
He was found guilty of involuntary manslaughter, was fined $100,
and spent 20 days in jail. After this incident, Cedeño never returned
to play winter ball in the Dominican winter league.

In his ruling on the situation, Baseball Commissioner Bowie
Kuhn wrote, "After some legal maneuvering, the charge was reduced
to involuntary manslaughter and he [Cedeño] was fined the
equivalent of $100 plus court costs. We made our best efforts to
determine if a cover-up had taken place, and whether there were any
facts beyond those brought out in the trial, but our efforts produced
nothing further. Under the circumstances, I took no disciplinary
action."[19]

Cedeño said, "I feel very sorry that this happened . . . that she
got herself killed. I will say it this way: God and me know I didn't

do it. She killed herself. I tried to take the gun away from her. I knew it was dangerous. I told her not to get it . . . because it was loaded. What else could I do? From now on, when I'm going to do something, I will think a lot about it. I'm sorry about what happened, but this will make me grow up faster. I think this will help me be a better person."[20]

The year after this incident Cedeño reached career highs with 57 stolen bases, 26 home runs, and 102 RBIs. He became the first player to hit 20 home runs and steal 50 bases in a season three times in his career. Joe Morgan of the Reds later matched that achievement. However, Cedeño struck out 103 times and his average dropped 51 points to .269. The pressure was beginning to show on the young superstar. In a 1975 spring training game, Cedeño smashed a water cooler after popping up.

He won his fourth Gold Glove in 1975, three times leaping over the center-field wall to take away home runs. New manager Bill Virdon said, "Potentially he [Cedeño] could be one of the best. And you don't just trade a man with that kind of talent. His top years could easily be ahead of him." But the Astros, even with Cedeño, finished in last place, an astounding 43½ games behind Cincinnati.

Over the next three years the Astros showed marked improvement. Yet 1978 proved disastrous for Cedeño. In late May he flied out in an RBI situation. When he returned to the dugout, he smashed his hand against the Plexiglas dugout roof, opening a 17-stitch cut. Houston management fined him $5,000 for his action, which they deducted from his $3.5 million, ten-year contract. When Cedeño returned to action three weeks later, he tore a ligament in his left knee sliding into second base. The injury and subsequent operation knocked him out for the year. Seeds of disappointment began to crop up when people began to speak of Cedeño's performance. Joe Morgan, Reds second baseman and former Astros teammate, typified these misgivings when he said, "I don't think Cedeño's been as good a player as I thought he would be."[21]

When Cedeño returned in 1979 the Astros made a strong run at the division title, falling to Cincinnati on the final weekend. With his knee repaired, Cedeño returned to the outfield in 1980, batting .309 with ten home runs and 73 RBIs. The Astros won a one-game playoff with Los Angeles to clinch their first divisional title in their 19-year history, but Cedeño's troubles were not over. He suffered a compound dislocation of his right ankle while trying to beat out a double play in the third game of the National League playoffs with Philadelphia. Houston lost the deciding fifth game in extra innings.

After the 1981 season Houston traded Cedeño to Cincinnati, where he put in three and a half years before being traded to St. Louis to fill in for Jack Clark in the team's drive for the 1985 pennant. Of the trade, Cedeño said, "I'm very happy an opportunity like this—to play with a contender—came around. Everywhere I've gone before, I've been expected to carry most of the weight. On this club, with these players, I don't have to do that. But I feel pretty sure I can help this team."[22] Cedeño homered on the first pitch thrown to him as a Cardinal, then pinch hit a grand slam against Atlanta a week later. In 34 games Cedeño hit a remarkable .434 with six home runs and 19 RBIs, with many clutch hits in key situations. St. Louis won the division and defeated Los Angeles in six games to advance to the World Series. Although St. Louis did not win the series, Cedeño, with his terrific talent, at least reached the Fall Classic. In a final attempt to reach 200 home runs, Cedeño signed on with the Dodgers in 1986. He was cut after 37 games, with the final count at 199.

Cedeño's first few years in the major leagues had created the expectation that he would join Mays, Aaron, and Clemente in the smallest circle of baseball's most talented performers. Even though he never soared to those heights, he reached stardom within three years of signing a contract for a $3,000 bonus. It was an extraordinary return in a short time on a meager investment and a lesson for all those major league organizations that were beginning to focus more energy and resources on the Dominican Republic and Latin America as inexpensive sources of great talent.

Pedro Guerrero

Regie Otero, scout for the Cleveland Indians, recognized this source of talent when he signed 16-year-old Pedro Guerrero in 1973 for $2,500. Guerrero grew up in San Pedro. He remembered, "I used to stand across from the shack where Rico Carty's aunt lived in the hope that I could see him drive up in his big car. I told myself that I wanted to be rich someday, just like he was."[23] In the meantime Guerrero built his strength by stacking heavy sugar sacks. He also played baseball whenever he could, and he listened to the Spanish language broadcasts of major league games during the summers.

The Indians sent young Guerrero to Sarasota of the Florida Rookie League. No one spoke Spanish, and Guerrero was terribly homesick. He later said, "I was playing in Sarasota, living in a motel. I had trouble ordering food. I got very depressed. I used to cry every day. I'd cry in the clubhouse, on the field, in my room. It was tough, but I made it, and the second year was much better."[24]

Meanwhile, Indians scout Otero moved over to the Dodgers, and he recommended that L.A. trade for Guerrero. At the time, Guerrero was beginning to feel comfortable with the Indians. He remembered, "There were more Spanish guys in spring training, and I had an idea of what to expect. I figured to go to [Class] A ball. Then one day in Tucson, they called me in the office. A lot of guys were getting released. I got worried. They said, 'We're sorry to tell you this, but you've been traded to the Dodgers.' I knew nothing about trades, I said I wouldn't go. I started crying again. I didn't know what they were saying or what was going on."[25]

In the end he did go. And it paid off for both Guerrero and the Dodgers. Guerrero worked up through the Dodgers' system and was called up to Los Angeles late in 1978. In Los Angeles, Steve Garvey stood in his way at first base. Ron Cey stood in his way at third base, so Guerrero focused on playing the outfield in Albuquerque. When he resurfaced with the Dodgers in 1980, Guerrero subbed for Davey Lopes at second base until Lopes was healthy, then moved to the outfield to keep his hot bat in the lineup. Late in the season, he damaged ligaments sliding back to second on a pickoff attempt. He decided that after that he would slide headfirst into bases to avoid further injury. After the 1980 season Guerrero married Denise Chavez, daughter of New Mexico State Senator Dennis Chavez.

In 1981 Guerrero opened the season in right field for Reggie Smith, who had undergone off-season shoulder surgery. Then in September Guerrero replaced Ron Cey at third when Cey broke his arm. Guerrero demonstrated a good attitude about the frequent changes, saying, "Sure, I'll play third base. I'll play anywhere, just so I'm in the lineup."[26]

The Dodgers gained a berth in the 1981 playoffs during the strike-shortened season. Guerrero homered against Houston, then against Montreal, both in important situations, but was otherwise in a slump. In the World Series against the Yankees, Guerrero played center field in the first game, right field in two others, and flip-flopped between center and right for the other three games. At the plate he caught fire, going 6 for 11.

In Game Five, with the series tied 2-2, Guerrero and catcher Steve Yeager hit sixth-inning, back-to-back home runs to turn a 1-0 Yankee lead into a 2-1 Dodger win. In Game Six, with Los Angeles one win away from the title, Guerrero hit a fifth-inning two-run triple for a 4-1 Los Angeles lead, followed by a two-run single in the sixth, and hit a solo home run in the eighth inning for a 9-2 Dodger win for the world championship. Guerrero, Cey, and Yeager were voted tri-MVPs.

After the final game, Guerrero credited first-base coach and countryman Manny Mota for his batting turnaround. "He had been telling me all along that I was hitting straight up instead of hitting down (in a crouch) as I did all season. Before the game tonight, Manny sat down with me at my locker for 10 or 15 minutes and reminded me to stay down and see the ball better. I saw it good all five times and hit it good all five times."[27]

Despite Guerrero's great series, trade rumors had him going to San Diego for shortstop Ozzie Smith. The trade did not take place, however, and Guerrero enjoyed an excellent 1982 season with 32 home runs, 100 RBIs, and a .304 average. His manager, Tommy Lasorda, always a motivator, said, "He can do it all . . . he can run, he can throw, he can steal a base (20 steals in 1982), he can beat you with the long ball, he can go get a ball, he can play left field, right field, center field, he can play first base, third base. Don't forget, he's even played second base—and y' know, he hasn't even reached the point where he knows what he's doing." Lasorda continued, "The thing about Pete is that he's not only a power hitter, he hits for a high average. He goes to all fields with the ball . . . clubs can't defense him in any one way."[28]

In 1983 the Dodgers traded Ron Cey to the Cubs and an-nounced that Guerrero would start at third base. Although he made the National League All-Star Team, Guerrero's defensive play suf-fered from some wild throws. Second baseman Steve Sax also had trouble throwing, but from less than half the distance. When Lasorda invited Guerrero into his office for a motivation session, he asked Guerrero what went through his mind when he played third. Guerrero responded, "I'm hoping the ball isn't hit to me." When Lasorda pressed him for another thought, Guerrero answered, "Second, I'm hoping the ball isn't hit to Sax."[29] When Guerrero's teammates heard his answer, they howled.

Despite his troubles at third, Guerrero hit 32 home runs, with 103 RBIs and a .298 average to join Duke Snider, Roy Campanella, and Gil Hodges as Dodgers with back-to-back 30-home-run seasons. The Dodgers won the division title, and Guerrero was signed to a $7 million, five-year contract.

After a slow start Guerrero finished the 1984 season with a .303 average, but much of his production came long after the pennant race was over. For 1985 Lasorda planned to move Guerrero from the outfield back to third base. Through June 1, Guerrero was hitting .268 with four home runs and 16 RBIs. Then Lasorda moved him to left field. Describing what happened, Lasorda said, "Son of a gun if he didn't catch fire. He homered that night, and it was just one after another after that." Guerrero hit 15 home runs in June to tie a record held by New York Yankee sluggers Babe Ruth and Roger Maris, and Robert ("Indian Bob") Johnson of the Philadelphia A's. The 15 home runs in June was a new National League record. Guerrero had 27 RBIs and raised his average to .324 in June. He stayed hot in July and batted .460, despite a week-long back sprain. Even with the back problem and a wrist injury, Guerrero finished the 1985 season with 33 home runs, a .320 batting average, and 87 runs knocked in. The Dodgers won the division by 5½, but fell to St. Louis in six games in the playoff.

In the final spring training exhibition game of 1986, Guerrero ruptured the tendon that holds the left kneecap in place during an aborted slide into third base. The Dodgers started the season on a downhill slide and ended in fifth place. The season was salvaged only by good seasons from Fernando Valenzuela and Steve Sax.

In 1987 Guerrero batted .338 and earned the Comeback Player of the Year Award, but Los Angeles finished in fifth place again. In 1988 Guerrero was batting .308 on June 5, when he went on the disabled list for 52 days because of a pinched nerve in his neck. On August 16 he was gone. The Dodgers traded him to St. Louis for left-hander John Tudor. Los Angeles won the world championship in 1988 on the strength of a strong Kirk Gibson–Orel Hershiser combination.

The trade was reminiscent of the 1966 Orlando Cepeda for Ray Sadecki trade. Cepeda was traded to St. Louis, where he enjoyed great success, while left-hander Sadecki was a disappointment with San Francisco. In 1989 Guerrero put on a one-man clutch hitting show to keep St. Louis in the pennant race late into 1989. He finished with a .311 average, 17 home runs, and 117 RBIs. John Tudor was injured for much of 1989, and signed as a free agent with St. Louis at season's end. Guerrero, bitter that Dodger fans and management had given up on him, made public statements against his treatment by the Dodgers. Tommy Lasorda used a combination of diplomacy and friendship with Guerrero to smooth relations before a Dodger Stadium salute to him in May 1989.

Scorned by Los Angeles fans and press as an underachiever, Guerrero was actually one of the best players in baseball in the 1980s. He finished the 1990 season with 206 home runs, tied with Felipe Alou's Dominican career home-run record. He has had three 100-RBI seasons and takes a .305 career average into 1991. Although his payoff was not as quick as Cedeño's, Guerrero continues to produce in the major leagues, 16 years after he was signed for $2,500.

The successes of Carty, Cedeño, and Guerrero taught the major leagues the economic lesson of big return on small investments. They also taught the leagues a lesson on the dangers of quick stardom for the unprepared.

19

A NEW BREED OF SCOUT

Since 1960 more ballplayers have made their way to the majors from the Dominican Republic than from any of its neighboring nations:

- Second baseman Julián Javiar performed steadily for the St. Louis Cardinals through the 1960s.
- In the 1980s San Pedro de Macorís native Joaquín Andújar won 20 games in two consecutive years, 127 games for his career, won the seventh game of the 1982 World Series, and was ejected from the seventh game of the 1985 World Series.
- Alfredo Griffin and Dámaso García made up the first Dominican double-play combination in an All-Star Game.
- Tony Peña won four Gold Gloves and displayed a great arm behind the plate.
- Mario Soto won 100 games and set a Cincinnati Reds' one-season strikeout record.
- Juan Samuel became the first player in major league history to achieve double figures in doubles, triples, home runs, and stolen bases in four consecutive seasons.
- Tony Fernández won Gold Gloves at shortstop.
- Junior Félix hit his first major league pitch for a home run.

- San Pedro de Macorís native George Bell hit 47 home runs and became the first Dominican to win an MVP Award, for Toronto in 1987.

- Julio Franco won the MVP in the 1990 All-Star Game.

- José Rijo won two games in the 1990 World Series, earning the series MVP.

Despite the glittering and growing array of Dominican baseball talent that has shone across the major league landscape, the Dominican Republic has become noted for one particular position: shortstop. On April 27, 1986, nine Dominican shortstops were in action around the major leagues. In 1987 70 Dominican shortstops were playing professional baseball in the United States.

Dominican talent, at all positions, has often come at bargain prices to the majors. But teams have also begun to face up to the fact that many of the players who are signed, like César Cedeño, struggle with the cultural challenges of moving to the United States and are often discarded without any nurturing. Of the old system, Felipe Alou said, "They sign 25 guys and maybe only one is a good player. It's like they throw a net in the ocean, hoping that maybe they'll get a big fish. The problem is, if they don't get a big fish, they'll throw all the smaller ones back. And if the competition is between keeping a $500 Latin player or an American player who gets a $15,000 bonus, who do you think the organization is going to keep?"[1]

In response to the abuses of the past, the major leagues have changed the way they scout in Latin America. In 1984 the major leagues created a 17-year-old age limit on the signing of young Latins. A new breed of scout has also evolved to cope with the special challenges of Latin recruiting. Former Phillies scouting supervisor Rubén Amaro asserts, "I tell my scouts that I don't want to hear them bragging, 'I signed a kid for $100.' That's not the point. The number one thing in Latin scouting, just like it used to be in the States, is getting to know the family, winning their confidence, establishing a reputation. We can afford to offer a fair contract and look after the kids we sign. If we pay to get a kid's teeth fixed or overcome what a bad diet did to him, and we make sure he gets eased into a whole different culture and language, then we're helping ourselves."[2]

One man whose scouting career embodies this approach is Epy Guerrero. A Dominican himself, Guerrero experienced some of the trials of young players when he played minor league baseball with Rico Carty in the 1960s. Guerrero remembers, "There were not too many players from here then. No Spanish instructors at the time. I had to go into a restaurant and buy Rico Carty food because he couldn't get into the restaurant. We were in Waco, Georgia. It was very tough for the black people."[3]

One of Guerrero's first recruits was César Cedeño. Although Cedeño put him on the map as a scout, the player's problems taught Guerrero some painful lessons about the trials of young Latin talent in the major leagues. Guerrero's new, more well-rounded approach to scouting has helped him build on the Latin scouting legacy of Joe Cambria and Howie Haak.

Epy Guerrero earned his first full-time scouting job from Houston's Latin American scouting supervisor, Pat Gillick, in 1966, based on the success of the Cedeño signing. Gillick and Guerrero later moved together to the New York Yankees, where Gillick headed scouting and player development. With the Yankees, Guerrero signed Dámaso García, Rafael Santana, and Domingo Ramos. In 1977 Gillick moved to the expansion Toronto Blue Jays and assigned Guerrero the job of Latin American scouting coordinator. Today Guerrero, nicknamed "The General" because his brother-in-law is in the military in the Dominican Republic, has ten full-time scouts working for him in Puerto Rico, Panama, Venezuela, the Dominican Republic, Mexico, Colombia, St. Martin, Curaçao, and Aruba.

One of the greatest success stories of Guerrero's nurturing was the development of shortstop Tony Fernández. Fernández grew up in a house just beyond the left-field fence of Stadium Tételo Vargas in San Pedro de Macorís. When Tony was a young boy, the owner of the Lucky Seven, a well-known Dominican baseball restaurant, learned of Fernández. The owner, exiled Cuban Evilio Oliva, recommended Fernández to fellow Cuban and Tigers scout Orlando Peña, saying that Fernández looked even better than shortstop Willie Miranda. Peña thought the prospect looked a little slow while running. Oliva called Guerrero, who arranged for surgery to remove a painful bone spur from Fernández's foot. Guerrero tested Fernández's speed with a stopwatch, saw he had become faster after the surgery, and signed him to a Toronto contract.[4] Fernández has become an All-Star and the best shortstop from San Pedro de Macorís, the little town that has become known as the City of Shortstops.

Guerrero's chief contribution to Latin scouting was his development of a Dominican training camp. He explained, "When I started scouting in 1966-1967, my purpose was to have my own ballpark. I bought the land in 1975. It was three cents a meter. Now that land goes for 20 cents a meter."[5] On the land, 15 miles from Santo Domingo but not near any city, Guerrero built Complejo Epy Deportivo, where the Blue Jays now house, feed, and train young Dominican prospects. The complex has a full-size ballpark where, from September to March, play starts at 9:00 a.m. From 35 to 40 kids stay there for a week at a time. Adjacent are chicken coops and three acres of vegetables to defray costs.

Epy's brother, Mario Guerrero, a former major leaguer and now a player agent, said, "People in Canada and the United States, they know they've got food on the table. The gang at the complex, they don't know if they're going to have it. They go looking for it. With Epy's complex, the food is there after practice. They've got a bed where they can sleep. All they have to do is work and play baseball. Most of the kids come from poor people, and there's nothing they can do, only play baseball. In the United States, there are different ways of making money. Here, the only way they can make money is baseball."[6]

In addition to the Blue Jays, 12 other major league teams operate baseball academies in the Dominican Republic today. Ramón Naranjo, former Red Sox scout and now the Yankees scout in the Dominican Republic, said in 1985, "The hardest part is getting some of them to go home on the weekends. I hear people in the United States say these kids ought to be in school, but that's ridiculous. Fewer than 20 percent of the kids in this country go to school. These complexes are the only places most of these kids get one square meal—let alone the three we give them. The big problem for years was that teams signed kids and took them to the States totally unprepared for that life. But not only do we work with them in terms of baseball, we also teach them some English and try to help them cope with society in the United States. Remember, you're dealing with kids who don't often know what a flush toilet is. It's just a shame that some backward people are trying to keep these kids from being helped. Yes, the Red Sox are one of the teams. I told Eddie Kasko for years that we need a complex, but he didn't want to spend the money. Money? Do you know what it costs the Yankees to operate our complex in San Cristóbal with eight instructors? One hundred and fifty thousand pesos. That's $50,000. Heck, you pay second-round draft choices for that kind of money."[7]

Today there are camps elsewhere in Latin America, but the Dominican Republic is still at the top of the recruiters' lists. Rafael Avila, Dodger head of Latin scouting, explained, "There are more players coming out of there [the Dominican Republic] than any place in the world. Remember what I said—hunger breeds players. They have a lot of other sports in Venezuela, and it's hard getting around because the country's so large. Puerto Rico is getting too Americanized. Kids want part-time jobs, not baseball. They want cars. Mexico is different, because American teams have had to buy the players from Mexican league owners. Nicaragua looked as if it were going to become a major area, because General Somoza pushed baseball so much, but the war's torn it apart. Panama has great leagues and great organization because of the Americans, but most of their players except Omar Moreno (and Juan Berenguer) moved to the States to play. Rod Carew and Ben Oglivie didn't play in Panama. They played in New York."[8]

Major League Baseball watches scouts' behavior and management of training complexes to ensure good treatment of the prospects and to prevent the signing of kids who do not have enough talent. Once the kids are signed to a professional contract, they can never regain amateur status and just play baseball for fun. However, signing a professional contract can be the first step toward a career that could land a young man in Milwaukee, Houston, Los Angeles, or Toronto.

20

REVOLUTIONARY BASEBALL

As baseball scouts scoured Latin America in search of talent, the borders of two countries remained closed to their scrutiny: Cuba and Nicaragua. Although these two countries divorced themselves from U.S. baseball, the sport is far from dead there. Baseball has survived the political and economic trials of revolution, as it has survived similar tests over the course of a century of history.

As the Dominican Republic was becoming a prime Latin talent source, Cuba was slipping into an isolation as deep as the Dominicans experienced under Trujillo. After Castro expropriated U.S.-owned businesses and embraced the Soviets, the United States cut Cuba off completely. In 1961 Castro countered the failed U.S. invasion of Cuba at the Bay of Pigs by inviting the Soviets to install nuclear weapons on the island. President John F. Kennedy managed to keep the missiles out after a confrontation in 1962, but the Soviet influence in Cuba remained.

The United States threw its biggest economic punch at Cuba by eliminating the annual purchase of Cuban sugar at highly subsidized

189

prices. The United States shifted the subsidy to the Dominican Republic and other sugar producers. When the United States choked off trade with Cuba, it also stopped the export of U.S. baseball equipment to the island. Castro reacted quickly and developed local manufacturing of baseballs, bats, gloves, shoes, and uniforms, all under the government brand name of "Batos."

Since Castro's takeover, Cuban summer baseball has grown stronger because no Cuban talent can leave the island. Because all players in Cuba are nominally amateur players, Cuba has performed extraordinarily well against amateur teams in the Pan American Games. After an initial win in 1963, Cuba won every game from 1967 to 1987, when it lost to Jim Abbott and the United States. Cuba overcame that defeat, however, and won its sixth straight Pan Am gold medal.

The Cuban government supported baseball with stadium expansion. In 1971 it added 20,000 seats to Gran Stadium, renamed Estadio Latinoamericano, for a total capacity of 55,000. A new 30,000-seat stadium was built in Matanzas, near the site of Cuba's first stadium in Palmar del Junco. This new stadium was named Estadio Victoria de Girón, dedicated to the Bay of Pigs victory over the United States. There are now nine baseball stadiums in Cuba, each of which holds more than 20,000 fans.

In the United States today there is little news or interest in Cuban baseball, although there are many Cuban players who have major league ability. Likewise, the Cuban public is not permitted to receive information about U.S. professional baseball, so visiting U.S. tourists are asked their opinions about Joe DiMaggio, Ted Williams, and Mickey Mantle—names that hearken back to the days of Ernest Hemingway and closer U.S.-Cuban relations.

In the mid-1970s a slight diplomatic thaw provided a forum for lively debate on U.S.-Cuban policy and baseball. An All-Star team of U.S. players was to face a Cuban All-Star team, but the State Department canceled the trip because of Cuba's involvement in Angola. Castro later invited the Yankees to play in Havana, but Commissioner Bowie Kuhn withheld permission, citing unequal advantage to that team in signing Cuban players if the barriers ever fell. Bill Veeck, White Sox owner, traveled to Cuba to evaluate talent and predicted future exhibitions between the two countries for diplomatic reasons, like the ping-pong diplomacy between China and the United States in 1972. An attempt to arrange an exhibition in Mexico in 1982 between the Seattle Mariners and the Cuban national team also fell through. It seems clear that until Fidel Castro and the U.S. State Department find a middle ground on international relations, there will be no U.S.-Cuban baseball outside of amateur tournaments and exhibitions.

In 1980 political negotiations between Castro and the Carter administration ended with the Mariel Boatlift exodus of 120,000 Cubans in small boats from the port of Mariel. Castro angrily encouraged the departure of certain political prisoners, criminals, and mental patients after President Jimmy Carter's unguarded remark that the United States would always welcome Cuban refugees "with open arms." Among those who left was baseball player Bárbaro Garbey. A year after his arrival, Garbey admitted that he had been forced to join the boatlift after Cuban officials discovered his part in a run-shaving scandal. Another gambling scandal hit Cuba in 1982, which led to two dozen people being permanently banned from the sport there.

Today there are ten million people living in Cuba, about one-third white, one-third mulatto, and one-third black. Thirty years after the revolution, Castro has built schools, hospitals, and public housing, raising the standard of living for the poorest in Cuba above pre-1959 levels. However, even Castro has been unable to change the basic economic reality of Cuba: Sugar still represents 80 percent of exports and suffers from declining world demand. The Soviet Union has traditionally bought Cuban sugar at artificially high prices. This and other Soviet subsidies to the Cuban economy have totalled over $5 billion per year. So, while no one in Cuba is starving, no one is enjoying prosperity, either. Food is still rationed, men and women get coupons for one or two new sets of clothing a year, and the few new cars on the streets are tiny Russian Ladas, which are dwarfed by the well-preserved Packards, Kaisers, Buicks, and Chevys from the 1950s. However, with the sweeping changes facing the USSR and the weakening Soviet economy, Castro may well lose the subsidies that have long sustained the Cuban economy.

But baseball will surely remain free in Cuba. From hundreds of towns and villages, teams will continue to compete in leagues to win the province championship. Each of the 14 province champions plays a 39-game season, and the top seven go on to a 54-game season, the

National Series. The players are amateurs and are given "baseball leaves" from their off-season jobs to play in these tournaments. Players make road trips in old buses and sleep and eat in makeshift quarters in the clubhouses, worse conditions than the lowest U.S. minor leagues.[1]

Because of the depressed economy, foul balls are thrown back from the stands and used long after they are stained dark. Although the scuffed balls give pitchers an advantage, the aluminum Batos bats usually make for explosive scores to delight fans. The fans are as loud and as partisan as ever, but with some changes. The umpire, almost as an extension of Castro himself, enjoys total control over the game and the crowd. The umpire's raised hand now silences a stadium full of fans. This respect for authority, in addition to control of beer and rum sales, has eliminated the violence common in the stands in the 1950s. The powerful umpire also keeps games under two hours in length.[2]

Only one other country in Latin America imitated Castro's defiant stand against the United States, and then only after a long battle with a U.S.-supported dictator similar to Cuba's Batista. As in Cuba, Nicaragua's separation followed a long history of U.S. intervention. U.S. troops first invaded Nicaragua in 1912 after an internal struggle to overthrow President José Santos Zelaya. The Marines occupied the country until 1933 with only a one-year hiatus in 1925-1926. In 1927 the U.S. Marines were called upon to fight liberal nationalist Augusto César Sandino, who was leading a guerilla war against the Marines and Nicaragua's National Guard. Sandino eventually agreed to lay down arms in a truce and was imprisoned.

When the Marines left Nicaragua in 1933, the Nicaraguan National Guard was left under the control of Anastasio "Tacho" Somoza. Somoza grew up in modest surroundings and was educated in Philadelphia at the Peirce School of Business Administration. He married Salvadora Debayle, a woman who came from a Nicaraguan society family. U.S. military forces worked well with Somoza and he strengthened his relationship with the National Guardsmen by calling for Sandino's execution in February of 1934. Guardsmen who had fought the rebels for years were then ordered to attack the villages that supported Sandino. Hundreds of villagers were killed, but Sandino's inspiration would resurface many years later.

In late 1936 Somoza staged a coup d'état. As the new leader he remained closely aligned with U.S. military interests, and he opened up the country to foreign investment. Somoza himself was a Philadelphia A's fan dating from his days as a student in that city. He declared baseball the national sport, and the game continued to develop and improve in Nicaragua. Retired Cuban Manuel Cueto brought a Cuban team to tour the country in the early 1930s and play against local competition. The team played 25 games and lost only one. In 1935 Nicaragua played its first international series in Panama and won 18 of 19 games against local teams. They continued on to El Salvador for the third Central American and Caribbean Games. Nicaragua tied for first place with Panama and Cuba, but finished third after a round-robin tie-breaker. Nicaragua also finished third in the 1939 baseball tournament at the Fourth Central American and Caribbean Games. Although Nicaragua did not participate in the 1946 version of these games, the country took part in the 1950 and 1954 games.

Nicaragua began its participation in the World Amateur Baseball Championships in Cuba in 1939. It finished second to the host team and went on to participate in 21 of the next 25 of these annual tournaments.

Major league teams did not scout the Nicaraguan amateur leagues. One left-handed pitcher, Francisco Dávila, reached Syracuse of AAA ball, but then went on to play in Jorge Pasquel's Mexican league in 1946 and did not return to the United States. José Angel "El Chino" Meléndez went to pitch in the Mexican league at age 30 in 1945. When the Brooklyn Dodgers traveled to Panama for spring training in 1947, Meléndez shut them out for six innings, 3-0.

After establishing himself in power, "Tacho" Somoza evolved into a moderate president. He maintained close ties with the United States and allowed the United States to use his country as the training base for the CIA invasion of Guatemala in 1954. Somoza was assassinated in 1956 during his campaign for reelection as president. His son Luís, educated at Berkeley, Louisiana State University, and the University of Maryland, assumed power and continued the moderate rule of his father.

In 1956 the Nicaraguan Professional League was established for winter baseball among four teams: El Boer, Oriental, Cinco Estrellas, and León. During the league's existence, many major league players performed in Nicaragua, including Zoilo Versalles, Marv Throneberry, Luís Tiant, Jim Kaat, George Scott, Ron Hansen, Jack Kralick, Phil Regan, Bert Campaneris, Ferguson Jenkins, and Lou Piniella. The Somozas had an investment in Cinco Estrellas ("Five Stars"), stocking the club with the best players.

One Cinco Estrellas player, Rigoberto Mena, was a fine-hitting shortstop. He had batted in front of slugger Hector Espino for the Monterrey Sultans in the Mexican league for nine years. Mena's career average was over .300, and he was elected to the Mexican Baseball Hall of Fame after his retirement in 1976. In the early 1960s the Detroit Tigers asked about Mena's contract, but Monterrey wanted too much for it.

In 1967 the ill Luís Somoza reluctantly permitted the rigged presidential election of his brother, Anastasio, who had previously held power as National Guard Commander. Luís died of a heart attack two months later. Soon after assuming power, President Anastasio Somoza refused to continue to provide funding for the baseball league because of a bad cotton crop and serious economic problems, and the league's existence came to an end.

In late November 1972 Nicaragua hosted the World Amateur Baseball Championships. The Nicaraguan team was very strong, led by pitchers Dennis Martínez and Tony Chévez, who would later become the country's first major leaguers. Pittsburgh Pirates star Roberto Clemente managed the Puerto Rican team at the tournament and made many friends in Managua. The Nicaraguans finished second in the tournament.

On December 23, 1972, a destructive earthquake shattered Managua and much of Nicaragua. Between 10,000 and 20,000 people died and $1 billion of property was destroyed, including Estadio Somoza, the stadium in Managua. International aid organizations sent money, food, and materials to rebuild the country. However, Somoza and the National Guard kept much of the aid for themselves, a move which marked the beginning of the downfall of the Somoza dynasty.

In 1973 Baltimore Orioles scout Ray Poitevint signed Dennis Martínez, a right-handed pitcher from Granada. After Martínez, four other Nicaraguans have appeared in the major leagues. Martínez made the Orioles team in 1976 and won 108 games for the Orioles through 1986 and another 55 for the Montreal Expos through 1990.

His 163-134 record over 15 years during the difficult times in his homeland and during his own battle with alcohol is a tribute to Martínez's emotional strength.

Tony Chévez, born in Telica, pitched for Baltimore in 1977. Al Williams, born in Pearl Lagoon on the east coast near Bluefields, was a starter for the Minnesota Twins from 1980 to 1984. Porfirio Altamirano, from Darillo, was discovered in the Venezuelan Winter League and pitched for Philadelphia and the Cubs from 1982 to 1984. But, because of his size and speed, the greatest expectations centered on outfielder David Green, son of Eduardo Green, a famous Nicaraguan player. Green was signed by the Milwaukee Brewers at age 17 in 1978 and was traded to the Cardinals in 1980. He enjoyed good years for St. Louis in 1983 and 1984, but has since been traded frequently and even played in Mexico and Japan.

The Nicaraguan League limped through the 1970s dominated by Granada, Estelí, and El Boer. León, Chinandega, the Buffaloes in Managua, and Cinco Estrellas occasionally challenged for the national title, but San Fernando in Masaya usually ended in last place. The teams played nine months of the year, with playoffs to determine the national champion.

The abuses of power by Somoza and his National Guard provided the spark for the anti-government Sandinista Front for National Liberation, named after César Sandino. After a number of anti-Somoza incidents, martial law was imposed and the National Guardsmen undertook a program to suppress Sandinista supporters. Somoza survived in power until July 19, 1979, when the Sandinista Front supporters entered Managua and took control.

After the Sandinistas attained power in Nicaragua, the United States provided financial support to the Contras, a group comprised of many former Nicaraguan National Guardsmen. The Sandinistas, in turn, received the support of Cuba's Fidel Castro. Although the United States imposed economic sanctions against Nicaragua, these were never of the magnitude imposed on Cuba. The Sandinistas did not interfere with the 43 U.S. multinational corporations, including Texaco, IBM, Monsanto, Caterpillar, Exxon, and John Deere, which still operate in Nicaragua today and account for 25 percent of the nation's industrial production.

While the war against the Contras drained the Nicaraguan economy, the Sandinistas, like the Cuban revolutionary government, recognized the importance of baseball to the people. Baseball was included in the Sandinistas' national budget, and the government subsidized a national amateur league of ten teams, which played from December through May. One team, Los Dantos, had traditionally been made up of soldiers, but as the war dragged on, the link between the military and Los Dantos was deemphasized. The Bluefields team was made up of English-speaking blacks. El Boer continued to be a popular team. Other teams represented geographical regions, industries, and government organizations. There was also a government-sponsored youth federation of four leagues for 22,000 players on over 1,000 teams.

In March 1980, before the Sandinistas fully embraced Castro, they encouraged the Baltimore Orioles to send local hero Dennis Martínez and a team of reserves for a two-game series against a local amateur All-Star team. The local All-Stars won one game and tied the other. Orioles coach Elrod Hendricks said, "They love baseball better than anything. And they know all the players. They used to be all Yankee fans in Nicaragua, but with Dennis an Oriole, they root for us now."[3] Nicaragua's four daily newspapers continued to report all the action in the U.S. major leagues—only U.S. player salaries were cut by Nicaraguan censors.

The Nicaraguan government constructed a rebuilt stadium on the site of the Somoza stadium. When the stadium opened in January 1985, it was called Estadio Rigoberto López Pérez in honor of the assassin of Anastasio Somoza, Sr. The construction of this and many smaller fields worried U.S. Lieutenant Colonel Oliver North, who feared that new baseball diamonds in Nicaragua reflected an increasing Cuban influence, just as in the 1960s Henry Kissinger had suspected greater Soviet involvement in Cuban affairs when aerial surveillance of Cuba revealed soccer fields. North was ignorant of Nicaragua's century-old love of baseball.[4]

Like the Cubans, the Sandinistas do not have access to hard currency and are forced to use aluminum bats and lifeless, locally made balls. Shortages are less obvious among the many vendors around the ballparks. Fried plantains, yuca, pork rinds, grilled meats, rice, beans, and fruits are all available for sale. The most common shortage is usually one of cups, so beer and soda are often served in plastic bags. Inside, the outfield fence is dominated by billboards with advertisements for Coca-Cola and Borden.

The national champion coming out of the Nicaraguan Winter League does not participate in the Caribbean World Series, which is for professionals only. However, the Nicaraguans frequently send teams to the amateur international competitions, including the World Amateur Championships, the Pan American Games, and the Olympics. In 1983 the Nicaraguans beat the United States, but lost their opening game against Japan 19-1. That night it was reported that "Even the Contras cried."[5] The United States gained revenge for its 1983 loss by thrashing Nicaragua 18-0 in the 1984 Olympics.

As Nicaragua ends its first century of baseball, the game is more important than ever to its people, for it provides an escape from the country's military and economic problems. Nicaraguan Bianca Jagger put it best during the 1987 Pan American Games in Indianapolis: "Here is a country the size of Iowa, a country of three million people, in the only arena where they can compete. Which is baseball."[6]

With the fall of the Berlin Wall in 1989, the unexpected may no longer seem so far-fetched. In February 1990 the opposition candidate, Violeta Barrios de Chamorro, defeated Daniel Ortega and the Sandinistas in free elections. The United States now has a wonderful opportunity to help rebuild friendship with the Nicaraguan people, and the game of baseball could play an important role in the process. At the same time, the United States should not forget its shared love of the sport with the Cubans, hosts of the 1991 Pan American Games in Havana. The opportunity for public relations may be as obvious as exhibitions, baseball equipment, and minor league contracts. Sugar subsidies can heal economic problems, but baseball can heal the emotional scars of years of adverse relations.

21

WORLD SERIES: CARIBBEAN STYLE

The imposition of revolutionary baseball in Cuba in the early 1960s ended the 82-year era of Cuban professional baseball. It also ended the reign of Cuban champions in the Caribbean World Series and put an end to the successful 12-year experiment in Latin unity. Without the participation of the Cubans, the other leagues could not bring themselves to continue the tournament, at least under the lofty title of the Caribbean World Series.

Yet the remaining Caribbean countries tried to keep the tournament afloat under the name "Inter-American Series." However, this new venture in Caribbean unification through baseball lasted only four years. Here, in summary, is a look at this four-year experiment.

Inter-American Series

1961 Site: Venezuela

- Teams: Rapiños, Venezuela; Valencia, Venezuela; Balboa, Panama; San Juan, Puerto Rico
- Champion: Valencia

1962 Site: Puerto Rico

- Teams: Santurce, Puerto Rico; Mayaguez, Puerto Rico; Leones de Caracas, Venezuela; Marlboro, Panama
- Champion: Santurce

1963 Site: Panama

- Teams: Chi-Bocas, Panama; El Boer, Nicaragua; Mayaguez, Puerto Rico; Valencia, Venezuela
- Champion: Chi-Bocas

1964 Site: Nicaragua

- Teams: Cinco Estrellas, Nicaragua; Marlboro, Panama; San Juan, Puerto Rico; Oriente, Venezuela
- Champion: Cinco Estrellas

The loss of this competition coincided with the decline of at least one of the winter league organizations. By the end of the 1960s, waning fan interest in Panama could only support three teams: the Cervecería Balboa Brewers, the Marlboro Smokers, and the Ramblers. As had been the pattern throughout the century, politics imposed limitations on the sport. In 1968 the Panamanian National Guard deposed President Arnulfo Arias and installed a military junta to lead the country. Lieutenant Colonel Omar Torrijos rose to prominence in the Guard. From that point, Torrijos ruled the country with a strong arm. Ironically, this strong control fostered the stability that made Panama a popular center for business and banking. Unlike most other Latin countries, Panama permits anyone to form and own corporations, register ships, and hold bank accounts. This freedom led to a considerable concentration of money, gained both legally and illegally, in Panama.

Despite his encouragement of outside investment, Torrijos dreamed of regaining control from the United States of the zone along each side of the canal. In 1978 he succeeded in negotiating a treaty with the Carter administration which provides for the gradual return of the Canal Zone to Panama by the end of the 20th century.

Two years after this great accomplishment, Torrijos died in a plane crash, and his chief of intelligence, Manuel Noriega, stepped into a power vacuum. Like many Panamanian leaders before him, Noriega reportedly profited greatly from his position. However,

Noriega made the mistake of flaunting his gains, many reportedly from control of the drug trade, before the U.S. press. In late 1989 President George Bush repeated a pattern of many U.S. leaders before him and sent U.S. troops into Panama. Noriega ultimately surrendered himself into the hands of U.S. soldiers, and the soldiers quickly began a staged withdrawal from the country. This time, they did not stay long enough to play baseball.

In the democratic, capitalistic countries, the winter leagues have fared much better. Puerto Rico, Venezuela, Mexico, and the Dominican Republic each have continued to build on their respective baseball traditions and form the core of the Latin leagues today. From these countries every year come teams that compete in the Caribbean World Series. This series was reinstituted in 1970 and has been played continually since (except for a 1981 players' strike) to establish an annual Caribbean champion. These core countries of the Latin leagues continue to build on their baseball traditions.

Puerto Rico

One reason Puerto Rican baseball is successful is the continuing support the game receives in the schools. Most of the other Latin countries' school systems cannot afford organized sports—they barely have enough money for a few books. Not so in Puerto Rico, where the school system benefits from U.S. support.

During the last century of U.S. control, Puerto Rico has not suffered the great social and political upheavals that have been seen in almost all of its neighboring countries. This political stability has facilitated the success of economic programs, still supported by Law #936, which was the centerpiece of the old Operation Bootstrap program. Puerto Rico is now home to more than 2,500 factories employing skilled workers. Less than five percent of the 3.3 million inhabitants work in agriculture. The success of these economic programs puts Puerto Rico about halfway between the wealthier Latin countries and the poorer states in the United States. The welfare safety net in the United States guarantees that there is no poverty comparable to that in neighboring countries. Today, the citizens of Puerto Rico frequently debate the benefits of graduating to U.S. statehood versus breaking away from the United States altogether.

Driving to a Puerto Rican baseball stadium on well-paved roads, it is common to get stuck in long lines of traffic. Puerto Ricans buy

new cars approximately every four years, and they love to drive them.
The stadiums are a little shinier and more modern than most other
Latin American baseball parks—they have the feel of U.S. minor
league facilities. The hot dogs and soda sold in the stands reinforce
the feeling that this is small-town USA. Then little differences crop
up. The empanadas (meat-filled pastries) are the first clue. Then the
piña coladas, so popular everywhere on the island, provide the next
assurance that this is not Kansas. The fans confirm it. They are
unmistakably Latin—emotional, enthusiastic, and celebratory. They
move to the salsa beat so popular there, and they are not above
throwing orange peels and setting off firecrackers.

Puerto Rico's Championship Years

The enthusiasm of the Puerto Rican fans
carried their winter champions to Caribbean World Series titles in
1951, 1953, 1954, and 1955. Santurce won three of the championships and Caguas claimed the 1954 crown.

1972 Site: Dominican Republic

Puerto Rico had participated in the revived Caribbean World
Series since it began in 1970, and it won its first crown in 1972 when
Ponce swept its first five games led by Sandy Alomar, Don Baylor,
Carlos May, Bernie Carbo, and Pat Corrales. Brothers José, Tommy,
and Hector Cruz were Ponce outfield reserves. Aragua, the
Venezuelan champ, won three of its six games, with manager Rod
Carew at second (.400) and David Concepción at short (.348). The
1972 Caribbean World Series was the first ever hosted by the
Dominican Republic.

1974 Site: Mexico

When Mexico hosted its first Caribbean World Series in 1974
in Hermosillo, Puerto Rico's Caguas squad won the tournament.
Two potential Hall of Famers highlighted the Caguas roster, with
Mike Schmidt at third and Gary Carter catching. Willie Montañez
played first, Otto Vélez, Jerry Morales, and Jay Johnstone played
the outfield, with Craig Swan, Eduardo Rodríguez, and Willie
Hernández anchoring the pitching staff. Venezuela did not send a
team because of a players' strike, so host Mexico entered both

Mazatlán and Obregon, with Licey representing the Dominican Republic.

1975 Site: Puerto Rico

The team from Bayamón retained the Caribbean World Series title for Puerto Rico in 1975 when it won on home turf. José Pagán was Bayamón's manager as outfielder Ken Griffey batted .500 (12 for 24 with a home run and three doubles) and first baseman Montañez had ten RBIs. Catcher Ellie Rodríguez, second baseman Félix Millán, and third baseman Art Howe contributed, while Eduardo Figueroa won Bayamón's opener. Joaquín Andújar posted a win for the Aguilas del Cibao (Dominican Republic). Hector Espino hit two home runs for Hermosillo (Mexico) against Aragua (Venezuela).

1978 Site: Mexico

When Mexico hosted the Caribbean World Series in 1978, Puerto Rico won again. The Indios de Mayaguez won their first five games. Manager Rene Lachman guided a team of Iván de Jesús, Ron LeFlore, Henry Cruz, Ed Romero, Jim Dwyer, and Luís Alvarado. Nicaraguan Tony Chévez, pitching for Caracas, struck out six straight hitters to set a Caribbean World Series record. George Brunet, who pitched for Panama in the 1950s, lost two games for Culiacán (Mexico) to finish with a 3-4 record for five Caribbean World Series.

1983 Site: Venezuela

The Puerto Rican team Lobos of Arecibo won the 1983 Caribbean World Series in Venezuela. After Licey (Dominican Republic) crushed Arecibo 17-2 in the opener, the Lobos won their next five games. Host La Guaira had Venezuelan hero David Concepción at short, Tony Armas and Luís Sálazar in the outfield, and Bo Díaz, in his record 30th consecutive game (1978-1983), behind the plate. The Tomateros ("Tomato Pickers") from Culiacán (Mexico) lost all six games, the first time any team lost all its games since Panama did in 1959.

1987 Site: Mexico

Caguas, Puerto Rico, won the 1987 Caribbean World Series in Mexico, the third Caribbean World Series title in Caguas history and the tenth for Puerto Rico. Puerto Rico set a new Caribbean World Series record with 14 home runs in the six games, breaking Panama's 12-home-run record from 1956. Cándido "Candy" Maldonado hit four, Carmelo Martínez and Germán Rivera smashed three each, and Henry Cotto and Hedi Vargas homered twice each. Cotto also stole three bases in one inning and four in one game, both new records, against Mazatlán (Mexico). Through the 1990 Caribbean World Series, Puerto Rico has won 10 of the 32 series.

Despite these victories, winter league baseball seems to have lost some of the excitement it once generated for Puerto Ricans. Basketball, cable television, and VCRs seem to be winning a greater portion of the entertainment dollar. In fact, attendance was so low at the last Caribbean World Series hosted by Puerto Rico in 1984 that the tournament has not returned there since. Perhaps the greater economic resources of the Puerto Rican League will enable the teams to weather abbreviated schedules and further declines in attendance until the next Roberto Clemente fires the imaginations of the Puerto Rican fans.

Venezuela

Of the Caribbean World Series' four original countries, Cuba and Panama have fallen by the wayside, and Puerto Rico struggles to survive local apathy, but Venezuela still thrives. In contrast to the shrinking Panamanian League of the 1960s, Venezuela's league expanded during the decade to its present six teams: La Guiara, Zulia, Caracas, Magallanes, Lara, and Aragua.

The Venezuelan economy took off in the 1970s as it became a founding member of OPEC and enjoyed a flood of oil-related income that sparked a decade-long economic boom. Like the Arab countries, Venezuela had been a leading oil producer for most of the century, but had never controlled the price it received for this limited natural resource. In 1974 the new president, Carlos Andrés Pérez, went further and nationalized the last foreign oil holdings although, unlike Castro, he compensated the oil giants for their lost assets.

Venezuela's Victories

1970 Site: Venezuela

In the 12 Caribbean World Series played from 1949 to 1960, only Venezuela did not win a championship. When the Caribbean

World Series resumed in 1970, Venezuela hosted the tournament and invited the Ponce Lions from Puerto Rico and Licey from the Dominican Republic. Cuban expatriate Orlando Peña pitched a 3-1 win for Magallenes (Venezuela) over Cuban expatriate Mike Cuellar, pitching for Ponce. Peña and another Cuban exile, Aurelio Monteagudo, each won two games. Catcher Ray Fosse, outfielders César Tóvar and Gonzalo Márquez, and pitchers Larry Jaster and Jay Ritchie had outstanding games for Magallenes. Venezuela won seven of the eight games to take the title. When third baseman Dámaso Blanco scored the winning run in the 11th inning of the decisive game against Ponce, a roar went up in the stands, and then the stadium erupted into the singing of the Venezuelan national hymn.

1979 Site: Puerto Rico

Venezuela experienced an eight-year drought until Magallenes won the 1979 Caribbean World Series in Puerto Rico. Manager-designated hitter Willie Horton watched his team get shut out 1-0 by the Aguilas del Cibao (Dominican Republic), then win five straight. Mike Norris pitched an 11-0 one-hitter (Tony Pérez had the only hit) over Caguas (Puerto Rico). Outfielder Jerry White (.522) and first baseman Mitchell Page (.417) led Magallenes. Navajoa (Mexico) shortstop Mario Mendoza batted .286, but finished with a .159 average in his five Caribbean World Series, well below his own "Mendoza line."

1982 Site: Mexico

After the 1981 Caribbean World Series was canceled by a players' strike in Venezuela, the Leones de Caracas won the 1982 tournament in newly named Hector Espino Stadium in Mexico. Espino played for Hermosillo, his fifth time in seven Caribbean World Series appearances for the Orangemen. He had only two hits in 18 at-bats, but finished his Caribbean World Series career with 46 hits (six home runs) in 155 at-bats for a .297 average. Fernando Valenzuela, in his only Caribbean World Series appearance, earned one of Hermosillo's two wins. Caracas, managed by Alfonso "Chico" Carrasquel, won five games to take the title. Bo Díaz hit two home runs and batted .400, and Tony Armas hit .375 with six RBIs for Caracas.

1984 Site: Puerto Rico

The Aguilas de Zulia, managed by Rubén Amaro, won the 1984 Caribbean World Series held in Puerto Rico. Puerto Rico's home team, possibly discouraged by dismal attendance, won only one game. Licey (Dominican Republic) won only one game, despite three home runs from George Bell. Los Mochis (Mexico) finished a strong 4-2, marking the last Caribbean World Series for third baseman Aurelio Rodríguez. Zulia had strong performances from third baseman Luís Salazar, catcher Bobby Ramos, first baseman Terry Francona, and left fielder Jerry White. Luís Leal, Nicaraguan Porfy Altamirano, Ron Meredith, and Derek Bothelo led the pitchers.

1989 Site: Mexico

Zulia, managed by Pete Mackanin, took the 1989 Caribbean World Series in Mazatlán, Mexico. Carlos Quintana and Phil Stephenson delivered key hits in Zulia's three extra-inning wins. Stephenson, Zulia first baseman, batted .385 with three home runs and seven RBIs as Zulia won five games. Defending champion Escogido (Dominican Republic) won only one game. Venezuela, after being shut out from 1949 through 1960, won five titles in the 1970-1990 period.

The legacy of Venezuela's oil boom years is now seen in gleaming skyscrapers, modern infrastructure, and a mass transit system that rivals Washington, D.C.'s subway system. Venezuela, roughly twice the size of California, has 18 million citizens with a per capita income that is four times that of its Caribbean neighbors in the Dominican Republic. Unfortunately, the other legacy of the oil boom is an overwhelming national debt. Like the Texans, the Venezuelans contracted too many loans under the assumption that oil prices would continue to increase. Times are rough today in Venezuela, although the country has fared better than many of its neighbors.

Baseball still commands the interest of the Venezuelan fans, although it competes with the other national passions of soccer, boxing, and bullfighting. The stadiums around the country are large and modern. Caracas games are still played in Estadio Universitario. Local favorites arepas (corn cakes) and meat cakes are available in the stands, along with beer and soda. Unlike the sugar-producing Caribbean, diet sodas are also readily available. In the 1980s the play has declined somewhat in Venezuela. Since baseball is not so deeply etched in the Venezuelan culture as in the Caribbean, the government has not seen the political necessity of preserving funding for the sport during hard times. The allowed number of "imported" players has thus been decreased from 11 to 7, and they are paid lower salaries. Ticket prices have also climbed.

Mexico

Joining Puerto Rico and Venezuela in the new Caribbean World Series, 1970s edition, was Mexico. Like Venezuela, Mexico enjoyed an oil-fueled boom in the 1970s followed by a crash in the 1980s, with the standard of living falling by 40 percent. The country is still ruled by the PRI, although it was widely reported that its 1988 presidential candidate, Salinas de Gortari, captured a majority of votes through ballot stuffing. His strongest opposition came from the son of Lázaro Cárdenas. Salinas de Gortari is struggling to control the country's huge economy.

The 82 million people spread across the Mexican territory, three times the size of Texas, support the largest baseball league structure in Latin America. The 15-team summer league complements the ten-team winter league. Winter play in the Mexican Pacific League takes place in the rugged western cities, where the rocky desert comes right to the very shore of the Pacific Ocean and the Sea of Cortez. The oceanside setting is confirmed by the cups of shrimp and the local beers available at the ballpark, including Sol, Pacífico, and Corona.

Mexico's Title Years

1976 Site: Dominican Republic

Mexico joined the Caribbean World Series in 1971 and won its first title in 1976. Hermosillo, managed by Benjamin "Cananea" Reyes, successfully defended its title to earn a visit to Santiago de los Caballeros in the Dominican Republic. First baseman Hector Espino and ageless pitcher George Brunet teamed with third baseman Celerino Sánchez, pitchers Ed (Cy) Acosta, and Vincente Romo. Imports Chet Lemon and Jerry Hairston contributed. After Hermosillo lost its opener to the Aguilas del Cibao, playing in their home park, the Orangemen won five straight. When Brunet retired the last Aragua (Venezuela) hitter, Hermosillo had won Mexico's first Caribbean World Series title.

1986 Site: Venezuela

Mexico did not win again for ten years. In 1986 Maracaibo, Venezuela hosted the tournament in Luís Aparicio Grande Stadium, named for Hall of Famer Luís Jr.'s father. Managing Mexicali, the Mexican representative, was Benjamín Reyes, manager of the 1976 victorious Mexican team. Mexicali lost two of its first three games on shutouts, 11-0 in the opener to La Guiara (Venezuela) and 6-0 to Luís de Leon of Mayaguez (Puerto Rico). However, for the first time in Caribbean World Series history, all four teams were tied at 2-2. Mexicali won its final two games, and the Aguilas del Cibao (Dominican Republic) stopped Venezuela in the final game to give Mexico its second title. Benjamín Reyes joined Napoleón Reyes (Marianao, Cuba, 1957-1958) as the only managers to win two Caribbean World Series.

Although they live far from the Caribbean, the Mexicans from the West Coast have a life much more similar to the Dominicans or Puerto Ricans than their compatriots in the huge metropolis of Mexico City might have. Mexican fans on the Pacific Coast have enthusiastically supported the Caribbean World Series each of the six times they have hosted since 1974.

Dominican Republic

If poverty is good for baseball, then the Dominican Republic is still far ahead of the competition. In the Dominican Republic, the fourth member country of the post-Cuba Caribbean World Series, per capita income is around $1,200 a year. The economy does not generate enough jobs for its seven million inhabitants. The presidency is back in the hands of Joaquín Balaguer, the man who moved the country into democracy following the Trujillo dictatorship. The Dominican economy still depends on exports of sugar, cacao, tobacco, and coffee, mostly to the United States.

To escape their troubles, the people look in their idle hours to the national hip-swinging dance merengue, dominoes, rum, cock-fighting, and sports. Boxing has always been popular and was the source of the country's first Olympic medal in 1984. Basketball has also been increasing in popularity, as illustrated by the selection of Tito Horford (University of Miami) and José Vargas (Louisiana State University) in the 1988 NBA draft. But baseball is still the national obsession.

Dominican Days

1971 Site: Puerto Rico

When Licey earned entry to the 1970 three-team Caribbean World Series in Venezuela, the Dominican Republic arrived at its proper place in the Latin baseball scene. When Licey traveled the next year to San Juan, Puerto Rico, for the 1971 Caribbean World Series, its manager, Manuel "Manny" Mota, singlehandedly led the team to a sweep of its six games by going 11 for 19 in the five games he played.

1973 Site: Venezuela

Tommy Lasorda managed the 1973 Licey team to the Caribbean World Series title in Venezuela. Caracas won its first three games, two on shutouts by Milt Wilcox and Cuban Diego Seguí, but lost its last three. Santurce (Puerto Rico), managed by Frank Robinson, enjoyed a strong team with Tony Pérez at first, José "Cheo" Cruz, Willie Crawford, and Don Baylor in the outfield, and Ellie Hendricks behind the plate. Yet Santurce won only three games. The Yaquis de Obregón (Mexico) won only one game. Lasorda's Licey team was led by Bobby Valentine at short, third baseman Steve Garvey, and top hitters Manny Mota and Jesús Rojas Alou. Pitcher Pedro Borbón won two starts, and Dick Tidrow won one.

1977 Site: Venezuela

Entering the 1977 Caribbean World Series, Caguas (Puerto Rico) was favored because the roster included Eddie Murray, José Cruz, Sixto Lezcano, Félix Millán, Jerry Morales, Kurt Bevacqua, John Wockenfuss, and Ed Whitson. But surprisingly, the team won just one game. Licey, managed by Bob Rodgers, was powered by the record-setting bat of Rico Carty. Carty had ten RBIs and five home runs in the series, the latter still a record. He hit home runs in the first four games, and one in the last. He also had three doubles and a single for ten hits in 21 at-bats (.476 batting average and 1.333

slugging average). Licey swept all six games and outscored its opponents 45-7. Ed Halicki and Odell Jones each won two games for Licey, while Pedro Borbón threw a shutout for the Dominicans. The win lifted Borbón's career won-loss record in Caribbean World Series competition to 5-0, trailing only Camilo Pascual (6-0) among all pitchers.

1980 Site: Dominican Republic

In 1980 Licey, managed by Dell Crandall, won its first four games on its home turf. Licey pitchers threw two shutouts, then Joaquín Andújar defeated Caracas and Luís Leal 3-1. A Tony Armas grand slam provided all the runs for Caracas over Mario Soto and Licey 4-2, but Hermosillo (Mexico) eliminated Caracas on the final day. Outfielders Miguel Diloné and Mickey Hatcher, catcher Mike Scioscia, second baseman Dámaso García, and shortstop Jerry Dybzinski all stood out for Licey.

1985 Site: Mexico

Licey, managed by Terry Collins, won its fifth Caribbean World Series title in 1985 in Mazatlán, Mexico. Glenn Davis smashed two home runs in the opener over La Guaira (Venezuela). Ralph Bryant and George Bell also added home runs for a 4-2 win. After a loss to Mexico, Mike Torrez and José Rijo combined for a 3-0 shutout of San Juan. Licey won its last four games to take the title.

1988 Site: Domincan Republic

Until 1988 no Dominican team besides Licey had won a Caribbean World Series title. In its home stadium Quisqueya in Santo Domingo, under the leadership of manager Phil Regan, Escogido finally won its first Caribbean World Series title. Rufino Linares batted .389 with five RBIs. Stan Javier (.421) and Luís Polonia played outfield with Linares. José Rijo, José Núñez, Luís Encarnación, and José Tapia won decisions. After the first four games, Caracas, managed by Bill Robinson, Mayaguez (Puerto Rico), managed by Jim Riggleman, Tijuana, managed by George Ficht, and Escogido were all tied 1-1. Then Escogido committed seven errors in an 8-6 loss to Caracas, which committed three, for a new, one-game record of ten errors. Escogido won its next three games for a 4-2 record and the title. Tony Armas hit two home runs to take the career Caribbean World Series lead with 11. Armas also holds the Caribbean World Series record with 32 RBIs.

1990 Site: Miami

The 1990 Caribbean World Series took place in the Orange Bowl in Miami, Florida. The continuing economic problems of Mexico, Venezuela, and the Dominican Republic led the leagues to try a new idea in 1990 for the series: They made a three-year commitment to hold the tournament in Miami, the first time the series had been played outside the member countries. Each team was guaranteed $60,000 toward expenses by the tournament's organizer. Also, Miami is a popular destination among well-to-do Latins, and it was hoped that more people might be inclined to travel to see the games. Finally, more than perhaps even the major leagues realized, the league organizers knew that Miami's population is over 50 percent Hispanic, many of whom are Cuban and Nicaraguan exiles who share the baseball passion of their homelands.

Escogido failed to repeat in Mazatlán in 1989, but traveled as the Dominican winter league champion for the third straight year in 1990. Under manager Felipe Rojas Alou, Escogido won five of its six games in the series and crushed San Juan 16-5 on the last day to claim the seventh Caribbean World Series title for the Dominican Republic.

The organizers did not actively promote the tournament, and consequently attendance was poor. A makeshift "Orange Monster," erected some 250 feet from home plate in left field, led to all sorts of home run records. Barry Jones of Puerto Rico tied Rico Carty's mark of five home runs in a Caribbean World Series. Jones, Carlos Baerga, and Hector Villanueva homered in succession in the final game, another record. A total of 48 home runs was hit in the 12 games, easily breaking the record of 30 by all teams in 1987. Escogido benefited from good pitching, highlighted by Bob Patterson's splendid 2-1 complete game victory. Reliever Melquiades Rojas pitched in three games and won two of them. Melido Pérez surrendered one run in seven innings. Outfielder Gerónimo Berróa smashed four home runs with eight RBIs.

1991 Site: Miami

The 1991 version of the Caribbean World Series represented an improvement in quality over the previous year. The organizers moved the tournament to the Roberto Maduro Stadium, the City of Miami ballpark named after the Cuban baseball owner.

Organizers also emphasized the commercial promotion and renamed the tournament Winterball I, with the sponsorship of Diet Pepsi. Billboards covered the outfield, advertising for American Airlines, Coors Light Beer, Marlboro cigarettes, and Hispanic magazines, among others.

The sound system, infield conditions, and outfield dimensions all approached major league quality. The organizers even changed the playoff system, which had been in effect for the 32 previous tournaments, implementing a six-game round robin to eliminate two countries, for a best-of-three final. Unfortunately, ticket prices at $8, $12, and $15 may have discouraged some fans from attending.

Even so, attendance increased over 1990, and those present saw a Dominican team that felt right at home. Roberto Maduro Stadium had served as the model in 1960 when Trujillo built ballparks in Santo Domingo, Santiago, and San Pedro de Macorís. So when Licey defeated defending champion Escogido in the Dominican League finals, it earned the right to play for the Caribbean World Series title in a stadium with dimensions identical to those of Estadio Quisqueya in Santo Domingo.

And the team members played like they were at home. Juan Guzmán, a Toronto prospect, stopped the Santurce (Puerto Rico) Cangrejeros in the opener 8-2. Former Atlanta outfielder Gerónimo Berróa homered and drove in three runs. In Licey's next game, White Sox pitcher Melido Pérez and three relievers shut out the Potros from Tijuana (Mexico) 4-0. Berróa sparked a four-run eighth inning with a two-run single. Licey leveled the Cardinales de Lara (Venezuela) 12-1 to sweep the preliminary round.

Santurce, Lara, and Tijuana each won one of their three games, forcing a day of playoff games, which Lara survived by winning twice. However, Licey bombarded Lara's exhausted pitching staff and swept the best-of-three final 13-1 and 13-4. In five games, Licey outscored the opposition by 50-8. The Dominicans thus claimed their eighth title, Licey's sixth.

Miami deserves the opportunity to host the Caribbean World Series again in 1992. The Mexican league president has announced hopes of hosting the 1993 tournament in Hermosillo, Mexico.

Dominican Baseball: A Final Observation

The 1991 Caribbean World Series was broadcast back to Santo Domingo by a Dominican television company. Reports were also carried in the six daily newspapers, which carry major league box scores all summer and Dominican box scores all winter. To keep fans abreast of future Caribbean World Series opponents, some newspapers even carry the results from the winter leagues in Puerto Rico, Mexico, and Venezuela.

Dominicans going home for lunch in Santo Domingo tune in to "Lucky Seven en el Aire" with Jorge Bournigal and Freddy Mondesí, who review the day in sports, concentrating on baseball, in both the big leagues and the winter leagues. They broadcast from a back room in the Lucky Seven Restaurant, a mecca for players, fans, management, and league administrators. Some major league games are also transmitted in Spanish over radio and television from a small studio off the main dining room. The trivia questions and the baseball commentary at the Lucky Seven challenge even the most knowledgeable U.S. fans.

Across the street from the restaurant and in countless spots across the country are small betting establishments, where fans wager pesos on the Cubs, Yankees, or Aguilas, based on the posted odds established by the house. Wagering is also common at the winter league games themselves. Fans bet on the outcome of the game, first hits made, first runs scored—even on individual pitches. One daring Dominican gambler once bet 15,000 pesos ($10,000 at the time) that U.S. slugger Mike Schmidt would hit the ball out of the infield on a specific at-bat. Schmidt grounded out, but the gambler had established for life his reputation as a high roller.

In the parking lots of baseball stadiums, skinny kids with dirty rags in their hands "protect" the cars of the more affluent fans. The tip for their services ranges between 50 centavos and one peso (a few U.S. cents). Other fans spend similar amounts to ride public transportation that travels along established routes through Dominican towns. Outside the stadium, women sell food cooked at home, ranging from roast chicken to empanadas. Others scalp tickets, even for games far from sellouts. Once inside the gate, armed soldiers check fans for guns, bottles, or other weapons.

In the stands vendors sell rum in plastic bottles to fans they seem to adopt. Wandering vendors also sell Presidente and Bohemia beer, Coca-Cola, Seven-Up, and the popular Rojo (red) soda. Vendors also take orders for pizza, empanadas, candy, cheeses, and fried plantain chips. The peanut sellers are always young, barefoot boys who sell handfuls of home-roasted peanuts wrapped in pieces of brown paper towels. If business looks slow for the peanut kids, they plop down in an aisle to talk about the game.

The teams' uniforms carry a sponsor's name, often that of a rum company. As each batter steps up to the plate, the announcer precedes his name with a plug for the company. The scoreboard shows the score, the number of strikes, and the number of outs. (The umpire uses hand signals to indicate how many balls have been called.) Scores from other games being played in the league are posted as well.

Games in the Dominican Republic rarely begin at the designated time, which is 8:00 p.m. on weeknights and Saturdays, 4:00 p.m. on Sundays. The pace of the game is slower than in the United States, as both pitcher and batter relish every moment in the spotlight. A contest usually takes three and a half hours to complete. Each Dominican team is only allowed three or four U.S. players, who usually come from a major league organization which has a relationship with the Dominican team. The U.S. players are minor leaguers or major leaguers with less than two full years in the majors. The clubs may substitute one U.S. player for another if one leaves because he is sick, homesick, injured, tired, fired, scared, or in a slump.

Traditionally around New Year's Day, the best imports take on the Dominican All-Stars in a game. The imports at these games attract much attention. The real stars of the winter league, though, are the Dominican major leaguers. When players of the caliber of Juan Marichal, Joaquín Andújar, or Mario Soto are scheduled to pitch, the stadiums fill up. The Alous, Manny Mota, Rico Carty, Tony Peña, Alfredo Griffin, Juan Samuel, and Julio Franco have all acknowledged their gratitude to the Dominican fans over the years by playing on a regular basis in the winter leagues.

✠✠✠✠✠✠✠✠✠✠✠✠✠✠✠✠

22

THE HALL OF FAME AND BEYOND

Over the last century a long and complex melodrama has played out in the Western Hemisphere. The characters were the Anglo-Saxons in North America and the Latins to the south. The relationship between the characters has been defined by the military and economic superiority of the United States, and a subplot to this drama is the story of baseball. Initially, through contact between upper classes, the sport spread south. Then, as baseball became a business, field hands became feature players, drawing customers to baseball stadiums across the region.

In time, players developed in the Latin leagues also filled rosters on the U.S. leagues. But these players have a curious status. Like migrant farm workers, they receive temporary visas to go north to supplement the local work force. At the end of the season, their visas expire and they must go home. The return home to winter leagues keeps players fit, but it reverses the progress made in learning English and adapting to U.S. culture. The players are suddenly pulled out of the melting pot of U.S. society, too soon to be remade into the cultural norm but too late to preserve their original identity.

215

Yet the young Latin American players continue to be drawn to U.S. organized baseball by the compelling economics of the baseball lottery. For, while major league teams may be required to pay little or no signing bonuses, the leagues pay the market price for big Latin talent once it has blossomed, rewarding the players with million-dollar contracts. Even the major league minimum, at $100,000, far exceeds salaries available for almost any honest employment in Latin American countries.

The baseball establishment, represented by the Baseball Writers Association of America (BBWAA), also has recognized the contribution of the elite players from Latin America by their election to the Baseball Hall of Fame in Cooperstown, New York. Roberto Clemente attained this honor through a special election after his tragic and untimely death. Martín Dihigo was selected by the Veterans' Committee for his performance in the previously unrecognized Negro leagues. In 1983 Juan Marichal became the first Latin to reach the Hall of Fame through the normal election process. The next year Luís Aparicio joined him, also through a vote by the BBWAA. Rod Carew became the first Latin elected in his first year of eligibility in January 1991, a tribute to the hitting skills which earned him seven batting titles. Tony Pérez, not yet eligible, waits in line.

With few exceptions, the media have lagged behind the baseball establishment in their recognition of Latin talent. This demonstrates that, for better or worse, U.S. society has never had much patience with those who refuse to jump into the melting pot. Thus, as with all immigrants, society puts the burden on the Latin ballplayer to learn the language and the culture of the United States. Unless the players do this successfully, the media will continue to perpetrate the stereotypes of pidgin English and misunderstood personalities.

These problems with the press can make it difficult for Latins to follow in the footsteps of Preston Gómez and Cookie Rojas into managerial positions. Whereas the players can respect a man for his ability, the press wants him to be easily understood and quotable. It is a shame that the major leagues, and many Latins themselves, have not found a way to overcome this barrier.

Successful presentation of Latin stars to mainstream baseball fans is only a question of good tutoring by the teams and maximum effort by the players themselves. The potential for bringing these players into the mainstream has been demonstrated by the success of stars like Fernando Valenzuela, Tony Peña, Luís Tiant, and Rod Carew. To expand on Tommy Lasorda's observations, such stardom is good for the players, the teams, and the business of baseball. May it continue to expand as baseball heads into the 21st century.

APPENDIX A

Player Profiles

Roberto Clemente

- Born August 18, 1934, Carolina, Puerto Rico. Died December 31, 1972, San Juan, Puerto Rico
- Debut date: April 17, 1955
- Elected National League MVP, 1966
- Played in 14 All-Star games for the National League from 1960–1971 and batted .323
- Led National League in batting average, 1961, 1964, 1965, and 1967
- Led National League in hits, 1964 and 1967
- Led National League in triples, 1969
- Awarded Gold Glove for fielding, 1961–1972
- Voted MVP of the 1971 World Series
- Hit safely in all 14 World Series games
- Elected to the Baseball Hall of Fame, Cooperstown, New York, 1973

	G	AB	H	2B	3B	HR	R	RBI	BB	SO	SB	BA
1955 Pit / N	124	474	121	23	11	5	48	47	18	60	2	.255
1956	147	543	169	30	7	7	66	60	13	58	6	.311
1957	111	451	114	17	7	4	42	30	23	45	0	.253
1958	140	519	150	24	10	6	69	50	31	41	8	.289
1959	105	432	128	17	7	4	60	50	15	51	2	.296
1960	144	570	179	22	6	16	89	94	39	72	4	.314
1961	146	572	201	30	10	23	100	89	35	59	4	.351
1962	144	538	168	28	9	10	95	74	35	73	6	.312
1963	152	600	192	23	8	17	77	76	31	64	12	.320
1964	155	622	211	40	7	12	95	87	51	87	5	.339
1965	152	589	194	21	14	10	91	65	43	78	8	.329
1966	154	638	202	31	11	29	105	119	46	109	7	.317
1967	147	585	209	26	10	23	103	110	41	103	9	.357
1968	132	502	146	18	12	18	74	57	51	77	2	.291
1969	138	507	175	20	12	19	87	91	56	73	4	.345
1970	108	412	145	22	10	14	65	60	38	66	3	.352
1971	132	522	178	29	8	13	82	86	26	65	1	.341
1972	102	378	118	19	7	10	68	60	29	49	0	.312
18 yrs	2433	9454	3000	440	166	240	1416	1305	621	1230	83	.317

LEAGUE CHAMPIONSHIP SERIES

	G	AB	H	2B	3B	HR	R	RBI	BB	SO	SB	BA
1970 Pit / N	3	14	3	0	0	0	1	1	0	4	0	.214
1971	4	18	6	0	0	0	2	4	1	6	0	.333
1972	5	17	4	1	0	1	1	2	3	5	0	.235
3 yrs	12	49	13	1	0	1	4	7	4	15	0	.265

WORLD SERIES

	G	AB	H	2B	3B	HR	R	RBI	BB	SO	SB	BA
1960 Pit / N	7	29	9	0	0	0	1	3	0	4	0	.310
1971	7	29	12	2	1	2	3	4	2	2	0	.414
2 yrs	14	58	21	2	1	2	4	7	2	6	0	.362

Juan Marichal

- Born October 20, 1938, Laguna Verde, Dominican Republic
- Debut date: July 19, 1960
- Pitched a 1-0 no-hit victory over the Houston Colt 45s on June 15, 1963
- Pitched for the National League in eight All-Star games (1962–1971) and achieved a 2-0 record and 0.50 ERA. Selected two other years but did not play
- Led National League in wins and innings pitched, 1963 and 1968
- Led National League in complete games, 1964 and 1968
- Led National League in shutout, 1965 and 1969
- Led National League in winning percentage, 1966
- Led National League in ERA, 1969
- Elected to the Baseball Hall of Fame, Cooperstown, New York, 1983

		W	L	PCT	ERA	G	GS	CG	IP	H	BB	SO	ShO
1960	SF / N	6	2	.750	2.66	11	11	6	81.1	59	28	58	1
1961		13	10	.565	3.89	29	27	9	185	183	48	124	3
1962		18	11	.621	3.36	37	36	18	262.2	233	90	153	3
1963		25	8	.758	2.41	41	40	18	321.1	259	61	248	5
1964		21	8	.724	2.48	33	33	22	269	241	52	206	4
1965		22	13	.629	2.13	39	37	24	295.1	224	46	240	10
1966		25	6	.806	2.23	37	36	25	307.1	228	36	222	4
1967		14	10	.583	2.76	26	26	18	202.1	195	42	166	2
1968		26	9	.743	2.43	38	38	30	325.2	295	46	218	5
1969		21	11	.656	2.10	37	36	27	300	244	54	205	8
1970		12	10	.545	4.11	34	33	14	243	269	48	123	1
1971		18	11	.621	2.94	37	37	18	279	244	56	159	4
1972		6	16	.273	3.71	25	24	6	165	176	46	72	0
1973		11	15	.423	3.79	34	32	9	209	231	37	87	2
1974	Bos / A	5	1	.833	4.87	11	9	0	57.1	61	14	21	0
1975	LA / N	0	1	.000	13.50	2	2	0	6	11	5	1	0
16 yrs		243	142	.631	2.89	471	457	244	3509.1	3153	709	2303	52
LEAGUE CHAMPIONSHIP SERIES													
1971	SF / N	0	1	.000	2.25	1	1	1	8	4	0	6	0
WORLD SERIES													
1962	SF / N	0	0		0.00	1	1	0	4	2	2	4	0

Rod Carew

- Born October 1, 1945, Gatun, Panama
- Debut date: April 11, 1967
- Elected American League Rookie of the Year, 1967
- Played in 15 All-Star games for the American League (1967–1984) and batted .244. Selected three other years but was replaced due to injury
- Elected American League MVP, 1977
- Led American League in batting average, 1969, 1972, 1973, 1974, 1975, 1977, and 1978
- Led American League in hits, 1973, 1974, and 1977
- Led American League in triples, 1973 and 1977
- Led American League in runs, 1977
- Elected to the Baseball Hall of Fame, Cooperstown, New York, 1991

	G	AB	H	2B	3B	HR	R	RBI	BB	SO	SB	BA
1967 Min / A	137	514	150	22	7	8	66	51	37	91	5	.292
1968	127	461	126	27	2	1	46	42	26	71	12	.273
1969	123	458	152	30	4	8	79	56	37	72	19	.332
1970	51	191	70	12	3	4	27	28	11	28	4	.366
1971	147	577	177	16	10	2	88	48	45	81	6	.307
1972	142	535	170	21	6	0	61	51	43	60	12	.318
1973	149	580	203	30	11	6	98	62	62	55	41	.350
1974	153	599	218	30	5	3	86	55	74	49	38	.364
1975	143	535	192	24	4	14	89	80	64	40	35	.359
1976	156	605	200	29	12	9	97	90	67	52	49	.331
1977	155	616	239	38	16	14	128	100	69	55	23	.388
1978	152	564	188	26	10	5	85	70	78	62	27	.333
1979 Cal / A	110	409	130	15	3	3	78	44	73	46	18	.318
1980	144	540	179	34	7	3	74	59	59	38	23	.331
1981	93	364	111	17	1	2	57	21	45	45	16	.305
1982	138	523	167	25	5	3	88	44	67	49	10	.319
1983	129	472	160	24	2	2	66	44	57	48	6	.339
1984	93	329	97	8	1	3	42	31	40	39	4	.295
1985	127	443	124	17	3	2	69	39	64	47	5	.280
19 yrs	2469	9315	3053	445	112	92	1424	1015	1018	1028	353	.328
LEAGUE CHAMPIONSHIPS												
1969 Min / A	3	14	1	0	0	0	0	0	1	4	0	.071
1970	2	2	0	0	0	0	0	0	0	1	0	.000
1979 Cal / A	4	17	7	3	0	0	4	1	0	0	1	.412
1982	5	17	3	1	0	0	2	0	4	4	1	.176
4 yrs	14	50	11	4	0	0	6	1	5	9	2	.220

Luís Aparicio

- Born April 29, 1934, Maracaibo, Venezuela
- Debut date: April 17, 1956
- Elected American League Rookie of the Year, 1956
- Played on ten American League All-Star teams (1958–1971) and batted .071
- Led American League in stolen bases, 1956–1964
- Led American League in at-bats, 1966
- Awarded Gold Glove for fielding, 1958–1962, 1964, 1966, 1968, and 1970
- Elected to the Baseball Hall of Fame, Cooperstown, New York, 1984

	G	AB	H	2B	3B	HR	R	RBI	BB	SO	SB	BA
1956 Chi / A	152	533	142	19	6	3	69	56	34	63	21	.266
1957	143	575	148	22	6	3	82	41	52	55	28	.257
1958	145	557	148	20	9	2	76	40	35	38	29	.266
1959	152	612	157	18	5	6	98	51	53	40	56	.257
1960	153	600	166	20	7	2	86	61	43	39	51	.277
1961	156	625	170	24	4	6	90	45	38	33	53	.272
1962	153	581	140	23	5	7	72	40	32	36	31	.241
1963 Bal / A	146	601	150	18	8	5	73	45	36	35	40	.250
1964	146	578	154	20	3	10	93	37	49	51	57	.266
1965	144	564	127	20	10	8	67	40	46	56	26	.225
1966	151	659	182	25	8	6	97	41	33	42	25	.276
1967	134	546	127	22	5	4	55	31	29	44	18	.233
1968 Chi / A	155	622	164	24	4	4	55	36	33	43	17	.264
1969	156	599	168	24	5	5	77	51	66	29	24	.280
1970	146	552	173	29	3	5	86	43	53	34	8	.313
1971 Bos / A	125	491	114	23	0	4	56	45	35	43	6	.232
1972	110	436	112	26	3	3	47	39	26	28	3	.257
1973	132	499	135	17	1	0	56	49	43	33	13	.271
18 yrs	2599	10230	2677	394	92	83	1335	791	736	742	506	.262
1959 Chi / A	6	26	8	1	0	0	1	0	2	3	1	.308
WORLD SERIES												
1966 Bal / A	4	16	4	1	0	0	0	2	0	0	0	.250
2 yrs	10	42	12	2	0	0	1	2	2	3	1	.286

Tony Pérez

- Born May 14, 1942, Camaguey, Cuba
- Debut date: July 26, 1964
- Played on seven National League All-Star teams from 1967–1976 and batted .125

		G	AB	H	2B	3B	HR	R	RBI	BB	SO	SB	BA
1964	Cin / N	12	25	2	1	0	0	1	1	3	9	0	.080
1965		104	281	73	14	4	12	40	47	21	67	0	.260
1966		99	257	68	10	4	4	25	39	14	44	1	.265
1967		156	600	174	28	7	26	78	102	33	102	0	.290
1968		160	625	176	25	7	18	93	92	51	92	3	.282
1969		160	629	185	31	2	37	103	122	63	131	4	.294
1970		158	587	186	28	6	40	107	129	83	134	8	.317
1971		158	609	164	22	3	25	72	91	51	120	4	.269
1972		136	515	146	33	7	21	64	90	55	121	4	.283
1973		151	564	177	33	3	27	73	101	74	117	3	.314
1974		158	596	158	28	2	28	81	101	61	112	1	.265
1975		137	511	144	28	3	20	74	109	54	101	1	.282
1976		139	527	137	32	6	19	77	91	50	88	10	.260
1977	Mon / N	154	559	158	32	6	19	71	91	63	111	4	.283
1978		148	544	158	38	3	14	63	78	38	104	2	.290
1979		132	489	132	29	4	13	58	73	38	82	2	.270
1980	Bos / A	151	585	161	31	3	25	73	105	41	93	1	.275
1981		84	306	77	11	3	9	35	39	27	66	0	.252
1982		69	196	51	14	2	6	18	31	19	48	0	.260
1983	Phi / N	91	253	61	11	2	6	18	43	28	57	1	.241
1984	Cin / N	71	137	33	6	1	2	9	15	11	21	0	.241
1985		72	183	60	8	0	6	25	33	22	22	0	.328
1986		77	200	51	12	1	2	14	29	25	25	0	.255
23 yrs		2777	9778	2732	505	79	379	1272	1652	925	1867	49	.279
LEAGUE CHAMPIONSHIP SERIES													
1970	Cin / N	3	12	4	2	0	1	1	2	1	1	0	.333
1972		5	20	4	1	0	0	0	2	0	7	0	.200
1973		5	22	2	0	0	1	1	2	0	4	0	.091
1975		3	12	5	0	0	1	3	4	1	2	0	.417
1976		3	10	2	0	0	0	1	3	1	2	0	.200
1983	Phi / N	1	1	1	0	0	0	0	0	0	0	0	1.000
6 yrs		20	77	18	3	0	3	6	13	3	16	0	.234
WORLD SERIES													
1970		5	18	1	0	0	0	2	0	3	4	0	.056
1972	Cin / N	7	23	10	2	0	0	3	2	4	4	0	.435
1975		7	28	5	0	0	3	4	7	3	9	1	.179
1976		4	16	5	1	0	0	1	2	1	2	0	.313
1983	Phi / N	4	10	2	0	0	0	0	0	0	2	0	.200
5 yrs		27	95	23	3	0	3	10	11	11	21	1	.242

Orlando Cepeda

- Born September 17, 1937, Ponce, Puerto Rico
- Debut date: April 15, 1958
- Elected National League Rookie of the Year, 1958
- Elected National League MVP, 1967
- Played in nine All-Star games for the National League from 1959–1967 and batted .037
- Led National League in RBI, 1961 and 1967
- Led National League in home runs, 1961

	G	AB	H	2B	3B	HR	R	RBI	BB	SO	SB	BA
1958 SF / N	148	603	188	38	4	25	88	96	29	84	15	.312
1959	151	605	192	35	4	27	92	105	33	100	23	.317
1960	151	569	169	36	3	24	81	96	34	91	15	.297
1961	152	585	182	28	4	46	105	142	39	91	12	.311
1962	162	625	191	26	1	35	105	114	37	97	10	.306
1963	156	579	183	33	4	34	100	97	37	70	8	.316
1964	142	529	161	27	2	31	75	97	43	83	9	.304
1965	33	34	6	1	0	1	1	5	3	9	0	.176
1966 2 teams		SF / N (19 games; .286)					StL / N (123 games; .303)					
total	142	501	151	26	0	20	70	73	38	79	9	.301
1967 StL / N	151	563	183	37	0	25	91	111	62	75	11	.325
1968	157	600	149	26	2	16	71	73	43	96	8	.248
1969 Atl / N	154	573	147	28	2	22	74	88	55	76	12	.257
1970	148	567	173	33	0	34	87	111	47	75	6	.305
1971	71	250	69	10	1	14	31	44	22	29	3	.276
1972 2 teams		Atl / N (28 games; .298)					Oak / A (3 games; .000)					
total	31	87	25	3	0	4	6	9	7	17	0	.287
1973 Bos / A	142	550	159	25	0	20	51	86	50	81	0	.289
1974 KC/ A	33	107	23	5	0	1	3	18	9	16	1	.215
17 yrs	2124	7927	2351	417	27	379	1131	1365	588	1169	142	.297
LEAGUE CHAMPIONSHIP SERIES												
1969 Atl / N	3	11	5	2	0	1	2	3	1	2	1	.455
WORLD SERIES												
1962 SF / N	5	19	3	1	0	0	1	2	0	4	0	.158
1967 StL / N	7	29	3	2	0	0	1	1	0	4	0	.103
1968	7	28	7	0	0	2	2	6	2	3	0	.250
3 yrs	19	76	13	3	0	2	4	9	2	11	0	.171

Luís Tiant

- Born November 23, 1940, Marianao, Cuba
- Debut date: July 19, 1964
- Pitched in three All-Star games for the American League from 1968–1976 and compiled an 0-2 record with a 3.00 ERA
- Led American League in shutouts, 1966, 1968, and 1974
- Led American League in ERA, 1968 and 1972
- Led American League in losses, 1969

	W	L	PCT	ERA	G	GS	CG	IP	H	BB	SO	ShO
1964 Cle / A	10	4	.714	2.83	19	16	9	127	94	47	105	3
1965	11	11	.500	3.53	41	30	10	196.1	166	66	152	2
1966	12	11	.522	2.79	46	16	7	155	121	50	145	5
1967	12	9	.571	2.74	33	29	9	213.2	177	67	219	1
1968	21	9	.700	1.60	34	32	19	258.1	152	73	264	9
1969	9	20	.310	3.71	38	37	9	249.2	229	129	156	1
1970 Min / A	7	3	.700	3.39	18	17	2	93	84	41	50	1
1971 Bos / A	1	7	.125	4.88	21	10	1	72	73	32	59	0
1972	15	6	.714	1.91	43	19	12	179	128	65	123	6
1973	20	13	.606	3.34	35	35	23	272	217	78	206	0
1974	22	13	.629	2.92	38	38	25	311	281	82	176	7
1975	18	14	.563	4.02	35	35	18	260	262	72	142	2
1976	21	12	.636	3.06	38	38	19	279	274	64	131	3
1977	12	8	.600	4.53	32	32	3	188.2	210	51	124	3
1978	13	8	.619	3.31	32	31	12	212.1	185	57	114	5
1979 NY / A	13	8	.619	3.90	30	30	5	196	190	53	104	1
1980	8	9	.471	4.90	25	25	3	136	139	50	84	0
1981 Pit / N	2	5	.286	3.95	9	9	1	57	54	19	32	0
1982 Cal / A	2	2	.500	5.76	6	5	0	29.2	39	8	30	0
19 yrs	229	172	.571	3.30	573	484	187	3485.2	3075	1104	2416	49
LEAGUE CHAMPIONSHIP SERIES												
1970 Min / A	0	0		13.50	1	0	0	.2	1	0	0	0
1975 Bos / A	1	0	1.000	0.00	1	1	1	9	3	3	8	0
2 yrs	1	0	1.000	0.93	2	1	1	9.2	4	3	8	0
WORLD SERIES												
1975 Bos / A	2	0	1.000	3.60	3	3	2	25	25	8	12	1

Tony Oliva

- Born July 20, 1940, Pinar del Rio, Cuba
- Debut date: September 9, 1962
- Elected American League Rookie of the Year, 1964
- Played in six All-Star games for the American League (1964–1970) and batted .263
- Led American League in batting average, 1964, 1965, and 1971
- Only rookie to win a batting title
- Only player to win a batting title, first two years
- Led American League in hits, 1964, 1965, 1966, 1969, and 1970
- Led American League in doubles, 1964, 1967, 1969, and 1970
- Led American League in runs, 1964

	G	AB	H	2B	3B	HR	R	RBI	BB	SO	SB	BA
1962 Min / A	9	9	4	1	0	0	3	3	3	2	0	.444
1963	7	7	3	0	0	0	0	1	0	2	0	.429
1964	161	672	217	43	9	32	109	94	34	68	12	.323
1965	149	576	185	40	5	16	107	98	55	64	19	.321
1966	159	622	191	32	7	25	99	87	42	72	13	.307
1967	146	557	161	34	6	17	76	83	44	61	11	.289
1968	128	470	136	24	5	18	54	68	45	61	10	.289
1969	153	637	197	39	4	24	97	101	45	66	10	.309
1970	157	628	204	36	7	23	96	107	38	67	5	.325
1971	126	487	164	30	3	22	73	81	25	44	4	.337
1972	10	28	9	1	0	0	1	1	2	5	0	.321
1973	146	571	166	20	0	16	63	92	45	44	2	.291
1974	127	459	131	16	2	13	43	57	27	31	0	.285
1975	131	455	123	10	0	13	46	58	41	45	0	.270
1976	67	123	26	3	0	1	3	16	2	13	0	.211
15 yrs	1676	6301	1917	329	48	220	870	947	448	645	86	.304

LEAGUE CHAMPIONSHIP SERIES

	G	AB	H	2B	3B	HR	R	RBI	BB	SO	SB	BA
1969 Min / A	3	13	5	2	0	1	3	2	1	3	1	.385
1970	3	12	6	2	0	1	2	1	0	1	0	.500
2 yrs	6	25	11	4	0	2	5	3	1	4	1	.440

WORLD SERIES

	G	AB	H	2B	3B	HR	R	RBI	BB	SO	SB	BA
1965 Min / A	7	26	5	1	0	1	2	2	1	6	0	.192

David Concepción

- Born June 17, 1948, Aragua, Venezuela
- Debut date: April 6, 1970
- Played in seven All-Star games for the National League (1975–1982) and batted .250. Selected for two other games but was replaced due to injury
- Voted MVP for the 1982 All-Star Game
- Awarded Gold Glove for fielding, 1974–1977, and 1979

	G	AB	H	2B	3B	HR	R	RBI	BB	SO	SB	BA
1970 Cin / N	101	265	69	6	3	1	38	19	23	45	10	.260
1971	130	327	67	4	4	1	24	20	18	51	9	.205
1972	119	378	79	13	2	2	40	29	32	65	13	.209
1973	89	328	94	18	3	8	39	46	21	55	22	.287
1974	160	594	167	25	1	14	70	82	44	79	41	.281
1975	140	507	139	23	1	5	62	49	39	51	33	.274
1976	152	576	162	28	7	9	74	69	49	68	21	.281
1977	156	572	155	26	3	8	59	64	46	77	29	.271
1978	153	565	170	33	4	6	75	67	51	83	23	.301
1979	149	590	166	25	3	16	91	84	64	73	19	.281
1980	156	622	162	31	8	5	72	77	37	107	12	.260
1981	106	421	129	28	0	5	57	67	37	61	4	.306
1982	147	572	164	25	4	5	48	53	45	61	13	.287
1983	143	528	123	22	0	1	54	47	56	81	14	.233
1984	154	531	130	26	1	4	46	58	52	72	22	.245
1985	155	560	141	19	2	7	59	48	50	67	16	.252
1986	90	311	81	13	2	3	42	30	26	43	13	.260
1987	104	279	89	15	0	1	32	33	28	24	4	.319
1988	84	197	39	9	0	0	11	8	18	23	3	.198
19 yrs	2488	8723	2326	389	48	101	993	950	736	1186	321	.267

LEAGUE CHAMPIONSHIP SERIES

	G	AB	H	2B	3B	HR	R	RBI	BB	SO	SB	BA
1970 Cin / N	3	0	0	0	0	0	0	0	0	0	0	
1972	3	2	0	0	0	0	0	0	0	0	0	.000
1975	3	11	5	0	0	1	2	1	1	2	2	.455
1976	3	10	2	1	0	0	4	0	2	1	0	.200
1979	3	14	6	1	0	0	1	0	0	3	0	.429
5 yrs	15	37	13	2	0	1	7	1	3	6	2	.351

WORLD SERIES

	G	AB	H	2B	3B	HR	R	RBI	BB	SO	SB	BA
1970 Cin / N	3	9	3	0	1	0	0	3	0	0	0	.333
1972	6	13	4	0	1	0	2	2	2	2	1	.308
1975	7	28	5	1	0	1	3	4	0	1	3	.179
1976	4	14	5	1	1	0	1	3	1	3	1	.357
4 yrs	20	64	17	2	3	1	6	12	3	6	5	.266

César Cedeño

- Born February 25, 1951, Santo Domingo, Dominican Republic
- Debut date: June 20, 1970
- Played in four All-Star games for the National League (1972–1976) and batted .333
- Led National League in doubles in 1971 and 1972
- Awarded Gold Glove for fielding, 1972–1976

	G	AB	H	2B	3B	HR	R	RBI	BB	SO	SB	BA
1970 Hou / N	90	355	110	21	4	7	46	42	15	57	17	.310
1971	161	611	161	40	6	10	85	81	25	102	20	.264
1972	139	559	179	39	8	22	103	82	56	62	55	.320
1973	139	525	168	35	2	25	86	70	41	79	56	.320
1974	160	610	164	29	5	26	95	102	64	103	57	.269
1975	131	500	144	31	3	13	93	63	62	52	50	.288
1976	150	575	171	26	5	18	89	83	55	51	58	.297
1977	141	530	148	36	8	14	92	71	47	50	61	.279
1978	50	192	54	8	2	7	31	23	15	24	23	.281
1979	132	470	123	27	4	6	57	54	64	52	30	.262
1980	137	499	154	32	8	10	71	73	66	72	48	.309
1981	82	306	83	19	0	5	42	34	24	31	12	.271
1982 Cin / N	138	492	142	35	1	8	52	57	41	41	16	.289
1983	98	332	77	16	0	9	40	39	33	53	13	.232
1984	110	380	105	24	2	10	59	47	25	54	19	.276
1985 2 teams		Cin / N (83 games; .241)				StL / N (28 games; .434)						
total	111	296	86	16	1	9	38	49	24	42	14	.291
1986 LA / N	37	78	18	2	1	0	5	6	7	13	1	.231
17 yrs	2006	7310	2087	436	60	199	1084	976	664	938	550	.285

DIVISIONAL PLAYOFF SERIES

1981 Hou / N	4	13	3	1	0	0	0	0	2	2	2	.231

LEAGUE CHAMPIONSHIP SERIES

1980 Hou / N	3	11	2	0	0	0	1	1	1	0	0	.182
1985 StL / N	5	12	2	0	0	0	2	0	2	3	0	.167
2 yrs	8	23	4	1	0	0	3	1	3	3	0	.174

WORLD SERIES

1985 StL / N	5	15	2	1	0	0	1	1	2	2	0	.133

José Cruz

- Born August 8, 1947, Arroyo, Puerto Rico
- Debut date: September 19, 1970
- Brothers Hector and Tommy also played Major League Baseball
- Played for the National League in the 1985 All-Star Game and was hitless in his only at-bat. Also a member of the 1980 All-Star team but did not play
- Led National League in hits, 1983

	G	AB	H	2B	3B	HR	R	RBI	BB	SO	SB	BA
1970 StL / N	6	17	6	1	0	0	2	1	4	0	0	.353
1971	83	292	80	13	2	9	46	27	49	35	6	.274
1972	117	332	78	14	4	2	33	23	36	54	9	.235
1973	132	406	92	22	5	10	51	57	51	66	10	.227
1974	107	161	42	4	3	5	24	20	20	27	4	.261
1975 Hou / N	120	315	81	15	2	9	44	49	52	44	6	.257
1976	133	439	133	21	5	4	49	61	53	46	28	.303
1977	157	579	173	31	10	17	87	87	69	67	44	.299
1978	153	565	178	34	9	10	79	83	57	57	37	.315
1979	157	558	161	33	7	9	73	72	72	66	36	.289
1980	160	612	185	29	7	11	79	91	60	66	36	.302
1981	107	409	109	16	5	13	53	55	35	49	5	.267
1982	155	570	157	27	2	9	62	68	60	67	21	.275
1983	160	594	189	28	8	14	85	92	65	86	30	.318
1984	160	600	187	28	13	12	96	95	73	68	22	.312
1985	141	544	163	34	4	9	69	79	43	74	16	.300
1986	141	479	133	22	4	10	48	72	55	86	3	.278
1987	126	365	88	17	4	11	47	38	36	65	4	.241
1988 NY / A	38	80	16	2	0	1	9	7	8	8	0	.200
19 yrs	2353	7917	2251	391	94	165	1036	1077	898	1031	317	.284
DIVISIONAL PLAYOFF SERIES												
1981 Hou / N	5	20	6	1	0	0	0	0	1	3	1	.300
LEAGUE CHAMPIONSHIP SERIES												
1980 Hou / N	5	15	6	1	1	0	3	4	8	1	0	.400
1986	6	26	5	0	0	0	0	2	1	8	0	.192
2 yrs	11	41	11	1	1	0	3	6	9	9	0	.268

Minnie Miñoso

- Born November 29, 1922, Havana, Cuba
- Debut date: April 19, 1949
- Named American League Rookie of the Year, 1951, by *The Sporting News*
- Played in all eight All-Star games in seven years for the American League (1951–1960) and batted .300
- Led American League in triples, 1951, 1954, and 1956
- Led American League in stolen bases, 1951, 1952, and 1953
- Led American League in doubles, 1957
- Led American League in hits, 1960
- Awarded Gold Glove for fielding, 1957, 1959, and 1960
- The only major league player to play in five decades (1940s–1980s)

		G	AB	H	2B	3B	HR	R	RBI	BB	SO	SB	BA
1949	Cle / A	9	16	3	0	0	1	2	1	2	2	0	.188
1951	2 teams		Cle / A	(8 games; .429)			Chi / A	(138 games; .324)					
total		146	530	173	34	14	10	112	76	72	42	31	.326
1952	Chi / A	147	569	160	24	9	13	96	61	71	46	22	.281
1953		157	556	174	24	8	15	104	104	74	43	25	.313
1954		153	568	182	29	18	19	119	116	77	46	18	.320
1955		139	517	149	26	7	10	79	70	76	43	19	.288
1956		151	545	172	29	11	21	106	88	86	40	12	.316
1957		153	568	176	36	5	12	96	103	79	54	18	.310
1958	Cle / A	149	556	168	25	2	24	94	80	59	53	14	.302
1959		148	570	172	32	0	21	92	92	54	46	8	.302
1960	Chi / A	154	591	184	32	4	20	89	105	52	63	17	.311
1961		152	540	151	28	3	14	91	82	67	46	9	.280
1962	StL / N	39	97	19	5	0	1	14	10	7	17	4	.196
1963	Was / A	109	315	72	12	2	4	38	30	33	38	8	.229
1964	Chi / A	30	31	7	0	0	1	4	5	5	3	0	.226
1976		3	8	1	0	0	0	0	0	0	2	0	.125
1980		2	2	0	0	0	0	0	0	0	0	0	.000
17 yrs		1841	6579	1963	336	83	186	1136	1023	814	584	205	.298

Mike Cuellar

- Born May 8, 1937, Las Villas, Cuba
- Debut date: April 18, 1959
- Pitched for the National League All-Star team, 1967, without decsion
- Pitched for the American League All-Star team, 1971, without decision
- Co-winner of the 1969 Cy Young Award
- Led the American League in wins, 1969
- Led the American League in winning percentage, 1970 and 1974
- Led the American League in starts, 1969
- Led the American League in complete games, 1969

	W	L	PCT	ERA	G	GS	CG	IP	H	BB	SO	ShO
1959 Cin / N	0	0		15.75	2	0	0	4	7	4	5	0
1964 StL / N	5	5	.500	4.50	32	7	1	72	80	33	56	0
1965 Hou / N	1	4	.200	3.54	25	4	0	56	55	21	46	0
1966	12	10	.545	2.22	38	28	11	227.1	193	52	175	1
1967	16	11	.593	3.03	36	32	16	246.1	233	63	203	3
1968	8	11	.421	2.74	28	24	11	170.2	152	45	133	2
1969 Bal / A	23	11	.676	2.38	39	39	18	290.2	213	79	82	5
1970	24	8	.750	3.47	40	40	21	298	273	69	190	4
1971	20	9	.690	3.08	38	38	21	292	250	78	124	4
1972	18	12	.600	2.57	35	35	17	248.1	197	71	132	4
1973	18	13	.581	3.27	38	38	17	267	265	84	140	2
1974	22	10	.688	3.11	38	38	20	269	253	86	106	5
1975	14	12	.538	3.66	36	36	17	256	229	84	105	5
1976	4	13	.235	4.96	26	19	2	107	129	50	32	1
1977 Cal / A	0	1	.000	18.90	2	1	0	3.1	9	3	3	0
15 yrs	185	130	.587	3.14	453	379	172	2807.2	2538	822	1632	36

LEAGUE CHAMPIONSHIP SERIES

	W	L	PCT	ERA	G	GS	CG	IP	H	BB	SO	ShO
1969 Bal / A	0	0		2.25	1	1	0	8	3	1	7	0
1970	0	0		12.46	1	1	0	4.1	10	1	2	0
1971	1	0	1.000	1.00	1	1	1	9	6	1	2	0
1973	0	1	.000	1.80	1	1	1	10	4	3	11	0
1974	1	1	.500	2.84	2	2	0	12.2	9	13	6	0
5 yrs	2	2	.500	3.07	6	6	2	44	32	19	28	0

WORLD SERIES

	W	L	PCT	ERA	G	GS	CG	IP	H	BB	SO	ShO
1969 Bal / A	1	0	1.000	1.13	2	2	1	16	13	4	13	0
1970	1	0	1.000	3.18	2	2	1	11.1	10	2	5	0
1971	0	2	.000	3.86	2	2	0	14	11	6	10	0
3 yrs	2	2	.500	2.61	6	6	2	41.1	34	12	28	0

Dolf Luque

- Born August 4, 1890, Havana, Cuba. Died July 3, 1957, Havana, Cuba
- Debut date: May 20, 1914
- Led the National League in shutouts, 1921, 1923, and 1925
- Led the National League in losses, 1922
- Led National League in wins, 1923
- Led National League in ERA, 1923 and 1925
- Led National League in winning percentage, 1923

	W	L	PCT	ERA	G	GS	CG	IP	H	BB	SO	ShO
1914 Bos / N	0	1	.000	4.15	2	1	1	8.2	5	4	1	0
1915	0	0		3.60	2	1	0	5	6	4	3	0
1918 Cin / N	6	3	.667	3.80	12	10	9	83	84	32	26	1
1919	9	3	.750	2.63	30	9	6	106	89	36	40	2
1920	13	9	.591	2.51	37	23	10	207.2	168	60	72	1
1921	17	19	.472	3.38	41	36	25	304	318	64	102	3
1922	13	23	.361	3.31	39	32	18	261	266	72	79	0
1923	27	8	.771	1.93	41	37	28	322	279	88	151	6
1924	10	15	.400	3.16	31	28	13	219.1	229	53	86	2
1925	16	18	.471	2.63	36	36	22	291	263	78	140	4
1926	13	16	.448	3.43	34	30	16	233.2	231	77	83	1
1927	13	12	.520	3.20	29	27	17	230.2	225	56	76	2
1928	11	10	.524	3.57	33	29	11	234.1	254	84	72	1
1929	5	16	.238	4.50	32	22	8	176	213	56	43	1
1930 Bkn / N	14	8	.636	4.30	31	24	16	199	221	58	62	2
1931	7	6	.538	4.56	19	15	5	102.2	122	27	25	0
1932 NY / N	6	7	.462	4.01	38	5	1	110	128	32	32	0
1933	8	2	.800	2.69	35	0	0	80.1	75	19	23	0
1934	4	3	.571	3.83	26	0	0	42.1	54	17	12	0
1935	1	0	1.000	0.00	2	0	0	3.2	1	1	2	0
20 yrs	193	179	.519	3.24	550	365	206	3220.1	3231	918	1130	26

WORLD SERIES

	W	L	PCT	ERA	G	GS	CG	IP	H	BB	SO	ShO
1919 Cin / N	0	0		0.00	2	0	0	5	1	0	6	0
1933 NY / N	1	0	1.000	0.00	1	0	0	4.1	2	2	5	0
2 yrs	1	0	1.000	0.00	3	0	0	9.1	3	2	11	0

Pedro Guerrero

- Born June 29, 1956, San Pedro de Macorís, Dominican Republic
- Debut date: September 22, 1978
- Played in all four All-Star games for the National League (1981–1989) and batted .000. Replaced for 1985 game because of injury
- Led National League in doubles, 1989
- Co-winner of 1981 World Series MVP Award
- Holds National League record for most home runs, month of June (15 in 1985)

	G	AB	H	2B	3B	HR	R	RBI	BB	SO	SB	BA
1978 LA / N	5	8	5	0	1	0	3	1	0	0	0	.625
1979	25	62	15	2	0	2	7	9	1	14	2	.242
1980	75	183	59	9	1	7	27	31	12	31	2	.322
1981	98	347	104	17	2	12	46	48	34	57	5	.300
1982	150	575	175	27	5	32	87	100	65	89	22	.304
1983	160	584	174	28	6	32	87	103	72	110	23	.298
1984	144	535	162	29	4	16	85	72	49	105	9	.303
1985	137	487	156	22	2	33	99	87	83	68	12	.320
1986	31	61	15	3	0	5	7	10	2	19	0	.246
1987	152	545	184	25	2	27	89	89	74	85	9	.338
1988 2 teams		LA / N	(59 games; .298)				StL / N (44 games; .268)					
total	103	364	104	14	2	10	40	65	46	59	4	.286
1989	162	570	177	42	1	17	60	117	79	84	2	.311
1990	136	498	140	31	1	13	42	80	44	70	1	.281
13 yrs	1378	4819	1470	249	27	206	679	812	561	1352	91	.305

DIVISIONAL PLAYOFF SERIES

	G	AB	H	2B	3B	HR	R	RBI	BB	SO	SB	BA
1981 LA / N	5	17	3	1	0	1	1	1	2	4	1	.176

LEAGUE CHAMPIONSHIP SERIES

	G	AB	H	2B	3B	HR	R	RBI	BB	SO	SB	BA
1981 LA / N	5	19	2	0	0	1	1	2	1	4	0	.105
1983	4	12	3	1	1	0	1	2	3	3	0	.250
1985	6	20	5	1	0	0	2	4	5	2	2	.250
3 yrs	15	51	10	2	1	1	4	8	9	9	2	.196

WORLD SERIES

	G	AB	H	2B	3B	HR	R	RBI	BB	SO	SB	BA
1981 LA / N	6	21	7	1	1	2	2	7	2	6	0	.333

Felipe Alou

- Born May 12, 1935, Haina, Dominican Republic
- Debut date: June 8, 1958
- Brothers Matty and Jesús also played Major League Baseball
- Played in two All-Star games for the National League (1962–1968) and batted .000 (0 for 0) with one RBI. He was selected for the 1966 All-Star Game, but did not play
- Led National League in hits, 1966 and 1968
- Led National League in runs, 1966
- Led National League in at-bats, 1966 and 1968

	G	AB	H	2B	3B	HR	R	RBI	BB	SO	SB	BA
1958 SF / N	75	182	46	9	2	4	21	16	19	34	4	.253
1959	95	247	68	13	2	10	38	33	17	38	5	.275
1960	106	322	85	17	3	8	48	44	16	42	10	.264
1961	132	415	120	19	0	18	59	52	26	41	11	.289
1962	154	561	177	30	3	25	96	98	33	66	10	.316
1963	157	565	159	31	9	20	75	82	27	87	11	.281
1964 Mil / N	121	415	105	26	3	9	60	51	30	41	5	.253
1965	143	555	165	29	2	23	80	78	31	63	8	.297
1966 Atl / N	154	666	218	32	6	31	122	74	24	51	5	.327
1967	140	574	157	26	3	15	76	43	32	50	6	.274
1968	160	662	210	37	5	11	72	57	48	56	12	.317
1969	123	476	134	13	1	5	54	32	23	23	4	.282
1970 Oak / A	154	575	156	25	3	8	70	55	32	31	10	.271
1971 2 teams		Oak / A	(2 games; .250)		NY / A	(131 games; .289)						
total	133	469	135	21	6	8	52	69	32	25	5	.288
1972 NY / A	120	324	90	18	1	6	33	37	22	27	1	.278
1973 2 teams		NY / A	(93 games; .236)		Mon / N	(19 games; .208)						
total	112	328	76	13	0	5	29	31	11	29	0	.232
1974 Mil / A	3	3	0	0	0	0	0	0	0	2	0	.000
17 yrs	2082	7339	2101	359	49	206	985	852	423	706	107	.286
LEAGUE CHAMPIONSHIP SERIES												
1969 Atl / N	1	1	0	0	0	0	0	0	0	0	0	.000
WORLD SERIES												
1962 SF / N	7	26	7	1	1	0	2	1	1	4	0	.269

Bert Campaneris

- Born March 9, 1942, Pueblo Nuevo, Cuba
- Debut date: July 23, 1964
- First player to play all nine positions in a nine inning game, September 8, 1965
- Tied major league record with two home runs in first game in majors, July 23, 1964, including first pitch of the game
- Played in five All-Star games for the American League (1968–1977)and batted .182. Also named a member of the 1972 American League All-Star team but did not play
- Led American League in stolen bases, 1965, 1966, 1967, 1968, 1970, and 1972
- Led American League in triples, 1965
- Led American League in hits, 1968
- Led American League in at-bats, 1968 and 1972

		G	AB	H	2B	3B	HR	R	RBI	BB	SO	SB	BA
1964	KC / A	67	269	69	14	3	4	27	22	15	41	10	.257
1965		144	578	156	23	12	6	67	42	41	71	51	.270
1966		142	573	153	29	10	5	82	42	25	72	52	.267
1967		147	601	149	29	6	3	85	32	36	82	55	.248
1968	Oak / A	159	642	177	25	9	4	87	38	50	69	62	.276
1969		135	547	142	15	2	2	71	25	30	62	62	.260
1970		147	603	168	28	4	22	97	64	36	73	42	.279
1971		134	569	143	18	4	5	80	47	29	64	34	.251
1972		149	625	150	25	2	8	85	32	32	88	52	.240
1973		151	601	150	17	6	4	89	46	50	79	34	.250
1974		134	527	153	18	8	2	77	41	47	81	34	.290
1975		137	509	135	15	3	4	69	46	50	71	24	.265
1976		149	536	137	14	1	1	67	52	63	80	54	.256
1977	Tex / A	150	552	140	19	7	5	77	46	47	86	27	.254
1978		98	269	50	5	3	1	30	17	20	36	22	.186
1979	2 teams	Tex / A (8 games; .111)				Cal / A	(85 games; .234)						
total		93	248	57	4	4	0	29	15	20	35	13	.230
1980	Cal / A	77	210	53	8	1	2	32	18	14	33	10	.252
1981		55	82	21	2	1	1	11	10	5	10	5	.256
1983	NY / A	60	143	46	5	0	0	19	11	8	9	6	.322
19 yrs		2328	8684	2249	313	86	79	1181	646	618	1142	649	.259

LEAGUE CHAMPIONSHIP SERIES

		G	AB	H	2B	3B	HR	R	RBI	BB	SO	SB	BA
1971	Oak / A	3	12	2	1	0	0	0	0	0	1	0	.167
1972		2	7	3	0	0	0	3	0	1	0	2	.429
1973		5	21	7	1	0	2	3	3	2	2	3	.333
1974		4	17	3	0	0	0	0	3	0	3	1	.176
1975		3	11	0	0	0	0	1	0	1	1	0	.000
1979	Cal / A	1	0	0	0	0	0	0	0	0	0	0	
6 yrs		18	68	15	2	0	2	7	6	4	7	6	.221

WORLD SERIES

		G	AB	H	2B	3B	HR	R	RBI	BB	SO	SB	BA
1972	Oak / A	7	28	5	0	0	0	1	0	1	4	0	.179
1973		7	31	9	0	1	1	6	3	1	7	3	.290
1974		5	17	6	2	0	0	1	2	0	2	1	.353
3 yrs		19	76	20	2	1	1	8	5	2	13	4	.263

Fernando Valenzuela

- Born November 1, 1960, Navajoa, Sonora, Mexico
- Debut date: September 15, 1980
- Elected National League Rookie of the Year, 1981
- Elected National League Cy Young Award winner, 1981
- Pitched 6-0 no-hitter over the St. Louis Cardinals on June 29, 1990
- Led National League in complete games, 1981, 1986, and 1987
- Led National League in shutouts, 1981
- Led National League in strikeouts, 1981
- Led National League in innings pitched, 1981
- Led National League in walks, 1984 and 1987
- Led National League in victories, 1986
- Pitched in five All-Star games for National League (1981–1986) with no decisions and 0.00 ERA. Named to 1983 team but did not pitch. Shares All-Star record for most consecutive strikeouts (five in 1986)
- Awarded Gold Glove for fielding, 1986

	W	L	PCT	ERA	G	GS	CG	IP	H	BB	SO	ShO
1980 LA / N	2	0	1.000	0.00	10	0	0	18	8	5	16	0
1981	13	7	.650	2.48	25	25	11	192	140	61	180	8
1982	19	13	.594	2.87	37	37	18	285	247	83	199	4
1983	15	10	.600	3.75	35	35	9	257	245	99	189	4
1984	12	17	.414	3.03	34	34	12	261	218	106	240	2
1985	17	10	.630	2.45	35	35	14	272.1	211	101	208	5
1986	21	11	.656	3.14	34	34	20	269.1	226	85	242	3
1987	14	14	.500	3.98	34	34	12	251	254	124	190	1
1988	5	8	.385	4.24	23	22	3	142.1	142	76	64	0
1989	10	13	.435	3.43	31	31	3	196.2	185	98	116	0
1990	13	13	.500	4.59	33	33	5	204	223	77	115	2
11 yrs	141	116	.549	3.31	331	320	107	2348.2	2099	915	1759	29
DIVISIONAL PLAYOFF SERIES												
1981 LA / N	1	0	1.000	1.06	2	2	1	17	10	3	10	0
LEAGUE CHAMPIONSHIP SERIES												
1981 LA / N	1	0	.500	2.45	2	2	0	14.2	10	5	10	0
1983	1	0	1.000	1.13	1	1	0	8	7	4	5	0
1985	1	0	1.000	1.88	2	2	0	14.1	11	10	13	0
3 yrs	3	1	.750	1.95	5	5	0	37	28	19	28	0
WORLD SERIES												
1981 LA / N	1	0	1.000	4.00	1	1	1	9	9	7	6	0

Rico Carty

- Born September 1, 1939, San Pedro de Macorís, Dominican Republic
- Debut date: September 15, 1963
- Played in one All-Star Game for the National League (1970) and was hitless in his only at-bat. First player to start an All-Star Game from write-in ballots
- Led National League in batting average, 1970

		G	AB	H	2B	3B	HR	R	RBI	BB	SO	SB	BA
1963	Mil / N	2	2	0	0	0	0	0	0	0	2	0	.000
1964		133	455	150	28	4	22	72	88	43	78	1	.330
1965		83	271	84	18	1	10	37	35	17	44	1	.310
1966	Atl / N	151	521	170	25	2	15	73	76	60	74	4	.326
1967		134	444	113	16	2	15	41	64	49	70	4	.255
1969		104	304	104	15	0	16	47	58	32	28	0	.342
1970		136	478	175	23	3	25	84	101	77	46	1	.366
1972		86	271	75	12	2	6	31	29	44	33	0	.277
1973	3 teams	Tex / A (86 games; .232)					Chi / N (22 games; .214)			Oak / A (7 games; .250)			
	total	115	384	88	13	0	5	29	42	44	50	2	.229
1974	Cle / A	33	91	33	5	0	1	6	16	5	9	0	.363
1975		118	383	118	19	1	18	57	64	45	31	2	.308
1976		152	552	171	34	0	13	67	83	67	45	1	.310
1977		127	461	129	23	1	15	50	80	56	51	1	.280
1978	2 teams	Tor / A (104 games; .284)					Oak / A (41 games; .277)						
	total	145	528	149	21	1	31	70	99	57	57	1	.282
1979	Tor / A	132	461	118	26	0	12	48	55	46	45	3	.256
	15 yrs	1651	5606	1677	278	17	204	712	890	642	663	21	.299
LEAGUE CHAMPIONSHIP SERIES													
1969	Atl / N	3	10	3	2	0	0	4	0	3	1	0	.300

Manny Sanguillen

- Born March 21, 1944, Colón, Panama
- Debut date: July 23, 1967
- Played in 1972 All-Star Game for the National League and had one hit in two at-bats (.500). Named to 1971 and 1975 National League All-Star teams, but did not play

	G	AB	H	2B	3B	HR	R	RBI	BB	SO	SB	BA
1967 Pit / N	30	96	26	4	0	0	6	8	4	12	0	.271
1969	129	459	139	21	6	5	62	57	12	48	8	.303
1970	128	486	158	19	9	7	63	61	17	45	2	.325
1971	138	533	170	26	5	7	60	81	19	32	6	.319
1972	136	520	155	18	8	7	55	71	21	38	1	.298
1973	149	589	166	26	7	12	64	65	17	29	2	.282
1974	151	596	171	21	4	7	77	68	21	27	2	.287
1975	133	481	158	24	4	9	60	58	48	31	5	.328
1976	114	389	113	16	6	2	52	36	28	18	2	.290
1977 Oak / A	152	571	157	17	5	6	42	58	22	35	2	.275
1978 Pit / N	85	220	58	5	1	3	15	16	9	10	2	.264
1979	56	74	17	5	2	0	8	4	2	5	0	.230
1980	47	48	12	3	0	0	2	2	3	1	3	.250
13 yrs	1448	5062	1500	205	57	65	566	585	223	331	35	.296

LEAGUE CHAMPIONSHIP SERIES

	G	AB	H	2B	3B	HR	R	RBI	BB	SO	SB	BA
1970 Pit / N	3	12	2	0	0	0	0	0	0	1	0	.167
1971	4	15	4	0	0	0	1	1	1	1	1	.267
1972	5	16	5	1	0	1	4	2	0	0	0	.313
1974	4	16	4	1	0	0	0	0	0	0	0	.250
1975	3	12	2	0	0	0	0	0	0	0	0	.167
5 yrs	19	71	17	2	0	1	5	3	1	2	1	.239

WORLD SERIES

	G	AB	H	2B	3B	HR	R	RBI	BB	SO	SB	BA
1971 Pit / N	7	29	11	1	0	0	3	0	0	3	2	.379
1979	3	3	1	0	0	0	0	1	0	0	0	.333
2 yrs	10	32	12	1	0	0	3	1	0	3	2	.375

APPENDIX B

Statistical Records of Latin
Americans Who Have Played
Major League Baseball

I. PLAYERS

Legend

G	Games
AB	At-bats
H	Hits
BA	Batting Average
P	Position(s)
T	Team(s)

Acosta, Mérito (brother of José)   b. May 19, 1896, Havana, Cuba
G: 175 / AB: 435 / H: 111 / BA: .255 / P: OF / T: Wash-A ; Phi-A

Aguayo, Luís   b. Mar 13, 1959, Vega Baja, Puerto Rico
G: 568; /AB: 1104 / H: 260 /BA: .236 / P: IF / T: Phil-N; NY-A; Cle-A

Alcaraz, Luís   b. Jun 20, 1941, Hummacao, Puerto Rico
G: 115 / AB: 365 / H: 70 / BA: .192 / P: IF / T: LA-N; KC-A

Alicea, Luís   b. Jul 29, 1965, Santurce, Puerto Rico
G: 93 / AB: 297 / H: 63 / BA: .212 / P: 2B / T: StL-N; Was-A

Almada, Mel   b. Feb 7, 1913, Hwatabampo, Sonora, Mexico
G: 646 / AB: 2483 / H: 706 / BA: .284 / P: OF / T: Bos-A, Was-A, StL-A, Bkn-N

Almeida, Rafael   b. Jul 30, 1887, Havana, Cuba
G: 102 / AB: 285 / H: 77 / BA: .270 / P: 3B; IF / T: Cin-N

Alomar, Roberto (son of Sandy)   b. Feb 5, 1968, Ponce, Puerto Rico
G: 448 / AB: 1754 / H: 497 / BA: .283 / P: 2B / T: SD-N

Alomar, Sandy, Sr. (father of Sandy & Roberto)   b. Oct 19, 1943, Salinas, Puerto Rico
G: 1481 / AB: 4760 / H: 1168 / BA: .245 / P: 2B / T: Mil-N; Atl-N; NYM-N; Chi-A; Cal-A; NY-A; Tex-A

Alomar, Sandy, Jr. (son of Sandy)   b. Jun 18, 1966, Salinas, Puerto Rico
G: 140 / AB: 465 / H: 133 / BA: .286 / P: C / T: SD-N; Cle-A

Alou, Felipe (brother of Jesús & Matty)   b. May 12, 1935, Haina, D.R.
G: 2082 / AB: 7339 / H: 2101 / BA: .286 / P: OF; 1B / T: SF-N; Mil-N; Atl-N; Oak-A; NY-A; Mon-A; Mil-A

Alou, Jesús (brother of Matty & Felipe)   b. Mar 24, 1942, Haina, D.R.
G: 1380 / AB: 4345 / H: 1216 / BA: .280 / P: OF / T: SF N; Hou N; Oak-A; NY-N

Alou, Matty (brother of Felipe & Jesús)   b. Dec 22, 1938, Haina, D.R.
G: 1667 / AB: 5789 / H: 1777 / BA: .307 / P: OF / T: SF-N; Pit-N; StL-N; Oak-A; NY-A; SD-N

Alvarado, Luís   b. Jan 15, 1949, Las Jas, Puerto Rico
G: 463 / AB: 1160 / H: 248 / BA: .214 / P: IF / T: Bos-A; Chi-A; StL-N; Cle-A; NY-N; Det-A

Alvarez, Orlando   b. Feb 28, 1952, Rio Grande, Puerto Rico
G: 25 / AB: 51 / H: 8 / BA: .157 / P: OF / T: LA-N; Cal-A

Alvarez, Ossie   b. Oct 19, 1933, Matanzas, Cuba
G: 95 / AB: 198 / H: 42 / BA: .212 / P: IF / T: Was-A; Det-A

Alvarez, Rogelio   b. Apr 18, 1938, Pinar Del Rio, Cuba
G: 17 / AB: 37 / H: 7 / BA: .189 / P: 1B / T: Cin-N

Amaro, Ruben   b. Jan 6, 1936, Veracruz, Mexico
G: 940 / AB: 2155 / H: 505 / BA: .234 / P: IF / T: StL-N; Phi-N; NY-A; Cal-A

Amoros, Sandy   b. Jan 30, 1930, Havana, Cuba
G: 517 / AB: 1311 / H: 334 / BA: .255 / P: OF / T: Bkn-N; LA-N; Det-A

Aparicio, Luís   b. Apr 29, 1934, Maracaibo, Venezuela
G: 2599 / AB: 10230 / H: 2677 / BA: .262 / P: SS / T: Chi-A; Bal-A; Bos-A

Aragón, Angel   b. Aug 2, 1893, Havana, Cuba
G: 33 / AB: 79 / H: 9 / BA: .114 / P: IF; OF / T: NY-A

Aragón, Jack   b. Nov 20, 1915, Havana, Cuba
G: 1 / AB: 0 / H: 0 / BA: .000 / P: R / T: NYG-N

Arcia, José   b. Aug 22, 1943, Havana, Cuba
G: 293 / AB: 615 / H: 132 / BA: .215 / P: IF / T: Chi-N; SD-N

Armas, Tony   b. Jul 2, 1953, Anzoatequi, Venezuela
G: 1432 / AB: 5164 / H: 1302 / BA: .252 / P: OF; DH/ T: Oak-A; Bos-A; Cal-A

Avila, Bobby   b. Apr 2, 1924, Veracruz, Mexico
G: 1300 / AB: 4620 / H: 1296 / BA: .281 / P: 2B / T: Cle-A; Bal-A; Bos-A; Mil-N

Aviles, Ramon   b. Jan 22, 1952, Manati, Puerto Rico
G: 117 / AB: 190 / H: 51 / BA: .268 / P: IF / T: Bos-A; Phi-N

Ayala, Benny   b. Feb 7, 1951, Yauco, Puerto Rico
G: 425 / AB: 865 / H: 217 / BA: .251 / P: OF; DH / T: NY-N; Bal-A; Cle-A

Azcue, Joe   b. Aug 18, 1939, Cienfuegos, Cuba
G: 909 / AB: 2828 / H: 712 / BA: .252 / P: C / T: Cin-N; KC-A; Cle-A; Cal-A ; Mil-A

Azocar, Oscar   b. Feb 21, 1965, Caracas, Venezuela
G: 65 / AB: 214 / H: 53 / BA: .248 / P: OF / T: NY-A

Baez, José   b. Dec 31, 1953, San Cristobal, D.R.
G: 114 / AB: 355 / H: 87 / BA: .245 / P: 2B / T: Sea-A

Baerga, Carlos   b. Nov 4, 1968, San Juan, Puerto Rico
G: 108 / AB: 312 / H: 81 / BA: .260 / P: 2B; 3B / T: Cle-A

Barranca, Germán   b. Oct 19, 1956, Veracruz, Mexico
G: 67 / AB: 62 / H: 18 / BA: .290 / P: IF / T: KC-A; Cin-N

Batista, Rafael   b. Oct 20, 1947, San Pedro de Macoris, D.R.
G: 22 / AB: 25 / H: 7 / BA: .280 / P: 1B / T: Hou-N

Becquer, Julio   b. Dec 20, 1931, Havana, Cuba
G: 488/ AB: 974 / H: 238 / BA: .244 / P: 1B / T: Was-A; LA-A; Min-A

Bell, George   b. Oct 21, 1959, San Pedro de Macoris, D.R.
G: 1181 / AB: 4528 / H: 1294 / BA: .286 / P: OF; DH / T: Tor-A

Bell, Juan   b. Mar 29, 1968, San Pedro de Macoris, D.R.
G: 13 / AB: 6 / H: 0 / BA: .000 / P: SS / T: Bal-A

Bellán, Esteban   b. 1850, Cuba
G: 59 / AB: 288 / H: 68 / BA: .236 / P: IF / T: Troy-NA; NYM-NA

Belliard, Rafael   b. Oct 24, 1961, Pueblo Nuevo, Mao, D.R.
G: 484 / AB: 1051 / H: 229 / BA: .218 / P: SS; 2B / T: Pit-N

Beníquez, Juan   b. May 13, 1950, San Sebastian, Puerto Rico
G: 1500 / AB: 4651 / H: 1274 / BA: .274 / P: OF; DH / T: Bos-A; Tex-A; NY-A; Sea-A; Cal-A; Bal-A; KC-A; Tor-A

Bernazard, Tony   b. Aug 24, 1956, Caguas, Puerto Rico
G: 1065 / AB: 3688 / H: 968 / BA: .262 / P: 2B / T: Mon-N; Chi-A; Sea-A; Cle-A; Oak-A

Bernhardt, Juan   b. Aug 31, 1953, San Pedro de Macoris, D.R.
G: 154 / AB: 492 / H: 117 / BA .238 / P: IF; DH / T: NY-A; Sea-A

Bernier, Carlos   b. Jan 28, 1929, Juana Diaz, Puerto Rico
G: 105 / AB: 310 / H: 66 / BA: .213 / P: OF / T: Pit-N

Berróa, Gerónimo   b. Mar 18, 1965, Santo Domingo, D.R.
G: 88 / AB: 140 / H: 36 / BA: .257 / P: OF / T: Atl-N

Blanco, Dámaso   b. Dec 11, 1941, Curiepe, Venezuela
G: 72 / AB: 33 / H: 7 / BA: .212 / P: IF / T: SF-N

Bonilla, Juan   b. Jan 12, 1956, Santurce, Puerto Rico
G: 429 / AB: 1462 /H: 375 / BA: .256 / P: 2B / T: SD-N; NY-A; Bal-A

Bravo, Angel   b. Aug 4, 1942, Maracaibo, Venezuela
G: 149 / AB: 218 / H: 54 / BA: .248 / P: OF / T: Chi-A; Cin-N; SD-N

Cabrera, Francisco   b. Oct 10, 1966, Santo Domingo, D.R.
G: 70 / AB: 163 / H: 43 / BA: .264 / P: C; 1B / T: Tor-A; Atl-N

Calderón, Iván   b. Mar 19, 1962, Fajardo, Puerto Rico
G: 660 / AB: 2433 / H: 665 / BA: .273 / P: OF / T: Sea-A; Chi-A

Calvo, Jack   b. Jun 11, 1894, Havana, Cuba
G: 33 / AB: 56 / H: 9 / BA: .161 / P: OF / T: Was-A

Campaneris, Bert   b. Mar 9, 1942, Pueblo Nuevo, Cuba
G: 2328 / AB: 8684 / H: 2249 / BA: .259 / P: SS / T: KC-A; Oak-A; Tex-A; Cal-A; NY-A

Campos, Frank   b. May 11, 1924, Havana, Cuba
G: 71 / AB: 147 / H: 41 / BA: .279 / P: OF / T: Was-A

Campusano, Sil   b. Dec 31, 1965, Mano Guayabo, D.R.
G: 139 / AB: 227 / H: 49 / BA: .216 / P: OF / T: Tor-A; Phi-N

Canseco, José   (brother of Ozzie)   b. Jul 2, 1964, Havana, Cuba
G: 699 / AB: 2644 / H: 715 / BA: .270 / P: OF / T: Oak-A

Canseco, Ozzie   (brother of José)   b. Jul 2, 1964, Havana, Cuba
G: 9 / AB: 19 / H: 2 / BA: .105 / P: OF / T: Oak-A

Cardenal, José   Oct 7, 1943, Matanzas, Cuba
G: 2017 / AB: 6964 / H: 1913 / BA: .275 / P: OF / T: Cal-A; Cle-A; StL-N; Chi-N

Cárdenas, Leo   Dec 17, 1938, Matanzas, Cuba
G: 1941 / AB: 6707 / H: 1725 / BA: .257 / P: SS / T: Cin-N; Min-A; Cal-A; Tex-A

Carew, Rod   b. Oct 1, 1945, Gatun, Panama
G: 2469 / AB: 9315 / H: 3053 / BA: .328 / P: 1B; 2B / T: Min-A; Cal-A

Carrasquel, Chico   b. Jan 23, 1926, Caracas, Venezuela
G: 1325 / AB: 4644 / H: 1199 / BA: .258 / P: SS / T: Chi-A; Cle-A; KC-A; Bal-A

Carty, Rico   b. Sep 1, 1939, San Pedro de Macoris, D.R.
G: 1651 / AB: 5606 / H: 1677 / BA: .299 / P: OF; DH / T: Mil-N; Atl-N; Tex-A; Chi-N; Oak-A; Cle-A; Tor-A

Casanova, Paul   b. Dec 21, 1941, Colon, Matanzas, Cuba
G: 859 / AB: 2786 / H: 627 / BA: .225 / P: C / T: Was A; Atl-N

Castillo, Carmen   b. Jun 8, 1958, San Pedro de Macoris, D.R.
G: 622 / AB: 1507 / H: 381 / BA: .253 / P: OF; DH / T: Cle-A; Min-A

Castillo, Juan   b. Jan 25, 1962, San Pedro de Macoris, D.R.
G: 199 / AB: 469 / H: 101 / BA: .215 / P: IF / T: Mil-A

Castillo, Manny   b. Apr 1, 1957, Santo Domingo, D.R.
G: 236 / AB: 719 / H: 174 / BA: .242 / P: 3B / T: KC-A; Sea-A

Castro, Louis   b. 1877, Cartagena, Colombia
G: 42 / AB: 143 / H: 35 / BA: .245 / P: 2B / T: Phi-A

Cedeño, Andujar   b. Aug 21, 1969, La Romana, D.R.
G: 7 / AB: 8 / H: 0 / BA: .000 / P: SS / T: Hou-N

Cedeño, César   b. Feb 25, 1951, Santo Domingo, D.R.
G: 2006 / AB: 7310 / H: 2087 / BA: .285 / P: OF / T: Hou-N; Cin-N; StL-N; LA-N

Cepeda, Orlando   b. Sep 17, 1937, Ponce, Puerto Rico
G: 2124 / AB: 7927 / H: 2351 / BA: .297 / P: 1B; OF; DH/ T: SF-N; StI-N; Atl-N; Oak-A; Bos-A; KC-A

Chacon, Elio   b. Oct 26, 1936, Caracas, Venezuela
G: 228 / AB: 616 / H: 143 / BA: .232 / P: IF / T: Cin-N; NY-N

Chavarría, Ossie   b. Aug 5, 1940, Colon, Panama
G: 124 / AB: 250 / H: 52 / BA: .208 / P: IF / T: KC-A

Clemente, Roberto   b. Aug 18, 1934, Carolina, Puerto Rico
G: 2433 / AB: 9454 / H: 3000 / BA: .317 / P: OF / T: Pit-N

Concepción, David   b. Jun 17, 1948, Aragua, Venezuela
G: 2488 / AB: 8723 / H: 2326 / BA: .267 / P: SS / T: Cin-N

Concepción, Onix   b. Oct 5, 1957, Dorado, Puerto Rico
G: 390 / AB: 1041 / H: 249 / BA: .239 / P: SS; 2B / T: KC-A; Pit-N

Conde, Ramón   b. Dec 29, 1934, Juana Diaz, Puerto Rico
G: 14 / AB: 16 / H: 0 / BA: .000 / P: 3B / T: Chi-A

Cora, Joey   b. May 14, 1965, Caguas, Puerto Rico
G: 140 / AB: 360 / H: 90 / BA: .250 / P: 2B; SS / T: SD-N

Cruz, Hector "Heity"   (brother of José & Tommy)   b. Apr 2, 1953, Arroyo, Puerto Rico
G: 624 / AB: 1607 / H: 361 / BA: .225 / P: OF; 3B / T: StL-N; Chi-N; SF-N; Cin-N

Cruz, José   (brother of Hector & Tommy)   b. Aug 8, 1947, Arroyo, Puerto Rico
G: 2353 / AB: 7917 / H: 2251 / BA: .284 / P: OF / T: StL-N; Hou-N; NY-A

Cruz, Tommy   (brother of José & Hector)   b. Feb 15, 1951, Arroyo, Puerto Rico
G: 7 / AB: 2 / H: 0 / BA: .000 / P: OF / T: StL-N; Chi-A

Cueto, Manuel   b. Feb 8, 1892, Guanajay, Cuba
G: 150 / AB: 379 / H: 86 / BA: .227 / P: OF; IF / T: StL-N; Cin-N

Davalillo, Pompeyo   (brother of Vic)   b. Jun 30, 1931, Caracas, Venezuela
G: 19 / AB: 58 / H: 17 / BA: .293 / P: SS / T: Was-A

Davalillo, Vic   (brother of Pompeyo)   b. Jul 31, 1936, Cabimas, Venezuela
G:1458 / AB: 4017 / H: 1122 / BA: .279 / P: OF / T: Cle-A; Cal-A; StL-N; Pit-N; Oak-A; LA-N

DeFreitas, Art   b. Apr 26, 1953, San Pedro de Macoris, D.R.
G: 32 / AB: 53 /H: 11 / BA: .208 / P: 1B / T: Cin-N

DeJesús, Iván   b. Jan 9, 1953, Santurce, Puerto Rico
G: 1371 / AB: 4602 / H: 1167 / BA: .254 / P: SS / T: LA-N; Chi-N; Phi-N; StL-N; NY-A; SF-N; Det-A

de la Hoz, Mike   b. Oct 2, 1938, Havana, Cuba
G: 494 / AB: 1114 / H: 280 / BA: .251 / P: IF / T: Cle-A; Mil-N; Atl-N

de la Rosa, Jesus   b. Jul 28, 1953, Santo Domingo, D.R.
G: 3 / AB: 3 / H: 1 / BA: .333 / P: PH / T: Hou-N

Delgado, Luís   b. Feb 2, 1954, Hatillo, Puerto Rico
G: 13 / AB: 22 / H: 4 / BA: .182 / P: OF / T: Sea-A

Delis, Juan   b. Feb 27, 1928, Santiago, Cuba
G: 54 / AB: 132 / H: 25 /BA: .189 /P: 3B /T: Was-A

de los Santos, Luís   b. Dec 29, 1966, San Cristobal, D.R.
G: 39 / AB: 109 / H: 24 / BA: .220 / P: 1B / T: KC-A

Destrade, Orestes   b. May 8, 1962, Santiago, Cuba
G: 45 / AB: 66 / H: 12 / BA: 182 / P: 1B / T: NY-A; Pit-N

Díaz, Bo   b. Mar 23, 1953, Cua, Venezuela
G: 993 / AB: 3274 / H: 834 / BA: .255 / P: C / T: Bos-A; Cle-A; Phi-N; Cin-N

Díaz, Edgar   b. Feb 8, 1964, Santurce, Puerto Rico
G: 91 / AB: 231 / H: 62 / BA: .268 / P: SS / T: Mil-A

Díaz, Mario   b. Jan 10, 1962, Humacao, Puerto Rico
G: 107 / AB: 191 / H: 42 / BA: .220 / P: SS / T: Sea-A; NY-N

Diloné, Miguel   b. Nov 1, 1954, Santiago, D.R.
G: 800 / AB: 2000 / H: 530 / BA: .265 / P: OF / T: Pit-N; Oak-A; Chi-N; Cle-A; Chi-A; Pit-N; Mon-N;
SD-N

Duncan, Mariano   b. Mar 13, 1963, San Pedro de Macoris, D.R.
G: 546 / AB: 1923 / H: 483 / BA: .251 / P: SS; 2B / T: LA-N; Cin-N

Escalera, Nino   b. Dec 1, 1929, Santurce, Puerto Rico
G: 73 / AB: 69 / H: 11 / BA: .159 / P: OF / T: Cin-N

Escobar, Angel   b. May 12, 1965, La Sabana, Venezuela
G: 3 / AB: 3 / H: 1 / BA: .333 / P: IF / T: SF-N

Espino, Juan   b. Mar 16, 1956, Bonao, D.R.
G: 49 / AB: 73 / H: 16 / BA: .219 / P: C / T: NY-A

Espinoza, Alvaro   b. Feb 19, 1962, Valencia, Venezuela
G: 369 / AB: 1043 / H: 264 / BA: .253 / P: SS / T: Min-A; NY-A

Estalella, Bobby   b. Apr 25, 1911, Cardenas, Cuba
G: 680 / AB: 2196 / H: 620 / BA: .282 / P: OF / T: Was-A; StL-A; Phi-A

Estrada, Francisco   b. Feb 12, 1948, Navojoa, Mexico
G: 1 / AB: 2 / H: 1 / BA: .500 / P: C / T: NY-N

Félix, Junior   b. Oct 3, 1967, Laguna Sabada, D.R.
G: 237 / AB: 878 / H: 229 / BA: .261 / P: OF / T: Tor-A

Fermín, Félix   b. Oct 9, 1963, Mao Valverde, D.R.
G: 370 / AB: 1053 / H: 262 / BA: .249 / P: SS / T: Pit-N; Cle-A

Fernández, Chico   b. Mar 2, 1932, Havana, Cuba
G: 856 / AB: 2778 / H: 666 / BA: .240 / P: SS / T: Bkn-N; Phi-N; Det-A; NY-N

Fernández, Chico   b. Apr 23, 1939, Havana, Cuba
G: 24 / AB: 18 / H: 2 / BA: .111 / P: IF / T: Bal-A

Fernández, Tony   b. Aug 6, 1962, San Pedro de Macoris, D.R.
G: 1028 / AB: 3952 / H: 1142 / BA: .289 / P: SS / T: Tor-A

Ferrer, Sergio   b. Jan 29, 1951, Santurce, Puerto Rico
G: 125 / AB: 178 / H: 43 / BA: .242 / P: SS / T: Min-A; NY-N

Figueroa, Jesús   b. Feb 20, 1957, Santo Domingo, D.R.
G: 115 / AB: 198 / H: 50 / BA: .253 / P: OF / T: Chi-N

Fleitas, Angel   b. Nov 10, 1914, Los Abreus, Cuba
G: 15 / AB: 13 / H: 1 / BA: .077 / P: SS / T: Was-A

Flores, Gil   b. Oct 27, 1952, Ponce, Puerto Rico
G: 185 / AB: 464 / H: 121 / BA: .261 / P: OF / T: Cal-A; NY-N

Franco, Julio   b. Aug 23, 1958, Hato Mayor, D.R.
G: 1221 / AB: 4720 / H: 1404 / BA: .297 / P:SS; 2B / T: Phi-N; Cle-A; Tex-A

Frías, Pepe   b. Jul 14, 1948, San Pedro de Macoris, D.R.
G: 723 / AB: 1346 / H: 323 / BA: .240 / P: SS; 2B / T: Mon-N; Atl-N; Tex-A; LA-N

Fuentes, Tito   b. Jan 4, 1944, Havana, Cuba
G: 1499 / AB: 5566 / H: 1491 / BA: .268 / P: 2B / T: SF-N; SD-N; Det-A; Oak-A

Galarraga, Andrés   Jun 18, 1961, Caracas, Venezuela
G: 740 / AB: 2707 / H: 748 / BA: .276 / P: 1B / T: Mon-N

Garbey, Bárbaro   b. Dec 4, 1956, Santiago, Cuba
G: 226 / AB: 626 / H: 167 / BA: .267 / P: 1B; OF / T: Det-A; Tex-A

García, Carlos   b. Oct 15, 1967, Tachira, Venezuela
G: 4 / AB: 4 / H: 2 / BA: .500 / P: SS / T: Pit-N

García, Chico   b. Dec 24, 1924, Veracruz, Mexico
G: 39 / AB: 62 / H: 7 / BA: .113 / P: 2B / T: Bal-A

García, Dámaso   b. Feb 7, 1957, Moca, D.R.
G: 1032 / AB: 3914 / H: 1108 / BA: .283 / P: 2B / T: NY-A; Tor-A; Atl-N; Mon-N

García, Leo   b. Nov 6, 1962, Santiago, D.R.
G: 54 / AB: 58 / H: 10 / BA: .172 / P: OF / T: Cin-N

García, Pedro   b. Apr 17, 1950, Guayama, Puerto Rico
G: 558 / AB: 1797 / H: 395 / BA: .220 / P: 2B / T: Mil-A; Det-A; Tor-A

Garrido, Gil   b. Jun 26, 1941, Panama City, Panama
G: 334 / AB: 872 / H: 207 / BA: .237 / P: IF / T: SF-N; Atl-N

Gerónimo, César   b. Mar 11, 1948, El Seibo, D.R.
G: 1522 / AB: 3780 / H: 977 / BA: .258 / P: OF / T: Hou-N; Cin-N; KC-A

Gil, Gus   b. Apr 19, 1939, Caracas, Venezuela
G: 221 / AB: 468 / H: 87 / BA: .186 / P: IF / T: Cle-A; Sea-A; Mil-A

Gómez, Chile   b. Mar 23, 1909, Villa Union, Mexico
G: 200 / AB: 627 / H: 142 / BA: .226 / P: IF / T: Phi-N; Was-A

Gómez, Leo   b. Mar 2, 1967, Canovanas, P.R.
G: 12 / AB: 39 / H: 9 / BA: .231 / P: 3B / T: Bal-A

Gómez, Luís   b. Aug 19, 1951, Guadalajara, Mexico
G: 609 / AB: 1251 / H: 263 / BA: .210 / P: SS / T: Min-A; Tor-A; Atl-N

Gómez, Preston   b. Apr 20, 1923, Central Preston, Cuba
G: 8 / AB: 7 / H: 2 / BA: .286 / P: IF / T: Was-A

González, Denny   b. Jul 22, 1963, Sabana Grande Boya, D.R.
G: 98 / AB: 262 / H: 54 / BA: .206 / P: IF / T: Pit-N; Cle-A

González, Eusebio   b. Jul 13, 1892, Havana, Cuba
G: 2 / AB: 2 / H: 1 / BA: .500 / P: SS / T: Bos-A

González, Fernando   b. Jun 19, 1950, Arecibo, Puerto Rico
G: 404 / AB: 1038 / H: 244 / BA: .235 / P: 2B / T: Pit-N; KC-A; NY-A; SD-N

González, José   b. Nov 23, 1964, Puerto Plata, D.R.
G: 337 / AB: 504 / H: 121 / BA: .240 / P: OF / T: LA-N

González, Juan   b. Oct 20, 1969, Vega Baja, Puerto Rico
G: 49 / AB: 150 / H: 35 / BA: .233 / P: OF / T: Tex-A

González, Julio   b. Dec 25, 1952, Caguas, Puerto Rico
G: 370 / AB: 969 / H: 228 / BA: .235 / P: IF / T: Hou-N; StL-N; Det-A

González, Mike   b. Sep 24, 1890, Havana, Cuba
G: 1042 / AB: 2829 / H: 717 / BA: .253 / P: C / T: Bos-N; Cin-N; StL-N; NYG-N; Chi-N

González, Orlando   b. Nov 15, 1951, Havana, Cuba
G: 79 / AB: 164 / H: 39 / BA: .238 / P: 1B; OF / T: Cle A; Phi N; Oak-A

González, Pedro   b. Dec 12, 1937, San Pedro de Macoris, D.R.
G: 407 / AB: 1084 / H: 264 / BA: .244 / P: IF / T: NY A; Cle A

González, Tony   b. Aug 28, 1936, Central Cunagua, Cuba
G: 1559 / AB: 5195 / H: 1485 / BA: .286 / P: OF / T: Cin-N; Phi-N; SD-N; Atl-N; Cal-A

Gotay, Julio   b. Jun 9, 1939, Fajardo, Puerto Rico
G: 389 / AB: 988 / H: 257 / BA: .260 / P: IF / T: StL-N; Pit-N; Cal-A; Hou-N

Green, David   b. Dec 4, 1960, Managua, Nicaraqua
G: 489 / AB: 1398 / H: 374 / BA: .268 / P: OF; 1B / T: StL-N; SF-N

Griffin, Alfredo   Oct 6, 1957, Santo Domingo, D.R.
G: 1744 / AB: 6185 / H: 1548 / BA: .250 / P: SS / T: Cle-A; Tor-A; Oak-A; LA-N

Guerra, Mike   b. Oct 11, 1912, Havana, Cuba
G: 565 / AB: 1581 / H: 382 / BA: .242 / P: C / T: Was-A; Phi-A; Bos-A

Guerrero, Mario   b. Sep 28, 1949, Santo Domingo, D.R.
G: 697 / AB: 2251 / H: 578 / BA: .257 / P: SS / T: Bos-A; StL-N; Cal-A; Oak-A

Guerrero, Pedro   b. Jun 29, 1956, San Pedro de Macoris, D.R.
G: 1378 / AB: 4819 / H: 1470 / BA: .305 / P: OF; 3B; 1B / T: LA-N; StL-N

Guillén, Ozzie   b. Jan 20, 1964, Oculare del Tuy, Venezuela
G: 929 / AB: 3277 / H: 870 / BA: .265 / P: SS / T: Chi-A

Gutiérrez, César   b. Jan 26, 1943, Coro, Venezuela
G: 223 / AB: 545 / H: 128 / BA: .235 / P: SS / T: SF-N; Det-A

Gutiérrez, Jackie   b. Jun 27, 1960, Cartagena, Colombia
G: 356 / AB: 957 / H: 227 / BA: .237 / P: SS / T: Bos-A; Bal-A; Phi-N

Hermoso, Angel   b. Oct 1, 1947, Carabobo, Venezuela
G: 91 / AB: 223 / H: 47 / BA: .211 / P: IF / T: Atl-N; Mon-N; Cle-A

Hernández, Carlos   b. May 24, 1967, San Felix, Bolivar, Venezuela
G: 10 / AB: 20 / H: 4 / BA: .200 / P: c / T: LA-N

Hernández, Enzo   b. Feb 12, 1949, Valle de Guanape, Venezuela
G: 714 / AB: 2327 / H: 522 / BA: .224 / P: SS / T: SD N; LA-N

Hernández, Jackie   b. Sep 11, 1940, Central Tinguaro, Cuba
G: 618 / AB: 1480 / H: 308 / BA: .208 / P: SS / T: Cal-A; Min-A; KC-A; Pit-N

Hernández, Leo   b. Nov 6, 1959, Santa Lucia, Venezuela
G: 85 / AB: 249 / H: 56 / BA: .226 / P: 3B /T: Bal-A; NY-A

Hernández, Pedro   b. Apr 4, 1959, La Romana, D.R.
G: 11 / AB: 9 / H: 0 / BA: .000 / P: DH / T: Tor-A

Hernández, Rudy   b. Oct 18, 1951, Empalme, Mexico
G: 8 / AB: 21 / H: 4 / BA: .190 / P: SS / T: Chi-A

Hernández, Sal   b. Jan 3, 1916, Havana, Cuba
G: 90 / AB: 244 / H: 61 / BA: .250 / P: C / T: Chi-N

Hernández, Toby   b. Nov 30, 1958, Calabozo, Venezuela
G: 3 / AB: 2 / H: 1 BA: .500 / P: C / T: Tor-A

Herrera, José   b. Apr 08, 1942, San Lorenzo, Venezuela
G: 80 / AB: 231 / H: 61 / BA: .264 / P: OF / T: Hou-N; Mon-N

Herrera, Mike   b. Dec 19, 1897, Havana, Cuba
G: 84 / AB: 276 / H: 76 / BA: .275 / P: IF / T: Bos-A

Herrera, Pancho   b. Jun 16, 1934, Santiago, Cuba
G: 300 / AB: 975 / H: 264 / BA: .271 / P: 1B / T: Phi-N

Infante, Alexis   b. Dec 4, 1961, Barquisimeto, Venezuela
G: 60 / AB: 55 / H: 6 / BA: .109 / P: IF / T: Tor-A: Atl-N

Isales, Orlando   b. Dec 22, 1959, Santurce, Puerto Rico
G: 3 / AB: 5 / H: 2 / BA: .400 / P: OF / T: Phi N

Izquierdo, Hank   b. Mar 20, 1931, Matanzas, Cuba
G: 16 / AB: 26 / H: 7 / BA: .269 / P: C / T: Min-A

Javier, Alfredo   b. Feb 4, 1954, San Pedro de Macoris, D.R.
G: 8 / AB: 24 / H: 5 / BA: .208 / P: OF / T: Hou-N

Javier, Julian   (father of Stan)   b. Aug 9, 1936, San Francisco de Macoris, D.R.
G: 1622 / AB: 5722 / H: 1469 / BA: .257 / P: 2B / T: StL-N; Cin-N

Javier, Stan   (son of Julian)   b. Sep 1, 1965, San Francisco de Macoris, D.R.
G: 507 / AB: 1288 / H: 323 / BA: .251 / P: OF / T: NY-A; Oak-A; LA-N

Jiménez, Elvio   (brother of Manny)   b. Jan 6, 1940, San Pedro de Macoris, D.R.
G: 1 / AB: 6 / H: 2 / BA: .333 / P: OF / T: NY A

Jiménez, Houston   b. Oct 30, 1957, Navojoa, Sonora, Mexico
G: 158 / AB: 411 / H: 76 / BA: .185 / P: SS / T: Min-A; Pit-N; Cle-A

Jiménez, Manny   (brother of Elvio)   b. Nov 19, 1938, San Pedro de Marcoris, D.R.
G: 429 / AB: 1003 / H: 273 / BA: .272 / P: OF / T: KC-A; Pit-N; Chi-N

José, Félix   b. May 8, 1965, Santo Domingo, D.R.
G: 154 / AB: 489 / H: 126 / BA: .258 / P: OF / T: Oak-A; StL-N

Joseph, Rick   b. Aug 24, 1939, Santa Fe, D.R.
G: 270 / AB: 633 / H: 154 / P: 1B; 3B; OF / T: KC-A; Phi-N

Kelly, Roberto   b. Oct 1, 1964, Panama City, Panama
G: 360 / AB: 1211 / H: 349 / BA: .288 / P: OF / T: NY-A

Laboy, Coco   b. Jul 3, 1940, Ponce, Puerto Rico
G: 420 / AB: 1247 / H: 291 / BA: .233 / P: 3B / T: Mon-N

Landestoy, Rafael   b. May 28, 1953, Bani, D.R.
G: 596 / AB: 1230 / H: 291 / BA: .237 / P: IF / T: LA-N; Hou-N; Cin-N;

Lee, Manny   b. Jun 17, 1965, San Pedro de Macoris, D.R.
G: 487 / AB: 1311 / H: 339 / BA: .259 / P: IF / T: Tor-A

Lewis, Allan   b. Dec 12, 1941, Colon, Panama
G: 156 / AB: 29 / H: 6 / BA: .207 / P: OF; PR / T: KC-A; Oak-A

Lezcano, Carlos   b. Sep 30, 1955, Arecibo, Puerto Rico
G: 49 / AB: 102 / H: 19 / BA: .186 / OF / T: Chi-N

Lezcano, Sixto   b. Nov 28, 1953, Arecibo, Puerto Rico
G: 1291 / AB: 4134 / H: 1122 / BA: .271 / P: OF / T: Mil-A; StL-N; SD-N; Phi-N; Pit-N

Librán, Francisco   b. May 6, 1948, Mayaguez, Puerto Rico
G: 10 / AB: 10 / H: 1 / BA: .100 / P: SS / T: SD-N

Linares, Rufino   b. Feb 28, 1951, Santo Domingo, D.R.
G: 207 / AB: 545 / H: 147 / BA: .270 / P: OF / T: Atl-N; Cal-A

Lind, José   b. May 1, 1964, Toabaja, Puerto Rico
G: 494 / AB: 1846 / H: 474 / BA: .257 / P: 2B / T: Pit-N

Liriano, Nelson   b. Jun 3, 1964, Santo Domingo, D.R.
G: 371 / AB: 1207 / H: 304 / BA: .252 / P: 2B / T: Tor-A; Min-A

Llenas, Winston   Sep 23, 1943, Santiago, D.R.
G: 300 / AB: 531 / H: 122 / BA: .230 / P: IF; OF / T: Cal-A

Lois, Alberto   May 6, 1956, Hato Mayor, D.R.
G: 14 / AB: 4 / H: 1 / BA: .250 / P: OF / T: Pit-N

López, Arturo   b. Jun 8, 1937, Mayaguez, Puerto Rico
G: 38 / AB: 49 / H: 7 / BA: .143 / P: OF / T: NY-A

López, Carlos   Sep 27, 1950, Mazatlan, Mexico
G: 237 / AB: 500 / H: 130 / BA: .260 / P: OF / T: Cal-A; Sea-A; Bal-A

López, Hector   b. Jul 9, 1929, Colon, Panama
G: 1450 / AB: 4644 / H: 1251 / BA: .269 / P: OF; IF / T: KC-A; NY-A

Maldonado, Candy   b. Sep 5, 1960, Humacao, Puerto Rico
G: 973 / AB: 2826 / H: 723 / BA: .256 / P: OF/ T: LA-N; SF-N; Cle-A

Mangual, Angel   (brother of Pepe)   b. Mar 19, 1947, Juana Diaz, Puerto Rico
G: 450 / AB: 1241 / H: 304 / BA: .245 / P: OF / T: Pit-N; Oak-A

Mangual, Pepe   (brother of Angel)   b. May 23, 1952, Ponce, Puerto Rico
G: 319 / AB: 972 / H: 235 / BA: .242 / P: OF / T: Mon-N; NY-N

Manrique, Fred   b. May 11, 1961, Edo Bolivar, Venezuela
G: 489 / AB: 1316 / H: 337 / BA: .256 / P: IF / T: Tor A; Mon-N; StL-N; Chi A; Tex A; Min-A

Mantilla, Félix   b. Jul 29, 1934, Isabela, Puerto Rico
G: 969 / AB: 2707 / H: 707 / BA: .261 / P: IF; OF / T: Mil-N; NY-A; Bos-A; Hou-N

Márquez, Gonzalo   b. Mar 31, 1946, Carupano, Venezuela
G: 76 / AB: 115 / H: 27 / BA: .235 / P: 1B / T: Oak-A; Chi-N

Márquez, Luís   b. Oct 28, 1925, Aguadilla, Puerto Rico
G: 99 / AB: 143 / H: 26 / BA: .182 / P: OF / T: Bos-N; Chi-N; Pit-N

Marsans, Armando   b. Oct 3, 1887, Matanzas, Cuba
G: 655 / AB: 2273 / H: 612 / BA: .269 / P: OF / T: Cin-N; StL-F; StL-A; NY-A

Martínez, Carlos   b. Aug 11, 1964, La Guiara, Venezuela
G: 218 / AB: 677 / H: 175 / BA: .258 / P: IF; OF / T: Chi-A

Martínez, Carmelo   b. Jul 28, 1960, Dorado, Puerto Rico
G: 895 / AB: 2631 / H: 652 / BA: .248 / P: OF; 1B / T: Chi-N; SD-N; Phi-N; Pit-N

Martínez, Hector   b. May 11, 1939, Las Villas, Cuba
G: 7 / AB: 15 / H: 4 / BA: .267 / P: OF / T: KC-A

Martínez, José   b. Jul 26, 1942, Cardenas, Cuba
G: 96 / AB: 188 / H: 46 / BA: .245 / P: IF / T: Pit-N

Martínez, Marty   b. Aug 23, 1941, Havana, Cuba
G: 436 / AB: 945 / H: 230 / BA: .243 / P: IF / T: Min-A; Atl-N; Hou-N; StL-N; Oak-A; Tex-A

Martínez, Teddy   b. Dec 10, 1947, Barahona, D.R.
G: 657 / AB: 1480 / H: 355 / BA: .240 / P: IF / T: NY-N; StL-N; Oak-A; LA-N

Martínez, Tony   b. Mar 18, 1941, Perico, Cuba
G: 73 / AB: 175 / H: 30 / BA: .171 / P: IF / T: Cle-A

Mata, Victor   b. Jun 17, 1961, Santiago, D.R.
G: 36 / AB: 77 / H: 24 / BA: .312 / P: OF / T: NY-A

McFarlane, Orlando   b. Jun 28, 1938, Oriente, Cuba
G: 124 / AB: 292 / H: 70 / BA: .240 / P: C / T: Pit-N; Det-A; Cal-A

Mejías, Roman   b. Aug 9, 1930, Abreus, Cuba
G: 627 / AB: 1768 / H: 449 / BA: .254 / P: OF / T: Pit N; Hou N; Bos A

Mejías, Sam   b. May 9, 1952, Santiago, D.R.
G: 334 / AB: 348 / H: 86 / BA: .247 / P: OF / T: StL-N; Mon-N; Chi-N; Cin-N

Meléndez, Francisco   b. Jan 25, 1964, Rio Piedras, Puerto Rico
G: 74 / AB: 84 / H: 18 / BA: .214 / P: 1B / T: Phi N; SF N; Bal A

Meléndez, Luís   b. Aug 11, 1949, Aibonito, Puerto Rico
G: 641 / AB: 1477 / H: 366 / BA: .248 / P: OF / T: StL N; SD N

Mendoza, Mario   b. Dec 26, 1950, Chihuahua, Mexico
G: 686 / AB: 1337 / H: 287 / BA: .215 / P: SS / T: Pit-N; Sea-A; Tex-A

Mendoza, Minnie   b. Nov 16, 1933, Ceiba Del Agua, Cuba
G: 16 / AB: 16 / H: 3 / BA: .188 / P: IF / T: Min-A

Mercado, Orlando   b. Nov 7, 1961, Arecibo, Puerto Rico
G: 253 / AB: 562 / H: 112 / BA: .199 / P: C / T: Sea-A; Tex-A; Det-A; LA-N; Oak-A; Min-A; Mon-N

Merced, Orlando   b. Nov 2, 1966, San Juan, Puerto Rico
G: 25 / AB: 24 / H: 5 / BA: .208 / P: 1B; OF / T: Pit-N

Millán, Félix   b. Aug 21, 1943, Yabucoa, Puerto Rico
G: 1480 / AB: 5791 / H: 1617 / BA: .279 / P: 2B / T: Atl-N; NY-N

Miñoso, Minnie   b. Nov 29, 1922, Havana, Cuba
G: 1841 / AB: 6579 / H: 1963 / BA: .298 / P: OF / T: Cle-A; Chi-A; StL-N; Was-A

Miranda, Willie   b. May 24, 1926, Velasco, Cuba
G: 824 / AB: 1914 / H: 423 / BA: .221 / P: SS / T: Was-A; Chi-A; StL-N; NY-A; Bal-A

Montañez, Willie   b. Apr 1, 1948, Catano, Puerto Rico
G: 1632 / AB: 5843 / H: 1604 / BA: .275 / P: 1B; OF / T: Cal-A; Phi-N; SF-N; Atl-N; NY-N; Tex-A;
SD-N; Mon-N; Pit-N

Monteagudo, Rene   b. Mar 12, 1916, Havana, Cuba
G: 156 / AB: 270 / H: 78 / BA: .289 / P: P; OF / T: Was-A; Phi-N

Montemayor, Felipe   b. Feb 7, 1930, Monterrey, Mexico
G: 64 / AB: 150 / H: 26 / BA: .173 / P: OF / T: Pit-N

Mora, Andrés   b. May 25, 1955, Rio Bravo, Mexico
G: 235 / AB: 700 / H: 156 / BA: .223 / P: OF / T: Bal-A; Cle-A

Morales, Jerry   b. Feb 18, 1949, Yabucoa, Puerto Rico
G: 1441 / AB: 4528 / H: 1173 / BA: .259 / P: OF / T: SD-N; Chi-N; StL-N; Det-A; NY-N

Morejón, Dan   b. Jul 21, 1930, Havana, Cuba
G: 12 / AB: 26 / H: 5 / BA: .192 / P: OF / T: Cin-N

Moreno, José   b. Nov 1, 1957, Santo Domingo, D.R.
G: 82 / AB: 97 / H: 20 / BA: .206 / P: OF; IF / T: NY-N; SD-N; Cal-A

Moreno, Omar   b. Oct 24, 1952, Puerto Armuelles, Panama
G: 1382 / AB: 4992 / H: 1257 / BA: .252 / P: OF / T: Pit N; Hou-N; NY-A; KC-A; Atl-N

Mota, Manny   b. Feb 18, 1938, Santo Domingo, D.R.
G: 1536 / AB: 3779 / H: 1149 / BA: .304 / P: OF / T: SF-N; Pit-N; Mon-N; LA-N

Muñoz, Pedro   b. Sep 19, 1968, Ponce, Puerto Rico
G: 22 / AB: 85 / H: 23 / BA: .271 / P: OF / T: Min-A

Murrell, Iván   b. Apr 24, 1945, Almirante, Panama
G: 564 / AB: 1306 / H: 308 / BA: .236/ P: OF; 1B / T: Hou-N; SD-N; Atl-N

Noble, Ray   b. Mar 15, 1919, Central Hatillo, Cuba
G: 107 / AB: 243 / H: 53 / BA: .218 / P: C / T: NY-N; NYG-N

Noboa, Junior   b. Nov 10, 1964, Azua, D.R.
G: 185 / AB: 309 / H: 75 / BA: .243 / P: IF / T: Cle-A; Cal-A; Mon-N

Norman, Nelson   b. May 23, 1958, San Pedro de Macoris, D.R.
G: 198 / AB: 429 / H: 95 / BA: .221 / P: SS / T: Tex-A; Pit-N; Mon-N

Offerman, José   b. Nov 8, 1968, San Pedro de Macoris, D.R.
G: 29 / AB: 58 / H: 9 / BA: .155 / P: SS / T: LA-N

Oglivie, Ben   b. Feb 11, 1949, Colon, Panama
G: 1754 / AB: 5913 / H: 1615 / BA: .273 / P: OF; DH / T: Bos-A; Det-A; Mil-A

Oliva, Tony   b. Jul 20, 1940, Pinar del Rio, Cuba
G: 1676 / AB: 6301 / H: 1917 / BA: .304 / P: OF; DH / T: Min-A

Olivares, Edward   b. Nov 5, 1938, Mayaguez, Puerto Rico
G: 24 / AB: 35 / H: 5 / BA: .143 / P: OF / T: StL-N

Olmo, Luís   Aug 11, 1919, Arecibo, Puerto Rico
G: 462 / AB: 1629 / H: 458 / BA: .281 / P: OF; IF / T: Bkn-N; Bos-N

Oquendo, José   b. Jul 4, 1963, Rio Peidras, Puerto Rico
G: 860 / AB: 2379 / H: 629 / BA .264 / P: IF; OF / T: NY-N; StL-N

Ordenana, Tony   b. Oct 30, 1918, Guanabacoa, Cuba
G: 1 / AB: 4 / H: 2 / BA: .500 / P: SS / T: Pit-N

Orta, Jorge   b. Nov 26, 1950, Mazatlan, Mexico
G: 1755 / AB: 5829 / H: 1619 / BA: .278 / P: IF; OF; DH / T: Chi-A; Cle-A; LA-N; Tor-A; KC-A

Ortiz, José   b. Jun 25, 1947, Ponce, Puerto Rico
G: 67 / AB: 123 / H: 37 / BA: .301 / P: OF / T: Chi-A; Chi-N

Ortiz, Junior   b. Oct 24, 1959, Humacao, Puerto Rico
G: 478 / AB: 1191 / H: 319 / BA: .268 / P: C / T: Pit-N; NY-N; Min-A

Ortiz, Roberto   (brother of Baby)   b. Jun 30, 1915, Camaguey, Cuba
G: 213 / AB: 659 / H: 168 / BA: .255 / P: OF / T: Was-A; Phi-A

Otero, Reggie   b. Sep 7, 1915, Havana, Cuba
G: 14 / AB: 23 / H: 9 / BA: .391 / P: 1B / T: Chi-N

Pagán, José   b. May 5, 1935, Barceloneta, Puerto Rico
G: 1326 / AB: 3689 / H: 922 / BA: .250 / P: IF / T: SF-N; Pit-N; Phi-N

Palmeiro, Rafael   b. Sep 24, 1964, Havana, Cuba
G: 568 / AB: 2031 / H: 602 / BA: .296 / P: OF; 1B /T: Chi-N; Tex-A

Paredes, Johnny   b. Sep 2, 1962, Maracaibo, Venezuela
G: 44 / AB: 105 / H: 20 / BA: .190 / P: 2B / T: Mon-N; Det-A

Parrilla, Sam   b. Jun 12, 1943, Santurce, Puerto Rico
G: 11 / AB: 16 / H: 2 / BA: .125 / P: OF / T: Phi-N

Paula, Carlos   b. Nov 28, 1927, Havana, Cuba
G: 157 / AB: 457 / H: 124 / BA: .271 / P: OF / T: Was-A

Pedrique, Al   b. Aug 11, 1960, Aragua, Venezuela
G: 174 / AB: 449 / H: 111 / BA: .247 / P: IF / T: Pit-N; Det-A

Peña, Bert   b. Jul 11, 1959, Santurce, Puerto Rico
G: 88 / AB: 153 / H: 31 / BA: .203 / P: IF / T: Hou-N

Peña, Geronimo   b. Mar 29, 1967, Santo Domingo, D.R.
G: 18 / AB: 45 / H: 11 / BA: .244 / P: 2B / T: StL-N

Peña, Roberto   b. Apr 17, 1937, Santo Domingo, D.R.
G: 587 / AB: 1907 / H: 467 BA: .245 / P: IF / T: Chi-N; Phi-N; SD-N; Oak-A; Mil-A

Peña, Tony   (brother of Ramón)   b. Jun 4, 1957, Monte Cristi, D.R.
G: 1350 / AB: 4676 / H: 1275 / BA: .273 / P: C / T: Pit-N; StL-N; Bos-A

Pérez, Tony   b. May 14, 1942, Camaguey, Cuba
G: 2777 / AB: 9778 / H: 2732 / BA: .279 / P: IF / T: Cin-N; Mon-N; Bos-A; Phi-N

Perezchica, Tony   b. Apr 20, 1966, Mexicali, Mexico
G: 11 / AB: 11 / H: 2 / BA: .181 / P: 2B / T: SF-N

Phillips, Adolfo   b. Dec 16, 1941, Bethania, Panama
G: 649 / AB: 1875 / H: 463 / BA: .247 / P: OF / T: Phi-N; Chi-N; Mon-N; Cle-A

Polidor, Gus   b. Oct 26, 1961, Caracas, Venezuela
G: 222 / AB: 428 / H: 89 / BA: .208 / P: IF / T: Cal-A; Mil-A

Polonia, Luís   b. Oct 12, 1964, Santiago, D.R.
G: 454 / AB: 1559 / H: 474 / BA: .304 / P: OF / T: Oak-A; NY-A; Cal-A

Ponce, Carlos   b. Feb 7, 1959, Rio Piedras, P.R.
G: 21 / AB: 62 / H: 10 / BA: .161 / P: 1B / T: Mil-A

Posada, Leo   b. Apr 15, 1936, Havana, Cuba
G: 155 / AB: 426 / H: 109 / BA: .256 / P: OF / T: KC -A

Power, Vic   b. Nov 1, 1931, Arecibo, P.R.
G: 1627 / AB: 6046 / H: 1716 / BA: .284 / P: 1B / T: Phi-A; KC-A; Cle-A; Min-A; LA-A; Phi-N; Cal-A

Prescott, Bobby   b. Mar 27, 1931, Colon, Panama
G: 10 / AB: 12 / H: 1 / BA: .083 / P: OF / T: KC-A

Pujols, Luís   b. Nov 18, 1955, Santiago, D.R.
G: 316 / AB: 850 / H: 164 / BA: .193 / P: C / T: Hou-N; KC-A; Tex-A

Quiñones, Luís   b. Apr 28, 1962, Ponce, Puerto Rico
G: 342 / AB: 786 / H: 179 / BA: .228 / P: IF / T: Oak-A; SF-N; Chi-N; Cin-N

Quiñones, Rey   b. Nov 11, 1963, Rio Piedras, Puerto Rico
G: 342 / AB: 1678 / H: 408 / BA: .243 / P: SS / T: Bos-A; Sea-A; Pit-N

Quintana, Carlos   b. Aug 26, 1965, Estado Mirana, Venezuela
G: 188 / AB: 595 / H: 165 / BA: .277 / P: 1B, OF / T: Bos-A

Ramírez, Mario   b. Sep 12, 1957, Yauco, Puerto Rico
G: 184 / AB: 286 / H: 55 / BA: .192 / P: SS / T: NY-N; SD-N

Ramírez, Milt   b. Apr 2, 1950, Mayaguez, Puerto Rico
G: 94 / AB: 152 / H: 28 / BA: .184 / P: IF / T: StL-N; Oak-A

Ramírez, Orlando   b. Dec 18, 1951, Cartagena, Colombia
G: 143 / AB: 281 / H: 53 / BA: .189 / P: SS / T: Cal-A

Ramírez, Rafael   b. Feb 18, 1958, San Pedro de Macoris, D.R.
G: 1365 / AB: 5085 / H: 1333 / BA: .262 / P: SS / T: Atl-N; Hou-N

Ramos, Bobby   b. Nov 5, 1955, Calabazar de Sagua, Cuba
G: 103 / AB: 232 / H: 44 / BA: .190 / P: C / T: Mon-N; NY-N

Ramos, Chucho   b. Apr 12, 1918, Maturin, Venezuela
G: 4 / AB: 10 / H: 5 / BA: .500 / P: OF / T: Cin-N

Ramos, Domingo   b. Mar 29, 1958, Santiago, D.R.
G: 507 / AB: 1086 / H: 261 / BA: .240 / P: IF / T: NY-A; Tor-A; Sea-A; Cle-A; Cal-A; Chi-N

Reyes, Gilberto   b. Dec 10, 1963, Santo Domingo, D.R.
G: 39 / AB: 51 / H: 7 / BA: .137 / P: C / T: LA-N; Mon-N

Reyes, Nap   b. Nov 24, 1919, Santiago, Cuba
G: 279 / AB: 931 / H: 264 / BA: .284 / P: IF / T: NY-N; NYG-N

Ríos, Juan   b. Jul 14, 1945, Mayaguez, Puerto Rico
G: 87 / AB: 196 / H: 44 / BA: .224 /P: IF / T: KC-A

Rivera, Bombo   b. Aug 2, 1952, Ponce, Puerto Rico
G: 335 / AB: 831 / H: 220 / BA: .265 / P: OF / T: Mon-N; Min-A; KC-A

Rivera, Germán   b. Jul 6, 1960, Santurce, Puerto Rico
G: 120 / AB: 280 / H: 72 / BA: .257 / P: 3B / T: LA-N; Hou-N

Rivera, Luís   b. Jan 3, 1964, Cidra, Puerto Rico
G: 407 / AB: 1238 / H: 283 / BA: .229 / P: SS / T: Mon-N; Bos-A

Roberts, Dave   b. Jun 30, 1933, Panama City, Panama
G: 91 / AB: 194 / H: 38 / BA: .196 / P: 1B; OF / T: Hou-N; Pit-N

Robles, Rafael   b. Oct 20, 1947, San Pedro de Macoris, D.R.
G: 47 / AB: 133 / H: 25 / BA: .188 / P: SS / T: SD-N

Robles, Sergio   b. Apr 16, 1946, Magdalena, Mexico
G: 16 / AB: 21 / H: 2 / BA: .095 / P: C / T: Bal-A; LA-N

Rodríguez, Aurelio   b. Dec 28, 1947, Cananea, Sonora, Mexico
G: 2017 / AB: 6611 / H: 1570 / BA: .237 / P: 3B / T: Cal-A; Was-A; Det-A; SD-N; NY-A; Chi-A; Bal-A

Rodríguez, Edwin   b. Aug 14, 1960, Ponce, Puerto Rico
G: 11 / AB: 22 / H: 5 / BA: .227 / P: IF / T: NY-A; SD-N

Rodríguez, Ellie   b. May 24, 1946, Fajardo, Puerto Rico
G: 775 / AB: 2173 / H: 533 / BA: .245 / P: C / T: NY-A; KC-A; Mil-A; Cal-A; LA-N

Rodríguez, Hector b. Jun 13, 1920, Alquizar, Cuba
G: 124 / AB: 407 / H: 108 / BA: .265 / P: 3B / T: Chi-A

Rodríguez, José b. Feb 23, 1894, Havana, Cuba
G: 58 / AB: 145 / H: 24 / BA: .166 / P: IF / T: NYG-N; NY-N

Rodríguez, Rubén b. Aug 4, 1964, Cabrera, D.R.
G: 4 / AB: 8 / H: 1 / BA: .125 / P: C / T: Pit-N

Rojas, Cookie b. Mar 6, 1939, Havana, Cuba
G: 1822 / AB: 6309 / H: 1660 / BA: .263 / P: IF; OF / T: Cin-N; Phi-N; StL-N; KC-A

Romero, Ed b. Dec 9, 1957, Santurce, Puerto Rico
G: 730 / AB: 1912 / H: 473 / BA: .247 / P: IF / T: Mil-A; Bos-A; Atl-N; Mil-A; Det-A

Roque, Jorge b. Apr 28, 1950, Ponce, Puerto Rico
G: 65 / AB: 139 / H: 19 / BA: .137 / P: OF / T: StL-N; Mon-N

Rosado, Luís b. Dec 6, 1955, Santurce, Puerto Rico
G: 11 / AB: 28 / H: 5 / BA: .179 / P: 1B; C / T: NY-N

Rosario, Jimmy b. May 5, 1945, Bayamon, Puerto Rico
G: 114 / AB: 231 / H: 50 / BA: .216 / P: OF / T: SF-N; Mil-A

Rosario, Santiago b. Jul 25, 1939, Guayanilla, Puerto Rico
G: 81 / AB: 85 / H: 20 / BA: .235 / P: 1B; OF / T: KC-A

Rosario, Victor b. Aug 26, 1966, Hato Mayor del Rey, D.R.
G: 9 / AB: 7 / H: 1 / BA: .143 / P: SS / T: Atl-N

Rosello, David b. Jun 25, 1950, Mayaguez, Puerto Rico
G: 422 / AB: 873 / H: 206 / BA: .236 / P: IF / T: Chi-N; Cle-A

Ruiz, Chico b. Dec 5, 1938, Santo Domingo, Cuba
G: 565 / AB: 1150 / H: 276 / BA: .240 / P: IF / T: Cin-N; Cal-A

Ruiz, Chico b. Nov 1, 1951, Santurce, Puerto Rico
G: 43 / AB: 72 / H: 21 / BA: .292 / P: IF / T: Atl-N

Salazar, Angel b. Nov 4, 1961, El Tigre, Venezuela
G: 383 / AB: 886 / H: 188 / BA: .212 / P: SS / T: Mon-N; KC-A; Chi-N

Salazar, Luis b. May 19, 1956, Barcelona, Venezuela
G: 1101 / AB: 3513 / H: 931 / BA: .265 / P: IF; OF / T: SD-N; Chi-A; Det-A; Chi-N

Salmon, Chico b. Dec 3, 1940, Colon, Panama
G: 658 / AB: 1667 / H: 415 / BA: .249 / P: IF; OF / T: Cle-A; Bal-A

Samuel, Amado b. Dec 6, 1938, San Pedro de Macoris, D.R.
G: 144 / AB: 368 / H: 79 / BA: .215 / P: IF / T: Mil-N; NY-N

Samuel, Juan b. Dec 9, 1960, San Pedro de Macoris, D.R.
G: 1081 / AB: 4328 / H: 1116 / BA: .258 / P: 2B; OF / T: Phi-N; NY-N; LA-N

Sánchez, Alejandro b. Feb 14, 1959, San Pedro de Macoris, D.R.
G: 109 / AB: 214 / H: 49 / BA: .229 / P: OF; DH / T: Phi-N; SF-N; Det-A; Min-A; Oak-A

Sánchez, Celerino   b. Feb 3, 1944, Veracruz, Mexico
G: 105 / AB: 314 / H: 76 / BA: .242 / P: IF; DH / T: NY-A

Sánchez, Orlando   b. Sep 7, 1956, Canovanas, Puerto Rico
G: 73 / AB: 110 / H: 24 / BA: .218 / P: C / T: StL-N; KC-A; Bal-A

Sanguillen, Manny   b. Mar 21, 1944, Colon, Panama
G: 1448 / AB: 5062 / H: 1500 / BA: .296 / P: C / T: Pit-N; Oak-A

Santana, Andres   b. Mar 19, 1968, San Pedro de Macoris, D.R.
G: 6 / AB: 2 / H: 0 / BA: .000 / P: SS / T: SF-N

Santana, Rafael   b. Jan 31, 1958, La Romana, D.R.
G: 668 / AB: 2021 / H: 497 / BA: .246 / P: SS / T: StL-N; NY-N; NY-A; Cle-A

Santiago, Benito   b. Mar 9, 1965, Ponce, Puerto Rico
G: 531 / AB: 1906 / H: 506 / BA: .265 / P: C / T: SD-N

Santo Domingo, Rafael   b. Nov 24, 1955, Orocovis, Puerto Rico
G: 7 / AB: 6 / H: 1 / BA: .167 / P: PH / T: Cin-N

Santovenia, Nelson   b. Jul 27, 1961, Pinar del Rio, Cuba
G: 250 / AB: 777 / H: 180 / BA: .232 / P: C / T: Mon-N

Sierra, Rubén   b. Oct 6, 1965, Rio Piedras, Puerto Rico
G: 748 / AB: 2882 / H: 790 / BA: .274 / P: OF / T: Tex-A

Silverio, Luís   b. Oct 23, 1956, Villa Gonzalez, D.R.
G: 8 / AB: 11 / H: 6 / BA: .545 / P: OF / T: KC-A

Silverio, Tom   b. Oct 14, 1945, Santiago, D.R.
G: 31 / AB: 30 / H: 3 / BA: .100 / P: OF / T: Cal-A

Sojo, Luís   b. Jan 3, 1966, Caracas, Venezuela
G: 33 / AB: 80 / H: 18 / BA: .225 / P: IF / T: Tor-A

Sosa, Sammy   b. Nov 10, 1968, San Pedro de Macoris, D.R.
G: 211 / AB: 715 / H: 171 / BA: .239 / P: OF / T: Tex-A; Chi-A

Stennett, Rennie   b. Apr 5, 1951, Colon, Panama
G: 1237 / AB: 4521 / H: 1239 / BA: .274 / P: 2B / T: Pit-N; SF-N

Suarez, Luís   b. Aug 24, 1916, Alto Songo, Cuba
G: 1 / AB: 2 / H: 0 / BA: .000 / P: 3B / T: Was-A

Sutherland, Leo   b. Apr 6, 1958, Santiago, Cuba
G: 45 / AB: 101 / H: 25 / BA: .248 / P: OF / T: Chi-A

Tartabull, Danny   (son of José)   b. Oct 30, 1962, San Juan, Puerto Rico
G: 691 / AB: 2435 / H: 685 / BA: .281 / P: OF; DH / T: Sea-A; KC-A

Tartabull, José   (father of Danny)   b. Nov 27, 1938, Ciefuegos, Cuba
G: 749 / AB: 1857 / H: 484 / BA: .261 / P: OF / T: KC-A; Bos-A; Oak-A

Taveras, Alex   b. Oct 9, 1955, Santiago, D.R.
G: 35 / AB: 53 / H: 11 / BA: .208 / P: IF / T: Hou-N; LA-N

Taveras, Frank b. Dec 24, 1949, Las Matas deSanta Cruz, D.R.
G: 1150 / AB: 4043 / H: 1029 / BA: .255 / P: SS / T: Pit-N; NY-N; Mon-N

Taylor, Tony b. Dec 19, 1935, Central Alara, Cuba
G: 2195 / AB: 7680 / H: 2007 / BA: .261 / P: IF / T: Chi-N; Phi-N; Det-A

Tejada, Wil b. Nov 12, 1962, Santo Domingo, D.R.
G: 18 / AB: 40 / H: 10 / BA: .250 / P: C / T: Mon-N

Thomas, Andres b. Nov 10, 1963, Boca Chica, D.R.
G: 577 / AB: 2103 / H: 493 / BA: .234 / P: SS /T: Atl-N

Thomas, Valmy b. Oct 21, 1928, Santurce, Puerto Rico
G: 252 / AB: 626 /H: 144 / BA: .230 / P: C / T: NY-N; SF-N; Phi-N; Bal-A; Cle-A

Torres, Félix b. May 1, 1932, Ponce, Puerto Rico
G: 365 / AB: 1191 / H: 302 / BA: .254 / P: 3B / T: LA-A

Torres, Gil b. Aug 23, 1915, Regla, Cuba
G: 346 / AB : 1271 / H: 320 / BA: .252 / P: IF / T: Was-A

Torres, Hector b. Sep 16, 1945, Monterrey, Mexico
G: 622 / AB: 1738 / H: 375 / BA: .216 / P: IF / T: Hou-N; Chi-N; Mon-N; SD-N; Tor-A

Torres, Ricardo b. 1894, Havana, Cuba
G: 22 / AB: 37 / H: 11 / BA: .297 / P: C; 1B / T: Was-A

Torres, Rusty b. Sep 30, 1948, Aguadilla, Puerto Rico
G: 654 / AB: 1314 / H: 279 / BA: .212 / P: OF / T: NY-A; Cle-A; Cal-A; Chi-A; KC-A

Tóvar, César b. Jul 3, 1940, Caracas, Venezuela
G: 1488 / AB: 5569 / H: 1546 / BA: .278 / P: OF; IF / T: Min-A; Phi-N; Tex-A; Oak-A; NY-A

Treviño, Alex (brother of Bobby) b. Aug 26, 1957, Monterrey, Mexico
G: 939 / AB: 2430 / H: 604 / BA: .249 / P: C / T: NY-N; Cin-N; Atl-N; SF-N; LA-N; Hou-N; Cin-N

Treviño, Bobby (brother of Alex) b. Aug 15, 1943, Monterrey, Mexico
G: 17 / AB: 40 / H: 9 / BA: .225 / P: OF / T: Cal-A

Trillo, Manny b. Dec 25, 1950, Carapito, Venezuela
G: 1780 / AB: 5950 / H: 1562 / BA: .263 / P: 2B / T: Oak-A; Chi-N; Phi-N; Cle-A; Mon-N; SF-N; Cin-N

Uribe, José b. Jan 21, 1959, San Cristobal, D.R.
G: 829 / AB: 2599 / H: 631 / BA: .243 / P: SS / T: StL-N; SF-N

Valdes, Roy b. Feb 20, 1920, Havana, Cuba
G: 1 / AB: 1 / H: 0 / BA: .000 / P: PH / T: Was-A

Valdespino, Sandy b. Jan 24, 1939, San Jose de las Lajas, Cuba
G: 382 / AB: 765 / H: 176 / BA: .230 / P: OF / T: Min-A; Atl-N; Hou-N; Sea-A; Mil-A; KC-A

Valdez, Julio b. Jun 3, 1956, San Cristobal, D.R.
G: 65 / AB: 87 / H: 18 / BA: .207 / P: SS; 2B / T: Bos-A

Valdivielso, José b. May 22, 1934, Matanzas, Cuba
G: 401 / AB: 971 / H: 213 / BA: .219 / P: SS / T: Was-A; Min-A

Valenzuela, Benny   b. Jun 02, 1933, Los Mochis, Mexico
G: 10 / AB: 14 / H: 3 / BA: .214 / P: 3B / T: StL-N

Valle, Hector   b. Oct 27, 1940, Vega Baja, Puerto Rico
G: 9 / AB: 13 / H: 4 / BA: .308 / P: C / T: LA-N

Vargas, Hedi   b. Feb 23, 1959, Guanica, Puerto Rico
G: 26 / AB: 39 / H: 10 / BA: .256 / P: 1B / T: Pit-N

Vega, Jesús   b. Oct 14, 1955, Bayamon, Puerto Rico
G: 87 / AB: 236 / H: 58 / BA: .246 / P: DH; 1B / T: Min-A

Velázquez, Freddie   b. Dec 6, 1937, Santo Domingo, D.R.
G: 21 / AB: 39 / H: 10 / BA: .256 / P: C / T: Sea-A; Atl-N

Velez, Otto   b. Nov 29, 1950, Ponce, Puerto Rico
G: 637 / AB: 1802 / H: 452 / BA: .251 / P: OF; DH / T: NY-A; Tor-A; Cle-A

Versalles, Zoilo   b. Dec 18, 1939, Havana, Cuba
G: 1400 / AB: 5141 / H: 1246 / BA: .242 / P: SS / T: Was-A; Min-A; LA-N; Cle-A

Vidal, José   b. Apr 3, 1940, Batey Lechugas, D.R.
G: 88 / AB: 146 / H: 24 / BA: .164 / P: OF / T: Cle-A; Sea-A

Villanueva, Hector   b. Oct 2, 1964, San Juan, Puerto Rico
G: 52 / AB: 114 / H: 31 / BA: .272 / P: C; 1B / T: Chi-N

Virgil, Ossie   (father of Ozzie)   b. May 17, 1933, Montecristi, D.R.
G: 324 / AB: 753 / H: 174 / BA: .231 / P: IF; OF; C / T: NY-N; Det-A; KC-A; Bal-A; Pit-N; SF-A

Virgil, Ozzie   (son of Ossie)   b. Dec 7, 1956, Mayaguez, Puerto Rico
G: 739 / AB: 2258 / H: 549 / BA: .243 / P: C / T: Phi-N; Atl-N; Tor-A

Vizcaíno, José   b. Mar 26, 1968, San Cristobal, D.R.
G: 44 / AB: 61 / H: 16 / BA: .262 / P: SS; 2B / T: LA-N

Vizquel, Omar   b. Apr 24, 1967, Caracas, Venezuela
G: 224 / AB: 642 / H: 148 / BA: .231 / P: SS / T: Sea-A

Webster, Ramón   b. Aug 31, 1942 , Colon, Panama
G: 380 / AB: 778 / H: 190 / BA: .244 / P: 1B / T: KC-A; Oak-A; SD-N; Chi-N

Young, Gerald   b. Oct 24, 1964, Tele, Honduras
G: 423 / AB: 1537 / H: 387 / BA: .252 / P: OF / T: Hou-N

II. PITCHERS

Legend

W	Wins
L	Losses
SV	Saves
G	Games Played
IP	Innings Pitched
SO	Strikeouts
ERA	Earned Run Average
T	Team(s)

Acosta, Cy   b. Nov 22, 1946, Sabino, Mexico
W: 13 / L: 9 / SV: 27 / G: 107 / IP: 186 / SO: 109 / ERA: 2.65 / T: Chi-A; Phi-N

Acosta, Ed   b. Mar 9, 1944, Boquete, Panama
W: 6 / L: 9 / SV: 1 / G: 57 / IP: 138 / SO: 70 / ERA: 4.04 / T: Pit-N; SD-N

Acosta José   b. Mar 4, 1891, San Antonio del Rio Blanco, Cuba
W: 10 / L: 10 / SV: 4 / G: 55 / IP: 213 / SO: 45 / ERA: 4.51 / T: Was-A; Chi-A

Agosto, Juan   b. Feb 23, 1958, Rio Pedras, Puerto Rico
W: 33 / L: 26 / SV: 27 / G: 426 / IP: 484 / SO: 245 / ERA: 3.62 / T: Chi-A; Min-A; Hou-N

Alba, Gibson   b. Jan 18, 1960, Santiago, D.R.
W: 0 / L: 0 / SV: 0 / G: 3 / IP: 3 / SO: 3 / ERA: 2.70 T: StL-N

Alcala, Santo   b. Dec 23, 1952, San Pedro de Macoris D.R.
W: 14/ L: 11 / SV: 2 / G: 68 / IP: 249 / SO: 140 / ERA: 4.76 / T: Cin-N; Mon-N

Aloma, Luís   b. Jul 23, 1923, Havana, Cuba
W: 18 / L: 3 / SV: 15 / G: 116 / IP: 235 / SO: 115 / ERA: 3.44 / T: Chi-A

Altamirano, Porfi   b. May 17, 1952, Darillo, Nicaragua
W: 7 / L: 4 / SV: 2 / G: 65 / IP: 91 / SO: 57 / ERA: 4.03 / T: Phi-N; Chi-N

Alvarez, Wilson   b. Mar 24, 1970, Maracaibo, Venezuela
W: 0 / L: 1 / SV: 0 / G: 1 / IP: 0 / SO: 0 / ERA: — / T: Tex-A

Amor, Vincente   b. Aug 8, 1932, Havana, Cuba
W: 1 / L: 3 / SV: 0 / G: 13 / IP: 33 / SO: 12 / ERA: 5.67 / T: Chi-N; Cin-N

Andújar, Joaquín   b. Dec 21, 1952, San Pedro de Macoris, D.R.
W: 127 / L: 118 / SV: 9 / G: 405 / IP: 2153 / SO: 1032 / ERA: 3.58 / T: Hou-N; StL-N; Oak-A

Aponte, Luís   b. Jun 14, 1953, El Tigre, Venezuela
W: 9 / L: 6 / SV: 7 / G: 110 / IP: 220 / SO: 113 / ERA: 3.27 / T: Bos-A; Cle-A

Aquino, Luís   b. May 19, 1964, Santurce, Puerto Rico
W: 12 / L: 10 / SV: 0 / G: 68 / IP: 250 / SO: 112 / ERA: 3.46 / T: Tor-A; KC-A

Arias, Rudy   b. Jun 6, 1931, Las Villas, Cuba
W: 2 / L: 0 / SV: 2 / G: 34 / IP: 44 / SO: 28 / ERA: 4.09 / T: Chi-A

Arroyo, Luís   b. Feb 18, 1927, Penuelas, Puerto Rico
W: 40 / L: 32 / SV: 44 / G: 244 / IP: 531 / SO: 336 / ERA: 3.93 / T: StL-N; Pit-N; Cin-N; NY-A

Barojas, Salomé   b. Jun 16, 1957, Cordoba, Mexico
W: 18 / L: 21 / SV: 35 / G: 179 / IP: 390 / SO: 177 / ERA: 3.95 / T: Chi-A; Sea-A; Phi-N

Barrios, Francisco   b. Jun 10, 1953, Hermosillo, Mexico
W: 38 / L: 38 / SV: 3 / G: 129 / IP: 718 / SO: 323 / ERA: 4.15 / T: Chi-A

Bauta, Ed   b. Jan 6, 1935, Florida, Camaguey, Cuba
W: 6 / L: 6 / SV: 11 / G: 97 / IP: 149 / SO: 89 / ERA: 4.35 / T: StL-N; NY-N

Bautista, José   b. Jul 25, 1964, Bani, D.R.
W: 10 / L: 19 / SV: 0 / G: 70 / IP: 276 / SO: 121 / ERA: 4.56 / T: Bal-A

Becquer, Julio   b. Dec 20, 1931, Havana, Cuba
W: 0 / L: 0 / SV: 0 / G: 2 / IP: 2 / SO: 0 / ERA: 15.43 / T: Was-A; LA-A; Min-A

Berenguer, Juan   b. Nov 30, 1954, Aguadulce, Panama
W: 63 / L: 54 / SV: 14 / G: 394 / IP: 1063 / SO: 877 / ERA: 3.88 / T: NY-N; KC-A; Tor-A; Det-A;
SF-N; Min-A

Bithorn, Hiram   b. Mar 18, 1916, Santurce, Puerto Rico
W: 34 / L: 31 / SV: 5 / G: 105 / IP: 510 / SO: 185 / ERA: 3.16 / T: Chi-N; Chi-A

Borbón, Pedro   b. Dec 2, 1946, Valverde De Mao, D.R.
W: 69 / L: 39 / SV: 80 / G: 593 / IP: 1026 / SO: 409 / ERA: 3.52 / T: Cal-A; Cin-N; SF-N; StL-N

Cano, José   b. Mar 7, 1962, Boca de Soco, D.R.
W: 1 / L: 1 / SV: 0 / G: 6 / IP: 23 / SO: 8 / ERA: 5.09 / T: Hou N

Carrasquel, Alex   b. Jul 24, 1912, Caracas, Venezuela
W: 50 / L: 39 / SV: 16 / G: 258 / IP: 861 / SO: 252 / ERA: 3.73 / T: Was-A; Chi-A

Castillo, Tony   b. Mar 1, 1963, Quibor, Venezuela
W: 7 / L: 3 / SV: 2 / G: 95 / IP: 118 / SO: 93 / ERA: 4.40 / T: Tor-A; Atl-N

Castro, Bill   b. Dec 13, 1953, Santiago, D.R.
W: 31 / L: 26 / SV: 45 / G: 303 / IP: 545 / SO: 203 / ERA: 3.33 / T: Mil-A; NY-A; KC-A

Cecena, José   b. Aug 20, 1963, Ciudad Obregon, Mexico
W: 0 / L: 0 / SV: 1 / G: 22 / IP: 20 / SO: 27 / ERA: 4.78 / T: Tex-A

Chávez, Nestor   b. Jul 6, 1947, Chacao, Venezuela
W: 1 / L: 0 / SV: 0 / G: 2 / IP: 5 / SO: 3 / ERA: 0.00 / T: SF-N

Chévez, Tony   b. Jun 20, 1954, Telica, Nicaragua
W: 0 / L: 0 / SV: 0 / G: 4 / IP: 8 / SO: 7 / ERA: 12.38 / T: Bal-A

Clarke, Webbo   b. Jun 8, 1928, Colon, Panama
W: 0 / L: 0 / SV: 0 / G: 7 / IP: 21 / SO: 9 / ERA: 4.64 / T: Was-A

Comellas, Jorge   b. Dec 7, 1916, Havana, Cuba
W: 0 / L: 2 / SV: 0 / G: 7 / IP: 12 / SO: 6 / ERA: 4.50 / T: Chi-N

Consuegra, Sandy   b. Sep 3, 1920, Potrerillos, Cuba
W: 51 / L: 32 / SV: 26 / G: 248 / IP: 809 / SO: 193 / ERA: 3.37 / T: Was-A; Chi-A; Bal-A; NY-N

Correa, Ed   b. Apr 29, 1966, Hato Rey, Puerto Rico
W: 16 / L: 19 / SV: 0 / G: 52 / IP: 283 / SO: 260 / ERA: 5.16 / T: Chi-A; Tex-A

Cruz, Victor   b. Dec 24, 1957, Rancho Viejo La Vega, D.R.
W: 18 / L: 23 / SV: 37 / G: 187 / IP: 271 / SO: 248 / ERA: 3.08 / T: Tor-A; Cle-A; Pit-N; Tex-A

Cuellar, Mike   b. May 8, 1937, Las Villas, Cuba
W: 185/ L: 130 / SV: 11 / G: 453 / IP: 2808 / SO: 1632 / ERA: 3.14 / T: Cin-N; StL-N; Hou-N; Bal-A;
Cal-A

Cueto, Berto   b. Aug 14, 1937, San Luis Pinar, Cuba
W: 1 / L: 3 / SV: 0 / G: 7 / IP: 21 / SO: 5 / ERA: 7.17 / T: Min-A

de la Cruz, Tommy   b. Sep 18, 1914, Marianao, Cuba
W: 9 / L: 9 / SV: 1 / G: 34 / IP: 191 / SO: 65 / ERA: 3.25 / T: Cin-N

DeLeón, José   b. Dec 20, 1960, La Vega, D.R.
W: 68 / L: 96 / SV: 4 / G: 233 / IP: 1417 / SO: 1225 / ERA: 3.79 / T: Pit-N; Chi-A; Stl-N

DeLeón, Luís   b. Aug 19, 1958, Ponce, Puerto Rico
W: 17 / L: 19 / SV: 32 / G: 207 / IP: 334 / SO: 248 / ERA: 3.13 / T: StL-N; SD-N; Bal-A; Sea-A

De Los Santos, Ramón   b. Jan 19, 1949, Santo Domingo, D.R.
W: 1 / L: 1 / SV: 0 / G: 12 / IP: 12 / SO: 7 / ERA: 2.25 / T: Hou-N

Dibut, Pedro   b. Nov 18, 1892, Cienfuegos, Cuba
W: 3 / L: 0 / SV: 0 / G: 8 / IP: 37 / SO: 15 / ERA: 2.70 / T: Cin-N

Donoso, Lino   b. Sep 23, 1922, Havana, Cuba
W: 4 / L: 6 / SV: 1 / G: 28 / IP: 97 / SO: 39 / ERA: 5.21 / T: Pit-N

Elvira, Narciso   b. Oct 29, 1967, Veracruz, Mexico
W: 0 / L: 0 / SV: 0 / G: 4 / IP: 5 / SO: 6 / ERA: 5.40 / T: Mil-A

Encarnación, Luís   b. Oct 20, 1963, Santo Domingo, D.R.
W: 0 / L: 0 / SV: 0 / G: 4 / IP: 10 / SO: 8 / ERA: 7.84 / T: KC-A

Escarrega, Ernesto   b. Dec 27, 1949, Los Mochis, Mexico
W: 1 / L: 3 / SV: 1 / G: 38 / IP: 74 / SO: 33 / ERA: 3.67 / T: Chi-A

Espinosa, Nino   b. Aug 15, 1953, Villa Altagracia, D.R.
W: 44 / L: 55 / SV: 0 / G: 140 / IP: 821 / SO: 338 / ERA: 4.17 / T: NY-N; Phi-N

Estrada, Oscar   b. Feb 15, 1904, Havana, Cuba
W: 0 / L: 0 / SV: 0 / G: 1 / IP: 1 / SO: 0 / ERA: 0.00 / T: StL-A

Figueroa, Ed   b. Oct 14, 1948, Ciales, Puerto Rico
W: 80 / L: 67 / SV: 1 / G: 200 / IP: 1309 / SO: 571 / ERA: 3.51 / T: Cal-A; NY-A; Tex-A; Oak-A

Flores, Jesse   b. Nov 2, 1914, Guadalajara, Mexico
W: 44 / L: 59 / SV: 6 / G: 176 / IP: 973 / SO: 352 / ERA: 3.18 / T: Chi-N; Phi-A; Cle-A

Fornieles, Mike   b. Jan 18, 1932, Havana, Cuba
W: 63 / L: 64 / SV: 55 / G: 432 / IP: 1157 / SO: 576 / ERA: 3.96 / T: Was-A; Chi-A; Bal-A; Bos-A;
Min-A

Fossas, Tony   b. Sep 23, 1957, Havana, Cuba
W: 4 / L: 5 / SV: 1 / G: 88 / IP: 96 / SO: 66 / ERA: 4.50 / T: Tex-A; Mil-A

Fuentes, Mickey   b. May 10, 1946, Loiza, Puerto Rico
W: 1 / L: 3 / SV: 0 / G: 8 / IP: 26 / SO: 14 / ERA: 5.19 / T: Sea-A

Galvez, Balvino   b. Mar 31, 1964, San Pedro de Macoris, D.R.
W: 0 / L: 1 / SV: 0 / G: 10 / IP: 20 / SO: 11 / ERA: 3.92 / T: LA-N

Garces, Rich   b. May 18, 1971, Maracay, Venezuela
W: 0 / L: 0 / SV: 2 / G: 5 / IP: 5 / SO: 1 / ERA: 1.59 / T: Min-A

García, Miguel   b. Apr 3, 1967, Caracas, Venezuela
W: 0 / L: 2 / SV: 0 / G: 14 / IP: 20 / SO: 11 / ERA: 8.41 / T: Cal-A; Pit-N

García, Ramón   b. Mar 5, 1924, La Esperanza, Cuba
W: 0 / L: 0 / SV: 0 / G: 4 / IP: 4 / SO: 12 / ERA: 17.18 / T: Was-A

Gómez, Luís   b. Aug 19, 1951, Guadalajara, Mexico
W: 0 / L: 0 / SV: 0 / G: 1 / IP: 1 / SO: 0 / ERA: 27.00 / T: Atl-N

Gómez, Rubén   b. Jul 13, 1927, Arroyo, Puerto Rico
W: 76 / L: 86 / SV: 5 / G: 289 / IP: 1454 / SO: 677 / ERA: 4.09 / T: NY-N; SF-N; Phi-N; Cle-A; Min-N

Gonzales, Germán   b. Mar 7, 1962, Rio Caribe, Venezuela
W: 3 / L: 2 / SV: 1 / G: 38 / IP: 50 / SO: 44 / ERA: 4.11 / T: Min-A

Gonzales, Julio   b. Dec 20, 1920, Havana, Cuba
W: 0 / L: 0 / SV: 0 / G: 13 / IP: 34 / SO: 5 / ERA: 4.72 / T: Was-A

González, Vince   b. Sep 28, 1925, Quivican, Cuba
W: 0 / L: 0 / SV: 0 / G: 1 / IP: 2 / SO: 1 / ERA: 27.00 / T: Was-A

Guante, Cecilio   b. Feb 1, 1960, Villa Mella, D.R.
W: 29 / L: 34 / SV: 35 / G: 363 / IP: 595 / SO: 473 / ERA: 3.48 / T: Pit-N; NY-A; Tex-A; Cle-A

Guzmán, José   b. Apr 9, 1963, Santa Isabel, Puerto Rico
W: 37 / L: 44 / SV: 0 / G: 101 / IP: 620 / SO: 411 / ERA: 4.21 / T: Tex-A

Guzmán, Santiago   b. Jul 25, 1949, San Pedro de Macoris, D.R.
W: 1 / L: 2 / SV: 0 G: 12 / IP: 32 / SO: 29 / ERA: 4.50 / T: StL-N

Heredia, Ubaldo   b. May 4, 1956, Ciudad Bolivar, Venezuela
W: 0 / L: 1 / SV: 0 / G: 2 / IP: 10 / SO: 6 / ERA: 5.40 / T: Mon-N

Hernaiz, Jesús   b. Jan 8, 1948, Santurce, Puerto Rico
W: 2 / L: 3 / SV: 1 / G: 27 / IP: 41 / SO: 16 / ERA: 5.93 / T: Phi-N

Hernández, Evelio   b. Dec 24, 1930, Guanabacoa, Cuba
W: 1 / L: 1 / SV: 0 / G: 18 / IP: 59 / SO: 24 / ERA: 4.45 / T: Was-A

Hernández, Guillermo "Willie"   b. Nov 14, 1954, Aguada, Puerto Rico
W: 70 / L: 63 / SV: 147 / G: 744 / IP: 1045 / SO: 788 / ERA: 3.38 / T: Chi-N; Phi-N; Det-A

Hernández, Manny   b. May 7, 1961, La Romana, D.R.
W: 2 / L: 7 / SV: 0 / G: 16 / IP: 50 / SO: 22 / ERA: 4.47 / T: Hou-N; NY-N

Hernández, Ramón   b. Aug 31, 1940, Carolina, Puerto Rico
W: 23 / L: 15 / SV: 46 / G: 337 / IP: 431 / SO: 255 / ERA: 3.03 / T: Atl-N; Chi-N; Pit-N; Chi-N

Hernández, Rudy   b. Dec 10, 1931, Santiago, D.R.
W: 4 / L: 2 / SV: 0 / G: 28 / IP: 44 / SO: 26 / ERA: 4.12 / T: Was-A

Herrera, Tito   b. Jul 26, 1926, Nuevo Laredo, Mexico
W: 0 / L: 0 / SV: 0 / G: 3 / IP: 2 / SO: 0 / ERA: 27.00 / T: StL-A

Higuera, Ted   b. Nov 9, 1958, Los Mochis, Mexico
W: 89 / L: 54 / SV: 0 / G: 181 / IP: 1255 / SO: 986 / ERA: 3.34 / T: Mil-A

Jiménez, Germán   b. Dec 5, 1962, Santiago, Mexico
W: 1 / L: 6 / SV: 0 / G: 15 / IP: 56 / SO: 26 / ERA: 5.01 / T: Atl-N

Jiménez, Juan   b. Mar 8, 1949, La Torre, D.R.
W: 0 / L: 0 / SV: 0 / G: 4 / IP: 4 / SO: 2 / ERA: 6.75 / T: Pit-N

Lauzerique, George   b. Jul 22, 1947, Havana, Cuba
W: 4 / L: 8 / SV: 0 / G: 34 / IP: 113 / SO: 73 / ERA: 5.00 / T: KC-A; Oak-A; Mil-A

Leal, Luís   b. Mar 21, 1957, Barquisimento, Venezuela
W: 51 / L: 58 / SV: 1 / G: 165 / IP: 947 / SO: 491 / ERA: 4.14 / T: Tor-A

León, Max   b. Feb 4, 1950, Pozo Hondo, Mexico
W: 14 / L: 18 / SV: 13 / G: 162 / IP: 311 / SO: 170 / ERA: 3.70 / T: Atl-N

León, Sid   b. Jan 4, 1911, Cruces, Cuba
W: 0 / L: 4 / SV: 0 / G: 14 / IP: 39 / SO: 11 / ERA: 5.35 / T: Phi-N

López, Aurelio   b. Sep 21, 1948, Tecamachalco, Mexico
W: 62 / L: 36 / SV: 93 / G: 459 / IP: 910 / SO: 635 / ERA: 3.56 / T: KC-A; StL-N; Det-A; Hou-N

López, Marcelino   b. Sep 23, 1943, Havana, Cuba
W: 31 / L: 40 / SV: 2 / G: 171 / IP: 653 / SO: 426 / ERA: 3.62 / T: Phi N; Cal A; Bal A; Mil Al Cle-A

López, Ramón   b. May 26, 1933, Las Villas, Cuba
W: 0 / L: 1 / SV: 0 / G: 4 / IP: 7 / SO: 2 / ERA: 5.14 / T: Cal A

Lugo, Urbano   b. Aug 12, 1962, Punto Fijo, Venezuela
W: 6 / L: 7 / SV: 0 / G: 50 / IP: 162 / SO: 91 / ERA: 5.31 / T: Cal-A; Mon-N; Det-A

Luna, Memo   b. Jun 25, 1930, Tacubaya, Mexico
W: 0 / L: 1 / SV: 0 / G: 1 / IP: 1 / SO: 0 / ERA: 27.00 / T: StL-N

Luque, Dolf   b. Aug 4, 1890, Havana, Cuba
W: 193 / L: 179 / SV: 28 / G: 550 / IP: 3220 / SO: 1130 / ERA: 3.24 / T: Bos-N; Cin-N; Bkn-N; NY-N

Machado, Julio   b. Dec 1, 1965, Zulia, Venezuela
W: 4 / L: 2 / SV: 3 / G: 47 / IP: 58 / SO: 53 / ERA: 2.62 / T: NY-N; Mil-A

Maestri, Hector   b. Apr 19, 1935, Havana, Cuba
W: 0 / L: 1 / SV: 0 / G: 2 / IP: 8 / SO: 3 / ERA: 1.13 / T: Was-A

Manon, Ramón   b. Jan 20, 1968, Santo Domingo, D.R.
W: 0 / L: 0 / SV: 0 / G: 1 / IP: 2 / SO: 2 / ERA: 13.50 / T: Tex-A

Maldonado, Carlos   b. Oct 18, 1966, Chepo, Panama
W: 0 / L: 0 / SV: 0 / G: 4 / IP: 6 / SO: 9 / ERA: 9.00 / T: KC-A

Manzanillo, Ravelo   b. Oct 17, 1963, San Pedro de Macoris, D.R.
W: 0 / L: 1 / SV: 0 / G: 2 / IP: 9 / SO: 10 / ERA: 5.79 / T: Chi-A

Marichal, Juan   b. Oct 20, 1937, Laguna Verde, D.R.
W: 243 / L: 142 / SV: 2 / G: 471 / IP: 3509 / SO: 2303 / ERA: 2.89 / T: SF-N; Bos-A; LA-N

Marrero, Connie   b. Apr 25, 1911, Las Villas, Cuba
W: 39 / L: 40 / SV: 3 / G: 118 / IP: 735 / SO: 297 / ERA: 3.67 / T: Was-A

Martínez, Dennis   b. May 14, 1955, Granada, Nicaragua
W: 163 / L: 134 / SV: 5 / G: 460 / IP: 2711 / SO: 1423 / ERA: 3.82 / T: Bal-A; Mon-N

Martínez, Ramon   b. Mar 22, 1968, Santo Domingo, D.R.
W: 27 / L: 13 / SV: 0 / G: 57 / IP: 368 / SO: 335 / ERA: 3.08 / T: LA-N

Martínez, Rogelio   b. Nov 5, 1918, Cidra, Cuba
W: 0 / L: 1 / SV: 0 / G: 2 / IP: 2 / SO: 0 / ERA: 27.00 / T: Was-A

Martínez, Silvio   b. Aug 19, 1955, Santiago, D.R.
W: 31 / L: 32 / SV: 1 / G: 107 / IP: : 583 / SO: 230 / ERA: 3.87 / T: Chi-A; StL-N

Melendez, José   b. Sep 2, 1965, Naguabo, Puerto Rico
W: 0 / L: 0 / SV: 0 / G: 3 / IP: 5 / SO: 7 / ERA: 11.81 / T: Sea-A

Mesa, José   b. May 22, 1966, Pueblo Viejo, D.R.
W: 4 / L: 5 / SV: 0 / G: 13 / IP: 78 / SO: 41 / ERA: 4.73 / T: Bal-A

Monge, Sid   b. Apr 11, 1951, Agua Prieta, Mexico
W: 49 / L: 40 / SV: 56 / G: 435 / IP: 764 / SO: 471 / ERA: 3.53 / T: Cal-A; Cle-A; Phi-N; SD-N; Det-A

Montalvo, Rafael   b. Mar 31, 1964, Rio Piedras, Puerto Rico
W: 0 / L: 0 / SV: 0 / G: 1 / IP: 1 / SO: 0 / ERA: 9.00 / T: Hou-N

Monteagudo, Aurelio   b. Nov 19, 1943, Caibarien, Cuba
W: 3 / L: 7 / SV: 4 / G: 72 / IP: 131 / SO: 58 / ERA: 5.05 / T: KC-A; Hou-N; Chi-A; KC-A; Cal-A

Monteagudo, Rene   b. Mar 12, 1916, Havana, Cuba
W: 3 / L: 7 / SV: 2 / G: 46 / IP: 168 / SO: 93 / ERA: 6.42 / T: Was-A; Phi-N

Montejo, Manny   b. Oct 16, 1935, Caibarien, Cuba
W: 0 / L: 0 / SV: 0 / G: 12 / IP: 16 / SO: 15 / ERA: 3.86 / T: Det-A

Monzant, Ray   b. Jan 4, 1933, Maracaibo, Venezuela
W: 16 / L: 21 / SV: 1 / G: 106 / IP: 316 / SO: 201 / ERA: 4.38 / T: NY-N; SF-N

Moreno, Angel   b. Jun 6, 1955, La Mendosa, Mexico
W: 4 / L: 10 / SV: 1 / G: 21 / IP: 80 / SO: 34 / ERA: 4.03 / T: Cal-A

Moreno, Julio   b. Jan 28, 1921, Guines, Cuba
W:18 / L: 22 / SV: 2 / G: 73 / IP: 336 / SO: 119 / ERA: 4.25 / T: Was-A

Moret, Roger   b. Sep 16, 1949, Guayama, Puerto Rico
W: 47 / L: 27 / SV: 12 / G: 168 / IP: 721 / SO: 408 / ERA: 3.67 / T: Bos-A; Atl-N; Tex-A

Muniz, Manny   b. Dec 31, 1947, Caguas, Puerto Rico
W: 0 / L: 1 / SV: 0 / G: 5 / IP: 10 / SO: 6 / ERA: 7.20 / T: Phi-N

Naranjo, Cholly   b. Nov 25, 1934, Havana, Cuba
W: 1 / L: 2 / SV: 0 / G: 17 / IP: 34 / SO: 26 / ERA: 4.46 / T: Pit-N

Navarro, Jaime (son of Julio)   b. Mar 27, 1967, Bayamon, Puerto Rico
W: 15 / L: 15 / SV: 1 / G: 51 / IP: 259 / SO: 131 / ERA: 3.89 / T: Mil-A

Navarro, Julio (father of Jaime)   b. Jan 9, 1936, Vieques, Puerto Rico
W: 7 / L: 9 / SV: 17 / G: 130 / IP: 212 / SO: 151 / ERA: 3.65 / T: LA-A; Det-A; Atl-N

Nieves, Juan   b. Jan 5, 1965, Santurce, Puerto Rico
W: 32 / L: 25 / SV: 1 / G: 94 / IP: 490 / SO: 352 / ERA: 4.71 / T: Mil-A

Núñez, Edwin   b. May 27, 1963, Humacao, Puerto Rico
W: 22 / L: 26 / SV: 42 / G: 284 / IP: 477 / SO: 362 / ERA: 3.83 / T: Sea-A; NY-N; Det-A

Núñez, José   b. Jan 13, 1964, Jarabacoa, D.R.
W: 9 / L: 10 / SV: 0 / G: 77 / IP: 197 / SO: 171 / ERA: 5.05 / T: Tor-A; Chi-N

Olivares, Omar   b. Jul 6, 1967, Mayaguez, Puerto Rico
W: 1 / L: 1 / SV: 0 / G: 9 / IP: 49 / SO: 20 / ERA: 2.92 / T: StL-N

Oliveras, Francisco   b. Jan 31, 1963, Santurce, Puerto Rico
W: 3 / L: 4 / SV: 0 / G: 12 / IP: 55 / SO: 24 / ERA: 4.53 / T: Min-A

Olivo, Chi Chi (brother of Diomedes)   b. Mar 18, 1928, Guayubin, D.R.
W: 7 / L: 6 / SV: 12 / G: 96 / IP: 141 / SO: 98 / ERA: 3.96 / T: Mil-N; Atl-N

Olivo, Diomedes (brother of Chi Chi)   b. Jan 22, 1919, Guayubin, D.R.
W: 5 / L: 6 / SV: 7 / G: 85 / IP: 107 / SO: 85 / ERA: 3.10 / T: Pit-N; StL-N

Ortiz, Baby (brother of Roberto)   b. Dec 5, 1919, Camaguey, Cuba
W: 0 / L: 2 / SV: 0 / G: 2 / IP: 13 / SO: 4 / ERA: 6.23 / T: Was-A

Palacios, Vicente   b. Jul 19, 1963, Veracruz, Mexico
W: 3 / L: 3 / SV: 3 / G: 20 / IP: 68 / SO: 36 / ERA: 4.19 / T: Pit-N

Palmero, Emilio   b. Jun 13, 1895, Guanabacoa, Cuba
W: 6 / L: 15 / SV: 0 / G: 41 / IP: 141 / SO: 48 / ERA: 5.17 / T: NY-N; StL-A; Was-A; Bos-N

Pascual, Camilo (brother of Carlos)   b. Jan 20, 1934, Havana, Cuba
W: 174 / L: 170 / SV: 10 / G: 529 / IP: 2930 / SO: 2167 / ERA: 3.63 / T: Was-A; Min-A; Was-A;
                       Cin-N; LA-N; Cle-A

Pascual, Carlos (brother of Camilo)   b. Mar 13, 1931, Havana, Cuba
W: 1 / L: 1 / SV: 0 / G: 2 / IP: 17 / SO: 3 / ERA: 2.12 / T: Was-A

Peña, Alejandro   b. Jun 25, 1959, Cambiaso, Puerto Plata, D.R.
W: 41 / L: 41 / SV: 37 / G: 333 / IP: 845 / SO: 647 / ERA: 2.95 / T: LA-N; NY-N

Peña, Hipólito   b. Jan 30, 1964, Fantino, D.R.
W: 1 / L: 7 / SV: 2 / G: 42 / IP: 48 / SO: 32 / ERA: 4.84 / T: Pit-N; NY-A

Peña, José　　　b. Dec 3, 1942, Ciudad Juarez, Mexico
W: 7 / L: 4 / SV: 5 / G: 61 / IP: 112 / SO: 82 / ERA: 4.97 / T: Cin-N; LA-N

Peña, Orlando　　　b. Nov 17, 1933, Victoria de las Tunas, Cuba
W: 56 / L: 77 / SV: 40 / G: 427 / IP: 1203 / SO: 818 / ERA: 3.70 / T: Cin-N; KC-A; Det-A; Bal-A

Peña, Ramón　　　(brother of Tony)　　　b. May 13, 1962, Santiago, D.R.
W: 0 / L: 0 / SV: 0 / G: 8 / IP: 18 / SO: 12 / ERA: 6.00 / T: Det-A; Cle-A; Pit-N; Bal-A; StL-N; Cal-A

Peraza, Luís　　　b. Jun 17, 1942, Rio Piedras, Puerto Rico
W: 0 / L: 0 / SV: 0 / G: 8 / IP: 9 / SO: 7 / ERA: 6.00 / T: Phi-N

Peraza, Oswaldo　　　b. Oct 19, 1962, Puerto Cabello, Venezuela
W: 5 / L: 7 / SV: 0 / G: 19 / IP: 86 / SO: 61 / ERA: 5.55 / T: Bal-A

Pérez, Melido　　　(brother of Pascual)　　　b. Feb 15, 1966, San Cristobal, D.R.
W: 37 / L: 39 / SV: 0 / G: 101 / IP: 587 / SO: 445 / ERA: 4.52 / T: KC-A; Chi-A

Pérez, Mike　　　b. Oct 19, 1964, Yauco, Puerto Rico
W: 1 / L: 0 / SV: 1 / G: 13 / IP: 13 / SO: 5 / ERA: 3.95 / T: Stl-N

Pérez, Pascual　　　(brother of Melido)　　　b. May 17, 1957, San Cristobal, D.R.
W: 65 / L: 64 / SV: 0 / G: 193 / IP: 1170 / SO: 781 / ERA: 3.45 / T: Pit-N; Atl-N; Mon-N; NY-A

Piña, Horacio　　　b. Mar 12, 1945, Coahuila, Mexico
W; 23 / L: 23 / SV: 38 / G: 314 / IP: 432 / SO: 278 / ERA: 3.25 / T: Cle-A; Was-A; Tex-A; Oak-A

Pizarro, Juan　　　b. Feb 7, 1937, Santurce, Puerto Rico
W: 131 / L: 105 / SV: 28 / G: 488 / IP: 2034 / SO: 1522 / ERA: 3.43 / T: Mil-N; Chi-A; Pit-N; Bos-A;
　　　　　　　　　　　　　　　　　　　　　　　　　Cle-A; Oak-A; Chi-N; Hou-N

Puente, Miguel　　　b. May 8, 1948, San Luis Potosi, Mexico
W: 1 / L: 3 / SV: 0 / G: 6 / IP: 19 / SO: 14 / ERA: 8.05 / T: SF-N

Pulido, Alfonso　　　b. Jan 23, 1957, Veracruz, Mexico
W: 1 / L: 1 / SV: 1 / G: 12 / IP: 34 / SO: 16 / ERA: 5.19 / T: Pit-N; NY-A

Quintana, Luís　　　b. Dec 25, 1951, Vega Baja, Puerto Rico
W: 2 / L: 3 / SV: 0 / G: 22 / IP: 20 / SO: 16 / ERA: 4.95 / T: Cal-A

Ramos, Pedro　　　b. Apr 28, 1935, Pinar del Rio, Cuba
W: 117 / L: 160 / SV: 55 / G: 582 / IP: 2355 / SO: 1305 / ERA: 4.08 / T: Was-A; Min-A; Cle-A; NY-A;
　　　　　　　　　　　　　　　　　　　　　　　　　Phi-N; Pit-N; Cin-N; Was-A

Rijo, José　　　b. May 13, 1965, San Cristobal, D.R.
W: 53 / L: 52 / SV: 3 / G: 193 / IP: 872 / SO: 753 / ERA: 3.60 / T: NY-A; Oak-A; Cin-N

Roche, Armando　　　b. Dec 7, 1926, Havana, Cuba
W: 0 / L: 0 / SV: 0 / G: 2 / IP: 6 / SO: 0 / ERA: 6.00 / T: Was-A

Rodríguez, Eduardo　　　b. Mar 6, 1952, Barceloneta, Puerto Rico
W: 42 / L: 36 / SV: 32 / G: 264 / IP: 734 / SO: 430 / ERA: 3.89 / T: Mil-A; KC-A

Rodríguez, Freddy　　　b. Apr 29, 1924, Havana, Cuba
W: 0 / L: 0 / SV: 2 / G: 8 / IP: 9 / SO: 6 / ERA: 8.68 / T: Chi-N; Phi-N

Rodríguez, Roberto   b. Nov 29, 1941, Caracas, Venezuela
W: 4 / L: 3 / SV: 7 / G: 57 / IP: 112 / SO: 91 / ERA: 4.82 / T: KC-A; Oak-A; SD-N; Chi-N

Rodríguez, Rosario   b. Jul 8, 1969, Los Mochis, Mexico
W: 1 / L: 1 / SV: 0 / G: 16 / IP: 14 / SO: 8 / ERA: 5.52 / T: Cin-N

Rojas, Melquiades   b. Dec 10, 1966, Haina, D.R.
W: 3 / L: 1 / SV: 1 / G: 23 / IP: 40 / SO: 26 / ERA: 3.60 / T: Mon-N

Rojas, Minnie   b. Nov 26, 1938, Remedios Las Villas, Cuba
W: 23 / L: 16 / SV: 43 / G: 157 / IP: 261 / SO: 153 / ERA: 3.00 / T: Cal-A

Román, José   b. May 21, 1963, Santo Domingo, D.R.
W: 1 / L: 8 / SV: 0 / G: 14 / IP: 44 / SO: 24 / ERA: 8.12 / T: Cle-A

Romero, Ramon   b. Jan 8, 1959, San Pedro de Macoris, D.R.
W: 2 / L: 3 / SV: 0 / G: 20 / IP: 67 / SO: 41 / ERA: 6.28 / T: Cle-A

Romo, Enrique   (brother of Vincente)   b. Jul 15, 1947, Santa Rosalia, Mexico
W: 44 / L: 33 / SV: 52 / G: 350 / IP: 603 / SO: 436 / ERA: 3.45 / T: Sea-A; Pit-N

Romo, Vicente   (brother of Enrique)   b. Apr 12, 1943, Santa Rosalia, Mexico
W: 32 / L: 33 / SV: 52 / G: 335 / IP: 645 / SO: 416 / ERA: 3.36 / T: LA-N; Cle-A; Bos-A; SD-N

Rubio, Jorge   b. Apr 23, 1945, Mexicali, Mexico
W: 2 / L: 3 / SV: 1 / G: 10 / IP: 42 / SO: 31 / ERA: 3.19 / T: Cal-A

Sánchez, Israel   b. Aug 20, 1963, Falcon Lasvias, Cuba
W: 3 / L: 2 / SV: 1 / G: 30 / IP: 45 / SO: 19 / ERA : 5.36 / T: KC-A

Sánchez, Luís   b. Aug 24, 1953, Cariaco, Venezuela
W: 28 / L: 21 / SV: 27 / G: 194 / IP: 370 / SO: 216 / ERA: 3.75 / T: Cal—A

Sánchez, Raul   b. Dec 12, 1930, Marianao, Cuba
W: 5 / L: 3 / SV: 5 / G: 49 / IP: 89 / SO: 48 / ERA: 4.62 / T: Was A; Cin-N

Santiago, José   b. Sep 4, 1928, Coamo, Puerto Rico
W: 3 / L: 2 / SV: 0 / G: 27 / IP: 56 / SO: 29 / ERA: 4.66 / T: Cle-A; KC-A

Santiago, José   b. Aug 15, 1940, Juana Diaz, Puerto Rico
W: 34 / L: 29 / SV: 8 / G: 163 / IP: 555 / SO: 404 / ERA: 3.74 / T: KC-A; Bos-A

Sarmiento, Manny   b. Feb 2, 1956, Cagua, Venezuela
W: 26 / L: 22 / SV: 12 / G: 228 / IP: 514 / SO: 283 / ERA: 3.48 / T: Cin-N; Sea-A; Pit-N

Scantlebury, Pat   b. Nov 11, 1925, Gatun, Canal Zone, Panama
W: 0 / L: 1 / SV: 0 / G: 6 / IP: 19 / SO: 10 / ERA: 6.63 / T: Cin-N

Seguí, Diego   b. Aug 17, 1937, Holguin, Cuba
W: 92 / L: 111 / SV: 71 / G: 639 / IP: 1808 / SO: 1298 / ERA: 3.81 / T: KC-A; Was-A; Sea-A; Oak-A;
Sea-A; StL-N; Bos-A

Segura, José   b. Jan 26, 1963, Barahona, D.R.
W: 0 / L: 1 / SV: 0 / G: 11 / IP: 14 / SO: 6 / ERA: 14.11 / T: Chi-A

Sierra, Candy   b. Mar 27, 1967, Rio Piedras, Puerto Rico
W: 0 / L: 1 / SV: 0 / G: 16 / IP: 27 / SO: 24 / ERA: 5.53 / T: SD N; Cin N

Solano, Julio   b. Jan 8, 1960, Agua Blanca, D.R.
W: 6 / L: 8 / SV: 3 / G: 106 / IP: 174 / SO: 102/ ERA: 4.55 / T: Hou-N; Sea-A

Solis, Marcelino   b. Jul 19, 1930, San Luis Potosi, Mexico
W: 3 / L: 3 / SV: 0 / G: 15 / IP: 52 / SO: 15 / ERA: 6.06 / T: Chi-N

Sosa, Elias   b. Jun 10, 1950, La Vega, D.R.
W: 59 / L: 51 / SV: 83 / G: 601 / IP: 919 / SO: 538 / ERA: 3.32 / T: SF-N; Stl-N; Atl-N; LA-N; Oak-A;
Mon-N; Det-A; SD-N

Sosa, José   b. Dec 28, 1952, Santo Domingo, D.R.
W: 1 / L: 3 / SV: 1 / G: 34 / IP: 59 / SO: 36 / ERA: 4.58 / T: Hou N

Soto, Mario   b. Jul 12, 1956, Bani, D.R.
W: 100 / L: 92 / SV: 4 / G: 297 / IP: 1730 / SO: 1449 / ERA: 3.47 / T: Cin-N

Straker, Les   b. Oct 10, 1959, Ciudad Bolivar, Venezuela
W: 10 / L: 15 / SV: 1 / G: 47 / IP: 237 / ERA: 4.22 / T: Min-A

Tiant, Luís   b. Nov 23, 1940, Marianao, Cuba
W: 229 / L: 172 / SV: 15 / G: 573 / IP: 3485 / SO: 2416 / ERA: 3.30 / T: Cle-A; Min-A; Bos-A; NY-A;
Pit-N; Cal-A

Torrealba, Pablo   b. Apr 28, 1948, Barquisimeto, Venezuela
W: 6 / L: 13 / SV: 5 / G: 111 / IP: 240 / SO: 113 / ERA: 3.26 / T: Atl-N; Oak-A; Chi-A

Torres, Angel   b. Oct 24, 1952, Las Ciengas, Azua, D.R.
W: 0 / L: 0 / SV: 0 / G: 5 / IP: 8 / SO: 8 / ERA: 2.25 / T: Cin-N

Tuero, Oscar   b. Dec 17, 1898, Havana, Cuba
W: 6 / L: 9 / SV: 4 / G: 58 / IP: 199 / SO: 58 / ERA: 2.88 / T: StL-N

Ullrich, Sandy   b. Jul 25, 1921, Havana, Cuba
W: 3 / L: 3 / SV: 1 / G: 31 / IP: 91 / SO: 28 / ERA: 5.04 / T: Was-A

Valdez, Efrain   b. Jul 11, 1966, Nizao de Bani, D.R.
W: 1 / L: 1 / SV: 0 / G: 13 / IP: 23 / SO: 13 / ERA: 3.04 / T: Cle-A

Valdez, Rafael   b. Dec 17, 1967, Nizao Bani, D.R.
W: 0 / L: 1 / SV: 0 / G: 3 / IP: 5 / SO: 3 / ERA: 11.12 / T: SD-N

Valdez, Rene   b. Jun 2, 1929, Guanabacoa, Cuba
W: 1 / L: 1 / SV: 0 / G: 5 / IP: 13 / SO: 10 / ERA: 5.54 / T: Bkn-N

Valdez, Sergio   b. Sep 7, 1964, Elias Pina, D.R.
W: 7 / L: 12 / SV: 0 / G: 54 / IP: 165 / SO: 112 / ERA: 5.39 / T: Mon-N; Atl-N; Cle-A

Valenzuela, Fernando   b. Nov 01, 1960, Navajoa, Mexico
W: 141 / L: 116 / SV: 2 / G: 331 / IP: 2348 / SO: 1759 / ERA: 3.31 / T: LA-N

Valera, Julio   b. Oct 13, 1968, San Sebastian, Puerto Rico
W: 1 / L: 1 / SV: 0 / G: 3 / IP: 13 / SO: 4 / ERA: 6.92 / T: NY-N

Vargas, Roberto   b. May 29, 1929, Santurce, Puerto Rico
W: 0 / L: 0 / SV: 2 / G: 25 / IP: 24 / SO: 13 / ERA: 8.76 / T: Mil N

Vásquez, Rafael   b. Jun 28, 1958, La Romana, D.R.
W: 1 / L: 0 / SV: 0 / G: 9 / IP: 16 / SO: 9 / ERA: 5.06 / T: Sea A

Velásquez, Carlos   b. Mar 22, 1948, Loiza, Puerto Rico
W: 2 / L: 2 / SV: 2 / G: 18 / IP: 38 / SO: 12 / ERA: 2.58 / T: Mil A

Wagner, Hector   b. Nov 26, 1968, Santo Domingo, D.R.
W: 0 / L: 2 / SV: 0 / G: 5 / IP: 23 / SO: 14 / ERA: 8.10 / T: KC-A

Williams, Al   b. May 6, 1954, Pearl Lagoon, Nicaragua
W: 35 / L: 38 / SV: 2 / G: 120 / IP: 642 / SO : 262 / ERA: 4.24 / T: Min A

Zabala, Adrian   b. Aug 26, 1916, San Antonio de los Banos, Cuba
W: 4 / L: 7 / SV: 1 / G: 26 / IP: 84 / SO: 27 / ERA: 5.02 T: NY N

Zamora, Oscar   b. Sep 23, 1944, Camaguay, Cuba
W: 13 / L: 14 / SV: 23 / G: 158 / IP: 225 / SO: 99 / ERA: 4.52 / T: Chi-N; Hou-N

NOTES

Chapter 1

1. Joseph L. Arbena, ed., *Sport and Society in Latin America* (Westport, CT: Greenwood Press, 1988), 118.
2. Angel Torres, *La Historia del Béisbol Cubano, 1878–1976* (Los Angeles: Angel Torres, 1976), 11.
3. Eladio Secades, "Primeras Noticias del Baseball," *Diario de la Marina,* 125th anniversary issue.
4. Arbena, *Sport and Society in Latin America,* 31-35.
5. Emilio E. Huyke, *Los Deportes en Puerto Rico* (Sharon, CT: Troutman Press), 80.
6. Carlos J. García, *Baseball para Siempre* (Mexico: E.I.S.W., 1979), 50.
7. *Ibid.*

Chapter 2

1. Latin Americans rightly point out that they, too, are "Americans." People from the United States are described as *North* Americans or *estadounidense.*
2. García, *Baseball para Siempre,* 242.
3. *Ibid.,* 264.
4. R.T. Martin, *Panama Morning Journal,* 2 January 1915.

Chapter 3

1. Charles C. Alexander, *Ty Cobb* (New York: Oxford University Press, 1984), 98-99.
2. Alexander, *John McGraw* (New York: Viking Penguin, 1988), 159.
3. John Holway, *Blackball Stars: Negro League Pioneers* (Westport, CT: Meckler Books, 1988), 56.
4. Edna and Art Rust, Jr., *Art Rust's Illustrated History of the Black Athlete* (New York: Doubleday, 1985), 15.
5. Holway, *Blackball Stars,* 129.
6. Rust and Rust, *Art Rust's Illustrated History of the Black Athlete,* 15.
7. Janet Bruce, *The Kansas City Monarchs: Champions of Black Baseball* (Lawrence, KS: The University Press of Kansas, 1985), 93.

Chapter 4

1. Lee Allen, *Cooperstown Corner: Columns from the Sporting News* (Cleveland: Society for American Baseball Research, Inc.), 7.
2. "Beisboleros," *Newsweek,* 29 May 1944, 90.
3. Rust and Rust, *Art Rust's Illustrated History of the Black Athlete,* 7.
4. Bruce Brown, "Cuban Baseball," *Atlantic Monthly,* June 1984, 111.

5. George Compton and Adolfo Solórzano Diaz, "Latins on the Diamond," *Americas* 3 (June 1951), 10.
6. Bob Rathgeber, *Cincinnati Reds Scrapbook* (JCP Corporation of Virginia, 1982), 54.
7. *Ibid.*
8. Frank Graham, "Adolfo Luque is Dead?"*New York Journal-American,* 17 July 1957.
9. Daniel C. Frio and Mark Onigman, "Good Field, No Hit: The Image of Latin American Baseball Players in the American Press, 1871-1946," *Revista/Review Interamericana,* Summer 1979, 204.
10. Milton Bracker, "Mexico's Raiders Ride Again," *Saturday Evening Post,* 8 March 1947, 146.
11. Holway, *Blackball Stars* , 59.

Chapter 5

1. Holway, *Blackball Stars,* 244.
2. *Ibid.,* 236-237.
3. Paul MacFarlane, ed.,*Daguerreotypes* (St. Louis: The Sporting News Publishing Company, 1981), 79.
4. Donn Rogosin, *Invisible Men: Life in Baseball's Negro Leagues* (New York: Atheneum Press, 1987), 156-157.

Chapter 6

1. LeRoy "Satchel" Paige, as told to David Lipman, *Maybe I'll Pitch Forever: A Great Baseball Player Tells the Hilarious Story Behind the Legend* (New York: Doubleday, 1962), 117.
2. Rogosin, *Invisible Men*, 167-168.

Chapter 7

1. Shirley Povich, *The Washington Senators,* (New York: G.P. Putnam's Sons, 1954), 206.
2. David Halberstam, *Summer of '49* (New York: William Morrow, 1989), 71.
3. Richard Goldstein, *Spartan Seasons: How Baseball Survived the Second World War* (New York: Macmillan, 1980), 187.
4. Kevin Kerrane, *Dollar Signs on the Muscle: The World of Baseball Scouting* (New York: Avon Books, 1985), 278.
5. *Ibid.,* 15.
6. Shirley Povich, *The Washington Senators*, 209-210.
7. Frio and Onigman, "Good Field, No Hit," *Revista/Review Interamericana,* 199-208.
8. Kerrane, *Dollar Sign on the Muscle,* 278.
9. Ray Fitzgerald, "Uncle Joe—Senators' Cuban Connection," *The Sporting News,* 21 June 1980, 17.
10. Peter Gammons, "Dominican Has Replaced Cuba as Prime Talent Source," *Baseball America,* 25 July 1985 and 9 August 1985.

Chapter 8

1. Janet Bruce, *The Kansas City Monarchs: Champions of Black Baseball*, 98.
2. Ray Gillespie, "Million Peso League," *Inter-American*, October 1946.
3. "Baseball 25 Grande," *Newsweek*, 15 April 1946, 82.
4. Tom Gorman and Jerome Holtzman, *Three and Two!* (New York: Charles Scribner's Sons, 1979), 25-26.
5. "Baseball 25 Grande," 82.

Chapter 9

1. Bruce Brown, "Cuban Baseball," *Atlantic Monthly*, June 1984, 78.
2. Jules Tygiel, *Baseball's Great Experiment: Jackie Robinson and His Legacy* (New York: Random House, 1984), 164-165.
3. *Ibid.*
4. Joe Donnelly, "Alou Bridged the Gap for Latin Americans," newspaper article dated 8 September 1971 at Baseball Hall of Fame Library.
5. Orestes Miñoso with Fernando Fernandez and Robert Kleinfelder, *Extra Innings: My Life in Baseball* (Chicago: Regnery Gateway, 1983), 12.
6. John C. Hoffman, "What You Say, Minnie's Hokay!" *Colliers*, 5 April 1952, 58.
7. A.S. "Doc" Young, *Great Negro Baseball Stars and How They Made the Major Leagues* (New York: A.S. Barnes, 1953), 176.
8. William Barry Furlong, "The White Sox Katzenjammer Kid," *Saturday Evening Post*, 10 July 1952, 78.
9. Donn Rogosin, *Invisible Men*, 6.
10. Young, *Great Negro Baseball Stars and How They Made the Major Leagues*, 167.
11. Hoffman, "What You Say, Minnie's Hokay!" 57.
12. Miñoso et al., *Extra Innings*, 49.
13. Hoffman, "What You Say, Minnie's Hokay!" 56.
14. John C. Hoffman, "Orestes Miñoso—Speed Merchant," *Baseball Stars of 1954*, compiled by Bruce Jacobs (New York: Lions Books, 1954), 83-84.
15. *Ibid.*
16. Miñoso et al., *Extra Innings*, 200.

Chapter 10

1. "Situacion Don Q," *Newsweek*, 9 January 1950, 62-64.
2. "Señor Mays—Big Hit in San Juan," *Colliers*, 7 January 1955, 49.
3. *Ibid.*, 50-51.
4. Rogosin, *Invisible Men*, 69.

Chapter 11

1. Ron Luciano and David Fisher, *Strike Two* (New York: Bantam Books, 1984), 78.
2. Howard Senzel, *Baseball and the Cold War: Being a Soliloquy on the Necessity of Baseball* (New York: Harcourt Brace Jovanovich, 1977), 73-74.

Chapter 12

1. Joseph Durso, "We Band of Brothers," *New York Times*, 14 August 1975.
2. Felipe Alou and Herm Weiskopf, *Felipe Alou . . . My Life and Baseball* (Waco, TX: Word Books, 1967), 29.
3. Alou and Weiskopf, *Felipe Alou*, 34-35.
4. Alou and Weiskopf, *Felipe Alou*, 43.
5. John Devaney, *Juan Marichal, Mister Strike* (New York: G.P. Putnam's Sons, 1970), 20-21.
6. Samuel Regalado, "Latin American Minor League Experience in Western Communities," paper on file at Baseball Hall of Fame Library.
7. "The Dandy Dominican," *Time,* 10 June 1966, 91.
8. Bob Stevens, "Felipe Suggests Latins Have Rep. in Frick's Office," *Sporting News,* 16 March 1963.
9. John Devaney, *Where are They Today? Great Sports Stars of Yesteryear* (New York: Crown Publishers, 1985), 4.
10. Alou and Weiskopf, *Felipe Alou,* 127-128.
11. Larry Gerlach, *The Men in Blue* (New York: The Viking Press, 1980), 202-203.
12. Jack Mann, "Battle of San Francisco," *Sports Illustrated,* 30 August 1965, 12-14.
13. John Roseboro with Bill Libby, *Glory Days with the Dodgers and Other Days with Others* (New York: Atheneum Press, 1978), 5-7.
14. Al Stump, "Always They Want More, More," *Saturday Evening Post,* 29 July 1967.
15. "Pitchmen," *Sports Illustrated,* 17 November 1969, 112.
16. Jim Ogle, "Yanks Book Alou as Florida Kid Tudor," *The Sporting News,* 16 September 1972 and "Old-Pro Felipe Perfect Model," *The Sporting News,* 28 April 1973.
17. "Felipe Alou Quits," article from Baseball Hall of Fame Library, 6 May 1974.

Chapter 13

1. Kal Wagenheim, *Clemente!* (New York: Waterfront, 1973), 35, 42.
2. *Ibid.,* 42.
3. Les Biederman, "Clemente: The Player Who Can Do it All," *The Sporting News,* 20 April 1968.
4. Wagenheim, *Clemente!,* 55.
5. *Ibid.,* 56-57.
6. Charles Lee, "Is Roberto Clemente as Good as He Thinks He Is?" *Sports Herald,* 1972, 71.
7. Wagenheim, *Clemente!,* 99.
8. Biederman, "Clemente: The Player Who Can Do it All," 11.
9. Jerry Izenberg, *Great Latin Sports Figures: The Proud People* (New York: Doubleday, 1976), 33-34.
10. Les Biederman, "Shoulder Sore, Clemente Says He May Retire," *The Sporting News,* 24 August 1969, 18.

11. David Wolf, "A Baseball Superstar Frustrated by Faint Praise," *Life*, 24 May 1968, 70-71.
12. "Two Lives and Two Loves, Clemente Tells Buc Fans," *The Sporting News*, 8 August 1970, 13.
13. C.R. Ways, "Nobody Does Anything Better than Me in Baseball," *New York Times Magazine*, 9 April 1972, 38-40.
14. Bob Broeg, "Spahn, Clemente, Irvin, Kelly Enter Hall of Fame," *The Sporting News*, 18 August 1973, 7.
15. *Ibid.*
16. Al Abrams, "Sidelights on Sports," *Pittsburgh Post-Gazette*, 11 March 1971, 42-44.
17. Charles Feeney, "$5,000 Manny Huge Pirate Treasure," *The Sporting News*, 1 May 1971, 3.
18. Al Abrams, "Super Stardom Ahead for Sanguillen?" *Baseball Digest*, 1970, 43.
19. *Ibid.*
20. Jess Peters, "Manny Sanguillen," *Black Sports*, October 1972, 41.
21. Charley Feeney, "Bucs Touting Manny as Mighty Fine Catcher," *The Sporting News*, 3 July 1971.
22. *Ibid.*
23. Ron Fimrite, "Two Catchers Cut from Royal Cloth, *Sports Illustrated*, 26 June 1972, 32.
24. Ray Blount, Jr., "Now Playing Right: Manny Sanguillen," *Sports Illustrated*, 19 March 1973.
25. "Manny's Task," *Newsweek*, 2 April 1973.
26. Bob Lenoir, "Manny Sanguillen . . . Out from Clemente's Shadow," *Baseball Digest*, undated article from Baseball Hall of Fame Library.
27. Lou Sahidi, *The Pirates: We are Family* (New York: Times Books, 1980), 162.
28. *Ibid.*, 171-172.
29. *Ibid.*
30. Kevin Kerrane, *Dollar Sign on the Muscle: The World of Baseball Scouting* (New York: Avon Books, 1985), 81.
31. *Ibid.*
32. *Ibid.*
33. Peter Gammons, "The Latin American Superscouts, *The Boston Globe*, 5 April 1985, 49.
34. Frank Deford, "Liege Lord of Latin Hopes," *Sports Illustrated*, 24 December 1973, 65.

Chapter 14

1. Gilbert Rogin, "Happy Little Luis," *Sports Illustrated*, 9 May 1960, 37-38.
2. Ed Prell, "Señor Shortstop of the White Sox," *The Saturday Evening Post*, 16 August 1958, 70.
3. Al Hirshberg, "He Makes the Go-Sox Go," *Journal American*, 21 July 1957.
4. Rogin, "Happy Little Luis," 32-34.
5. *Ibid.*, 34.

6. Margery Miller Welles, "Youth Section," *Christian Science Monitor,* 13 April 1956.
7. Rogin, "Happy Little Luis," 38.
8. *Ibid.,* 31.
9. "Sharpest Shortstop," *Newsweek,* 29 June 1959.
10. Rogin, "Happy Little Luis," 34.
11. Frank Robinson, *My Life in Baseball* (New York: Doubleday, 1968), 174.
12. Ron Fimrite, "Even the President Worried," *Sports Illustrated,* 14 June 1971, 54.
13. Larry Claflin, "L'il Looie Nearing End of Line, but it's More than Year Away," *The Sporting News,* 2 October 1971.
14. Peter Gammons, "Boston Massacre Throws Big Burden on Youth," *The Sporting News,* 13 April 1974.
15. Larry Whiteside, *Boston Globe,* 6 July 1983.
16. From 1983 induction speech, Baseball Hall of Fame, Cooperstown, New York.
17. A.S. ("Doc") Young, "Home Run King of the Giants," *Ebony,* July 1962, 50.
18. Orlando Cepeda with Bob Markus, *High and Inside—Orlando Cepeda's Story* (South Bend, IN: Icarus Press, 1983), 8.
19. Orlando Cepeda with Charles Epstein, *My Ups and Downs in Baseball* (New York: G.P. Putnam's Sons, 1968), 31.
20. A.S. ("Doc") Young, "Home Run King of the Giants," 47.
21. Tim Cohane, "Orlando Cepeda—Can He Slug His Way out of the Doghouse?" *Look,* 21 May 1963, 87.
22. "Proof of the Pluses," *Time,* 17 November 1967, 73.
23. Mark Mulvoy, "Cha Cha Goes Boom, Boom, Boom," *Sports Illustrated,* 24 July 1967, 20.
24. Alvin Dark and John Underwood, *When in Doubt, Fire the Manager* (New York: E.P. Dutton, 1980), 95.
25. Bob Stevens and Richard Keller, *Orlando Cepeda—the Baby Bull* (San Francisco: Woodford Publishing, 1987), 19.
26. "Proof of the Pluses," *Time,* 73.
27. Cepeda and Markus, *High and Inside,* 3.
28. Bob Price, "Cuellar Masters Screwjie," *The Sporting News,* 20 June 1964.
29. Ken Nigro, "Mike Cuellar, the Diamond's Happy Warrior," *Super Sports,* September 1972, 44.
30. Morris Siegel, "'Tonto' has Quiet Ride," *Baltimore Star,* no date, Baseball Hall of Fame Library.
31. Nigro, "Mike Cuellar, the Diamond's Happy Warrior," 44.
32. Lowell Reidenbaugh, "Shaky at Start, Cuellar Finishes like a Champ," *The Sporting News,* 31 October 1970, 39.
33. Nigro, "Mike Cuellar, the Diamond's Happy Warrior," 42.

Chapter 15

1. Bill Libby, "Bert Campaneris and the Better Life," *Sport,* December 1968, 70.

2. *Ibid.*
3. *Ibid.*
4. Bill Libby, *Charlie O. and the Angry A's* (New York: Doubleday, 1975), 159.
5. *Ibid.*
6. Bob Hertzel, "Rose to Campy: Bats Don't Carry Here," *Cincinnati Enquirer,* 14 October 1972, 31.
7. W. Leggett, "Hares Against Hairs," *Sports Illustrated,* 8 October 1973, 35.
8. Bill Libby, *Charlie O. and the Angry A's,* 280.
9. *The Sporting News,* 4 October 1980.
10. Steve Wulf, "In Philadelphia, They're the Wheeze Kids," *Sports Illustrated,* 14 March 1983, 27.
11. Marty Bell, "Dave Concepcion," *Sport,* October 1978, 46.
12. William Leggets, "Red Menace from Staid Cincy," *Sports Illustrated,* 20 April 1970.
13. Earl Lawson, "Reds Entertain Big Hopes for Lil David's Comeback," *The Sporting News,* 17 November 1973.
14. Lacy J. Banks, "Duo Sparks Cincinnati Machine," *Ebony,* September 1970, 70.
15. "Big Red Machine," *Time,* 24 August 1970, 35.
16. Ed Rumill, "Concepcion's Bat Comes Alive," *Christian Science Monitor,* 5 June 1973.
17. Bell, "Dave Concepcion," 46.
18. Earl Lawson, "Long-Awaited Family Reunion Sends Perez into Orbit," *The Sporting News,* 27 January 1973, 39.
19. Earl Lawson, "Perez Getting Hits as Reds Need 'Em," *The Sporting News,* 8 September 1973, 18.
20. Earl Lawson, "Concepcion Delivers as Reds' New Goliath," *The Sporting News,* 5 May 1973, 13.
21. Earl Lawson, "Concepcion Almost Immaculate as Shortstop," *The Sporting News,* 26 April 1975, 3.
22. Bob Rathgeber, "Man's Best Friend—Tony Perez," *Cincinnati Reds Scrapbook* (JCP Corporation of Virginia, 1982), 132.
23. Douglas S. Looney, "Hello Ypsilanti, Goodby," *Sports Illustrated,* 26 June 1976, 54.
24. "Perez Trade Angers Fans," Associated Press, 18 December 1976.
25. Wulf, "In Philadelphia, They're the Wheeze Kids," 32.
26. Tom Callahan, "The Complexities of Complexions," *Time,* 22 June 1987, 50.
27. "Perez Sees Bad Signs," *The Sporting News,* 23 August 1980, 12.
28. Hal Bodley, "When Perez Talks, Phils Will Listen," *The Sporting News,* 21 March 1983, 33.
29. Roger Angell, *Season Ticket: A Baseball Companion* (New York: Ballantine Books, 1988), 163-164.
30. Bell, "Dave Concepcion," 46.
31. Baseball Notebook, *The Sporting News,* 24 October 1988.
32. Bell, "Dave Concepcion," 46.

Chapter 16

1. Rod Carew with Ira Berkow, *Carew* (New York: Simon and Schuster, 1979), 15.
2. *Ibid.*, 15.
3. Jerry Izenberg, *Great Latin Sports Figures: The Proud People* (New York: Doubleday and Company, 1976), 96.
4. "Baseball's Best Hitter Goes for Glory," *Time*, 18 July 1977, 61.
5. Carew and Berkow, *Carew*, 63.
6. Ron Fimrite, "Portrait of the Artist as a Hitter," *Sports Illustrated*, 13 June 1983, 86.
7. Carew and Berkow, *Carew*, 108-109.
8. Peter Carry, "Baseball's Week," *Sports Illustrated*, 9 June 1969, 108.
9. Bob Fowler, "Oliva's 1967 Tip Helped Carew to Batting Title," *The Sporting News*, 28 October 1972, 19.
10. Fimrite, "Portrait of the Artist as a Hitter," 87.
11. "No Top Pay, Very Little Ink, Carew Only a Permanent King," Associated Press, 28 September 1975.
12. Scorecard, *Sports Illustrated*, 11 July 1977, 10.
13. Peter Bonaventure, "How Carew Does It," *Newsweek*, 11 July 1977, 46-47.
14. Ted Williams with John Underwood, "I Hope Rod Carew Hits .400," *Sports Illustrated*, 29 June 1977, 20-22.
15. Jack Hines, "The Total Gamer," *Sport*, August 1979, 15-16.
16. Rod Carew with Frank Pace and Armen Keteyian, *Rod Carew's Art and Science of Hitting* (New York: Penguin Books, 1986), 170.
17. Murray Chass, "Carew's Credentials for Hall are of Impeccable Variety," *New York Times*, January 1991, B7-B8.
18. Leonard Lewin, "Oliva, The Natural," *New York Post*, 20 September 1965.
19. Max Nichols, ". . . Says Griffith," *The Sporting News*, 16 May 1964, 3.
20. *Ibid.*
21. *Ibid.*
22. Phil Elderkin, "Oliva—Saved by Designated Hitter Rule," *Christian Science Monitor*, 12 June 1965.
23. *Carew and Berkower*, 84-85.
24. Bob Snyder, "I'd Get Hurt All Over Again—Tony Oliva," *Syracuse Herald American*, 24 August 1980.
25. *Carew and Berkower*, 84-85.
26. Bob Fowler, "Oliva, Even as Spear Carrier, Has Champion's Touch," *The Sporting News*, 29 May 1976, 8.
27. Mel Antoney, "Oliva Savors 'the feeling' Again," *USA Today*, 16 October 1987.
28. Tim Horgan, "Luis Tiant–All Man," *Boston Herald American*, 12 June 1974.
29. Tom Fitzpatrick, "The Most Popular Indian," *Sport*, September 1968, 73.
30. *Ibid.*
31. Mike Lamey, "Life is Lots of Fun for Luis but He Frets over Injury," *The Sporting News*, 20 June 1970, 10.

32. Luís Tiant and Joe Fitzgerald, *El Tiante, the Luís Tiant Story* (New York: Doubleday, 1976).
33. *Ibid.,* 157.
34. Peter Gammons, "El Tiante," *Boston Globe,* 21 July 1974.
35. Peter Gammons, "Tiant Terrific—And Bosox Fans Let him Know it," *The Sporting News,* 4 October 1975, 19.
36. Lowell Reidenbaugh, "Luis Retraces his Steps, Makes Bosox Run Legal," *The Sporting News,* 25 October 1975, 8.
37. Jayson Stark, "Jose Cruz: Astros' Invisible Superstar," *The Sporting News,* 24 June 1985, 25.
38. Jerry Sullivan, "Jose Cruz Steps Out," *Sport,* September 1985, 59-60.
39. Harry Shattuck, "Speeding Astros Credit Cruz for Igniting Fuse," *The Sporting News,* 21 August 1976, 24.
40. Harry Shattuck, "Optimists Unlimited in Houston Dugout," *The Sporting News,* 5 May 1979, 34.
41. Jose Cruz as told to George Vass, "The Game I'll Never Forget," *Baseball Digest,* December 1985, 87-89.
42. "Complete Player? Astros' Jose Cruz," *The Sporting News,* 11 July 1983, 42.
43. "The Ponce de Leon of the Astros," *Texas Monthly,* June 1986, 125.

Chapter 17

1. Leo Banks, "Babe Ruth of Mexico," *Sport,* February 1985, 70.
2. *Ibid.,* 74.
3. *Ibid.,* 70.
4. *Ibid.,* 68.
5. *Ibid.,* 74.
6. Scott Ostler, "He Has Baseball World in His Hands," *The Sporting News,* 23 May 1981.
7. Furmen Bisher, "Valenzuela," *The Sporting News,* 13 June 1981.
8. Ostler, "He Has Baseball World in His Hands."
9. *Ibid.*
10. S.H. Burchard, *Sports Star: Fernando Valenzuela* (San Diego: Harcourt Brace Jovanovich, 1982).
11. "Caught on the Fly," *The Sporting News,* 2 February 1982.
12. "They Said It," *Sports Illustrated,* 28 December 1981, 18.
13. Stan Isle, "Kuhn Denies Backing Share-Wealth Scheme," *The Sporting News,* 17 May 1982, 7.
14. Stan Isle, "Caught on the Fly."
15. Murray Chass, "Fernando's $1 Million Tops Pay Awards," *The Sporting News,* 7 March 1983, 60-62.
16. *The Sporting News,* 10 June 1985, 7.
17. Tony Castro, "Something Screwy Going on Here," *Sports Illustrated,* 8 July 1985, 31-37.
18. Stan Isle, "An Old Semipro Lives out a Baseball Fantasy," *The Sporting News,* 3 March 1986, 8.
19. Gordon Verrell, "Fernando Makes 20, the Hard Way," *The Sporting News,* 6 October 1986, 16.

20. Fernando Paramo, "Sport Interview: Fernando Valenzuela," *Sport,* July 1986, 22.
21. Sam McManis, "Mania No Mas," *Los Angeles Times,* 17 March 1988.
22. McManis, "Trying to Get the Snap Back," *Los Angeles Times,* 14 June 1988, 1, 6.

Chapter 18

1. Bernard Diederich, "Baseball in Their Blood: The San Pedro Syndrome," *Caribbean Review,* vol. 4, no. 4, 15.
2. Russell Schneider, "Carty Kayoes his Hard-Luck Hoodoo," *The Sporting News,* 28 August 1976.
3. Bob Wolf, "Carty in Front as Braves Toss Mitts at Mets," *The Sporting News,* 8 August 1964, 21.
4. Wayne Minshew, "Shoe Salesman in Deep Shock," *The Sporting News,* 22 July 1967.
5. "Rico Curious about Smoke, Conducts a One-Man Probe," *The Sporting News,* 22 July 1967.
6. Dick Young, "Rico Carty," *Daily News,* 4 June 1970.
7. Wayne Minshew, "Even the Mayor Doused in Atlanta Celebration," *The Sporting News,* 18 October 1969.
8. Wayne Minshew, "Braves, Carty Beaten," *The Sporting News,* 11 September 1971, 14.
9. Schneider, "Carty Kayoes His Hard-Luck Hoodoo."
10. Diederich, "Baseball in Their Blood," 15.
11. Bill Gutman, *At Bat #2* (New York: Grosset & Dunlap, 1974), 112-147.
12. John Wilson, "Cesar Cedeño . . . The Next Super Star?" *The Sporting News,* 19 August 1972.
13. Harold Peterson, "Hail Cesar! and Hello," *Sports Illustrated,* 7 August 1972, 42.
14. Gutman, *At Bat #2,* 123.
15. *Ibid.,* 128-129.
16. Ron Fimrite, "Now Let us Render unto Cesar," *Sports Illustrated,* 21 May 1973, 41-43.
17. Ben Henkey, "Bench and Gibson Reign on N.L. Fielding Team," *The Sporting News,* 24 November 1973, 31.
18. "Hot Dog and Pudge," *Time,* 16 July 1973, 38.
19. Bowie Kuhn, *Hardball, the Education of a Baseball Commissioner* (New York: McGraw Hill, 1988), 201.
20. Joe Heiling, "Cesar Set for Brickbats," *The Sporting News,* 9 February 1974, 33.
21. Abby Mendelson, "Whatever Happened to Cesar Cedeño," *Baseball Quarterly,* Winter 1978-79, 45-47, 57.
22. Rick Hummel, "Price is Right in Cedeño Deal," *The Sporting News,* 16 September 1985, 19.
23. Ross Newman, "The Great Escape" (Part III), *Los Angeles Times,* 7 January 1985, 16.
24. *Ibid.*

25. *Ibid.*
26. Gordon Verrell, "Dodgers' Guerrero is Wanted Man," *The Sporting News,* 19 December 1981, 46.
27. Dave Nightengale, "Lemon Takes Rap . . . Dodgers Take Series," *The Sporting News,* 14 November 1981, 40.
28. Gordon Verrell, "Guerrero Glistens while Others Fail," *The Sporting News,* 7 June 1982, 36.
29. Tim McCarver, "Baseball '85: Sneak Preview," *Sport,* 66.

Chapter 19

1. Bill Brubaker, "Hey Kid—Wanna be a Star?" *Sports Illustrated,* 13 July 1981, 71.
2. Kerrane, *Dollar Sign on the Muscle: The World of Baseball Scouting,* 278.
3. Larry Millson, *Ballpark Figures: The Blue Jays and the Business of Baseball,* 217.
4. Steve Wulf, "Standing Tall at Short," *Sports Illustrated,* 9 February 1987, 138.
5. Millson, *Ballpark Figures,* 219-220.
6. *Ibid.*
7. Peter Gammons, "The Winter Game, "*Boston Globe,* 25 January 1985, 62.
8. Peter Gammons, "Dominican has Replaced Cuba as Prime Talent Source," *Baseball America,* 25 July 1985 and 9 August 1985, 8.

Chapter 20

1. "Cuba Si, Baseball Si." *Sports Illustrated,* 24 November 1975, 65.
2. Thomas Boswell, "Cuban Baseball: The Only Way of Life," *The Miami Herald,* 30 April 1978.
3. Ken Nigro, "Sobering Sight in Nicaragua—Gun-Toting Kids," *The Sporting News,* 5 April 1980.
4. Phillip Bennett, "Game Didn't Help Them Escape Long," *Boston Globe,* 13 August 1987.
5. Leslie Bernstein, "On the Scene: While War Rages, Baseball Remains the National Passion in Nicaraga," *Sports Illustrated,* 19 August 1985.
6. "Even the Contras Cried," *Mother Jones,* July 1985, 13-14.
7. John Powers, "Games of Ball and Politics,"*Boston Globe,* 13 August 1987.

Chapter 21

Note: The primary sources for chapters 11 and 21 on the Caribbean World Series were *Series del Caribe 1949-1986* and *Guia de las Series del Caribe 1949-1988,* both written by Alfonso Araujo Bojorquez, the former published by Impressions Gassos, Ciudad Obregon, Sonora, Mexico, the latter with no publisher name evident. Other sources include *Momentos Inolvidables del Béisbol Profesional Venezolano 1946-1984,* written by Alexis Salas H., published by Miguel Angel Garcia e Hijo s.r.l., Caracas, Venezuela, 1985, and *Serie del Caribe 88,* Volume II, written by Jose Antero Nunez, General de Brigada, published by Impresos Urbina, C.C., Caracas, 1988.

BIBLIOGRAPHY

Abrams, Al. "Sidelights on Sports." *Pittsburgh Post-Gazette,* 11 March 1971.

———. "Super Stardom Ahead for Sanguillen?" Baseball Hall of Fame Library Collection: *Baseball Digest* article, n.d.

Alexander, Charles C. *John McGraw.* New York: Viking Penguin Inc., 1988.

———. *Ty Cobb.* New York: Oxford University Press, 1984.

Allen, Lee. *The Cincinnati Reds.* New York: G.P. Putnam's Sons, 1948.

———. *Cooperstown Corner: Columns From the Sporting News.* Cleveland: Society for American Baseball Research, Inc., n.d.

Alou, Felipe, and Herm Weiskopf. *Felipe Alou . . . My Life and Baseball.* Waco, TX: Word Books, 1967.

Alvarez Bajares, Rodolfo, and Oscar Arango Cadavid. *Alfonso "Chico" Carrasquel: Idolo de Siempre.* Caracas: Ediciones Culturales y Deportivas, C.A., 1986.

Anderson, Sparky, and Si Burick. *The Main Spark: Sparky Anderson and the Cincinnati Reds.* New York: Doubleday, 1978.

Angell, Roger. *Season Ticket: A Baseball Companion.* New York: Ballantine Books, 1988.

Antoney, Mel. "Oliva Savors 'The Feeling' Again." *USA Today,* 16 October 1987.

Arbena, Joseph L., ed. *Sport and Society in Latin America.* New York: Greenwood Press, 1988.

Banks, Lacy J. "Duo Sparks Cincinnati Machine." *Ebony,* September 1970.

Banks, Leo. "Babe Ruth of Mexico." *Sport,* February 1985.

"Baseball 25 Grande." *Newsweek,* 15 April 1946.

"Baseball Notebook." *The Sporting News,* 24 October 1988.

"Baseball's Best Hitter Goes for Glory." *Time,* 18 July 1977, 61.

"Beisboleros," *Newsweek,* 29 May 1944.

Bell, Ian. *The Dominican Republic.* Boulder, CO: Westview Press, 1981.

Bell, Marty. "Dave Concepcion." *Sport,* October 1978.

Benítez, Leo. *Las Grandes Ligas 1900-1980.* 2d ed. Caracas: Publicaciones Seleven, 1980.

———. *Registro del Béisbol Professional de Venezuela 1965-1985.* Caracas: Impresos Urbina C.A., 1985.

Benjamin, Thomas, and William McNellie. *Other Mexicos: Essays on Regional Mexican History, 1876-1911.* Albuquerque: The University of New Mexico Press, 1984.

Bennett, Phillip. "Game Didn't Help Them Escape Long." *Boston Globe,* 13 August 1987.

Biederman, Les. "Clemente: The Player Who Can Do it All." *The Sporting News,* 20 April 1968.

———. "Shoulder Sore, Clemente Says He May Retire." *The Sporting News,* 24 August 1968.

"Big Red Machine." *Time,* 24 August 1970.

Bisher, Furman. "Valenzuela Already Steeped in Legends." *The Sporting News,* 13 June 1981.

Blount, Ray, Jr. "Now Playing Right: Manny Sanguillen." *Sports Illustrated,* 19 March 1973.

Bodley, Hal. "When Perez Talks, Phils Will Listen." *The Sporting News,* 21 March 1983.

Bojórquez, Alfonso Araujo. *Guia de las Series del Caribe 1949-1988.*

———. *Series del Caribe 1949-1986.* Cíudad Obregón, Sonora, Mexico: Impresiones Gassos, 1986.

Bonaventure, Peter. "How Carew Does it." *Newsweek,* 11 July 1977, 46-47.

Bracker, Milton. "Mexico's Raiders Ride Again." *Saturday Evening Post,* 8 March 1947.

Brashler, William. *Josh Gibson: A Life in the Negro Leagues.* New York: Harper and Row, 1978.

Broeg, Bob. "Spahn, Clemente, Irvin, Kelly Enter Hall of Fame." *The Sporting News,* 18 August 1973.

Brosnan, Jim. *Great Baseball Pitchers.* New York: Random House, 1965.

Brown, Bruce. "Cuban Baseball." *Atlantic Monthly,* June 1984.

Brubaker, Bill. "Hey, Kid—Wanna Be a Star?" *Sports Illustrated,* 13 July 1981.

Bruce, Janet. *The Kansas City Monarchs: Champions of Black Baseball.* Lawrence, KS: University Press of Kansas, 1985.

Burchard, S.H. *Fernando Valenzuela: Sports Star.* San Diego: Harcourt Brace Jovanovich, 1982.

Burns, E. Bradford. *At War in Nicaragua: The Reagan Doctrine and the Politics of Nostalgia.* New York: Harper and Row, 1987.

Callahan, Tom. "The Complexities of Complexions." *Time,* 22 June 1987.

Carew, Rod, and Ira Berkow. *Carew.* New York: Simon and Schuster, 1979.

Carew, Rod, with Frank Pace and Armen Keteyian. *Rod Carew's Art and the Science of Hitting.* New York: Penguin Books, 1986.

Carry, Peter. "Baseball's Week." *Sports Illustrated,* 9 June 1969, 108.

Castro, Tony. "Something Screwy Going on Here." *Sports Illustrated,* 8 July 1985.

Cepeda, Orlando, with Bob Markus. *High and Inside: Orlando Cepeda's Story.* South Bend, IN: Icarus Press, 1983.

Cepeda, Orlando, with Charles Epstein. *My Ups and Downs in Baseball.* New York: G.P. Putnam's Sons, 1968.

Chass, Murray. "Carew's Credentials for Hall are of Impeccable Variety." *New York Times,* 3 January 1991, B7-B8.

Chass, Murray. "Fernando's $1 Million Tops Pay Awards." *The Sporting News,* 7 March 1983.

Christine, Bill. *Roberto!* New York: Stadia Sports Publishing, 1973.

Clafin, Larry. "Li'l Looie Nearing End of Line, but It's More than Year Away." *The Sporting News,* 2 October 1971.

Cohane, Tim. "Orlando Cepeda—Can He Slug his Way out of the Doghouse?" *Look,* 21 May 1963.

"Complete Player? Astros' Jose Cruz." *The Sporting News,* 11 July 1983.

Compton, George C., and Adolfo Solórzano Diaz. "Latins on the Diamond." *Americas,* vol. 3, June 1951.

Couzens, Gerald Secor. *A Baseball Album.* New York: Lippincott and Crowell, 1980.

Cropenz, Richard C. *Baseball: America's Diamond Mine 1919-1941.* Orlando: University Presses of Florida, 1980.

Cruz, Hector J. *Juan Marichal: La Historia de su Vida.* Santo Domingo: Turideportes S.A., 1984.

Cruz, Jose, as told to George Vass. "The Game I'll Never Forget." *Baseball Digest,* December 1985.

Dark, Alvin, and John Underwood. *When in Doubt, Fire the Manager.* New York: E.P. Dutton, 1980.

Davids, L. Robert, ed. *Minor League Baseball Stars.* Cooperstown, NY: Society for American Baseball Research, 1978.

Deane, Bill. *Award Voting: A History of the Most Valuable Player, Rookie of the Year, and Cy Young Awards.* Kansas City, MO: Society for American Baseball Research, 1988.

DeFord, Frank. "Liege Lord of Latin Hopes." *Sports Illustrated,* 24 December 1973.

del Rosario, Rubén, Esther Melon de Díaz, and Edgar Martínez Masdeu. *Breve Enciclopedia de la Cultura Puertorriqueña.* San Juan, Puerto Rico: Editorial Cordillera, Inc.

Devaney, John. *Juan Marichal, Mister Strike.* New York: G.P. Putnam's Sons, 1970.

———. *Where Are They Today? Great Sport Stars of Yesteryear.* New York: Crown Publishers, 1985.

Diederich, Bernard. "Baseball in Their Blood: The San Pedro Syndrome." *Caribbean Review,* vol. 4, no. 4.

Dolson, Frank. *Beating the Bushes.* South Bend, IN: Icarus Press, 1982.

"Dominican Dandy." *Time,* 10 June 1966.

Donnelly, Joe. "Alou Bridged the Gap for Latin Americans." Baseball Hall of Fame Library newspaper article, 8 September 1971.

Durso, Joseph. "We Band of Brothers." *New York Times,* 14 August 1975.

Einstein, Charles, ed. *The Baseball Reader: Favorites from the Fireside Books of Baseball.* New York: McGraw-Hill, 1983.

Elderkin, Phil. "Oliva—Saved by Designated Hitter Rule." *Christian Science Monitor,* 12 June 1965.

Feeney, Charles. "Bucs Touting Manny as a Mighty Fine Catcher." *The Sporting News,* 3 July 1971.

———. "$5,000 Manny Huge Pirate Treasure." *The Sporting News,* 1 May 1971.

"Felipe Alou Quits." Baseball Hall of Fame Library newspaper article, 6 May 1974.

Figueredo, Jorge, ed. *Momentos Estelares*. Miami: Internal Trading Corporation, 1981.

Fimrite, Ron. "Even the President Worried." *Sports Illustrated,* 14 June 1971.

————. "Now Let Us Render unto Cesar." *Sports Illustrated,* 21 May 1973.

————. "Portrait of the Artist as a Hitter." *Sports Illustrated,* 13 June 1983.

————. "Two Catchers Cut from Royal Cloth." *Sports Illustrated,* 26 June 1972.

Fitzgerald, Ray. "Uncle Joe—Senators' Cuban Connection. *The Sporting News,* 21 June 1980.

Fitzpatrick, Tom. "The Most Popular Indian." *Sport,* September 1968.

Fowler, Bob. "Oliva, Even as Spear Carrier, Has Champion's Touch." *The Sporting News,* 29 May 1976.

————. "Oliva's 1967 Tip Helped Carew to Batting Title." *The Sporting News,* 28 October 1972.

Frio, Daniel C., and Mark Onigman. "Good Field, No Hit: The Image of Latin American Baseball Players in the American Press, 1871-1946." *Revista/Review Inter-Americana* 9 (Summer 1979).

Furlong, William Barry. "The White Sox Katzenjammer Kid." *Saturday Evening Post,* 10 July 1952.

Gammons, Peter. "Boston Massacre Throws Big Burden on Youth." *The Sporting News,* 13 April 1974.

————. "Dominican has Replaced Cuba as Prime Talent Source." *Baseball America,* 25 July 1985 and 9 August 1985.

————. "El Tiante." *Boston Globe,* 21 July 1974.

————. "The Latin American Superscouts." *The Boston Globe,* 5 April 1985.

————. "Tiant Terrific—And Bosox Fans Let Him Know It." *The Sporting News,* 4 October 1975.

————. "The Winter Game." *Boston Globe,* 25 January 1985.

García, Carlos. *Béisbol para Siempre*. Mexico: I.E.S.A., 1979.

Gerlach, Larry. *The Men in Blue*. New York: The Viking Press, 1980.

Gillespie, Ray. "Million Peso League." *Inter-American,* October 1946.

Goldstein, Richard. *Spartan Seasons: How Baseball Survived the Second World War*. New York: Macmillan, 1980.

Gorman, Tom, and Jerome Holtzman. *Three and Two!* New York: Charles Scribner's Sons, 1979.

Graham, Frank. "Adolfo Luque is Dead?" *New York Journal-American,* 17 July 1957.

Gunther, John. *Inside South America*. New York: Harper and Row, 1966.

Gutman, Bill. *At Bat #2 Bonds*Cedeno*Fisk*Rose*. New York: Grosset & Dunlop, 1974.

Halberstam, David. *Summer of '49*. New York: William Morrow, 1989.

Hanson, Roger D. *The Politics of Mexican Development*. Baltimore: The Johns Hopkins Press, 1971.

Harris, Phillip R., and Robert T. Moran. *Managing Cultural Differences*. Houston: Gulf Publishing Company, 1979.

Heiling, Joe. "Cesar Set for Brickbats." *The Sporting News,* 9 February 1974.

Henderson, Robert W. *Baseball and Rounders*. New York: New York Public Library, 1939.

Henkey, Ben. "Bench and Gibson Reign on N.L. Fielding Team." *The Sporting News*, 24 November 1973.

Hertzel, Bob. "Rose to Campy: Bats Don't Carry Here." *Cincinnati Enquirer*, 14 October 1972.

Hines, Jack. "The Total Gamer." *Sport*, August 1979, 15-16.

Hirshberg, Al. "He Makes the Go-Sox Go." *Journal American*, 21 July 1957.

Hoffman, John C. *Baseball Stars of 1954*. New York: Lions Books, 1954.

———. "Orestes Miñoso—Speed Merchant." *Baseball Stars of 1954*, compiled by Bruce Jacobs. New York: Lions Books, 1954.

———. "What You Say, Minnie's Hokay!" *Colliers*, 5 April 1952.

Holway, John. *Blackball Stars: Negro League Pioneers*. Westport, CT: Meckler Books, 1988.

Horgan, Tim. "Luís Tiant—All Man." *Boston Herald American*, 12 June 1974.

"Hot Dog and Pudge." *Time*, 16 July 1973.

Hummel, Rick. "Price is Right in Cedeño Deal." *The Sporting News*, 16 September 1985.

Huyke, Emilo E. *Los Deportes en Puerto Rico*. Sharon, CT: Troutman Press.

Isle, Stan. *The Sporting News*, 17 May 1982.

———. *The Sporting News*, 28 June 1982.

———. "An Old Semipro Lives out a Baseball Fantasy." *The Sporting News*, 3 March 1986.

Izenberg, Jerry. *Great Latin Sports Figures: The Proud People*. New York: Doubleday, 1976.

James, Bill. *The Bill James Historical Abstract*. New York: Villard Books, 1986.

James, Bill, John Dewan, and Project Scoresheet. *The Great American Baseball Stat Book*. New York: Ballantine Books, 1987.

Jimenez, O., and Dr. Jose de Jesus. *Archivo de Baseball*. Santiago, Dominican Republic: Amigo del Hogar, 1977.

Kerrane, Kevin. *Dollar Sign on the Muscle: The World of Baseball Scouting*. New York: Avon Books, 1985.

Kiersh, Edward. *Where Have You Gone, Vince DiMaggio?* New York: Bantam Books, 1983.

Kuhn, Bowie. *Hardball, the Education of a Baseball Commissioner*. New York: McGraw-Hill, 1988.

Lamey, Mike. "Life is Lots of Fun for Luis but He Frets Over Injury." *The Sporting News*, 20 June 1970.

Lasorda, Tommy, and David Fisher. *The Artful Dodger*. New York: Avon Books, 1985.

Lawson, Earl. "Concepcion Almost Immaculate as Shortstop." *The Sporting News*, 26 April 1975.

———. "Concepcion Delivers as Reds' New Goliath." *The Sporting News*, 5 May 1973.

———. Long-Awaited Family Reunion Sends Perez into Orbit." *The Sporting News*, 27 January 1973.

————."Perez Getting Hits as Reds Need 'Em." *The Sporting News*, 8 September 1973.

————. "Reds Entertain Big Hopes for Lil David's Comeback." *The Sporting News*, 17 November 1973.

Lee, Charles. "Is Roberto Clemente as Good as He Thinks He Is?" *Sports Herald*, 1972.

Leggets, William. "Red Menace from Staid Cincy." *Sports Illustrated*, 20 April 1970.

Lenoir, Bob. "Manny Sanguillen . . . Out from Clemente's Shadow." Hall of Fame Library Collection, *Baseball Digest* article, n.d.

Leones de Caracas. "La Fiebre del Béisbol." Team program, 1986.

Lewin, Leonard. "Oliva, The Natural." *New York Post*, 20 September 1965.

Libby, Bill. "Bert Campaneris and the Better Life." *Sport*, December 1968.

————. *Charlie O. and the Angry A's*. New York: Doubleday, 1975.

Lindberg, Richard. *Sox: The Complete Record of Chicago White Sox Baseball*. New York: Macmillan, 1984.

Littwin, Mike. *Fernando!* New York: Bantam Books, 1981.

Looney, Douglas S. "Hello Ypsilanti, Goodby." *Sports Illustrated*, 26 June 1976.

Los Doce Mundos del Caribe. Spain: Ediciones Cid, 1963.

Lowenthal, Abraham F. *The Dominican Intervention*. Cambridge, MA: Harvard University Press, 1972.

Luciano, Ron, and David Fisher. *Strike Two*. New York: Bantam Books, 1984.

————. *The Umpire Strikes Back*. New York: Bantam Books, 1982.

MacFarlane, Paul, ed. *Daguerreotypes*. St. Louis: The Sporting News Publishing Company, 1981.

Mann, Jack. "Battle of San Francisco." *Sports Illustrated*, 30 August 1965.

"Manny's Task." *Newsweek*, 2 April 1973.

Marazzi, Rich, and Len Fiorito. *Aaron to Zipfel*. New York: Avon Books, 1985.

————. *Aaron to Zuverink*. Briarcliff Manor, NY: Stein and Day, 1982.

Marichal, Juan, with Charles Einstein. *A Pitcher's Story*. New York: Doubleday, 1967.

McCarver, Tim. "Baseball '85: Sneak Preview." *Sport*. January 1985, 66.

McManis, Sam. "Mania No Mas." *Los Angeles Times*, 17 March 1988.

————. "Trying to Get the Snap Back." *Los Angeles Times*, 14 June 1988.

Mendelson, Abby. "Whatever Happened to Cesar Cedeño." *Baseball Quarterly*, Winter 1978-79.

Millson, Larry. *Ballpark Figures: The Blue Jays and the Business of Baseball*. Toronto: McClelland and Stewart, 1987.

Miñoso, Orestes, with Fernando Fernandez and Robert Kleinfelder. *Extra Innings: My Life in Baseball*. Chicago: Regnery Gateway, 1983.

Minshew, Wayne. "Braves, Carty Beaten." *The Sporting News*, 11 September 1971.

————. "Even the Mayor Doused in Atlanta Celebration." *The Sporting News*, 18 October 1969.

————. "Shoe Salesman in Deep Shock." *The Sporting News*, 22 July 1967.

Mulvoy, Mark. "Cha Cha Goes Boom, Boom, Boom." *Sports Illustrated*, 24 July 1967.

Musicant, Ivan. *The Banana Wars: A History of United States Military Intervention in Latin America from the Spanish-American War to the Invasion of Panama*. New York: Macmillan, 1990.

Musick, Phil. *Who was Roberto? A Biography of Roberto Clemente*. New York: Doubleday, 1974.

Newman, Ross. "The Great Escape." *Los Angeles Times*, 7 January 1985.

Nichols, Max. *The Sporting News*, 16 May 1964.

Nightengale, Dave. "Lemon Takes Rap . . . Dodgers Take Series." *The Sporting News*, 14 November 1981, 40.

Nigro, Ken. "Mike Cuellar, the Diamond's Happy Warrior." *Super Sports*, September 1972.

———. "Sobering Night in Nicaragua—Gun-Toting Kids. *The Sporting News*, 5 April 1980.

"No Top Pay, Very Little Ink, Carew Only a Permanent King." Associated Press, 28 September 1975.

Núñez, José Antero. *Serie del Caribe 88*. Volumen II, Caracas: Impresos Urbina C.A., 1988.

Ogle, Jim. "Old-Pro Felipe Perfect Model." *Sunday Star Ledger*, 28 April 1973.

———. "Yanks Book Alou as Florida Kid Tutor." *Sunday Star Ledger*, 16 September 1972

Oliva, Tony, with Bob Fowler. *Tony O! The Trials and Triumphs of Tony Oliva*. New York: Hawthorne Books, 1973.

Keller, Rich. *Orlando Cepeda: The Baby Bull*. San Francisco: Woodford Publishing, 1987.

Ostler, Scott. "He Has Baseball World in his Hands." *The Sporting News*, 23 May 1981.

Paige, LeRoy "Satchel," as told to David Lipman. *Maybe I'll Pitch Forever: A Great Baseball Player Tells the Hilarious Story Behind the Legend*. New York: Doubleday, 1962.

Palmer, R.R., and Joel Colton. *A History of the Modern World*. New York: Alfred A. Knopf, 1967.

Paramo, Fernando. "Sport Interview: Fernando Valenzuela." *Sport*, July 1986.

Pendle, George. *A History of Latin America*. London: Penguin Books, 1973.

"Perez Sees Bad Signs." *The Sporting News*, 23 August 1980.

"Perez Trade Angers Fans." Associated Press, 18 December 1976.

Peters, Jess. "Manny Sanguillen." *Black Sports*, October 1972.

Peterson, Harold. "Hail, Cesar! and Hello." *Sports Illustrated*, 7 August 1972.

Peterson, Robert. *Only the Ball was White: A History of Legendary Black Players and All-Black Professional Teams*. New York: McGraw-Hill, 1984.

Picon-Salas, Mariano, Augusto Mijares, Ramón Díaz-Sánchez, Eduardo Arcila Farias, and Juan Liscano. *Venezuela Independiente 1810-1960*. Caracas: Fundacion Eugenio Mendoza, 1962.

Piña, Tony. *Guía del Béisbol Professional Dominicano*. Santo Domingo: Editorama, S.A., 1983-1988.

———. *Los Grandes Finales*. Santo Domingo: Editora Colegial Quisqueyana, S.A., 1983.

"The Selling Game." *Sports Illustrated,* 17 November 1969.

"The Ponce de Leon of the Astros." *Texas Monthly,* June 1986.

Povich, Shirley. *The Washington Senators.* New York: G.P. Putnam's Sons, 1954.

Powers, John. "Games of Ball and Politics." *Boston Globe,* 13 August 1988.

Prell, Ed. "Senor Shortstop of the White Sox." *The Saturday Evening Post,* 16 August 1958.

Price, Bob. "Cuellar Masters Screwjie." *The Sporting News,* 20 June 1974.

"Proof of the Pluses." *Time,* 17 November 1967.

Rathgeber, Bob. *Cincinnati Reds Scrapbook.* JCP Corporation of Virgina, 1982.

Regalado, Samuel. "Latin American Minor League Experience in Western Communities." Baseball Hall of Fame Library Collection, paper on file.

Reichler, Joseph L. *The Great All-Time Baseball Record Book.* New York: Macmillan, 1981.

———, ed. *The Baseball Encyclopedia.* 7th ed. New York: Macmillan, 1988.

Reidenbaugh, Lowell. "Luis Retraces his Steps, Makes Bosox Run Legal." *The Sporting News,* 25 October 1975.

———. "Shaky at Start, Cuellar Finishes Like a Champ." *The Sporting News,* 31 October 1970.

"Rico Curious about Smoke, Conducts a One-Man Probe." *The Sporting News,* 22 July 1967.

Riley, James A. *The All-Time All-Stars of Black Baseball.* TK Publishers, 1983.

Robinson, Frank. *My Life in Baseball.* New York: Doubleday, 1968.

Rodman, Seldon. *A Short History of Mexico.* New York: Stein and Day, 1982.

Rogin, Gilbert. "Happy Little Luis." *Sports Illustrated,* 9 May 1960.

Rogosin, Donn. *Invisible Men: Life in Baseball's Negro Leagues.* New York: Atheneum Press, 1983.

Roseboro, John, with Bill Libby. *Glory Days with the Dodgers and Other Days with Others.* New York: Atheneum Press, 1978.

Rumill, Ed. "Concepcion's Bat Comes Alive." *Christian Science Monitor,* 5 June 1973.

Rust, Art, Jr. *Get that Nigger off the Field.* New York: Delacorte Press, 1976.

———. *Recollections of a Baseball Junkie.* New York: William Morrow, 1985.

Rust, Edna, and Art Rust, Jr. *Art Rust's Illustrated History of the Black Athlete.* New York: Doubleday, 1985.

Sahidi, Lou. *The Pirates: We are Family.* New York: Times Books, 1980.

Salas H., Alexis. *Momentos Inolvidables del Béisbol Professional Venezolano 1946–1984.* Venezuela: Miguel Angel Garcia e Hijo, s.r.l., 1985.

Schneider, Russell. "Carty Kayoes his Hard-Luck Hoodoo." *The Sporting News,* 28 August 1976.

"Scorecard." *Sports Illustrated,* 11 July 1977.

Secades, Eladio, "Primeras Noticias del Baseball," *Diario de la Marina,* 125th anniversary issue. Havana: 1957.

Seda, Jose. *Béisbol.* Universidad de Puerto Rico, 1959.

"Señor Mays—Big Hit in San Juan." *Colliers,* 7 January 1955.

Senzel, Howard. *Baseball and the Cold War: Being a Soliloquy on the Necessity of Baseball.* New York: Harcourt Brace Jovanovich, 1977.

Seymour, Harold. *Baseball: The Early Years*. New York: Oxford University Press, 1960.

"Sharpest Shortstop." *Newsweek*, 29 June 1959.

Shattuck, Harry. "Optimists Unlimited in Houston Dugout." *The Sporting News*, 5 May 1979.

———. "Speeding Astros Credit Cruz for Igniting Fuse." *The Sporting News*, 21 August 1976.

Shlain, Bruce. *Oddballs: Baseball's Greatest Pranksters, Flakes, Hot Dogs, and Hotheads*. New York: Penguin Books, 1989.

Siegel, Morris. "'Tonto' Has Quiet Ride." Baseball Hall of Fame Library Collection, newspaper article, n.d.

"Situacion Don Q." *Newsweek*, 9 January 1950.

Smith, Ira. *Baseball's Famous Pitchers: Capers Cut and Records Made by Fifty-Three Pitching Greats*. New York: A.S. Barnes and Company, 1954.

Smith, Myron J., Jr. *Baseball: A Comprehensive Bibliography*. Jefferson, NC: McFarland and Company, 1986.

Snow, Peter G. *Government and Politics in Latin America*. New York: Holt, Rinehart and Winston, 1967.

Snyder, Bob. "I'd Get Hurt All Over Again—Tony Oliva." *Syracuse Herald American*, 24 August 1980.

Stark, Jayson. "Jose Cruz: Astros' Invisible Superstar." *The Sporting News*, 24 June 1985.

The Sporting News. *Official Baseball Register*. St. Louis: The Sporting News Publishing Company, 1990.

———. *Baseball Guide*. St. Louis: The Sporting News Publishing Company, 1990.

———. *The Complete Baseball Record Book*. St. Louis: The Sporting News Publishing Company, 1989.

Stevens, Bob. *"Felipe Suggests Latins have Rep. in Frick's Office."* *The Sporting News*, 16 March 1963.

Stump, Al. "Always They Want More, More." *Saturday Evening Post*, 29 July 1967.

Sullivan, Jerry. "Jose Cruz Steps Out." *Sport*, September 1985.

Sultanes: Aniversario 50. Asociacion de Equipos Profesinales de Béisbol de la Liga Mexicana A.C., 1988.

Szulc, Tad. *Dominican Diary*. New York: Dell Publishing Company, 1965.

———. *Fidel*. New York: Avon Books, 1986.

Terzian, James. *The Kid from Cuba: Zolio Versailles*. New York: Doubleday, 1967.

Thorn, John, and John Holway. *The Pitcher*. New York: Prentice Hall Press, 1987.

Thorn, John, and Pete Palmer, eds. *Total Baseball*. New York: Warner Books, Inc., 1989.

Tiant, Luís, and Joe Fitzgerald. *El Tiante: The Luís Tiant Story*. New York: Doubleday, 1976.

Torres, Angel. *La Historia del Béisbol Cubano 1876-1976*. Los Angeles: Angel Torres, 1976.

"Two Lives and Two Loves, Clemente Tells Buc Fans." *The Sporting News*, 8 August 1970.

Tygiel, Jules. *Baseball's Great Experiment: Jackie Robinson and His Legacy.* New York: Random House, 1984.

Vene, Juan. *La Historia de la Series Mundiales 1903-1986.* Caracas, Venezuela: Minnesota Baseball Company, 1985.

Verrell, Gordon. "Dodgers' Guerrero is Wanted Man." *The Sporting News,* 19 December 1981.

————. "Fernando Makes 20, the Hard Way." *The Sporting News,* 6 October 1986.

————. "Guerrero Glistens While Others Fail." *The Sporting News,* 7 June 1982, 36.

Wagerheim, Kal. *Clemente!* New York: Waterfront, 1973.

Ways, C.R. "Nobody Does Anything Better than Me in Baseball." *New York Times Magazine,* 9 April 1972.

Welles, Margery Miller. "Youth Section." Baseball Hall of Fame Library Collection: newspaper article, 13 April 1956.

Whiteside, Larry. Baseball Hall of Fame Library Collection: article from *The Boston Globe,* 6 July 1983.

Wiarda, Howard J., and Harvey F. Kline. *Latin American Politics and Development.* Boston: Houghton Mifflin, 1979.

Williams, Ted, with John Underwood. "I Hope Rod Carew Hits .400." *Sports Illustrated,* 29 June 1977, 20-22.

Wilson, John. "Cesar Cedeño . . . The Next Super Star?" *The Sporting News,* 19 August 1972.

Wolf, Bob. "Carty in Front as Braves Toss Mitts at Mets." *The Sporting News,* 8 August 1964.

Wolf, David. "A Baseball Superstar Frustrated by Faint Praise." *Life,* 25 May 1968.

Wulf, Steve. "In Philadelphia, They're the Wheeze Kids." *Sports Illustrated,* 14 March 1983.

Young, A.S. "Doc." *Great Negro Baseball Stars and How They Made the Major Leagues.* New York: A.S. Barnes and Company, 1953.

————. "Home Run King of the Giants." *Ebony,* July 1962.

Young, Dick. "Rico Carty." *Daily News,* 4 June 1970.

Index

Oglivie, Ben, 187
Oliva, Antonio "Tony," 135, 137–138,
  141–145, 149, 172
Oliva, Pedro
  See Oliva, Antonio
Olivo, Diómedes, 99
Olmo, Luís, 45, 50, 67
Oriental (Nicaragua), 193
Oriente (Venezuela), 69, 200
Orosco, Jesse, 166
Ortega, Daniel, 197
Ortiz, Roberto, 44, 50
Osborne, Tiny, 29
Osteen, Claude, 150
Otero, Regie, 178, 179
Ott, Mel, 29
Owen, Mickey, 50–51, 52, 68

P

Pagán, José, 83, 96, 111, 117, 203
Page, Mitchell, 205
Paige, Satchel, 23, 39, 49, 109
Palmer, Jim, 117, 118, 124
Palmeiro, Rafael, 1, 75
Panther, Jim, 173
Pappas, Milt, 107
Parker, Dave, 134
Partlow, Roy, 54
Pascual, Camilo, 68, 69, 73, 210
Pascual, Carlos, 73
Pasquel, Bernardo, 50, 51
Pasquel, Francisco, 49
Pasquel, Jorge, 49–52, 61, 193
Patterson, Bob, 211, 212
Paul, Gabe, 147
Paula, Carlos, 69, 75
Pedroza, Eustaquio, 20, 21, 22
Peña, Orlando, 69, 185, 205
Peña, Tony, 99, 163, 183, 214, 217
Pérez, Atanasio "Tony," 5, 125–134,
  135, 205, 209, 216
Pérez, Carlos Andrés, 204
Pérez, Melido, 211
Perry, Gaylord, 139
Perry, Jim, 116
Petway, Bruce, 21
Pinelli, Babe, 29
Piniella, Lou, 194
Pizarro, Juan, 69, 104, 147
Plank, Eddie, 21
Poitevint, Ray, 194
Polonia, Luís, 210
Pompez, Alex, 33, 56–57, 79, 81

Ponce Lions (Puerto Rico), 62, 162, 202,
  205
Porras, Belisario, 17
Potros de Tijuana (Mexico), 210, 212
Powell, Boog, 133
Power, Victor Pellot, 68, 69, 142
Prío, Carlos, 71
Puckett, Kirby, 145
Puebla (Mexico), 30, 50, 159
Puerto Vallarta (Mexico), 60

Q

Quintana, Carlos, 206

R

Ramos, Bobby, 206
Ramblers (Panama), 200
Ramos, "Chucho," 45
Ramos, Domingo, 185
Ramos, Pedro, 68, 69
Rapiños (Venezuela), 69, 199
Rapp, Vern, 138
Raschi, Vic, 58
Reagan, Ronald, 160
Reed, Howie, 86
Regan, Phil, 194, 210
Reiser, Pete, 137
Reuss, Jerry, 161
Reyes, Benjamín "Cananea," 207, 208
Reyes, Napoleón, 50, 69, 208
Reynolds, Allie, 58, 65
Rice, Jim, 132
Richards, Paul, 58, 59
Richardson, Spec, 175
Rickey, Branch, 53–54, 90, 99
Riggleman, Jim, 210
Righetti, Dave, 162
Rigney, Bill, 82
Rijo, José, 1, 184, 210
Ripken, Cal, 165
Ritchie, Jay, 205
Rivera, Germán, 204
Rivera, Jim, 68, 106
Rixey, Eppa, 28
Rizzuto, Phil, 65, 107
Robinson, Bill, 210
Robinson, Brooks, 108, 128, 133
Robinson, Frank, 107, 111, 209
Robinson, Humberto, 69
Robinson, Jackie, 54–55, 60, 80, 132,
  136, 137
Rodgers, Andre, 78
Rodgers, Bob, 210